UK illustrative financial statements for 2013 year ends

UK Accounting Consulting Services
PricewaterhouseCoopers LLP

Published by

Bloomsbury Professional

Bloomsbury Professional, an imprint of Bloomsbury Publishing plc, Maxwelton House, 41–43 Boltro Road, Haywards Heath, West Sussex, RH16 1BJ

This book has been prepared for general guidance on matters of interest only, and does not constitute professional advice. You should not act upon the information contained in this book without obtaining specific professional advice. Accordingly, to the extent permitted by law, PricewaterhouseCoopers LLP (and its members, employees and agents) and publisher accept no liability, and disclaim all responsibility, for the consequences of you or anyone else acting, or refraining from acting, in reliance on the information contained in this document or for any decision based on it, or for any consequential, special or similar damages even if advised of the possibility of such damages.

All rights reserved. No part of this publication may be reproduced in any material form (including photocopying or storing it in any medium by electronic means and whether or not transiently or incidentally to some other use of this publication) without the written permission of PricewaterhouseCoopers LLP except in accordance with the provisions of the Copyright, Designs and Patents Act 1988 or under the terms of a licence issued by the Copyright Licensing Agency Ltd, Saffron House, 6–10 Kirby Street, London EC1 N 8TS. Applications for the copyright owner's written permission to reproduce any part of this publication should be addressed to the publisher.

Warning: The doing of an unauthorised act in relation to a copyright work may result in both a civil claim for damages and criminal prosecution.

ISBN 978 1 78043 257 1

British Library Cataloguing-in-Publication Data.
A catalogue record for this book is available from the British Library.

© 2013 PricewaterhouseCoopers Printed in Great Britain

Preface

This publication provides example sets of financial statements for the year ended 31 December 2013. These example financial statements will assist you in preparing financial statements by illustrating the required disclosure and presentation for UK groups and UK companies, whether reporting under IFRS or UK GAAP.

IFRS GAAP plc
An example annual report including the consolidated financial statements of IFRS GAAP plc group of companies. The annual report has been prepared to show the disclosures and format that might be expected for a group of its size that prepares its financial statements in accordance with IFRS, UK law and UK Listing Rules requirements, for a fictional corporate entity (IFRS GAAP plc).

GAAP UK Group Limited
An example annual report including the consolidated financial statements of the GAAP UK Group Limited. The annual report has been prepared to show the disclosures and format that might be expected for a group of its size that prepares its financial statements in accordance with the Companies Act and UK Accounting Standards. GAAP UK Group Limited is a fictional unlisted company that is incorporated in the UK. It has a number of UK and overseas investments, including subsidiaries and joint ventures.

UK GAAP Limited
An example set of financial statements for UK GAAP Limited. These financial statements have been prepared to show how an unlisted UK company might prepare its financial statements in accordance with the Companies Act and UK Accounting Standards.

PricewaterhouseCoopers LLP
London
October 2013

Contents

1 IFRS GAAP plc 1001
2 GAAP UK Group Limited 2001
3 UK GAAP Limited 3001

IFRS GAAP Plc

Example annual report under IFRS

Introduction

This example annual report presents an illustrative set of consolidated financial statements, prepared in accordance with International Financial Reporting Standards (IFRS) as endorsed by the EU , for a fictional manufacturing, wholesale and retail group (IFRS GAAP plc) and the requirements of a UK listed entity. IFRS GAAP plc is an existing preparer of IFRS consolidated financial statements.

This publication is based on the requirements of IFRS standards and interpretations for financial years beginning on or after 1 January 2013.

> Areas in which we have made significant changes to this example annual report since 2012 have been highlighted in pink and include:
> - The Strategic report requirements and related amendments to the Directors' report;
> - The Directors' Remuneration report requirements;
> - Updated illustrative Auditor's report for listed companies;
> - Application of IFRSs 10, 11 and 12 (IFRS GAAP plc has early adopted these standards);
> - Application of IFRS 13;
> - IAS 19 revised;
> - IAS 1 Presentation changes; and
> - IFRS 7 Offsetting disclosures.

We have attempted to create a realistic set of financial statements for a corporate entity. However, by necessity we illustrate disclosures that for many entities may be immaterial. Determining the level of disclosure is a matter of judgement, and naturally disclosure of immaterial items is not required. Certain types of transaction have been excluded, as they are not relevant to the group's operations. The example disclosures, if material, for some of these additional items have been included in appendix II. The forthcoming IFRS requirements are outlined in a table in appendix III.

PwC commentary has been provided, in grey boxes, to explain the detail behind the presentation of a number of challenging areas. We draw your attention in particular to our commentary on the income statement, statement of comprehensive income, balance sheet, statement of changes in equity, statement of cash flows, statement of significant accounting policies and financial risk management.

Guidance and further information

References to source material are given in the left hand margin. IFRS 1, 'First-time adoption of International Financial Reporting Standards', is not applicable. Guidance on financial statements for first-time adopters of IFRS is available at www.pwc.com/ifrs.

IFRS GAAP plc – year ended 31 December 2013

If you require further guidance on UK law and the accounting requirements affecting companies' financial statements under IFRS, the PwC 'Manual of Accounting – IFRS for the UK 2014' may be of assistance.

The example disclosures should not be considered the only acceptable form of presentation and are intended for guidance only. The form and content of each reporting entity's financial statements are the responsibility of the entity's management. Alternative presentations to those proposed in this publication may be equally acceptable if they comply with the specific disclosure requirements prescribed in IFRS.

These illustrative financial statements do not show all conceivable disclosures, should not be used as a checklist and are not a substitute for reading the standards and interpretations themselves or for professional judgement as to fairness of presentation. They do not cover all possible disclosures that IFRS requires. Further specific information may be required in order to ensure fair presentation under IFRS. We recommend that readers refer to our publication 'IFRS disclosure checklist 2013'.

The names of the undertakings and persons included in the annual report are used for illustration only; any resemblance to any existing undertaking or person is not intended.

IFRS GAAP Plc

Example annual report for the year ended 31 December 2013

Contents

	Page
Strategic report	1
Appendix 1 – Financial Reporting Council – 'Exposure Draft : Guidance on the Strategic report' – Overview and Principles	3
Appendix 2 – Accounting Standards Board –'Reporting Statement: Operating and financial review	6
Directors' report	13
Remuneration report	19
Corporate governance report	31
Statement of directors' responsibilities	49
Independent auditors' report to the members of IFRS GAAP plc	51
Financial statements	56
Consolidated income statement	56
Consolidated statement of comprehensive income	58
Consolidated and Parent Company balance sheets	66
Consolidated statement of changes in equity	71
Consolidated and Parent Company statements of cash flows	74
Notes to the consolidated financial statements:	
1 General information	78
2 Summary of significant accounting policies:	78
2.1 Basis of preparation	78
2.1.1 Going concern	78
2.1.2 Changes in accounting policies and disclosures	79
2.2 Consolidation	81
2.3 Segment reporting	83
2.4 Foreign currency translation	83
2.5 Property, plant and equipment	84
2.6 Intangible assets	85
2.7 Impairment of non-financial assets	86
2.8 Non-current assets (or disposal groups) held for sale	87
2.9 Financial assets	87
2.9.1 Classification	87
2.9.2 Recognition and measurement	87
2.10 Offsetting financial instruments	88
2.11 Impairment of financial assets	88
2.12 Derivative financial instruments and hedging activities	89
2.13 Inventories	91
2.14 Trade receivables	91
2.15 Cash and cash equivalents	91
2.16 Share capital	91
2.17 Trade payables	92
2.18 Borrowings	92
2.19 Borrowing costs	92
2.20 Compound financial instruments	92
2.21 Current and deferred income tax	93
2.22 Employee benefits	94
2.23 Share-based payments	95
2.24 Provisions	96
2.25 Revenue recognition	96
2.26 Interest income	97
2.27 Dividend income	98
2.28 Leases	98
2.29 Dividend distribution	98
2.30 Exceptional items	98

3	Financial risk management		101
	3.1 Financial risk factors		101
	3.2 Capital management		106
	3.3 Fair value classification		106
	3.4 Offsetting financial assets and financial liabilities		110
4	Critical accounting estimates and judgements		119
	4.1 Critical accounting estimates and assumptions		119
	4.2 Critical judgements in applying the entity's accounting policies		120
5	Segment information		121
6	Exceptional items		126
7	Other income		127
8	Other (losses)/gains – net		127
9	Expenses		127
	9(a) Expenses by nature		127
	9(b) Auditor remuneration		128
10	Employees		128
	10(a) Employee benefit expense		128
	10(b) Average number of people employed		129
11	Finance income and costs		129
12	Investments		130
	12(a) Investments in associates		130
	12(b) Investments in joint venture		133
	12(c) Principal subsidiaries		136
	12(d) Investment in subsidiaries		138
13	Income tax expense		139
14	Earnings per share		142
15	Net foreign exchange gains/(losses)		143
16	Property, plant and equipment		143
17	Intangible assets		148
18	Financial instruments		152
	18(a) Financial instruments by category		152
	18(b) Credit quality of financial assets		154
19	Available-for-sale financial assets		155
20	Derivative financial instruments		156
21	Trade and other receivables		157
22	Inventories		160
23	Financial assets at fair value through profit or loss		160
24	Cash and cash equivalents		160
25	Non-current assets held for sale and discontinued operations		161
26	Share capital and premium		162
27	Share-based payments		163
28	Retained earnings		164
29	Other reserves		165
30	Trade and other payables		168
31	Borrowings		168
32	Deferred income tax		171
33	Post-employment benefits		173
	33(a) Defined benefit pension plans		173
	33(b) Post-employment medical benefits		177
	33(c) Post-employment benefits (pension and medical)		179
34	Dividends per share		181
35	Provisions for other liabilities and charges		181
36	Cash generated from operations		183
37	Contingencies		184
38	Commitments		184
39	Business combinations		185
40	Transactions with non-controlling interests		188

41	Related parties	189
42	Events after the reporting period	192
43	Changes in accounting policies	194

Appendices

Appendix I – Alternative presentation 206
   Consolidated statement of cash flows – direct method 206
   Consolidated statement of comprehensive income – single statement, showing
   expenses by function 207
Appendix II – Areas not illustrated in financial statements of IFRS GAAP plc 209
   1. Biological assets 209
   2. Construction contracts 213
   3. Oil and gas exploration assets 215
   4. Leases: accounting by lessor 218
   5. Government grants 220
   6. Revenue recognition: multiple-element arrangements 220
   7. Customer loyalty programmes 221
   8. Put option arrangements 221
   9. Foreign currency translations 221
   10. Share-based payments – modification and cancellation 222
Appendix III – New standards and amendments 223
Appendix IV – IFRS 9, 'Financial instruments' 227

IFRS GAAP plc – year ended 31 December 2013

Strategic report

Strategic report for the year ended 31 December 2013

CA06 s414A The directors present their strategic report on the group for the year ended 31 December 2013.

Review of the business[1]

The report should include a review of the business containing:

CA06 s414C(2)(a)
- a fair review of the business of the company; and

CA06 s414C(2)(b)
- a description of the principal risks and uncertainties facing the company.

Where non-GAAP numbers are disclosed, it should be clear that these differ from the GAAP numbers; the equivalent GAAP number should be disclosed; and there should be a reconciliation between the GAAP and non-GAAP numbers, together with relevant comment. This disclosure may be necessary to ensure that the annual report is fair, balanced and understandable.

CA06 s414C(3) The review is a balanced and comprehensive analysis of:

- the development and performance of the business of the company during the financial year; and
- the position of the company at the end of the year,

consistent with the size and complexity of the business.

CA06 s414C(4) The review must, to the extent necessary for an understanding of the development, performance or position of the business of the company, include[2]:

CA06 s414C(4)(a)
- analysis using financial key performance indicators; and

CA06 s414C(2)(b)
- where appropriate, analysis using other key performance indicators, including information relating to environmental matters and employee matters.

CA06 s414C(7) The review should, to the extent necessary for an understanding of the development, performance or position of the business of the company include:

CA06 s414C(7)(a)
- the main trends and factors likely to affect the future development, performance and position of the business;

CA06 s414C(7)(b)
- information about:
    (i) environmental matters (including the impact of the company's business on the environment),
    (ii) the company's employees, and
    (iii) social, community and human rights issues,

including information about any policies of the company in relation to these matters and their effectiveness.

If the report does not contain information and analysis of each type mentioned above, it should state which of those types of information it does not contain.

---

[1] The information that is required to be included in the strategic report may be included in an Operating and Financial Review incorporated into the strategic report by cross-reference. The ASB statement of best practice "Reporting statement: Operating and financial review" is included as an appendix to this section.
[2] This disclosure is applicable to quoted companies.

IFRS GAAP plc – year ended 31 December 2013

UKCGC C1.1, 1.2 CA06 s414C(8)(a)	**Review of strategy and business model**[1] A description of the company's strategy.
CA06 s414C(8)(b)	A description of the company's business model.
	Gender of directors and employees[2]
CA06 s414C(8)(c)(i); (10)(a)	A breakdown at the end of the financial year –
CA06 s414C(8)(c)(ii), (10)(b)	(i) the number of persons of each sex who were directors of the [parent] company; (ii) the number of persons of each sex who were senior managers of the company, other than the persons in (i) above. This must include employees who were directors of undertakings included in the consolidation; (iii) the number of persons of each sex who were employees of the group.
CA06 s414C(9)	A senior manager is an employee who has responsibility for planning, directing or controlling the activities of the company or a strategically significant part of the company.
	General
CA06 s414C(11); SI 2008/410 7 Sch 1A.	Disclosure may include any matters that are directors' report disclosure requirements but considered by the directors to be of strategic importance to the company. (If this is the case, the directors' report includes a cross-reference to the relevant information in the strategic report.)
CA06 s414C(12)	The report must, where appropriate, include references to, and additional explanations of, amounts included in the financial statements of the company.
CA06 s414C(14)	The report need not disclose any information about impending developments or matters in the course of negotiation if, in the opinion of the directors, such disclosure would be seriously prejudicial to the interests of the company.

CA06 s414D(1) By order of the board

CA06 s414D(1) AB Smith
Company Secretary[3]
26 February 2014

---

[1] This disclosure is applicable to quoted companies.
[2] This disclosure is applicable to quoted companies.
[3] The strategic report has to be signed by the company secretary or a director after it has been approved by the board of directors. The copy of the strategic report that is delivered to the Registrar of Companies must be manually signed by the company secretary or a director.

Strategic Report

Appendix 1 Financial Reporting Council – Exposure Draft: Guidance on the Strategic Report – Overview and Principles

In August 2013 the Financial Reporting Council (FRC) issued an "Exposure Draft: Guidance on the Strategic Report" (ED) to provide non-mandatory guidance to preparers. The existing guidance on the business review (the part of the directors' report that the strategic report will replace) is the Accounting Standards Board's (ASB) "Reporting Statement: Operating and Financial Review" (RS). At the time of writing, the FRC exposure draft is open for comment.

FRC ED Intro (vii) The draft guidance aims to be:

(a) principles-based;
(b) shorter and more streamlined than the RS;
(c) mindful of recent developments in narrative reporting best practice; and
(d) aligned with the requirements in the UK Corporate Governance Code.

The Accounting Council, in providing advice to the FRC on issuing the exposure draft, noted that the final guidance will replace the ASB's Reporting Statement. We provide illustrative disclosure requirements of the RS in Appendix 2 "ASB Reporting Statement: Operating and financial review" as this is current guidance until it is replaced by the new FRC guidance

The exposure draft is structured into various sections with each section identifying –

- main principles or content elements; and
- supporting guidance including summary of legal requirements and where applicable, examples and linkage examples.

In this appendix we summarise the principles identified in the ED.

Scope

FRC ED 2.1 The draft guidance has been written with quoted companies in mind. It may also serve as best practice guidance for other entities preparing strategic reports.

Purpose of the annual report

FRC ED 3.4 The purpose of the annual report is to provide shareholders with relevant information that is useful for making resource allocation decisions and assessing management's stewardship.

FRC ED 3.8 The annual report as a whole should be fair, balanced and understandable.

Placement of information in the annual report

FRC ED 3.10 The placement of information in the annual report should facilitate the communication of the information contained within it.

Strategic reports and materiality

FRC ED 5.1 Information is material if its omission from or misrepresentation in the strategic report might reasonably be expected to influence the economic decisions shareholders make on the basis of the annual report as a whole. Such information should be included in the strategic report.

IFRS GAAP plc – year ended 31 December 2013

Conversely, the inclusion of immaterial information can obscure key messages and impair the understandability of information provided in the strategic report. Immaterial information should be exclude from the strategic report.

The purpose of the strategic report

FRC ED 6.1 The strategic report should provide shareholders of the company with the ability to assess how the directors have performed their duty to promote the success of the company for their collective benefit.

FRC ED 6.6 The strategic report should be fair[1], balanced[2] and understandable[3].

FRC ED 6.11 The strategic report should be concise.

FRC ED 6.16 Where appropriate, information in the strategic report should have a forward-looking orientation.

FRC ED 6.19 The strategic report should provide information that is entity-specific.

FRC ED 6.21 The strategic report should highlight relationships and interdependencies (linkages) between information presented in different parts of the annual report.

FRC ED 6.26 The structure and presentation of the strategic report should be reviewed annually to ensure that it continues to meet its objectives in an efficient and effective manner.

The content elements of the strategic report

FRC ED 6.31 The strategic report should include a description of the entity's principal objectives and its strategies for achieving those objectives[4].

FRC ED 6.37 The strategic report should include a description of the entity's business model.[5]

FRC ED 6.42 To the extent necessary for an understanding of the development, performance or position of the entity's business, the strategic report should include the main trends and factors likely to affect the future development, performance or position of the business.[6]

FRC ED 6.49 The strategic report should include a description of the principal risks and uncertainties facing the entity[7], together with an explanation of how they are managed or mitigated.

FRC ED 6.55 The analysis in the strategic report should include the financial and non-financial key performance indicators (KPIs)[8] utilised by the directors to measure progress towards achieving a particular objective or strategy.

FRC ED 6.60 The strategic report should provide an analysis of the development and performance of the business in the financial year and of its position at the end of that year.[9]

FRC ED 6.64 To the extent necessary for an understanding of the development, performance or position of the entity's business, the strategic report should include information about:

---

[1] Companies Act 2006 Section 414C(2)(a).
[2] Companies Act 2006 Section 414C(3).
[3] 2012 UK Corporate Governance Code C.1.1.
[4] Companies Act 2006 Section 414C(8)(a).
[5] Companies Act 2006 section 414C(8)(b).
[6] Companies Act 2006 Section 414C(7)(a).
[7] Companies Act 2006 Section 414C(2)(b).
[8] Companies Act 2006 Section 414C(4).
[9] Companies Act 2006 Section 414C(2)(a) and (3).

> (a) environmental matters (including the impact of the business of the entity in the environment)[1];
> (b) the entity's employees[2]; and
> (c) social, community and human rights issues[3].

FRC ED 6.68 The strategic report should provide a breakdown showing, as at the end of the financial year[4]:

> (a) the number of persons of each sex who are directors of the company;
> (b) the number of persons of each sex who were senior managers of the entity (other than persons falling within sub-paragraph (a)); and
> (c) the number of persons of each sex who were employees of the entity.

FRC ED 6.72 To the extent that they are matters which are considered to be of strategic importance to the entity, the strategic report should also include information which would otherwise be disclosed in the directors report[5].

---

[1] Companies Act 2006 Section 414C(7)(b)(i).
[2] Companies Act 2006 Section 414C(7)(b)(ii).
[3] Companies Act 2006 Section 414C(7)(b)(iii).
[4] Companies Act 2006 Section 414C(8)(c).
[5] Companies Act 2006 Section 414C(11).

IFRS GAAP plc – year ended 31 December 2013

Strategic Report

Appendix 2   Accounting Standards Board – 'Reporting statement: Operating and financial review'

RS (OFR) DV — The ASB has published 'Reporting statement: Operating and financial review' ('RS (OFR)'), which is a statement of best practice on the OFR. It is written with quoted companies in mind but is also applicable to any other entity that produces an OFR. Where an entity includes an operating and financial review in the financial statements, it is recommended that it complies with the RS (OFR). There is some overlap between certain recommendations of the RS (OFR) and the disclosure requirements of law and regulation set out elsewhere in this document. Legal and regulatory disclosure requirements applying to other sections of the annual report can be included in the OFR, provided that there are specific cross-references to the locations of the relevant disclosures in the OFR.

Group operating and financial review

Principles

CC C.1
RS (OFR) p15 — The board should present a balanced and understandable assessment of the group's position and prospects. Where non-GAAP historical numbers are disclosed, they should be clearly identified as such and reconciled to the statutory numbers, with sufficient prominence being given to the statutory numbers and to the reconciliation. The operating and financial review should give a balanced picture of performance; non-statutory numbers should be presented in a manner that achieves this objective. They should supplement and not replace statutory numbers, and their purpose should be clearly stated. The descriptions of non-GAAP historical numbers should not imply any representation about future performance.

For example, terms such as 'normalised', 'sustainable' or 'maintainable' earnings could be taken to imply an element of forecasting. Instead, 'adjusted' or more specific terms (such as 'profit before tax and exceptionals') can be used.

RS (OFR) p4 — The OFR should set out an analysis of the business through the eyes of the board of directors.

RS (OFR) p5 — The OFR should reflect the directors' view of the business. The entity should disclose appropriate elements of information used in managing the entity, including its subsidiary undertakings. Where appropriate, the review may give greater emphasis to those matters that are significant to the entity and its subsidiary undertakings taken as a whole. Such matters may include issues specific to business segments where relevant to the understanding of the business as a whole. The presentation of the OFR should complement the format of the annual report as a whole.

RS (OFR) p6 — The OFR should focus on matters that are relevant to the interests of members.

RS (OFR) p7 — Members' needs are paramount when directors consider what information should be contained in the OFR. Information in the OFR will also be of interest to users other than members – for example, other investors, potential investors, creditors, customers, suppliers, employees and general society. The directors should consider the extent to which they should report on issues relevant to the other users where, because of the influence on the performance of the business and its value, they are also of significance to members. The OFR should not, however, be seen as a replacement for other forms of reporting addressed to a wider stakeholder group.

RS (OFR) p8 — The OFR should have a forward-looking orientation, identifying those trends and factors relevant to the members' assessment of the current and future performance of the business and the progress towards the achievement of long- term business objectives.

RS (OFR) p9 The particular factors discussed should be those that have affected development, performance, and position during the financial year and those which are likely to affect the entity's future development, performance and position.

RS (OFR) p10 Given the nature of some forward-looking information, in particular elements that cannot be objectively verified but have been made in good faith, directors may want to include a statement in the OFR to treat such elements with caution, explaining the uncertainties underpinning such information.

RS (OFR) p11 The OFR should comment on the impact on future performance of significant events after the balance sheet date.

RS (OFR) p12 The OFR should discuss predictive comments, both positive and negative, made in previous reviews whether or not these have been borne out by events.

RS (OFR) p13 The OFR should complement as well as supplement the financial statements, in order to enhance the overall corporate disclosure.

RS (OFR) p14 In complementing the financial statements, the OFR should provide useful financial and non-financial information about the business and its performance that is not reported in financial statements but that the directors' judge might be relevant to the members' evaluation of past results and assessment of future prospects.

RS (OFR) p15 In supplementing the financial statements, the OFR should, where relevant:

- provide additional explanations of amounts recorded in the financial statements; and
- explain the conditions and events that shaped the information contained in the financial statements.

Where amounts from the financial statements have been adjusted for inclusion in the OFR, that fact should be highlighted and a reconciliation provided.

RS (OFR) p16 The OFR should be comprehensive and understandable.

RS (OFR) p17 Directors should consider whether the omission of information might reasonably be expected to influence significantly the assessment made by members.

RS (OFR) p18 The recommendation for the OFR to be comprehensive does not mean that the OFR should cover all possible matters: the objective is quality not quantity of content. It is neither possible nor desirable for a reporting statement to list all the elements that might need to be included, as these will vary depending on the nature and circumstances of the particular business and how the business is run.

RS (OFR) p19 Directors should consider the evidence underpinning the information to be included in the OFR. Where relevant, directors should explain the source of the information and the degree to which the information is objectively supportable, to allow members to assess the reliability of the information presented for themselves.

RS (OFR) p20 Directors should consider the key issues to include in the OFR that will provide members with focused and relevant information. The inclusion of too much information may obscure judgements and will not promote understanding. Where additional information is discussed elsewhere in the annual report, or in other reports, cross-referencing to those sources will assist members.

RS (OFR) p21 The OFR should be written in a clear and readily understandable style.

IFRS GAAP plc – year ended 31 December 2013

RS (OFR) p22   The OFR should be balanced and neutral, dealing even-handedly with both good and bad aspects.

RS (OFR) p23   The directors should ensure that the OFR retains balance and that members are not misled as a result of the omission of any information on unfavourable aspects.

RS (OFR) p24   The OFR should be comparable over time.

RS (OFR) p25   Disclosure should be sufficient for the members to be able to compare the information presented with similar information about the entity for previous financial years. Comparability enables identification of the main trends and factors, and their analysis, over successive financial years. Directors may wish to consider the extent to which the OFR is comparable with reviews prepared by other entities in the same industry or sector.

RS (OFR) p79   No disclosure of information should be made about impending developments or about matters in the course of negotiation that would, in the opinion of the directors, be seriously prejudicial to the interests of the entity.

Disclosure framework

RS (OFR) p27   The OFR should provide information to assist members to assess the strategies adopted by the entity and the potential for those strategies to succeed. The key elements of the disclosure framework necessary to achieve this are:

- the nature of the business, including a description of the market, competitive and regulatory environment in which the entity operates, and the entity's objectives and strategies;
- the development and performance of the business, both in the financial year under review and in the future;
- the resources, principal risks and uncertainties and relationships that may affect the entity's long-term value; and
- the position of the business, including a description of the capital structure, treasury policies and objectives and liquidity of the entity, both in the financial year under review and the future.

Details of particular matters

RS (OFR) p28   To the extent necessary to meet the recommendations set out in paragraph above, the OFR should include information about:

- environmental matters (including the impact of the business of the entity on the environment);
- the entity's employees;
- social and community issues;
- persons with whom the entity has contractual or other arrangements that are essential to the business of the entity;
- receipts from, and returns to, members of the entity in respect of shares held by them; and
- all other matters the directors consider to be relevant.

RS (OFR) p29   The OFR should, in particular, include:

- the entity's policies on environmental matters, the entity's employees and social and community issues; and
- the extent to which those policies have been successfully implemented.

The nature, objectives and strategies of the business

RS (OFR) p30, 31   The OFR should include a description of the business and the external environment in which it operates as context for the directors' discussion and analysis of performance and financial position. This description is recommended in order to provide members with an understanding of the industry/industries in which the entity operates; its main products, services, customers, business processes and distribution methods; the structure of the business; and its economic model, including an overview of the main operating facilities and their location.

RS (OFR) p32 Every entity is affected by its external environment. Depending on the nature of the business, the OFR should include discussion of matters such as the entity's major markets and competitive position within those markets and the significant features of the legal, regulatory, macro-economic and social environment that influence the business.

RS (OFR) p33-35 The OFR should discuss the objectives of the business to generate or preserve value over the longer-term. Objectives will often be defined in terms of financial performance; however, objectives in non-financial areas should also be discussed where appropriate. The nature of the industry will affect the directors' determination of an appropriate time perspective for reporting in the OFR.

RS (OFR) p36 The OFR should set out the directors' strategies for achieving the objectives of the business.

RS (OFR) p38-40 It should include the key performance indicators, both financial and, where appropriate, non-financial, used by the directors to assess progress against their stated objectives. The KPIs disclosed should be those that the directors judge are effective in measuring the delivery of their strategies and managing their business. Regular measurement using KPIs should enable an entity to set and communicate its performance targets and to measure whether it is achieving them. Comparability will be enhanced if the KPIs disclosed are accepted and widely used, either within the industry sector or more generally.

RS (OFR) p41-42 Directors should also consider the extent to which other performance indicators and evidence should be included in the OFR. These could be narrative evidence describing how the directors manage the business or quantified measures used to monitor the entity's external environment and/ or progress towards the achievement of its objectives.

Current and future development and performance

RS (OFR) p44-46 Trends and factors in development and performance suggested by an analysis of the current and previous financial years should be highlighted. Development and performance should be described in the context of the strategic objectives of the business. The OFR should cover significant aspects of the statements of financial performance and, where appropriate, should be linked to other aspects of performance. It should set out the directors' analysis of the effect on current development and performance of changes during the financial year in the industry, or the external environment in which the business operates and of developments within the business.

RS (OFR) p43, 47-49 The OFR should describe the significant features of the development and performance of the business in the financial year covered by the financial statements, focusing on those business segments that are relevant to an understanding of the development and performance as a whole. It should analyse the main trends and factors that directors consider likely to impact future prospects. The main trends and factors likely to affect the future development and performance will vary according to the nature of the business; they might include the development of known new products and services or the benefits expected from capital investment. The OFR should discuss the current level of investment expenditure together with planned future expenditure and should explain how that investment is directed to assist the

IFRS GAAP plc – year ended 31 December 2013

achievement of business objectives. Any assumptions underlying the main trends and factors should be disclosed. Directors should consider the potential future significance of issues in deciding whether or not to include an analysis of them in the OFR.

Resources

RS (OFR) p50-51 The OFR should include a description of the resources available to the entity and how they are managed. It should set out the key strengths and resources, tangible and intangible, available to the business, that will assist it in the pursuit of its objectives and, in particular, those items that are not reflected in the balance sheet. Depending on the nature of the business, these may include: corporate reputation and brand strength; natural resources; employees; research and development; intellectual capital; licences, patents, copyright and trademarks; and market position.

Principal risks and uncertainties

RS (OFR) p52-56 The OFR should include a description of the principal risks and uncertainties facing the entity, together with a commentary on the directors' approach to them. Different industries and entities use different risk models or approaches for identifying and managing risk, although all entities face and should disclose strategic, commercial, operational and financial risks where these may significantly affect the entity's strategies and development of the entity's value. The principal risks and uncertainties facing entities will vary according to the nature of the business; some risks, such as the risk to reputation, are likely to be common to all.

RS (OFR) p55-56 The description of the principal risks and uncertainties should cover the exposure to negative consequences as well as potential opportunities. The directors' policy for managing principal risks should be disclosed. The OFR should cover the principal risks and uncertainties necessary for an understanding of the objectives and strategies of the business, both where they constitute a significant external risk to the entity, and where the entity's impact on other parties through its activities, products or services, affects its performance. Directors should consider the full range of business risks.

Relationships

RS (OFR) p57-58 The OFR should include information about the significant relationships with stakeholders other than members that are likely, directly or indirectly, to influence the performance of the business and its value. In deciding what should be included in the OFR, directors should take a broad view in considering the extent to which the actions of stakeholders other than members can affect an entity's performance and value.

RS (OFR) p59 Where necessary for an understanding of the business, the OFR should describe receipts from, and returns to, shareholders in relation to shares held by them. This should include a description of any distributions, capital raising and share repurchases.

Financial position

RS (OFR) p60-62 The OFR should contain an analysis of the financial position and a discussion of the capital structure of the entity. This should include the sources of funding and may include targeted ratio of liabilities to equity. The analysis, while based on the financial statements, should comment on the events that have impacted the financial position of the entity during the financial year and future factors that are likely to affect the financial position going forward. The analysis should supplement the disclosures required in accounting standards – in particular, those required by IFRS 7, 'Financial instruments: Disclosures'. The OFR should highlight accounting policies set out in the notes to the financial statements. It should discuss those accounting policies that are critical to an understanding of the performance and financial position of the entity, focusing on those which have required the particular exercise of judgement in their application and to which the results are most sensitive. In addition, it should draw attention to the accounting policies that have changed during the financial year under review.

RS (OFR) p65-67 The OFR should set out the entity's treasury policies and objectives. It should also discuss the implementation of these policies in the financial year under review. The purpose and effect of major financing transactions undertaken up to the date of approval of the financial statements should be explained. The effect of interest costs on profits and the potential impact of interest rate changes should also be discussed.

RS (OFR) p63-64 The OFR should contain a discussion of the capital structure of the entity. This could include the balance between equity and debt, the maturity profile of debt, the type of capital instrument used, currency, regulatory capital and interest rate structure. The discussion should include comments on short and longer-term funding plans to support the directors' strategies to achieve the entity's objectives. In addition, the discussion should comment on why the entity has adopted its particular capital structure.

Cash flows

RS (OFR) p68 The OFR should discuss the cash inflows and outflows during the financial year, along with the entity's ability to generate cash, to meet known or probable cash requirements and to fund growth.

RS (OFR) p69-70 Any discussion should supplement the information provided in the financial statements by, for example, commenting on any special factors that have influenced cash flows in the financial year and those that may have a significant effect on future cash flows. Where entities have cash that is surplus to future operating requirements and current levels of distribution, the discussion should include future plans for making use of the excess cash. Analysis of profit by segment might be indicative of the cash flow generated by each segment, but this will not always be so — for example, because of fluctuations in capital expenditure and depreciation. Where segment cash flows are significantly out of line with segment revenues or profits, this should be indicated and explained.

Liquidity

RS (OFR) p71 The OFR should discuss the entity's current and prospective liquidity. Where relevant, this should include commentary on the level of borrowings, the seasonality of borrowing requirements (indicated by the peak level of borrowings during that period) and the maturity profile of both borrowings and undrawn committed borrowing facilities.

RS (OFR) p72-74 The discussion on liquidity should discuss the ability of the entity to fund its current and future operations and stated strategies. It should cover internal sources of liquidity, referring to any restrictions on the ability to transfer funds from one part of the group to meet the obligations of another part of the group where these represent, or might foreseeably come to represent, a significant restraint on the group. Such constraints would include exchange controls and taxation consequences of transfers. Where the entity has entered into covenants in financing contracts that could restrict the use of financing arrangements or credit facilities, and negotiations with the lenders on the operation of these covenants are taking place or are expected to take place, this fact should be indicated in the OFR. Where a breach of a covenant has occurred or is expected to occur, the OFR should give details of the measures taken or proposed to remedy the situation.

Key performance indicators

RS (OFR) p75 The entity should provide information that enables members to understand each KPI disclosed in the OFR.

RS (OFR) p76 For each KPI disclosed in the OFR:

- the definition and its calculation method should be explained;
- its purpose should be explained;
- the source of underlying data should be disclosed and, where relevant, assumptions explained;
- quantification or commentary on future targets should be provided;
- where information from the financial statements has been adjusted for inclusion in the OFR, that fact should be highlighted and a reconciliation provided;
- where available, corresponding amount for the financial year immediately preceding the current year should be disclosed; and
- any changes to KPIs should be disclosed, and the calculation method used compared to previous financial years – including significant changes in the underlying accounting policies adopted in the financial statements – should be identified and explained.

RS (OFR) p77 Quantification or commentary on future targets is about communicating the direction the entity is taking by, for example, setting out future strategies and goals.

Other performance indicators

RS (OFR) p78 Where a quantified measure other than a KPI is included, the OFR should disclose:

- the definition and its calculation method; and
- where available, the corresponding amount for the financial year immediately preceding the current year.

RS (OFR) p80 Entities are encouraged to include a statement as to whether the OFR is prepared in accordance with this Reporting Statement and contain particulars of, and reasons for any departure.

Directors' report

Group directors' report for the year ended 31 December 2013

CA06 s415(1) — The directors present their report and the audited financial statements for the year ended 31 December 2013.

SI 2008/410 Reg 10 — *Note: The directors' report should also comply with the relevant requirements of Schedule 7 to SI 2008/410.*

General Information

1p138(a) and (c) — There should be disclosure of the:

- domicile and legal form of entity;
- country of incorporation;
- address of the registered office or principal place of business, if different[1]; and
- the name of the parent and the ultimate parent of the group.

Branches outside the UK

SI 2008/410 7 Sch 7(1)(d) — The directors' report should disclose the existence of any branches that operate outside of the UK.

Future developments

SI 2008/410 7 Sch 7(1)(b) — The directors' report should contain an indication of the likely future developments in the group's business.

This disclosure is likely to be relevant to the strategic report. It could be included in the strategic report and incorporated into the directors' report by cross reference.

Dividends

CA06 s416(3) — Details of the recommended dividend should be provided.

Waiver of dividends

LR 9.8.4R (12), (13) LR 9.8.5R — Details should be disclosed of any arrangement under which a shareholder has waived or agreed to waive any dividends or future dividends. Waivers of less than one per cent of the total value of any dividend are not required to be disclosed provided that some payment has been made on each share of the relevant class during the relevant calendar year.

Research and development

SI 2008/410 7 Sch 7(1)(c) — The directors' report should provide an indication of the group's research and development activities.

DV — It is recommended that a statement is included with regard to the charge to the income statement for the year (which should be separately disclosed in the notes to financial statements).

---

[1] This disclosure can be given in the note to the financial statements and not in the directors' report.

IFRS GAAP plc – year ended 31 December 2013

Political donations and political expenditure

SI 2008/410 7 Sch 3

If the company and/or any of its subsidiaries made any donations to a registered political party, other political organisation in the EU (including the UK) or any independent election candidate, or if it incurred EU political expenditure exceeding £2,000 in the financial year, the directors' report should disclose:

- EU donations – the name of the political party and total amount given per party, by the entity and each subsidiary that has donated such expenditure individually.
- EU political expenditure – total amount incurred in the financial year by the company and each subsidiary that has incurred such expenditure individually.

SI 2008/410 7 Sch 4

Total contributions to non-EU political parties should be disclosed for the group as a whole in aggregate. (There is no threshold for this disclosure.)

Post balance sheet events

SI 2008/410 7 Sch 7(1)(a)

The directors' report should include particulars of any important events affecting the company or group since the year end.

Similar to the disclosure on future developments, this disclosure is likely to fit well with the strategic report. It might therefore be appropriate to include therein and cross reference.

Directors and directors' interests

CA06 s416(1)(a)

The names of all persons who were directors during any part of the period should be provided.

DV

Changes in directors since the end of the financial year and the dates of any appointments and/ or resignations of directors occurring during the financial year should be provided.

DV

Information regarding the retirement of the directors at the AGM and whether they offer themselves for election should be disclosed.

LR9.8.6R(1)

All interests in respect of which transactions are notifiable to the company under DTR 3.1.2 R[1], including spouse and children's interests for individuals who are directors at the end of the period under review, should be disclosed.

LR 9.8.6R(1) (a) (b)

All changes in directors' interests that have occurred between the end of the period under review and a date not more than one month prior to the date of the notice of the annual general meeting should be disclosed. If there is no change, a statement to that effect is required.[2]

Further information about the directors' interests is provided in the directors' remuneration report.

Directors' third-party and pension scheme indemnity provisions

CA06 s236(2)(1) – (5)

The directors' report needs to include a statement if a qualifying third-party indemnity provision and/or qualifying pension scheme indemnity provision (whether made by the company or otherwise) has been in place for one or more directors of the company or of an associated company at any time during the financial year or at the date of approval of the directors' report.

---

[1] In accordance with DTR 3.1.2R, 'interests' includes shares of the issuer, or derivatives or any other financial instruments relating to those shares. A definition of financial instruments is available in DTR 3.1.23R.

[2] The information may be included with the disclosures of directors' interests in the directors' remuneration report instead of here.

Employees[1]

SI 2008/410 7 Sch 10(1), 11(3)

A statement is required describing the action that has been taken during the period to introduce, maintain or develop arrangements aimed at involving UK employees in the entity's affairs. This statement should discuss the group's policy on:

- systematic provision of relevant information to employees;
- regular consultation with employees or their representatives so that the employees' views may be taken into account in making decisions that are likely to affect their interests;
- encouragement of employees' participation in the group's performance by employee share schemes or other means; and
- achieving awareness on the part of all employees of the financial and economic factors affecting the group's performance.

SI 2008/410 7 Sch 10(3)

A statement should be included as to the UK policy for giving full and fair consideration to applications for employment that disabled people make to the company, the policy for employment, training, career development and promotion of disabled people and for the continuing employment and training of employees who have become disabled while employed by the company.

Financial instruments

SI 2008/410 7 Sch 6

Where material for the assessment of the assets, liabilities, financial position and profit or loss of the group, the directors' report must contain an indication of:

- the financial risk management objectives and policies of the entity, including the policy for hedging each major type of forecasted transaction for which hedge accounting is used; and
- the exposure of the entity to price risk, credit risk, liquidity risk and cash flow risk.[2]

Purchase of own shares and sale of treasury shares

SI 2008/410 7 Sch 7,8 SI2008/410 7 Sch 8, 9

Where a public company purchases or places a charge on its own shares, there are specific disclosures to be made. These disclosures are:

Share purchases

- the number and nominal value of the shares purchased, the aggregate amount of the consideration paid by the company for such shares and the reasons for their purchase;

Shares otherwise acquired or charged

- the number and nominal value of the shares otherwise acquired by the company (whether acquired by the company, its nominee or another person) or charged during the financial year;
- the maximum number and nominal value of shares that – having been so acquired or charged (whether or not during that year) – are held at any time during the year;
- the number and nominal value of the shares so acquired or charged by the company that are disposed of by the company (or the other person) or cancelled by the company during the year;
- for each of the above, the percentage of the called-up share capital that shares of that description represent;

---

[1] The requirements only apply if the company employed on average more than 250 employees in the UK each week during the financial year (7 Sch 10(1), 11(1)).
[2] These disclosures are also requirements of IFRS 7 and could be cross referenced to the financial statements.

IFRS GAAP plc – year ended 31 December 2013

- where any of the shares have been charged, the amount of the charge in each case; and
- where any of the shares have been disposed of by the company or the person who acquired them for money or money's worth, the amount or value of the consideration in each case.

LR 9.8.6R(4)(a), (b), (c), (d) Details of any shareholders' authority for the company's purchase of its own shares still valid at the end of the period under review. Where any such purchases are made or are proposed to be made, other than through the market or by tender to all shareholders, details should be given of the names of the sellers of such shares purchased in the period. In respect of purchases, made other than through the market or by tender to all shareholders, or options or contracts to make such purchases entered into since the year end, the information listed above should be given. Details should be given of the names of the purchasers of treasury shares sold or proposed to be sold for cash (other than through the market or in connection with an employees' share scheme, or where sales are not pursuant to an opportunity available to all holders of the company's securities on the same terms) during the period under review.

Substantial shareholdings

LR 9.8.6R(2)(a), (b) Particulars, as at a date not more than a month prior to the date of the notice of the general meeting, should be given of substantial shareholdings (material interests of three per cent or more and non-material interests of 10 per cent or more) disclosed to the company, in any part of the company's share capital. Where there have been no such disclosures, this fact should be stated.

Placing of shares

LR 9.8.4R(9) Where a listed company is a subsidiary undertaking of another company, particulars should be given of the participation by its parent company in any placing made during the period under review.

Contracts of significance

LR 9.8.4R(10)(b) LR 9.8.4R(11) Particulars should be given of any contract of significance (including contracts for the provision of services) between the company (including subsidiary undertakings) and controlling shareholder subsisting in the period. 'Significance' is defined as one per cent or more of the relevant transactions for the group.

LR 9.8.4R(10)(a) Disclosure is required of the particulars of any contract of significance to which the company or one of its subsidiaries is a party and in which a director of the company is or was materially interested.

LR9.8.4R (3) LR 11.1.10R (2)(c) Details should be disclosed of small related-party transactions notified to the Financial Conduct Authority.

Takeover Directive requirements

DTR 7.2.6 The following information should be disclosed if the company has securities (shares or debentures) carrying voting rights admitted to trading on a regulated market at the end of the year:

SI 2008/410 7 Sch 13(2)(a)
- The structure of the company's capital including:
    (a) the rights and obligations attached to each class of shares; (b) where there are two or more classes, the percentage of the total share capital represented by each class; and
    (b) where there are two or more classes, the percentage of the total share capital represented by each class.

SI 2008/410 7 Sch 13(3)	A company's capital includes any securities in the company that are not admitted to trading on a regulated market.
SI 2008/410 7 Sch 13(2)(b)	■ Details of any restrictions on the transfer of securities in the company, including limitations on the holding of securities and requirements to obtain the approval of the company or of other holders prior to a transfer of securities.
SI 2008/410 7 Sch 13(2)(c)	■ In respect of each person with a significant direct or indirect holding of securities in the company, the identity of the person, the size of the holding and the nature of the holding.
SI 2008/410 7 Sch 13(2)(d)	■ In the case of each person who holds securities carrying special rights with regard to control of the company, the identity of the person and the nature of the rights.
SI 2008/410 7 Sch 13(2)(e)	■ Where the company has an employees' share scheme and shares to which the scheme relates have rights with regard to control of the company that are not exercisable directly by the employees, details of how these rights are exercisable.
SI 2008/410 7 Sch 13(2)(f)	■ Details of any restrictions on voting rights, including limitations on voting rights of holders of a given percentage or number of votes; deadlines for exercising voting rights; and arrangements by which, with the company's co-operation, financial rights carried by securities are held by a person other than the holder of the securities.
SI 2008/410 7 Sch 13(2)(g)	■ Details of any agreements between holders of securities that are known to the company and may result in restrictions on the transfer of securities or on voting rights.
SI 2008/410 7 Sch 13(2)(h)	■ Details of any rules that the company has about the appointment and replacement of directors, and details of any rules about the amendment of the company's articles of association.
SI 2008/410 7 Sch 13(2)(i)	■ Details of the powers of the company's directors, including in particular any powers in relation to the issuing or buying back by the company of its shares.
SI 2008/410 7 Sch 13(2)(j)	■ Details of any significant arrangements to which the company is a party that take effect, alter or terminate upon a change of control of the company following a takeover bid, and the effects of any such agreements. This does not apply if disclosure would be seriously prejudicial to the company and the company is not under any other obligation to disclose it.
SI 2008/410 7 Sch 13(2)(k)	■ Details of any agreements between the company and its directors or employees providing for compensation for loss of office or employment (through resignation, purported redundancy or otherwise) that occurs because of a takeover bid.
SI 2008/410 7 Sch 14	■ Details of any other information and explanations required in respect of the details included above.

By virtue of DTR 7.2.6R, the information required by 7 Sch 13(2)(c), (d), (f), (h) and (i) may be in a separate report (for example, a corporate governance statement) published with the annual report, provided there is a specific cross-reference to the disclosures from the directors' report.

Greenhouse gas emissions

SI 2008/410 7 Sch 15(2) (SI 2013/1970)	■ The annual quantity of emissions in tonnes of carbon dioxide equivalent from activities for which the company is responsible including: (a) the combustion of fuel; and (b) the operation of any facility.
SI 2008/410 7 Sch 15(3) (SI 2013/1970)	■ The annual quantity of emissions in tonnes of carbon dioxide equivalent resulting from the purchase of electricity, heat, steam or cooling by the company for its own use.[1]

---

[1] Disclosure is only required to the extent practical but where not practical the report must state what information is not included and why [SI 2008/410 7 Sch 15(4) amended by SI 2013/1970].

IFRS GAAP plc – year ended 31 December 2013

SI 2008/410 7 Sch 15(3) (SI 2013/1970)	■ Description of the methodologies used to calculate the information above.
SI 2008/410 7 Sch 17 (SI 2013/1970)	■ At least one ratio which expresses the annual emissions in relation to a quantifiable factor associated with the company's activities.
SI 2008/410 7 Sch 18, 19 (SI 2013/1970)	■ Comparative information is not required for the first year that the information above is provided.
	■ If the reporting period for the above information is different to that of the directors' report, then that fact must be stated.

AGM notice

LR13.8.8R Where the shareholders of a listed company are sent a notice of a meeting which includes any business other than routine business at an AGM, an explanatory circular must accompany the notice. If the other business is to be considered at or on the same day as an AGM, the explanation may be incorporated in the directors' report.

Auditor and disclosure of information to auditor

CA06 s418(2) The report should contain a statement to the effect that, in the case of each of the persons who are directors at the time when the report is approved, the following applies:

- As far as the director is aware, there is no relevant audit information of which the company's auditor is unaware; and
- The director has taken all the steps that he/she ought to have taken as a director in order to make him/herself aware of any relevant audit information and to establish that the company's auditor is aware of that information.

DV
CA06 s489(1) The auditors, PricewaterhouseCoopers LLP, have indicated their willingness to continue in office, and a resolution that they be re-appointed will be proposed at the annual general meeting.

DTR 7.2.1, 7.2.9

Corporate governance

The company's statement on corporate governance can be found in the corporate governance report on pages 31 to 48 of these financial statements. The corporate governance report forms part of this directors' report and is incorporated into it by cross-reference.

DTR 7.2.10R states that an issuer that is required to prepare a group directors' report must include in that report a description of the main features of the group's internal control and risk management systems in relation to the process for preparing consolidated financial statements. This may be included in the corporate governance statement, where the corporate governance statement is incorporated into the directors' report by cross-reference.

CA06 s419(1) By order of the board

CA06 s419(1) AB Smith

Company Secretary[1]
26 February 2014

---

[1] The directors' report has to be signed by the company secretary or a director after it has been approved by the board of directors. The copy of the directors' report that is delivered to the Registrar of Companies must be manually signed by the company secretary or a director

IFRS GAAP plc – year ended 31 December 2013

Remuneration report

Requirements for the directors' remuneration[1] report

The details of compliance and policy are usually set out as a remuneration committee report. Section 422(1) of the Companies Act 2006 requires this to be approved by the board, as it is the board's responsibility to report to shareholders. Schedule 8 to SI 2013/1981, the UK Corporate Governance Code and paragraph 9.8.8R of the Listing Rules contain information to be included in the report.

8 Sch Part 1(1) The remuneration report must include the following[2]:

**SI 2013/1981
8 Sch Part 2**

Annual Statement

Statement by chair of remuneration committee[3]

**SI 2013/1981
8 Sch Part 2(3)
LR 9.8.8R(1)**[4]

A summary for the relevant financial year of:

(a) the major decisions on directors' remuneration;
(b) any substantial changes relating to directors' remuneration made during the year; and
(c) the context in which those changes occurred and decisions have been taken.

**SI 2013/1981
8 Sch Part 3**

Annual report on remuneration

Information required to be audited

Single total figure of remuneration for each director (audited)

**SI 2013/1981
8 Sch Part 3
(4)(1), 5(1)
LR 9.8.8R(2)(a), (b)**

For each person who has served as a director of the company at any time during the year, set out in a table in the format below, the information prescribed.

**SI 2013/1981
8 Sch Part 3
(4)(2)**

The report may set out separate tables for directors who perform executive functions and those who do not[5] (i.e non-executive).

**SI 2013/1981
8 Sch Part 3
(4)(3)**

Unless otherwise indicated the sums set out in the table are in respect of the relevant financial year and relate to the director's performance of, or agreement to perform, qualifying services.

**SI 2013/1981
8 Sch Part 3
(6)(1)
LR 9.8.8R(2)(a)**

In addition to the columns described, columns:

(a) must be included to set out any other items in the nature of remuneration (other than payments to past directors) which are not set out in the columns headed (a) to (e); and

---

[1] The new requirements do not apply to financial years ending before 30 September 2013 when the previous requirements apply.[8Sch 4].
[2] Nothing in the Schedule prevents the directors setting out any such additional information as they think fit and any item may be shown in greater detail than required by the schedule. [8 Sch 2(2)]
[3] If there is no chair the report should be by the director nominated by the directors to make the statement [8Sch Part 2(3)].
[4] See Financial Conduct Authority Consultation Paper "Consequential Changes to the Listing Rules resulting from the BIS Directors' Remuneration Reporting Regulations and Narrative Reporting Regulations" (ref CP13/7*), issued in August 2013. Appendix 1 "Comparison of Listing Rule 9.8.8R and the new BIS Directors' Remuneration Reporting Regulations" provides an analysis of the regulations for the purpose of comparison against the requirements of the relevant listing rules.
[5] Information may, in respect of directors who do not perform an executive function, be omitted or modified where that requirement is not applicable to such a director and in such a case, particulars of, and the reasons for, the omission or modification must be given in the report. [8 Sch Part 1 2(4)].

IFRS GAAP plc – year ended 31 December 2013

	(b) may be included if there are any sub-totals or other items which the directors consider necessary in order to assist the understanding of the table.
SI 2013/1981 8 Sch Part 3 (7) (2)	Where it is necessary to assist the understanding of the table by the creation of sub-totals the columns headed (a) to (e) may be set out in any order other than the one set out below.
SI 2013/1981 8 Sch Part 3 (6)(2)	Any additional columns must be inserted before the column marked "Total".

Single total figure table[1]

	(a)	(b)	(c)	(d)	(e)	
SI 2013/1981 8 Sch Part 3 (5)(1); SI 2013/1981 8 Sch Part 3 (7); LR 9.8.8R(2)(a),(b)	Total amount of salary and fees	All taxable benefits	Money and other assets received or receivable as a result of the achievement of performance measures and targets relating to a period ending in that financial year.	Money and other assets receivable for periods of more than one financial year	All pension related benefits	Total
	2013 2012	2013 2012	2013 2012	2013 2012	2013 2012	2013 2012
	Director 1					
	Director 2					

SI 2013/1981 8 Sch Part 3 (9)(1) LR 9.8.8R(2)(b)	Each column in the table must contain, in such a manner to permit comparison, two amounts as follows: (a) the amount set out in the corresponding column in the report prepared in respect of the preceding financial year; and (b) the amount for the relevant financial year.
SI 2013/1981 8 Sch Part 3 (9)(2)	When an amount is given for the preceding financial year and that amount, when disclosed in the preceding financial year was, or included, an estimated amount, then in the relevant financial year: (a) it must be given as an actual amount; (b) the amount representing the difference between the estimate and the actual must not be included in the column relating to the relevant financial year; and (c) details of the calculation of the revised amount must be given in a note to the table.
SI 2013/1981 8 Sch Part 3 (8)(2)	Where any money, or other assets, reported in respect of any previous financial year are the subject of a recovery of the amount paid or the withholding of any amount for any reason in the relevant financial year: (a) the recovery or withholding so attributable must be shown in a separate column in the table as a negative value and deducted from the column headed "Total"; and (b) an explanation for the recovery or withholding and the basis of the calculation must be given in a note to the table.

[1] The directors may choose to display the table using alternative orientation. [8Sch Part 3 (5)(2)]

SI 2013/1981 8 Sch Part 3 (8)(3)	Where the calculations (other than in respect of a recovery or withholding) result in a negative value, the result must be expressed as zero in the relevant column in the relevant column in the table.
SI 2013/1981 8 Sch Part 3 (7); (10); (11).	Detailed requirements on the calculations, presentation and definitions of the amounts in the table are provided in paragraphs 7, 10 and 11 of Part 3 to the Schedule.
SI 2013/1981 8 Sch Part 3 (12)(1); LR 9.8.8R(2)(a)	A summary of the types of benefits in column (b) and the value, where significant, must be disclosed after the table.
SI 2013/1981 8 Sch Part 3 (12)(2);12(3) LR 9.8.8R(2)(a)	For every component of money and assets received and receivable in column (c) and (d), the relevant details must be disclosed after the table. The relevant details include; (i) details of performance measures and relative weighting; (ii) the performance target set at the beginning of the performance period and value of award achievable; (iii) for each performance measure details of actual performance and the resulting level of award; and (iv) particulars of how any discretion was exercised and the resulting level of award.
SI 2013/1981 8 Sch Part 3 (12)(4)	If amounts in column (c) and (d) (money and assets receivable) are deferred; (i) the amount must be stated; (ii) the percentage deferred; (iii) whether it was deferred cash or shares; and (iv) whether the deferral was subject to any conditions other than performance measures.
SI 2013/1981 8 Sch Part 3 (12)(5)	Where additional columns are included for other items in the nature of remuneration; the following must be disclosed, in a note to the table: (i) the basis on which the sums were calculated; and (ii) any details necessary for an understanding of the sums including performance measures or, if none, an explanation of why not.

Total pension entitlements (audited)

SI 2013/1981 8 Sch Part 3 (13)(1)	For each person who served as a director at any time during the relevant financial year and who has a prospective entitlement to defined benefits, cash balance benefits or benefits under a hybrid arrangement the report must disclose: ■ details of the rights as at the end of the year, including the person's normal retirement date (as per the pension scheme rules or otherwise determined); ■ a description of any additional benefit receivable in the event of early retirement; and ■ separate details relating to each type of benefit, where a person has rights under more than one type of pension benefit.

Scheme interests awarded during the financial year (audited)

SI 2013/1981 8 Sch Part 3 (14)(1) LR 9.8.8R(2)(a) SI 2013/1981 8 Sch Part 3 (14)(1)(a)	For each person who served as a director at any time during the relevant financial year a table setting out: ■ details of scheme interests awarded during the relevant financial year; and

IFRS GAAP plc – year ended 31 December 2013

SI 2013/1981
8 Sch Part 3
(14)(1)(b);
14(2);14(3)
LR 9.8.8R(2)(d)
LR
9.8.8R(3),(4)
	■ For each scheme interest:
	  ■ A description of the type of interest awarded;
	  ■ A description of the basis on which the award is made;
	  ■ The face value of the award (as defined);
	  ■ The percentage of the scheme interests that would be receivable if minimum performance was achieved; and
	  ■ For a share option an explanation of any difference between the exercise price per share and either share price at date of grant or average price.

Payments to past directors (audited)

SI 2013/1981 8 Sch Part 3 (15)	The report must contain details of any payment of money or other assets to any person who was not a director of the company at the time the payment was made, but who had been a director of the company before that time.
SI 2013/1981 8 Sch Part 3 (15)(a) – (f) LR 9.8.8R(2)(c).	The following are excluded from the above disclosure: ■ Any payments for payments for loss of office (see below); ■ Any payments shown in the single total figure table; ■ Payments disclosed in a previous directors' remuneration report; ■ Any payments below a *de minimis* threshold, which is stated in the report ■ Payments of regular pension benefits commenced in a previous year or dividend payments in respect of scheme interests retained after leaving office; and ■ Payments in respect of employment with or any contractual service performed other than as a director.

Payments for loss of office (audited)

SI 2013/1981 8 Sch Part 3 (16)(a) – (f)	The report must set out, for each person who has served as a director at any time during that year, or any previous year:
LR 9.8.8R(2)(a)	■ The total amount of any payment for loss of office paid to or receivable, in respect of that financial year broken down into each component and the value of each component; ■ An explanation of how each component was calculated; ■ Any other payments in connection with the termination of qualifying services, including the treatment of outstanding incentive awards that vest on or following termination;and ■ Where any discretion was exercised, an explanation of how it was exercised.
SI 2013/1981 8 Sch Part 3 (16)	The company can exclude amounts below a *de minimis* threshold set by the company and stated in the report.

Statement of directors' shareholding and share interests (audited)

SI 2013/1981 8 Sch Part 3 (17) LR 9.8.8R(2)(d)	The report must set out, for each person who has served as a director at any time during that year:
SI 2013/1981 8 Sch Part 3 (17)(a)	■ Statements of any requirements or guidelines for the director to own shares in the company and state whether or not those requirements or guidelines have been met; and

SI 2013/1981
8 Sch Part 3
(17)(b)
LR 9.8.8R(6)
	■ In a table or tables
	  ■ The total number of interests of the director, including interests of connected persons;
	  ■ Total number of scheme interests differentiating between shares and share options and those with or without performance measures;

- Details of those scheme interests (which may exclude any details included elsewhere in the report); and
- Details of share options which are vested but unexercised and exercised in the relevant financial year.

Information not required to be audited

Performance graph

SI 2013/1981 8 Sch Part 3 18(1)(a)(b)

A performance graph showing the company's total shareholder return compared with a broad equity market index chosen by the company over the five preceding financial years (including the financial year covered by the report), and the name of and reasons for the choice of broad equity market index.

Chief executive officer's remuneration

SI 2013/1981 8 Sch Part 3 18(2)(a)(b)(c)

A table showing, for each of the financial years, for the director undertaking the role of the chief executive officer:

- Total remuneration (as set out in the single total figure table);
- The sum in column (c) of the table as a percentage of the maximum that could have been paid in the financial year; and
- The sum in column (d) of the table as a percentage of the number of shares vesting against the maximum number of shares that could have been received or where paid in money and other assets as a percentage of the maximum that could have been paid.

In the first year of preparing this report 5 years information is required increasing annually thereafter to 10 years information.

SI 2013/1981 8 Sch Part 3 19(1)(a)(b)

In relation to remuneration in each of columns (a), (b) and (c) of the single total figure table the following information, in a manner which permits comparison:

- The percentage change from the preceding financial year; and

SI 2013/1981 8 Sch Part 3 19(3)

- The average percentage change from the preceding financial year in respect of the employees of the company (or group if the company is a parent company) as a whole.

SI 2013/1981 8 Sch Part 3 19(2)

Where the company considers the comparator group of employees as a whole is inappropriate, another group may be used, providing there is a statement setting out why the other group was chosen.

Relative importance of spend on pay

SI 2013/1981 8 Sch Part 3 20 (1) (a)(b)(c)

A table or graph that shows for the relevant financial year, and the preceding financial year, the actual expenditure and the difference in spend between those years on:

(a) remuneration paid to or receivable by all employees of the group;

(b) distributions to shareholders by way of dividends and share buyback; and

(c) any other significant payments or distributions or other uses of profit or cash deemed to assist in understanding the relevant importance of spend on pay.

SI 2013/1981 8 Sch Part 3 20(2)

An explanation of why the matters in (c) above were chosen and how the amounts were calculated.

SI 2013/1981 8 Sch Part 3 20(3)

Where the amounts in (c) above are not the same as in the previous year, an explanation for the change must be given.

IFRS GAAP plc – year ended 31 December 2013

Statement of implementation of remuneration policy in the following financial year

SI 2013/1981 8 Sch Part 3 21(1)) — A statement[1] describing how the company intends to implement the approved directors' remuneration policy in the next financial year.

SI 2013/1981 8 Sch Part 3 21(2)) — The statement must include:

- performance measures and relative weightings for each measure; and
- performance targets determined for the performance measures and how awards will be calculated.

SI 2013/1981 8 Sch Part 3 21(3)) — A statement of details of any change in the way the remuneration policy will be implemented in the next financial year compared to how it was implemented in the relevant financial year[2].

Consideration by the directors of matters relating to directors' remuneration (remuneration committee)

SI 2013/1981 8 Sch Part 3 22(1)) — Names of the members of the remuneration committee (at any time when directors' remuneration for the year is considered)[3].

SI 2013/1981 8 Sch Part 3 22(b) — The names of any person(s) providing advice to the remuneration committee that has materially assisted the committee with their decisions.

For any adviser to the remuneration committee, who is not a director of the company:

SI 2013/1981 8 Sch 22(c)(i)
SI 2013/1981 8 Sch Part 3 22(c)(ii)
SI 2013/1981 8 Sch Part 3 22(c)(iii)
SI 2013/1981 8 Sch Part 3 22(c)(iv)

- disclosure of the nature of any other services, performed by the adviser, to the company during the year;
- whether the adviser was appointed by the remuneration committee and how they were selected;
- whether, and how, the remuneration committee satisfied itself that the advice received was objective and independent; and
- the amount of the fee or other charge paid for the other services and the basis on which it was charged.

Statement of voting at general meeting

SI 2013/1981 8 Sch Part 3 23(a) and (b) LR 9.8.8R(1) — A statement of the percentage votes cast for and against and number of votes withheld at the last general meeting which considered resolutions of the following kind:

- the resolution to approve the directors' remuneration report; and
- the resolution to approve the directors' remuneration policy.

SI 2013/1981 8 Sch Part 3 23(c) LR 9.8.8R(1) — Where there was a significant percentage of votes against either resolution, a summary of the reasons for those votes (as far as known to the directors) and any actions taken by the directors in response to those votes.

---

[1] This statement need not include information elsewhere in the report.
[2] This disclosure is only required where this is not the first year of the approved remuneration policy. [8 Sch 21 (3)].
[3] The board should establish a remuneration committee of at least three (smaller companies:two) independent, non-executive directors. The chairman may also be a member, but not chair, of the committee if he/she is considered to be independent. The committee should make available its terms of reference. The committee should be responsible for setting remuneration for all executive directors and the chairman and also monitoring the remuneration for senior management. The board should determine the remuneration of non-executive directors. Shareholders should be invited to approve all new long-term incentive schemes. [UKCGC D.2.1-2.4].

IFRS GAAP plc – year ended 31 December 2013

SI 2013/1981 8 Sch Part 4	**Director's Remuneration policy**[1]
	Future policy table
SI 2013/1981 8 Sch Part 4 25(1),(2) LR 9.8.8R(1)	A table describing each of the components[2] of the remuneration package for the directors' which are in the remuneration policy. If a general policy table is prepared the table must include any particular arrangements specific to an individual director.
SI 2013/1981 8 Sch Part 4 26(a)-(e). LR 9.8.8R(1) LR 9.8.8R(7)	The table must include the following information: ■ how the component supports the short and long term objectives of the group (or company); ■ an explanation of how that component of the package operates; ■ the maximum that may be paid, in monetary terms or otherwise; ■ If applicable, an explanation of the framework using in assessing performance, including performance measures, their weighting, the amount that may be paid for minimum performance and for any further levels of performance; and ■ an explanation of provisions for recovery of amounts paid or withholding of amounts payable.
SI 2013/1981 8 Sch Part 4 27(a)-(e) LR 9.8.8R(7)	Notes to the table must include: ■ why performance measures were chosen and how any targets are set; ■ if applicable, an explanation of why there are no performance measures for any component, other than salary, fees, benefit or pension; ■ for any new component of the remuneration package why that component is now included; ■ any changes that have been made to any previous component and why they were made; and ■ an explanation of any differences in remuneration policy between that for directors and that for employees generally.
SI 2013/1981 8 Sch Part 4 28(a)-(c) LR 9.8.8R(1)	Information on non-executive directors may be set out in a separate table; if so the table must disclose the approach to determining: ■ the fee payable to such directors; ■ any additional fees for other duties; and ■ such other items as are considered to be in the nature of remuneration.
	Approach to recruitment remuneration
SI 2013/1981 8 Sch Part 4 29(1)-(3)	A statement of the principles applied when agreeing the various components of the remuneration package for the appointment of directors. Disclosure of components for inclusion and the approach adopted, and the maximum level of variable remuneration which may be granted, expressed in monetary terms or otherwise.
SI 2013/1981 8 Sch Part 4 29(1),(2),(4)	Remuneration representing compensation for the forfeit of any variable remuneration arrangements with a previous employer is not included in the maximum remuneration above, but is subject to separate disclosure.

[1] This is a separate part of the report [SI 2013/1981 8 Sch Part 4para 24(1)]. Where the resolution to approve a directors' remuneration policy includes the continuation of previous policy, this must be stated and the relevant provisions should be identified and for what period they shall apply. [para 24(2)]. Where the policy allows the directors' to exercise discretion on any aspect of the policy, the policy must set out the extent of that discretion in respect of any such variation, change or amendment [para 24(4)]. On the first occasion of a resolution approving the policy it should set out the date from which the policy is to take effect.
[2] Components include, but are not limited to, those items included in the single total figure table. [para 25(3)].

IFRS GAAP plc – year ended 31 December 2013

SI 2013/1981 8 Sch Part 4 30,32	*Service contracts and letters of appointment*
SI 2013/1981 8 Sch Part 4 30(1)-(3) LR 9.8.8R(7)	A description of any obligation in service contract or contracts, or proposed in service contracts to be entered into, which could give rise to, or impact on, remuneration payments or payments for loss of office, unless disclosed elsewhere in the report.
SI 2013/1981 8 Sch Part 4 31 LR 9.8.8R(7)	Where directors service contracts are not kept available for inspection at the registered office, disclosure of where they are kept and, if available on a website, a link to that website.
SI 2013/1981 8 Sch Part 4 32	The above disclosures apply to letters of appointment of directors.
LR 9.8.8R (8)	Details of any director's service contract that has a notice period in excess of one year or one with provisions for pre-determined compensation on termination that exceeds one year's salary and benefits in kind, including the reasons for such a notice period[1].
LR 9.8.8R (9)	Details of the unexpired term of any director's service contract for a director proposed for election or re-election at the forthcoming annual general meeting.
LR 9.8.8R(9)	If any director proposed for election or re-election at the forthcoming annual general meeting does not have a director's service contract, a statement to that effect.
	Illustration of application of remuneration policy
SI 2013/1981 8 Sch Part 4 33 LR 9.8.8R(1)	For each director (other than a director not performing an executive function), a bar chart indicating the level of remuneration receivable by the director in accordance with the policy in the first year to which the policy applies.
SI 2013/1981 8 Sch Part 4 34 LR 9.8.8R(1)	The bar chart must contain separate bars representing: (a) minimum remuneration receivable; (b) remuneration receivable if, in respect of performance measures and targets, the director was performing in line with the company's expectation; and (c) maximum remuneration receivable, excluding share price appreciation. Each bar must contain separate parts representing: (a) salary, fees, benefits, pension and any other item included in minimum remuneration; (b) remuneration where performance measures or targets relate to one financial year; and (c) remuneration where performance measures or targets relate to more than one financial year. Each bar must show: (a) percentage of the total comprised by each part; and (b) total value of remuneration expected for each bar.
SI 2013/1981 8 Sch Part 4 35	Description of the basis of calculation and assumptions used to compile the charts[2].

---

[1] The FCA consultation paper CP13/7* notes that these requirements are not in the BIS regulations. The consultation paper proposes removing this rule.

[2] It is not necessary for any matter to be included in the narrative description which has been set out in the future policy table prepared under (SI 2013/1981 Part 4) paragraph 25.

Policy on payment for loss of office

SI 2013/1981 8 Sch Part 4 36 LR 9.8.8R(8)	A description of the company's policy on setting of notice periods under service contracts.
SI 2013/1981 8 Sch Part 4 37(a)-(c)	A description of the principles for determining payments for loss of office including: (a) an indication of how each component of the payment will be calculated; (b) whether, and how, the circumstances of the director's loss of office and performance during the period of qualifying service are relevant to the exercise of any discretion; and (c) any contractual provision agreed prior to 27 June 2012 that could impact on the amount of the payment.

Statement of consideration of employment conditions elsewhere in the company

SI 2013/1981 8 Sch Part 4 38	A statement of how the pay and employment conditions of employees of the company and elsewhere in the group were taken into account when determining the policy for directors' remuneration.
SI 2013/1981 8 Sch Part 4 39	Disclosure of: (a) whether, and how, the company consulted with employees when drawing up the directors' remuneration policy; and (b) whether any remuneration comparison measures were used and, if so, what they were and how the information was taken into account.

Statement of consideration of shareholder views

SI 2013/1981 8 Sch Part 4 40	A statement of whether, and how, any views on directors' remuneration, expressed to the company by shareholders, have been taken into account in the formulation of the policy.

Other matters – omission of information and explanation

SI 2013/1981 8 Sch Part 1 2(5), (6)	Any requirement to provide information in respect of performance measures or targets does not require disclosure of information, which in the opinion of the directors' is commercially sensitive. The particulars of, and the reasons for, the omission must be given in the report and an indication of when (if at all) the information is to be reported to members.
SI 2013/1981 8 Sch Part 1 2(4)	Information may, in respect of non-executive directors, be omitted or modified where the requirement is not applicable to such a director. Particulars of, and the reasons for, the omission or modification must be given in the report.
APB 2002/2 p 12-16	Where the remuneration report does not clarify which parts of the report have been audited, such clarification in the audit report.

Listing rules – additional requirements

LR 9.8.4R(5)	Details should be given of any arrangement under which a director has waived or agreed to waive any emoluments from the company or any subsidiary.
LR 9.8.4R(6)	Where a director has agreed to waive future emoluments, details should be given of such waiver together with details relating to emoluments that were waived in the year.

IFRS GAAP plc – year ended 31 December 2013

LR9.8.8R(1) – (8), (10)	The FCA Consultation paper CP13/7 compared the Listing Rules 9.8.8R with the Directors' Remuneration Reporting Regulations. The only rule where the consultation paper definitively concluded to retain a rule was LR9.8.8R(9).
LR9.8.8R(9)	Details of the unexpired term of any director's service contract, of a director proposed for election or re-election at the forthcoming annual general meeting, and if there is no such contract a statement to that effect.
LR9.8.8R(10)	Disclosure of the policy on the granting of options or awards under its employee's share schemes and other long term incentive schemes.
	Explanations and justifications of any departure from the policy in the period under review and any changes in the policy from the preceding year[1].
LR 9.4.3R	Additional disclosures are required in the first annual report published following the date on which the relevant director becomes eligible to participate in an arrangement in which that director is the only participant and the arrangement is established specifically to facilitate, in unusual circumstances, the recruitment or retention of that director.

Shareholder approval

CA06 s439(1)	The board should put an ordinary resolution to shareholders for the approval of the remuneration report, other than the part containing the directors' remuneration policy (see CA06 s439A).
CA06 s439A(1)	At least every third year the board must put an ordinary resolution to shareholders for the approval of the directors' remuneration policy.

Corporate governance requirements

UKCGC D.1 Main principle	Levels of remuneration should be sufficient to attract, retain and motivate directors of the quality required to run the company successfully. A significant portion of executive director's remuneration should be structured to link rewards to corporate and individual performance.
UKCGC D.1.1	In designing schemes of performance-related remuneration, remuneration committees should follow the provisions of Schedule A to the UK Corporate Governance Code. These include:
UKCGC Sch A	■ Performance targets should be relevant, stretching and designed to promote the long-term success of the company.
UKCGC Sch A	■ Executive share options should not be offered at a discount save as permitted by LR 9.4.4R.
UKCGC Sch A	■ Share options and other long term incentive schemes should normally be phased rather than awarded in large blocks.
UKCGC Sch A	■ Shares granted or other forms of deferred remuneration should not vest, and options should not be exercisable, in less than three years.
UKCGC D1.2	Where a company releases an executive director to serve as a non-executive director elsewhere, a statement as to whether or not the director will retain such earnings, and if so, what the remuneration is.
UKCGC D.1.3	The remuneration of all non-executive directors should reflect the time commitment and responsibilities of the role. Their remuneration should not include share options or other performance related elements.

---

[1] The FCA consultation paper CP13/7* notes that this requirement is not in the BIS regulations. It proposes eliminating this from the Listing Rules.

UKCGC D.1.4	The remuneration committee should carefully consider what compensation commitments (including pension contributions and all other elements) its directors' terms of appointment would entail in the event of early termination. The aim should be to avoid rewarding poor performance. They should take a robust line on reducing compensation to reflect departing directors' obligations to mitigate loss.
UKCGC D.1.5	Notice or contract periods should be set at one year or less. If it is necessary to offer a longer notice or contract periods to new directors from outside, such periods should reduce to one year or less after the initial period.
UKCGC Main Principle D.2	There should be a formal and transparent procedure for developing policy on executive remuneration and for fixing the remuneration packages of individual directors. No director should be involved in deciding his or her own remuneration.
UKCGC D.2.1 UKCGC D.2.2	To avoid potential conflicts of interest, boards of directors should set up remuneration committees of independent non-executive directors to make recommendations to the board, within agreed terms of reference, on the company's framework of executive remuneration and its cost; and to determine on their behalf the level and structure of remuneration for senior management, including pension rights and any compensation payments.
	The remuneration committee's terms of reference, explaining its role and the authority delegated to it by the board, should be publicly available (that is, available on request and on the company's web site).
UKCGC D.2.1	The remuneration committee should consist of at least three, or in the case of smaller companies, two, independent non-executive directors. The company chairman may also be a member of, but not chair, the committee if he or she was considered independent on appointment as chairman.
UKCGC D.2.2	The definition of senior management is determined by the board but would normally include the first layer of management below board level.
UKCGC D.2 Supporting principle	The chairman of the board should ensure that the company maintains contact as required with its principal shareholders about remuneration.
UKCGC D.2.3	The board itself, or where required by the Articles of Association the shareholders, should determine the remuneration of non-executive directors within the limits set by the Articles. Where permitted by the Articles, the board may delegate this responsibility to a committee, which may include the chief executive.
UKCGC D.2.4	Shareholders should be invited specifically to approve all new long-term incentive schemes (including share option schemes) that potentially commit shareholders' funds over more than one year or dilute the equity, except as permitted by LR 9.4.2R and significant changes to existing schemes.

Other areas of guidance

Executive remuneration is an area of investor focus. In addition to the requirements above, Remuneration committees should, amongst others, consider:

- Association of British Insurers – ABI Principles of Remuneration;
- National Association of Pension Funds – 'Remuneration principles for building and reinforcing long-term business success';
- RiskMetric Group's '2010 RiskMetrics U.K. Remuneration Guidance'; and
- RREV '2012 RREV U.K. Remuneration Guidance'.

IFRS GAAP plc – year ended 31 December 2013

Interests in shares (and derivatives or any other financial instrument relating to those shares)[1]

LR 9.8.6R(1) The interests of the directors and their connected persons in the shares of the company and other group members were:

	1 January 2013	**31 December 2013**
The company – ordinary shares 1p		
Executive directors		
Director 1		
Director 2		
Director 3		
Director 4		
Non-executive directors		
Director 5		
Director 6		
X Limited – ordinary shares C1		
Executive directors		
Director 1		
Y Limited – preference shares 50c		
Non-executive directors		
Director 7		

LR 9.8.6R(1) There has been no change in the interests set out above between 31 December 2013 and 26 February 2014.

On behalf of the board

R Graham
Chairman of the remuneration committee[2]
26 February 2014

---

[1] This disclosure is required by the Listing Rules.
[2] The remuneration report should be approved by the board and signed on its behalf by a director or the company secretary. The remuneration report includes the requirements of Schedule 8 to SI 2013/1981. In addition, Schedule 5 to SI 2008/410 requires certain aggregate information on emoluments to be included by quoted companies in the notes to the financial statements.

Corporate governance report

Introduction

This report sets out the disclosure requirements for a UK premium listed company preparing its corporate governance statement. Premium listed companies are those companies with equity listings which are subject to the more stringent, super-equivalent UK listing requirements as set out in the FCA's Listing Rules (see Issue 2 of the Financial Conduct Authority (FCA) (previously FSA) Listing Regime FAQs published in June 2010). The relevant corporate governance disclosure requirements are set out in three places:

- FCA Listing Rule 9.8.6 R (which includes the 'comply or explain' requirement);
- FCA Disclosure and Transparency Rules (DTR) Section 7.1 and 7.2 (which set out certain mandatory disclosures); and
- The UK Corporate Governance Code (UKCGC - issued in September 2012) and associated guidance from the Financial Reporting Council (FRC).

The provisions of the UKCGC are set out under each section of a suggested governance report below. The order of the sections does not follow the UKCGC exactly, reflecting normal practice among premium listed companies. The order used by companies should be driven by how best to communicate their messages on governance rather than the order of the provisions of the UKCGC.

Those provisions and other rules that require specific disclosures in the corporate governance statement are given immediately after the relevant principles, in normal font. The remaining provisions relating to each principle are given in *italics* for information purposes.

Commentary

The corporate governance disclosures included in these illustrative financial statements are based on the requirements for a UK premium listed company. Overseas premium listed companies (that is, companies incorporated overseas but with a premium listing in the UK) are also required to comply with the UKCGC. The FCA has not, however, applied Listing Rule 9.8.6(3), which requires "a statement made by the directors that the business is a going concern" to overseas premium listed companies. Notwithstanding this, provision C.1.3 of the UKCGC states that "the directors should report in annual and half yearly financial statements that the business is a going concern..." so any failure of an overseas premium listed company to do this would need to be explained under Listing Rule 9.8.6(6).

Overseas companies (whether standard or premium listed) are required to comply with DTR 7.2 (Corporate Governance statements) but not DTR 7.1 (Audit Committees). The requirements are summarised in the table below.

IFRS GAAP plc – year ended 31 December 2013

	UK premium	UK standard	Overseas premium	Overseas standard
Listing Rule 9.8.6(5) and (6) (Compliance statement)	✓	✗	✓	✗
The UKCGC ('comply or explain')	✓	✗	✓	✗
Listing Rule 9.8.6(3) (Going concern statement)	✓	✗	✗ (though UKCGC provision C.1.3 requires similar going concern disclosures)	✗
FCA Corporate Governance Rules				
DTR 7.1 (Audit Committees)	✓	✓	✗	✗
DTR 7.2 (Corporate Governance Statement)	✓	✓	✓	✓
Auditors' Report (LR 9.8.10) – 9 code provisions	✓	✗	✓ (though APB guidance relates only to UK companies)	✗

DTR reporting requirements – all companies

DTR 7.2.1R The issuer must include a corporate governance statement in its directors' report. This statement must be included as a specific section of the directors' report and must contain at least the information set out in DTR 7.2.2R to 7.2.7R and, where consolidated accounts are prepared, DTR 7.2.10R.

DTR 7.2.2R The corporate governance statement must contain a reference to: (1) the corporate governance code to which the issuer is subject, (2) the governance code which the issuer may have voluntarily decided to apply; and/or (3) all relevant information about the corporate governance practices applied beyond the requirements under national law.

DTR 7.2.3R (1) An issuer which is complying with DTR 7.2.2R (1) or (2) must:

(a) state in its directors' report where the relevant corporate governance code is publicly available; and

(b) to the extent that it departs from that corporate governance code, explain which parts of the corporate governance code it departs from and the reasons for doing so.

(2) Where DTR 7.2.2R(3) applies, the issuer must make its corporate governance practices publicly available and state in its directors' report where they can be found.

(3) If an issuer has decided not to apply any provision of a corporate governance code referred to under DTR 7.2.2R(1) and (2), it must explain its reasons for that decision.

IFRS GAAP plc – year ended 31 December 2013

Commentary

In effect DTR 7.2.3R means that a company that voluntarily applies any corporate governance code must report against it; it is not permitted voluntarily to put in place the governance processes to apply a code without reporting against it.

DTR 7.2.5R The corporate governance statement must contain a description of the main features of the issuer's internal control and risk management systems in relation to the financial reporting process.

DTR 7.2.6R The corporate governance statement must contain the information required by paragraph 13(2)(c), (d), (f), (h) and (i) of Schedule 7 to the Large and Medium-sized Companies and Groups (Accounts and Reports) Regulations 2008 (SI 2008/410) (information about share capital required under Directive 2004/25/EC (the Takeover Directive)) where the issuer is subject to the requirements of that paragraph. (For disclosure requirements refer to the Directors' Report).

DTR 7.2.7R The corporate governance statement must contain a description of the composition and operation of the issuer's administrative, management and supervisory bodies and their committees.

DTR 7.2.9R An issuer may elect that instead of including its corporate governance statement in its directors' report, the information required by DTR 7.2.1R to DTR 7.2.7R may be set out:

(1) in a separate report published together with and in the same manner as its annual report. In the event of a separate report, the corporate governance statement must contain either the information required by DTR 7.2.6R or a reference to the directors' report where that information is made available; or
(2) by means of a reference in its directors' report to where such document is publicly available on the issuer's website.

Commentary

Although DTR 7.2.9R is relevant to all listed companies, a premium listed company is subject to Listing Rule requirements and will therefore have to include the corporate governance information within its annual report rather than only on its website.

DTR 7.2.10R Subject to DTR 7.2.11R, an issuer which is required to prepare a group directors' report within the meaning of section 415(2) of the Companies Act 2006 must include in that report a description of the main features of the group's internal control and risk management systems in relation to the process for preparing consolidated accounts. In the event that the issuer presents its own annual report and its consolidated annual report as a single report, this information must be included in the corporate governance statement required by DTR 7.2.1R.

DTR 7.2.11R An issuer that elects to include its corporate governance statement in a separate report as permitted by DTR 7.2.9(1) must provide the information required by DTR 7.2.10R in that report.

IFRS GAAP plc – year ended 31 December 2013

34

> ### Commentary
>
> **DTR 7.2.4G**
> **DTR 7.2.8G**
> The DTR requirements above apply to both premium and standard listed companies. There are a number of overlaps between the provisions in the UKCGC and the DTR requirements. These are explained in the guidance provisions from the DTR set out below. Where there are additional disclosure requirements in the DTR, these are included under the relevant area of governance in this chapter.
>
> A listed company which complies with LR 9.8.6R(6) (the comply or explain rule in relation to the UKCGC) will satisfy the requirements of DTR 7.2.2R and 7.2.3R.
>
> In the FCA's view, the information specified in provisions A.1.1, A.1.2, B.2.4, C.3.8 and D.2.1 of the UKCGC will satisfy the requirements of DTR 7.2.7R.

Chairman's introduction

UKCGC Preface para 6
The UKCGC encourages personal reporting by the chairman on how the principles relating to the role and effectiveness of the board have been applied (sections A & B of the UKCGC). Most companies now do this, usually as an introduction to the corporate governance report, and some also have personal reporting from the chairmen of board committees.

Compliance

LR 9.8.6(5)
A statement must be made of how the company has applied the main principles of the UKCGC in a manner that enables shareholders to evaluate how the principles have been applied. The form and content of this part of the statement are not prescribed. The intention is for companies to explain their governance policies in light of the UKCGC principles, and the 'comply or explain' section in the 'preamble' to the UKCGC contains some guidance in this area.

LR 9.8.6(6)
DTR 7.2.3R (1)(b), (2), (3)
A statement must be made as to whether the company has complied throughout the accounting period with all relevant UKCGC provisions. Where the company has not complied with all of the provisions, or has complied for only part of the accounting period, a statement to that effect must be made specifying the provisions that have not been complied with and where details of the company's corporate governance practices can be found. Reasons must also be given for any non-compliance, and where relevant, the period of non-compliance must be stated. It is considered best practice for the company to set out the steps it is taking, or will be taking, towards full compliance in the future, if indeed the board judges full compliance to be best for the business.

> ### Commentary
>
> A listed company that complies with LR 9.8.6R(6) (the comply-or-explain rule in relation to the UKCGC) will satisfy the requirements of DTR 7.2.2R and 7.2.3R.
>
> The FRC issued 'What constitutes an explanation under comply-or-explain' in February 2012. These features have now been incorporated in the introductory section of the 2012 edition of the Code

IFRS GAAP plc – year ended 31 December 2013

The board and its committees

Main principle A.1	Every company should be headed by an effective board which is collectively responsible for the long-term success of the company.
Main principle A.2	There should be a clear division of responsibilities at the head of the company between the running of the board and the executive responsibility for the running of the company's business. No one individual should have unfettered powers of decision.
Main principle A.3	The chairman is responsible for leadership of the board and ensuring its effectiveness on all aspects of the role.
Main principle A.4	As part of their role as members of a unitary board, non-executive directors should constructively challenge and help develop proposals on strategy.
Main principle B.5	The board should be supplied in a timely manner with information in a form and of a quality appropriate to enable it to discharge its duties.
UKCGC A.1.1	A statement should be made about how the board operates, including a high-level statement of which types of decisions are taken by the board and which are delegated to management.
DTR 7.2.7R	The corporate governance statement must contain a description of the composition and operation of the company's administrative, management and supervisory bodies and their committees.

Commentary

The above provisions overlap; the DTR confirms that, if a company provides the information specified by UKCGC A.1.1 above, it will satisfy the relevant requirements of DTR 7.2.7R.

UKCGC A.1.2	The annual report should identify: ■ The chairman. ■ The deputy chairman (where applicable). ■ The chief executive. ■ The senior independent director. ■ The chairmen and members of each of the nomination, audit and remuneration committees.
UKCGC A.1.2	It should also set out the number of meetings of the board and each committee and individual attendance by directors.
DTR 7.1.5R	The company must make a statement available on how the audit committee (or equivalent body) carries out its responsibilities and how it is composed.

Commentary

The above provisions overlap; the DTR confirms that, if a company provides the information specified by UKCGC A.1.2 above and UKCGC C.3.3, it will satisfy the relevant requirements of DTR 7.1.5 and DTR 7.2.7.

IFRS GAAP plc – year ended 31 December 2013

Other related provisions

UKCGC A.1.1 (a) The board should meet sufficiently regularly to discharge its duties effectively. There should be a formal schedule of matters specifically reserved for its decision.

UKCGC A.2.1 (b) The roles of chairman and chief executive should not be exercised by the same individual. The division of responsibilities between the chairman and chief executive should be clearly established, set out in writing and agreed by the board.

UKCGC A.1.3 (c) The company should arrange appropriate insurance cover in respect of legal action against its directors.

UKCGC A.4.3 (d) Where directors have concerns which cannot be resolved about the running of the company or a proposed action, they should ensure that their concerns are recorded in the board minutes. On resignation, non-executive directors should provide a written statement to the chairman, for circulation to the board, if they have any such concerns.

UKCGC B.2.1, C.3.3, D.2.1 (e) The terms of reference of the nomination, audit and remuneration committees, including each committee's role and authority delegated to it by the board, should be made available. The recommendation can be met by making the information available on the company's web site.

UKCGC B.5.1 (f) All directors, especially non-executive directors, should have access to independent professional advice, at the expense of the company, where they judge it necessary to discharge their responsibilities as directors. Committees should be provided with sufficient resources to undertake their duties.

UKCGC B.5.2 (g) All directors should have access to the advice and services of the company secretary who is responsible to the board for ensuring that board procedures are complied with. The appointment and removal of the company secretary should be a matter for the board as a whole.

Board balance and independence

Main principle B.1 The board and its committees should have the appropriate balance of skills, experience, independence and knowledge of the company to enable them to discharge their respective duties and responsibilities effectively.

UKCGC B.1.1 The annual report should identify each non-executive director that the board considers to be independent. If the board considers a director to be independent, but circumstances or relationships exist that may appear relevant to that decision, disclosure should be made of the reasons for determining that director to be independent.

Companies Act 2006 s171-177 The Companies Act 2006 introduced a duty to avoid a conflict of interest: a director must avoid any situation where he/she has a conflict, although such conflicts may be authorised by non-interested directors as long as there is authority in the company's Articles for this to happen. It is recommended that companies include a transparent disclosure in their corporate governance statement in confirming to shareholders that the conflicts authorisation procedures have been followed.

Other related provisions

UKCGC B.1.1 (a) The board should determine whether each non-executive director is independent in character and judgement and whether there are relationships or circumstances which are likely to affect a director's independence. These include:

- Employment with the company or group within the last five years.
- A material business relationship within the last three years between the company and the director, or a body of which he/she is a partner, shareholder, director or senior employee.
- Any entitlement to remuneration from the company other than a director's fee or participation in the share option or performance-related pay scheme or membership of the company's pension scheme.
- Close family ties between the director and any of the company's advisers, directors or senior employees.
- A cross-directorship or significant links with other directors through involvement in other companies or bodies.
- Representing a significant shareholder.
- More than nine years' service on the board.

UKCGC B.1.2 (b) At least half the board, excluding the chairman, should comprise independent non-executive directors. A smaller company (that is, a company below the FTSE 350 throughout the year immediately prior to the reporting year) should have at least two independent non-executive directors.

UKCGC C.3.1, UKCGC D.2.1 (c) The board should establish both an audit committee and a remuneration committee of at least three, or in the case of smaller companies (that is, those below the FTSE 350 throughout the year immediately prior to the reporting year) two independent non-executive directors.

UKCGC D.2.1 (d) The company chairman may also be a member of, but not chair, the remuneration committee if he or she was considered independent on appointment.

UKCGC C.3.1 (e) For smaller companies, the company chairman may also be a member of, but not chair, the audit committee if he or she was considered independent on appointment. This is in addition to the two independent non-executive directors.

UKCGC B.2.1 (f) The nomination committee should have a majority of independent non-executive directors. The chairman or an independent non-executive director should be chair of the committee. The chairman should not chair the nomination committee when it is dealing with the appointment of a successor to the chairmanship.

UKCGC A.4.1 (g) An independent non-executive director should be appointed by the board as the senior independent director. The director should provide a sounding board for the chairman and serve as an intermediary for other directors. This director should also be available to shareholders if they have concerns which contact through the normal channels of chairman, chief executive or finance director has failed to resolve or for which such contact is inappropriate.

UKCGC A.3.1 (h) A chief executive should not go on to be chairman of the same company. If, exceptionally, the board decides that a chief executive should become chairman, the board should consult major shareholders in advance and set out its reasons for that appointment at the time of appointment and in the next annual report.

UKCGC A.3.1 (i) On appointment, the chairman should meet the independence criteria set out in B.1.1.

Appointments to the board

Main principle B.2 There should be a formal, rigorous and transparent procedure for the appointment of new directors to the board.

Main principle B.3 All directors should be able to allocate sufficient time to the company to discharge their responsibilities effectively.

Main principle B.4	All directors should receive induction on joining the board and should regularly update and refresh their skills and knowledge.
UKCGC B.3.1	Disclosure should be made of the chairman's other significant commitments before his/her appointment. Any changes to these should be reported to the board as they arise and their impact explained in the next annual report.

Other related provisions

UKCGC B.2.1	(a)	There should be a nomination committee which should lead the process for board appointment and make recommendations to the board.
UKCGC B.2.3	(b)	Non-executive directors should be appointed for specified terms subject to re-election and to statutory provisions relating to the removal of a director. Any term beyond six years for a non-executive director should be subject to particularly rigorous review and should take into account progressive refreshing of the board.
UKCGC B.3.1	(c)	The nomination committee should prepare a job specification for the appointment of a chairman, including an assessment of the time commitment expected, recognising the need for availability in the event of crises.
UKCGC B.3.2	(d)	The terms and conditions of appointment of non-executive directors should be made available for inspection (at the company's registered office during business hours and at the AGM (for 15 minutes before the meeting and during the meeting). This information may be made available on the company's website.
UKCGC B.3.2	(e)	Letters of appointment should set out the expected time commitment. Non-executive directors should undertake that they will have sufficient time to meet what is expected of them. Their other significant commitments should be disclosed to the board before appointment, along with an indication of the time involved, and upon subsequent changes.
UKCGC B.3.3	(f)	The board should not agree to a full time executive director taking on more than one non-executive directorship in a FTSE 100 company nor the chairmanship of such a company.
UKCGC B.4.1	(g)	The chairman should ensure that new directors receive a full, formal and tailored induction on joining the board. The directors should avail themselves of opportunities to meet major shareholders.
UKCGC B.4.2	(h)	The chairman should regularly review and agree with each director their training and development needs.

Re-election of directors

Main principle B.7	All directors should be submitted for re-election at regular intervals, subject to continued satisfactory performance.

Other related provisions

UKCGC B.7.1	(a)	All directors of FTSE 350 companies should be subject to annual re-election by shareholders. All other directors should be subject to election by shareholders at the first AGM after their appointment and to re-election thereafter at intervals of no more than three years. Non-executive directors who have served longer than nine years should be subject to annual re-election.
UKCGC B.7.1	(b)	In the papers sent out to shareholders the names of directors submitted for election or re-election should be accompanied by sufficient biographical details to enable shareholders to make an informed decision on their election.

UKCGC B.7.2	(c) The board should set out to shareholders in the AGM papers why they believe an individual should be elected as a non-executive director. When proposing re-election, the chairman should confirm that, following formal performance evaluation, the individual's performance continues to be effective and to demonstrate commitment to the role.

Performance evaluation

Main principle B.6	The board should undertake a formal and rigorous annual evaluation of its own performance and that of its committees and individual directors.
UKCGC B.6.1	The report should state how performance evaluations of the board, its committees and its individual directors have been conducted.
UKCGC B.6.2	Where an external facilitator is used to evaluate the board, they should be identified in the annual report and a statement made as to whether the facilitator has any other connection with the company.

Other related provisions:

UKCGC B.6.2	(a) All FTSE 350 companies should engage an external party to evaluate the performance of the board at least every three years.
UKCGC A.4.2, UKCGC B.6.3	(b) The chairman should hold meetings with the non-executive directors without the executive directors present.
	(c) The non-executive directors, led by the senior independent director, should be responsible for performance evaluation of the chairman, taking into account the views of the executive directors.

Report of the nomination committee

UKCGC B.2.4	A separate section describing the work of the nomination committee should be given in the annual report. This should include the process used in relation to board appointments. This section should include a description of the board's policy on diversity, including gender, any measurable objectives that it has set for implementing the policy, and progress on achieving the objectives. An explanation should be given if neither an external search consultancy nor open advertising has been used in the appointment of a chairman or a non-executive director. Where an external search consultancy has been used, it should be identified in the report and a statement should be made as to whether it has any other connection with the company.

Commentary

The above provision overlaps and, the DTR confirms that, if a company provides the information specified by UKCGC B.2.4 above, it will satisfy the relevant requirements of DTR 7.2.7.

Other related provisions

UKCGC B.2.1	(a) The nomination committee should lead the process for board appointments and make recommendations to the board. The majority of the committee should be independent non-executive directors. The chairman should chair the committee, but the chairman should not chair the nomination committee when it is dealing with the appointment of a successor to the chairmanship.

| UKCGC B.2.2 | (b) The nomination committee should evaluate the balance of skills, experience, independence and knowledge of the board and, in the light of this evaluation, prepare a description of the role and responsibilities required for a particular appointment. |

Commentary

In February 2011, Lord Davies published his report *Women on Boards*. This is in line with supporting principle B.2, which states that 'the search for board candidates should be conducted, and appointments made, on merit, against objective criteria and with due regard for the benefits of diversity on the board, including gender'. Lord Davies recommended that FTSE 350 companies should set out their targets for female board representation by 2013 and 2015.

Audit committee and auditors

| Main principle C.3 | The board should establish formal and transparent arrangements for considering how they should apply the corporate reporting and risk management and internal control principles and for maintaining an appropriate relationship with the company's auditors. |

Report of the audit committee

Commentary

The FRC Guidance on Audit Committees (ACG) (formerly known as the Smith Guidance) was updated in 2012 at the same time as the UKCGC. It is designed to assist company boards in making suitable arrangements for their audit committees in carrying out their role. The disclosure recommendations of the ACG have been included below. FRC 'Guidance' does not form part of the UKCGC and is therefore not subject to the comply-or-explain mechanism, but it is intended to assist with implementing the relevant provisions of the UKCGC.

| ACG 5.1, UKCGC C.3.8 | A separate section of the annual report should describe the work of the committee in discharging its responsibilities. |

| UKCGC C.3.8, ACG 5.2 | The report should include:
■ a summary of the role of the audit committee;
■ the names and qualifications of all members of the audit committee during the period;
■ the number of audit committee meetings;
■ the significant issues that the committee considered in relation to the financial statements, and how these issues were addressed;
■ an explanation of how it has assessed the effectiveness of the external audit process and the approach taken to the appointment or reappointment of the external auditor, and information on the length of tenure of the current audit firm and when a tender was last conducted;
■ and, if the external auditor provides non-audit services, an explanation of how auditor objectivity and independence is safeguarded. |

| ACG 4.46 | The explanation of how auditor objectivity and independence is safeguarded should:
■ describe the work of the committee in discharging its responsibilities; |

IFRS GAAP plc – year ended 31 December 2013

41

- set out the audit committee's policy on the engagement of the external auditor to supply non-audit services in sufficient detail to describe each of the elements in paragraph 4.39 (see below), or cross-refer to where this information can be found on the company's website;
- set out or cross-refer to the fees paid to the auditor for audit services, audit related services and other non-audit services; and if the auditor provides non-audit services other than audit related services, explain for each significant engagement, or category of engagement, what the services are, why the audit committee concluded it was in the interests of the company to purchase them from the external auditor (rather than another supplier) and how auditor objectivity and independence has been safeguarded.

UKCGC C.3.4, ACG 4.5	Where requested by the board, the audit committee should provide advice on whether the annual report and accounts, taken as a whole, is fair, balanced and understandable and provides the information necessary for shareholders to assess the company's performance, business model and strategy.

Commentary

Although this is not strictly a disclosure provision of the UKCGC, it is likely that an audit committee which advises the board on this matter will want to indicate this in the audit committee report.

UKCGC C.3.6, ACG 4.11	Where there is no internal audit function, the reasons for its absence should be explained.
UKCGC C.3.7, ACG 4.20	The audit committee should have primary responsibility for making a recommendation to the board on the appointment, reappointment and removal of the external auditors. FTSE 350 companies should put the external audit contract out to tender at least every ten years. If the board does not accept the audit committee's recommendation, the annual report and any papers recommending appointment or reappointment should include a statement from the audit committee explaining its recommendation and the reasons why the board has taken a different position.
ACG 4.26	The audit committee section of the annual report should include an explanation of how the committee has assessed the effectiveness of the external audit process and of the approach taken to the appointment or reappointment of the external auditor, in order that shareholders can understand why it recommended either to reappoint, or change, the auditors. It should also include information on the length of tenure of the current audit firm, when a tender was last conducted, and any contractual obligations that acted to restrict the audit committee's choice of external auditors.
	Other related provisions
ACG 4.39	*The audit committee should set and apply a formal policy specifying the types of non-audit service (if any):*
	- *for which the use of the external auditor is pre-approved (that is, approval has been given in advance as a matter of policy, rather than the specific approval of an engagement being sought before it is contracted);*
	- *for which specific approval from the audit committee is required before they are contracted; and*
	- *from which the external auditor is excluded.*
UKCGC C.3.1,	(a) The audit committee should consist of at least three, or in the case of smaller companies, (that is, those below the FTSE 350 throughout the year immediately

ACG 2.1 and 2.3	prior to the reporting year), two independent non-executive directors. In smaller companies the chairman may be a member of, but not chair, the committee in addition to the independent non-executive directors, provided he or she was considered independent on appointment as chairman. The board should satisfy itself that at least one member of the audit committee has recent and relevant financial experience.
DTR 7.1.1R, 7.1.2G	(b) The audit committee should have at least one member who is independent; at least one member should have competence in accounting and/or auditing. These requirements may be satisfied by the same member or by different members of the committee.

Commentary

This is a relaxation for smaller companies that were below the FTSE 350 throughout the year immediately prior to the reporting year and was introduced to help smaller companies comply with this Code provision.

There is a difference between the Code recommendation and the DTR requirement as to the composition of the audit committee; however, if a company complies with the Code provision, it will fulfil the DTR requirement.

DTR 7.1.4R	(c) A company must base any proposal to appoint the auditor on a recommendation by the audit committee (or equivalent body).
UKCGC C.3.2, ACG 2.2	(d) The audit committee should have written terms of reference setting out its responsibilities that should include:
	■ Monitoring the integrity of the company's financial statements and announcements relating to financial performance and reviewing significant financial reporting judgements contained in them.
	■ Reviewing the company's financial and non-financial internal controls and risk management systems (to the extent that these are not delegated to another committee made up of independent non-executive directors).
	■ Monitoring and reviewing the effectiveness of the group's internal audit function.
	■ Making recommendations to the board relating to the appointment, reappointment and removal of the external auditor and approving the remuneration and terms of engagement of the external auditor.
	■ Reviewing and monitoring the external auditor's independence and objectivity and the effectiveness of the audit processes, taking into consideration relevant UK professional and regulatory developments.
	■ Developing and implementing a policy on the engagement of the external auditor to supply non-audit services, taking into account relevant ethical guidance, and reporting to the board, identifying matters where action or improvement is needed.
	■ Reporting to the board on how it has discharged its responsibilities.
DTR 7.1.3R	(e) As a minimum, the audit committee must:
	■ monitor the financial reporting process;
	■ monitor the effectiveness of the company's internal control, internal audit where applicable, and risk management systems;
	■ monitor the statutory audit of the annual and consolidated accounts;
	■ review and monitor the external auditor's independence and the provision of additional services.

Commentary

The above provisions overlap, and the DTR confirms, that if a company provides the information specified by C.3.2 above, it will satisfy the requirements of DTR 7.1.3R.

UKCGC C.3.6, ACG 4.11   (f) The audit committee should monitor and review the effectiveness of the internal audit activities. Where there is no internal audit function, the audit committee should consider annually whether there is a need for one and make a recommendation to the board.

UKCGC C.3.5   (g) The audit committee should review arrangements by which staff of the company may, in confidence, raise concerns about possible improprieties in matters of financial reporting or other matters. It should ensure the proportionate and independent investigation of such matters and follow up actions.

Remuneration committee

Commentary

The corporate governance report normally contains information on remuneration committee membership, meetings (including attendance), performance evaluation and, sometimes, the matters from Section D set out below. The disclosures on remuneration policy and amounts paid are always set out in the separate Remuneration report.

UKCGC D.1.2   Where an executive director serves as a non-executive director elsewhere, the remuneration report should state whether or not the director will retain such earnings and, if so, what the remuneration is.

UKCGC D.2.1   Where remuneration consultants are appointed, they should be identified in the annual report and a statement made as to whether they have any other connection with the company.

Other related provisions

UKCGC D.2.1   The board should establish a remuneration committee of at least three, or in the case of smaller companies' two, independent non-executive directors. In addition the company chairman may also be a member of, but not chair, the committee if he or she was considered independent on appointment as chairman. The remuneration committee should make available its terms of reference, explaining its role and the authority delegated to it by the board.

Risk and internal control

Main principle C.2   The board is responsible for determining the nature and extent of the significant risks it is willing to take in achieving its strategic objectives. The board should maintain sound risk management and internal control systems.

UKCGC C.2.1   The board should at least annually conduct a review of the effectiveness of the company's risk management and internal control systems and should report to shareholders that they have done so. The review should cover all material controls, including financial, operational and compliance controls and risk management systems.

IFRS GAAP plc – year ended 31 December 2013

DTR 7.2.5R   The corporate governance statement must include a description of the main features of the company's internal control and risk management systems in relation to the financial reporting process.

DTR 7.2.10R   Where the issuer is required to prepare a group directors' report, they should include a description of the main features of the group's internal control and risk management systems in relation to the process for preparing consolidated accounts.

> **Commentary**
>
> The DTR requirement differs from the recommendation in the UKCGC; however, the FRC envisage that both could be met by a single internal control statement.

Reporting under the Turnbull guidance (2005)

TG 34
- The board should, as a minimum, disclose that there is an ongoing process for identifying, evaluating and managing the significant risks faced by the company, that it has been in place for the year under review and up to the date of approval of the annual report, that it is regularly reviewed by the board and accords with the Turnbull guidance (2005).

TG 33
- The annual report should include such meaningful, high-level information as the board considers necessary to assist shareholders' understanding of the main features of the company's risk management processes and system of internal control, and should not give a misleading impression.

TG 35
- The board should acknowledge that it is responsible for the company's system of internal control and for reviewing its effectiveness. It should also explain that such a system is designed to manage rather than eliminate the risk of failure to achieve business objectives and can only provide reasonable, but not absolute assurance against material misstatement or loss.

TG 36
- The board should summarise the process it (where applicable, through its committees) has applied in reviewing the effectiveness of the system of internal control and confirm that necessary actions have been or are being taken to remedy any significant failings or weaknesses identified from that review. It should also disclose the process it has applied to deal with material internal control aspects of any significant problems disclosed in the annual report.

TG 37
- Where a board cannot make one or more of the disclosures in paragraphs 34 and 36 described above, it should state this fact and provide an explanation. The Listing Rules require the board to disclose if it has failed to conduct a review of the effectiveness of the company's system of internal control.

TG 38
- Where material joint ventures and associates have not been dealt with as part of the group for the purposes of applying this guidance, this should be disclosed.

Other aspects of the Turnbull guidance

TG 26   *Effective monitoring on a continuous basis is an essential component of a sound system of internal control. The board cannot, however, rely solely on the embedded monitoring processes within the company to discharge its responsibilities. It should regularly receive and review reports on internal control. In addition, the board should undertake an annual assessment for the purposes of making its public statement on internal control to ensure that it has considered all significant aspects of internal control for the company for the year under review and up to the date of approval of the annual report.*

TG 30	For the purpose of making its public statement on internal control the board should undertake an annual assessment. The assessment should consider issues dealt with in reports reviewed by it during the year together with any additional information necessary to ensure that the board has taken account of all significant aspects of internal control for the company for the year under review and up to the date of approval of the annual report.
TG 31	The board's annual assessment should, in particular, consider: ■ The changes since the last annual assessment in the nature and extent of significant risks and the company's ability to respond to changes in its business and the external environment. ■ The scope and quality of management's ongoing monitoring of risks and of the system of internal control and, where applicable, the work of its internal audit function and other providers of assurance. ■ The extent and frequency of the communication of the results of the monitoring to the board (or board committee(s)) that enables it to build up a cumulative assessment of the state of control in the company and the effectiveness with which risk is being managed. ■ The incidence of significant control failings or weaknesses that have been identified at any time during the period and the extent to which they have resulted in unforeseen outcomes or contingencies that have had, could have had, or may in the future have, a material impact on the company's financial performance or condition. ■ The effectiveness of the company's public reporting processes.

Requirements from the Takeover Directive

DTR 7.2.6R	The corporate governance statement must contain the information required by paragraph 13(2)(c), (d), (f), (h) and (i) of Schedule 7 to the Large and Medium-sized Companies and Groups (Accounts and Reports) Regulations 2008 (SI 2008/410) (information about share capital required under Directive 2004/25/EC (the Takeover Directive) where the issuer is subject to the requirements of that paragraph.

> **Commentary**
>
> These disclosures are similar to the Takeover Directive requirements usually given in the Directors' Report. These disclosures must either be repeated in the corporate governance statement or cross-referred to the relevant part of the Directors' Report.

Financial reporting

Main principle C.1	The board should present a fair, balanced and understandable assessment of the company's position and prospects.
Supporting principle	The board should establish arrangements that will enable it to ensure that the information presented is fair, balanced and understandable.
UKCGC C.1.1	The directors should explain in the annual report their responsibility for preparing the annual report and accounts, and state that they consider the report and accounts, taken as a whole, is fair, balanced and understandable and provides the information necessary for shareholders to assess the company's performance, business model

and strategy. There should be a statement by the auditor about their reporting responsibilities.

> **Commentary**
>
> The UKCGC does not specify where the 'fair, balanced and understandable' statement by the directors should be given in the annual report. It is likely to be incorporated into the Directors' responsibilities statement.

UKCGC C.1.2 The directors should include in the annual report an explanation of the basis on which the company generates or preserves value over the longer term (the business model) and the strategy for delivering the objectives of the company.

LR 9.8.6R(3), UKCGC C.1.3 There must be a statement by the directors in both the annual and half-yearly statements, that the business is a going concern, with supporting assumptions or qualifications as necessary. This statement should cover both the parent company and the group as a whole.

> **Commentary**
>
> A going concern statement is required in both the annual and half-yearly financial statements.
>
> The FRC Guidance 'Going concern and liquidity risk: Guidance for Directors of UK Companies 2009" ('GC') provides a framework to assist directors, audit committees and finance teams, of all sizes of company, in determining whether it is appropriate to adopt the going concern basis for preparing financial statements (both annual and half yearly) and in making balanced, proportionate and clear disclosures.

GC principle 3 Directors should make balanced, proportionate and clear disclosures about going concern for the financial statements to give a true and fair view. Directors should disclose if the period that they have reviewed is less than twelve months from the date of approval of annual and half-yearly financial statements and explain their justification for limiting their review period.

GC para 80 It is helpful to investors and other stakeholders if all of these disclosures are brought together in a single place in the company's financial statements. It may be necessary to provide a cross reference to that single place from other parts of the annual report. If it is not practicable to provide all of the information in a single place, it is still helpful if the key disclosures are brought together by way of a note that includes appropriate cross-references to information in the financial statements and from the financial statements to information included elsewhere in the annual report. Refer to note 2.1.1 of the IFRS GAAP Plc financial statements for illustrative going concern disclosures.

GC para 81 Balanced, proportionate and clear disclosures would include the following components:

- the key disclosures or references thereto;
- the particular factors which the directors have considered in reaching a conclusion on going concern; and
- a concluding statement as to whether the use of the going concern basis of accounting is appropriate, explaining the basis of that conclusion.

GC para 83

Examples illustrating such disclosures and how they can be brought together are included in Appendix I for small companies and in Appendix II for other companies of the FRC guidance 'Going concern and liquidity risk: Guidance for Directors of UK Companies 2009'.

> **Commentary**
>
> In January 2013 the FRC published a consultation paper setting out proposed measures to implement a number of the Sharman Inquiry's recommendations aimed at improving the reporting regime relating to going concern and liquidity risks.
>
> In June 2013 the FRC confirmed that it plans to issue further consultation documents in autumn 2013 covering SMEs, proposed changes to the Code, and integrated going concern and risk management Code guidance. In the meantime, the FRC has encouraged companies to 'consider and abide by' the principles of the Sharman Inquiry.

Dialogue with shareholders

Main principle E.1 — There should be a dialogue with shareholders based on the mutual understanding of objectives. The board as a whole has responsibility for ensuring that a satisfactory dialogue with shareholders takes place.

UKCGC E.1.2 — Disclosure should be made of the steps that the board has taken to ensure that the members of the board, and in particular the non-executive directors, develop an understanding of the views of the major shareholders (for example through direct face-to-face contact, analysts' or brokers' briefings and surveys of shareholder opinion) about their company.

Other related provisions

UKCGC E.1.1 — (a) The chairman should ensure that the views of shareholders are communicated to the board as a whole.

UKCGC E.1.1 — (b) The chairman should discuss governance and strategy with major shareholders. Non-executive directors should be offered the opportunity to attend scheduled meetings with major shareholders and should expect to attend if requested by major shareholders. The senior independent director should also attend sufficient meetings with a range of major shareholders to listen to their views in order to help develop a balance of understanding of their concerns.

Constructive use of the AGM

Main principle E.2 — The board should use the AGM to communicate with investors and to encourage their participation.

Other related provisions

UKCGC E.2.3 — (a) The chairman should arrange for the chairmen of the audit, remuneration and nomination committees to attend the AGM to answer questions and for all directors to attend.

UKCGC E.2.1 — (b) The company should propose a separate resolution on each substantially separate issue and should in particular propose a resolution at the AGM relating to the report and accounts. For each resolution, proxy appointment forms should provide shareholders with the option to direct their proxy to vote either for or against the resolution or to withhold their vote. The proxy form and any announcement of the results of a vote should make clear that a 'vote withheld' is not a vote in law and will not be counted in the calculation of the proportion of votes for and against the resolution.

UKCGC E.2.2 (c) The company should ensure that all valid proxy appointments received for general meetings are properly recorded and counted. For each resolution, after a vote has been taken, except where taken on a poll, the company should ensure that the following information is given at the general meeting and made available as soon as reasonably practicable on the company's web site:

- the number of shares in respect of which proxy appointments have been validly made; and
- the number of votes (i) for, and (ii) against the resolution, and (iii) the number of shares in respect of which the vote was directed to be withheld.

UKCGC E.2.4 (d) The company should arrange for the Notice of the AGM and related papers to be sent to shareholders at least 20 working days before the meeting.

Statement of directors' responsibilities

The directors are responsible for preparing the Annual Report and the financial statements in accordance with applicable law and regulations.

Company law requires the directors to prepare financial statements for each financial year. Under that law the directors have prepared the group and parent company financial statements in accordance with International Financial Reporting Standards (IFRSs) as adopted by the European Union. Under company law the directors must not approve the financial statements unless they are satisfied that they give a true and fair view of the state of affairs of the group and the company and of the profit or loss of the group for that period. In preparing these financial statements, the directors are required to:

- select suitable accounting policies and then apply them consistently[1];
- make judgements and accounting estimates that are reasonable and prudent[2];
- state whether applicable IFRSs as adopted by the European Union have been followed, subject to any material departures disclosed and explained in the financial statements[3]; and
- prepare the financial statements on the going concern basis unless it is inappropriate to presume that the company will continue in business[4].

The directors are responsible for keeping adequate accounting records that are sufficient to show and explain the company's transactions and disclose with reasonable accuracy at any time the financial position of the company and the group and enable them to ensure that the financial statements and the directors' remuneration report comply with the Companies Act 2006 and, as regards the group financial statements, Article 4 of the IAS Regulation. They are also responsible for safeguarding the assets of the company and the group and hence for taking reasonable steps for the prevention and detection of fraud and other irregularities.

UKCGC C.1.1 Having taken advice from the Audit Committee, the directors consider that the Annual Report, taken as a whole, is fair, balanced and understandable and provides the information necessary for shareholders to assess the company's performance, business model and strategy.

Directors' statement pursuant to the Disclosure and Transparency Rules

DTR 4.1.12R Each of the directors, whose names and functions are listed in [refer to section of annual report containing details of directors] confirm that, to the best of each person's knowledge and belief:

- the financial statements, prepared in accordance with IFRSs as adopted by the EU, give a true and fair view of the assets, liabilities, financial position and profit [loss] of the group and company; and
- the strategic report and report contained in the annual report include a fair review of the development and performance of the business and the position of the company and group, together with a description of the principal risks and uncertainties that they face.

---

[1] Reference to the company has been deleted as the parent company takes exemption under section 408 of the Companies Act 2006 and does not present the parent company income statement.
[2] Paragraph 29 of Part 2 of Schedule 1 to SI 2008/410 requires that the amount of any item 'shall be determined on a prudent basis'.
[3] This bullet does not apply to small and medium-sized companies as defined by CA06.
[4] This bullet can be omitted if the directors have voluntarily given a separate statement about going concern.

The directors are responsible for the maintenance and integrity of the group web site, www.IFRSGAAPplc.com. Legislation in the UK governing the preparation and dissemination of financial statements may differ from legislation in other jurisdictions.

By order of the board

AB Smith

Company Secretary
26 February 2014

Notes:

(a) There is no requirement for the corporate governance report to be signed. However, it is good practice for the company secretary or the senior non-executive director to sign it.

(b) The statement by the directors should be made in accordance with what is known to them at the date on which they approve the financial statements; in practice directors will need to perform their work to a date before the approval of the financial statements and update their work as appropriate.

LR 9.8.10R	The Listing Rules require that the auditors should review the following aspects of the company's 'statement of compliance' with the Combined Code of corporate governance:
UKCGC C.1.1	■ Directors' responsibility statement for preparing the financial statements and auditors' reporting responsibilities.
UKCGC C.2.1	■ Directors' report to shareholders on the company's system of internal controls.
UKCGC C.3.1-7■	Disclosure relating to the audit committee and auditors.
	The Listing Rules require that the auditors review the:
LR 9.8.10R(1)	■ Directors' statement on going concern [LR9.8.6R(3)].
LR 9.8.11R	■ Detailed disclosure in the directors' remuneration report relating to total remuneration, share options, long-term incentive schemes and pension entitlements (as disclosed in accordance with LR 9.8.8R (2),(3), (4), (5),(11) and (12)).

Independent auditor's report to the members of IFRS GAAP plc

> **Warning:** This audit report format was current at the date of going to print. However it may not be the most up-to-date version. It should not be used without checking that it is the appropriate version, and in any case will need to be tailored to incorporate information specific to the entity being audited.

Report on the financial statements

Our opinion

In our opinion:

- The financial statements give a true and fair view of the state of the Group's and of the Parent Company's affairs as at 31 December 2013 and of the Group's profit and of the Group's and Parent Company's cash flows for the year then ended;
- The Group financial statements have been properly prepared in accordance with International Financial Reporting Standards (IFRSs) as adopted by the European Union;
- The Parent Company financial statements have been properly prepared in accordance with IFRSs as adopted by the European Union and as applied in accordance with the provisions of the Companies Act 2006; and
- The financial statements have been prepared in accordance with the requirements of the Companies Act 2006 and, as regards the Group financial statements, Article 4 of the IAS Regulation.

This opinion is to be read in the context of what we say below.

What we have audited

The Group financial statements and Parent Company financial statements (the "financial statements"), which are prepared by IFRS GAAP plc, comprise:

- the Group and Parent Company statements of financial position as at 31 December 2013;
- the Group income statement and statement of comprehensive income for the year then ended;
- the Group and Parent Company statements of changes in equity and statements of cash flows for the year then ended; and
- the notes to the financial statements, which include a summary of significant accounting policies and other explanatory information.

The financial reporting framework that has been applied in their preparation comprises applicable law and IFRSs as adopted by the European Union and, as regards the Parent Company, as applied in accordance with the provisions of the Companies Act 2006.

What an audit of financial statements involves

We conducted our audit in accordance with International Standards on Auditing (UK and Ireland) (ISAs (UK & Ireland)). An audit involves obtaining evidence about the amounts and disclosures in the financial statements sufficient to give reasonable assurance that the financial statements are free from material misstatement, whether caused by fraud or error. This includes an assessment of:

- whether the accounting policies are appropriate to the Group's and Parent Company's circumstances and have been consistently applied and adequately disclosed;

- the reasonableness of significant accounting estimates made by the directors; and
- the overall presentation of the financial statements.

In addition, we read all the financial and non-financial information in the IFRS GAAP plc Annual Report (the "Annual Report") to identify material inconsistencies with the audited financial statements and to identify any information that is apparently materially incorrect based on, or materially inconsistent with, the knowledge acquired by us in the course of performing the audit. If we become aware of any apparent material misstatements or inconsistencies we consider the implications for our report.

Overview of our audit approach

[This section will be specific to the circumstances of the entity being audited, and the wording below is therefore only illustrative.]

Materiality

We set certain thresholds for materiality. These helped us to determine the nature, timing and extent of our audit procedures and to evaluate the effect of misstatements both individually and on the financial statements as a whole.

Based on our professional judgment, we determined materiality for the Group financial statements as a whole to be C2.4[1] million.

We agreed with the Audit Committee that we would report to them misstatements identified during our audit above C120,000[1] as well as misstatements below that amount that, in our view, warranted reporting for qualitative reasons.

Overview of the scope of our audit

The Group is structured along eight business segments being structured into geographic and product lines for reporting purposes. The Group financial statements are a consolidation of 21[1] reporting units, comprising the group's operating businesses and centralised functions.

In establishing the overall approach to the group audit, we determined the type of work that needed to be performed at reporting units by us, as the group engagement team, or component auditors from other PwC network firms, operating under our instruction. Where the work was performed by component auditors, we determined the level of involvement we needed to have in the audit work at those reporting units to be able to conclude whether sufficient appropriate audit evidence had been obtained as a basis for our opinion on the Group financial statements as a whole.

Accordingly, of the group's 21[1] reporting units, we identified 15[1] which, in our view, required an audit of their complete financial information, either due to their size, their risk characteristics or because some are covered on a rotational basis over a 3 year cycle. Specific audit procedures on certain balances and transactions were performed at a further 2[1] reporting units due to specific risks identified. This, together with additional procedures performed at the Group level, gave us the evidence we needed for our opinion on the Group financial statements as a whole.

[1] For illustrative purposes only.

Areas of particular audit focus

In preparing the financial statements, the directors made a number of subjective judgements, for example in respect of significant accounting estimates that involved making assumptions and considering future events that are inherently uncertain. We primarily focused our work in these areas by assessing the directors' judgements against available evidence, forming our own independent judgements, and evaluating the disclosures in the financial statements.

In our audit, we tested and examined information, using sampling and other auditing techniques, to the extent we considered necessary to provide a reasonable basis for us to draw conclusions. We obtained audit evidence through testing the effectiveness of controls, substantive procedures or a combination of both. As there is always a risk that any system of internal control will be overridden and this is always an area of focus in our audit.

We considered the following areas to be those that required particular focus in the current year. This is not a complete list of all risks or areas of focus identified by our audit.

Area of focus	How the scope of our audit addressed the area of focus
Matters in this section will be specific to the entity being audited.	This disclosure will be established by the auditors based on their responses to the areas of focus.
We have not provided information in these illustrative financial statements.	
Sources of information will include;	
• The auditor's audit plan • Management's assessment of principal risks • Auditing standards	

We discussed these areas of focus with the Audit Committee. The Audit Committee's report on those matters that they considered to be significant issues in relation to the financial statements is set out on page 40.

Going Concern

Under the Listing Rules we are required to review the directors' statement in relation to going concern. We have nothing to report having performed our review.

As noted in the directors' statement, set out on page 49, the directors have concluded that it is appropriate to prepare the Group's and Parent Company's financial statements using the going concern basis of accounting. The going concern basis presumes that the Group and Parent Company have adequate resources to remain in operation, and that the directors intend them to do so, for at least one year from the date the financial statements were signed. As part of our audit we have concluded that the directors' use of the going concern basis is appropriate.

However, because not all future events or conditions can be predicted, these statements are not a guarantee as to the Group's and the Parent Company's ability to continue as a going concern.

Opinions on matters prescribed by the Companies Act 2006

In our opinion:

- the information given in the Strategic Report and the Directors' Report for the financial year for which the financial statements are prepared is consistent with the financial statements;
- the part of the Directors' Remuneration Report to be audited has been properly prepared in accordance with the Companies Act 2006.

Other matters on which we are required to report by exception

Adequacy of accounting records and information and explanations received

Under the Companies Act 2006 we are required to report to you if, in our opinion:

- we have not received all the information and explanations we require for our audit; or
- adequate accounting records have not been kept by the Parent Company, or returns adequate for our audit have not been received from branches not visited by us; or
- the Parent Company financial statements and the part of the Directors' Remuneration Report to be audited are not in agreement with the accounting records and returns.

We have no exceptions to report arising from this responsibility.

Directors' remuneration

Under the Companies Act 2006 we are required to report if, in our opinion, certain disclosures of directors' remuneration specified by law have not been made, and under the Listing Rules we are required to review certain elements of the report to shareholders by the Board on directors' remuneration.

We have no exceptions to report arising from these responsibilities.

Corporate Governance Statement

Under the Listing Rules we are required to review the part of the Corporate Governance Statement relating to the Company's compliance with nine provisions of the UK Corporate Governance Code ('the Code').

We have nothing to report having performed our review.

On page 49 of the Annual Report, as required by the Code Provision C.1.1, the directors state that they consider the Annual Report taken as a whole to be fair, balanced and understandable and provides the information necessary for members to assess the Group's performance, business model and strategy. On page 40, as required by C3.8 of the Code, the Audit Committee has set out the significant issues that it considered in relation to the financial statements, and how they were addressed. Under ISAs (UK & Ireland) we are required to report to you if, in our opinion:

- the statement given by the directors is materially inconsistent with our knowledge of the Group acquired in the course of performing our audit; or
- the section of the Annual Report describing the work of the Audit Committee does not appropriately address matters communicated by us to the Audit Committee.

We have no exceptions to report arising from this responsibility.

Other information in the Annual Report

Under ISAs (UK & Ireland), we are required to report to you if, in our opinion, information in the Annual Report is:

- materially inconsistent with the information in the audited financial statements; or
- apparently materially incorrect based on, or materially inconsistent with, our knowledge of the Group and Parent Company acquired in the course of performing our audit; or
- is otherwise misleading.

We have no exceptions to report arising from this responsibility.

Responsibilities for the financial statements and the audit

Our responsibilities and those of the directors

As explained more fully in the Directors' Responsibilities Statement set out on page 49, the directors are responsible for the preparation of the Group and Parent Company financial statements and for being satisfied that they give a true and fair view.

Our responsibility is to audit and express an opinion on the Group and Parent Company financial statements in accordance with applicable law and ISAs (UK & Ireland). Those standards require us to comply with the Auditing Practices Board's Ethical Standards for Auditors.

This report, including the opinions, has been prepared for and only for the Company's members as a body in accordance with Chapter 3 of Part 16 of the Companies Act 2006 and for no other purpose. We do not, in giving these opinions, accept or assume responsibility for any other purpose or to any other person to whom this report is shown or into whose hands it may come save where expressly agreed by our prior consent in writing.

John Smith (Senior Statutory Auditor)
for and on behalf of PricewaterhouseCoopers LLP
Chartered Accountants and Statutory Auditors
London
26 February 2014

IFRS GAAP plc – year ended 31 December 2013

(All amounts in C thousands unless otherwise stated)

Consolidated income statement[1]

			Note	Group Year ended 31 December 2013	2012 Restated
1p10(b)					
1p113, 1p38					
		Continuing operations			
1p82(a)		Revenue	5	211,034	112,360
1p99, 1p103		Cost of sales	6	(77,366)	(46,682)
1p103		**Gross profit[2]**		133,668	65,678
1p99, 1p103		Distribution costs		(52,529)	(21,213)
1p99, 1p103		Administrative expenses		(30,105)	(10,511)
1p99, 1p103		Other income	7	2,750	1,259
1p85		Other (losses)/gains – net	8	(90)	63
1p85		**Operating profit[2]**		53,694	35,276
1p85		Finance income	11	1,730	1,609
1p82(b)		Finance costs	11	(8,173)	(12,197)
1p85		Finance costs – net	11	(6,443)	(10,588)
1p82(c)		Share of profit of investments accounted for using the equity method	12	1,682	1,022
1p85		**Profit before income tax**		48,933	25,710
1p82(d),12p77		Income tax expense	13	(14,611)	(8,670)
1p85		**Profit for the year from continuing operations**		34,322	17,040
IFRS5p33(a)		**Discontinued operations**			
		Profit for the year from discontinued operations (attributable to owners of the parent)	25	100	120
1p81A(a)		**Profit for the year**		34,422	17,160
		Profit attributable to:			
1p81B(a)(ii)		– Owners of the parent		31,874	16,304
1p81B(a)(i), IFRS12p12(e)		– Non-controlling interests	12	2,548	856
				34,422	17,160
		Earnings per share from continuing and discontinued operations attributable to owners of the parent during the year (expressed in C per share)			
		Basic earnings per share			
33p66		From continuing operations	14	1.35	0.79
33p68		From discontinued operations[3]		0.01	0.01
33p66		From profit for the year		1.36	0.80
		Diluted earnings per share			
33p66		From continuing operations	14	1.21	0.74
33p68		From discontinued operations		0.01	0.01
33p66		From profit for the year		1.22	0.75

The notes on pages 78 to 205 are an integral part of these consolidated financial statements.

---

[1] This income statement presents expenses by function. See Commentary, paras 12 and 13.
[2] IAS 1 does not prescribe the disclosure of operating profit and gross profit on the face of the income statement. However, entities are not prohibited from disclosing this or a similar line item.
[3] EPS for discontinued operations may be given in the notes to the financial statements instead of the income statement.

(All amounts in C thousands unless otherwise stated)

CA06 s408 The company has elected to take the exemption under section 408 of the Companies Act 2006 not to present the parent company profit and loss account.

The profit for the parent company for the year was C9,098 (2012: C10,491).

IFRS GAAP plc – year ended 31 December 2013

(All amounts in C thousands unless otherwise stated)

Consolidated statement of comprehensive income

		Note	Group Year ended 31 December 2013	2012 Restated
	Profit for the year		34,422	17,160
	Other comprehensive income:			
1p82A	**Items that will not be reclassified to profit or loss**			
16p39	Gains on revaluation of land and buildings	29	755	759
19p93B	Remeasurements of post employment benefit obligations	28,33	83	(637)
			838	122
1p82A	**Items that may be subsequently reclassified to profit or loss**			
IFRS7p20(a)(ii)	Change in value of available-for-sale financial assets	29	362	912
IFRS3p59	Reclassification of revaluation of previously held interest in ABC Group	7,29,39	(850)	–
1p85	Impact of change in Euravian tax rate on deferred tax[1]	28,32	(10)	–
IFRS7p23(c)	Cash flow hedges	29	64	(3)
1p85	Net investment hedge	29	(45)	40
21p52(b)	Currency translation differences	29	2,401	(922)
1p82A	Share of other comprehensive income of investments accounted for using the equity method	29	(86)	91
			1,836	118
	Other comprehensive income for the year, net of tax	13	2,674	240
1p81A(c)	**Total comprehensive income for the year**		37,096	17,400
	Attributable to:			
1p81B(b)(ii)	– Owners of the parent		34,296	16,584
1p81B(b)(i)	– Non-controlling interests	12	2,800	816
	Total comprehensive income for the year		37,096	17,400
	Total comprehensive income attributable to equity shareholders arises from:			
	– Continuing operations		34,196	16,464
IFRS5p33(d)	– Discontinued operations	25	100	120
			34,296	16,584

Items in the statement above are disclosed net of tax. The income tax relating to each component of other comprehensive income is disclosed in note 13.

The notes on pages 78 to 205 are an integral part of these consolidated financial statements.

---

[1] The impact of change in Euravian tax rate is shown for illustrative purposes. UK Companies with 31 December 2013 year ends will need to consider the impact of the reduction in tax rates in the Finance Act 2013.

Commentary — income statement and statement of comprehensive income

The commentary that follows explains some of the key requirements in IAS 1, 'Presentation of financial statements', and other requirements that impact the income statement/statement of comprehensive income.

1p10A 1. Entities have a choice of presenting a statement of profit and loss and other comprehensive income:
(a) An entity may present a single statement of profit or loss and other comprehensive income, with profit or loss and other comprehensive income presented in two sections. The sections shall be presented together, with the profit or loss section presented first followed directly by the other comprehensive income section; or
(b) An entity may present the profit or loss section in a separate statement of profit or loss. If so, the separate statement of profit or loss shall immediately precede the statement presenting comprehensive income, which shall begin with profit or loss.

The main difference between these two options is that in option (a), profit for the year is shown as a sub-total rather than the 'bottom line', and the statement continues down to total comprehensive income for the year.

1p81A 2. The statement of profit and loss and other comprehensive income shall include:
(a) profit or loss
(b) total other comprehensive income
(c) comprehensive income for the period, being the total of (a) and (b)

1p81B 3. The following items are disclosed as allocations for the period:
(a) profit or loss attributable to:
    (i) non-controlling interests; and
    (ii) owners of the parent
(b) total comprehensive income for the period attributable to:
    (i) non-controlling interests; and
    (ii) owners of the parent

IFRS5p33(d) (c) the amount of income attributable to owners of the parent from:
    (i) continuing operations; and
    (ii) discontinued operations.

1p82 4. The profit or loss section or the statement of profit and loss includes, as a minimum, the following line items:
(a) revenue;
(b) finance costs;
(c) share of the profit or loss of associates and joint ventures accounted for using the equity method;
(d) tax expense;
(e) a single amount for the total of discontinued operations.

1p82A 5. The other comprehensive income section shall present items classified by nature (including share of the other comprehensive income of associates and joint ventures accounted for using the equity method) and grouped in those that, in accordance with other IFRSs:
(a) will not be reclassified subsequently to profit or loss; and

IFRS GAAP plc – year ended 31 December 2013

(All amounts in C thousands unless otherwise stated)

(b) will be reclassified subsequently to profit or loss when specific conditions are met.

1p85

6. Additional line items, headings and subtotals are presented in the statement of comprehensive income and the income statement (where presented) when such presentation is relevant to an understanding of the entity's financial performance.

7. Additional sub-headings should be used with care. The apparent flexibility in IAS 1 can only be used to enhance users' understanding of the GAAP-compliant numbers. It cannot be used to detract from the GAAP numbers. Set out below are overall principles that entities should apply when presenting additional line items, headings, sub-totals and alternative performance measures:

(a) GAAP numbers should be given at least equal prominence to non-GAAP numbers.
(b) Additional line items, sub-totals and columns may be used, but only if they do not detract from the GAAP numbers by introducing bias or by overcrowding the income statement.
(c) Each additional line item or column should contain all the revenue or expenses that relate to the particular line item or column inserted.
(d) Each additional line item or column should contain only revenue or expense that is revenue or expense of the entity itself.
(e) Items may be segregated (for example, by use of columns or sub-totals) where they are different in nature or function from other items in the income statement.
(f) It is generally not permissible to mix natural and functional classifications of expenses where these categories of expenses overlap.
(g) Terms used for additional line items and sub-totals should be defined if they are not terms recognised in IFRS.
(h) Additional line items, columns and sub-totals should only be presented when they are used internally to manage the business.
(i) Various presentations will be acceptable individually, but consideration should be given to the aggregate effect of these presentations, so that the overall message of the income statement is not distorted or confused.
(j) The presentation method should generally be consistent from year to year.
(k) The presentation method should comply with any local regulatory rules.

8. Earnings before interest and tax (EBIT) may be an appropriate sub-heading to show in the income statement. This line item usually distinguishes between the pre-tax profits arising from operating activities and those arising from financing activities.

9. In contrast, a sub-total for earnings before interest, tax, depreciation and amortisation (EBITDA) can only be included as a sub-total where the entity presents its expenses by nature and provided the sub-total does not detract from the GAAP numbers either by implying that EBITDA is the 'real' profit or by overcrowding the income statement so that the reader cannot determine easily the entity's GAAP performance. Where an entity presents its expenses by function, it will not be possible to show depreciation and amortisation as separate line items in arriving at operating profit, because depreciation and amortisation are types of expense, not functions of the business. In this case, EBITDA can only be disclosed by way of supplemental information in a box, in a footnote, in the notes or in the review of operations.

(All amounts in C thousands unless otherwise stated)

Material items of income and expense

1p97 10. When items of income and expense are material, their nature and amount is disclosed separately either in the income statement or in the notes. In the case of IFRS GAAP plc, these disclosures are made in note 6. Some entities provide this information in the income statement in the form of additional analysis boxes or columns. Further discussion is available in PwC's 'IFRS manual of accounting'.

1p85, 97 11. IAS 1 does not provide a specific name for the types of items that should be separately disclosed. Where an entity discloses a separate category of 'exceptional', 'significant' or 'unusual' items either in the income statement or in the notes, the accounting policy note should include a definition of the chosen term. The presentation and definition of these items should be applied consistently from year to year.

Analysis of expenses by nature or function

1p99 12. Where an entity classifies its expenses by nature, it must ensure that each class of expense includes all items related to that class. Material restructuring cost may, for example, include redundancy payments (employee benefit cost), inventory write-downs (changes in inventory) and impairments in property, plant and equipment. It is not normally acceptable to show restructuring costs as a separate line item in an analysis of expenses by nature where there is an overlap with other line items.

13. Entities that classify their expenses by function include the material items within the function to which they relate. In this case, material items can be disclosed as footnotes or in the notes to the financial statements.

Operating profit

1BC56 14. An entity may elect to include a sub-total for its result from operating activities. This is permitted, but management should ensure that the amount disclosed is representative of activities that would normally be considered to be 'operating'. Items that are clearly of an operating nature (for example, inventory write-downs, restructuring and relocation expenses) are not excluded simply because they occur infrequently or are unusual in amount. Nor can expenses be excluded on the grounds that they do not involve cash flows (for example, depreciation or amortisation). As a general rule, operating profit is the subtotal after 'other expenses' – that is, excluding finance costs and the share of profits of equity-accounted investments – although in some circumstances it may be appropriate for the share of profits of equity-accounted investments to be included in operating profit (see paragraph 16 below).

Re-ordering of line items

1p86 15. The line items and descriptions of those items are re-ordered where this is necessary to explain the elements of performance. However, entities are required to make a 'fair presentation' and should not make any changes unless there is a good reason to do so.

16. The share of profit of associates is normally shown after finance costs; this recognises that the share of profits from associates arises from what is essentially an investing activity, rather than part of the group's operating activities. However, where associates (and joint ventures) are an integral vehicle for the conduct of the group's

operations and its strategy, it may be more appropriate to show finance costs after the share of profit of associates and joint ventures. In such cases, it may be appropriate either to insert a sub-total 'profit before finance costs' or to include the share of profits from associates and joint ventures in arriving at operating profit (if disclosed). It would not be appropriate to include the share of associates and joint ventures within 'revenue' (and, therefore, within 'gross profit').

17. Finance income cannot be netted against finance costs; it is included in 'other revenue/other income' or shown separately in the income statement. Where finance income is an incidental benefit, it is acceptable to present finance income immediately before finance costs and include a sub-total of 'net finance costs' in the income statement. Where earning interest income is one of the entity's main line of business, it is presented as 'revenue'.

Discontinued operations

1p82(ea), IFRS5p33(a)(b)
18. As stated in paragraph 4(e) above, entities disclose a single amount in the statement of comprehensive income (or separate income statement), comprising the total of discontinued operations. Paragraph 33 of IFRS 5, 'Non-current assets held for sale and discontinued operations', also requires an analysis of this single amount. This analysis may be presented in the notes or in the statement of comprehensive income (separate income statement). If it is presented in the income statement, it should be presented in a section identified as relating to discontinued operations – that is, separate from continuing operations. The analysis is not required for disposal groups that are newly acquired subsidiaries that meet the criteria to be classified as held for sale on acquisition.

Earnings per share

33p66
19. IAS 33, 'Earnings per share', requires an entity to present in the statement of comprehensive income basic and diluted earnings per share (EPS) for profit or loss from continuing operations attributable to the ordinary equity holders of the parent entity and for total profit or loss attributable to the ordinary equity holders of the parent entity for each class of ordinary shares. Basic and diluted EPS are disclosed with equal prominence for all periods presented.

33p67A
20. If an entity presents a separate income statement, basic and diluted earnings per share are presented at the end of that statement.

33p73
21. Earnings per share based on alternative measures of earnings may also be given if considered necessary but should be presented in the notes to the financial statements only.

33p67
22. If diluted EPS is reported for at least one period, it should be reported for all periods presented, even if it equals basic EPS. If basic and diluted EPS are equal, dual presentation can be accomplished in one line in the statement of comprehensive income.

33p68
23. An entity that reports a discontinued operation discloses the basic and diluted amounts per share for the discontinued operation either in the statement of comprehensive income or in the notes to the financial statements.

33p69, 41, 43
24. Basic and diluted EPS are disclosed even if the amounts are negative (that is, a loss per share). However, potential ordinary shares are only dilutive if their

(All amounts in C thousands unless otherwise stated)

conversion would increase the loss per share. If the loss decreases, the shares are anti-dilutive.

33p4   25. When an entity presents both consolidated financial statements and separate financial statements prepared in accordance with IAS 27, 'Consolidated and separate financial statements', the disclosures required by IAS 33 need to be presented only on the basis of the consolidated information. An entity that chooses to disclose EPS based on its separate financial statements presents such EPS information only in its separate statement of comprehensive income.

Components of other comprehensive income

1p7   26. Components of other comprehensive income (OCI) are items of income and expense (including reclassification adjustments) that are not recognised in profit or loss as required or permitted by other IFRSs. They include: changes in the revaluation surplus relating to property, plant and equipment or intangible assets; remeasurements of post employment defined benefit obligations; gains and losses arising from translating the financial statements of a foreign operation; gains and losses on re-measuring available-for-sale financial assets; and the effective portion of gains and losses on hedging instruments in a cash flow hedge.

1p91, 90   27. Entities may present components of other comprehensive income either net of related tax effect or before related tax effects. If an entity choses to present the items net of tax, the amount of income tax relating to each component of OCI, including reclassification adjustments, is disclosed in the notes.

1p92, 94   28. An entity discloses separately any reclassification adjustments relating to components of other comprehensive income either in the statement of comprehensive income or in the notes.

1p7, 95   29. Reclassification adjustments are amounts reclassified to profit or loss in the current period that were recognised in other comprehensive income in the current or previous periods. They arise, for example, on disposal of a foreign operation, on derecognition of an available-for-sale financial asset and when a hedged forecast transaction affects profit or loss.

1p82A   30. IAS 1 has been amended, effective for annual periods beginning on or after 1 July 2012. The amendment requires items of OCI, classified by nature (including share of the other comprehensive income of associates and joint ventures accounted for using the equity method), to be grouped into those that will be reclassified subsequently to profit or loss when specific conditions are met and those that will not be reclassified to profit or loss. The amendment also requires entities that present items of OCI before related tax effects with the aggregate tax shown separately to allocate the tax between the items that might be reclassified subsequently to the profit or loss section and those that will not be reclassified.

1p107   31. The amount of dividends recognised as distributions to owners during the period and the related amount per share are presented either in the statement of changes in equity or in the notes. Dividends cannot be displayed in the statement of comprehensive income or income statement.

(All amounts in C thousands unless otherwise stated)

Consistency

1p45 32. The presentation and classification of items in the financial statements is retained from one period to the next unless:
(a) it is apparent, following a significant change in the nature of the entity's operations or a review of its financial statements that another presentation or classification would be more appropriate, addressing the criteria for the selection and application of accounting policies in IAS 8, 'Accounting policies, changes in accounting estimates and errors'; or
(b) IFRS requires a change in presentation.

Materiality and aggregation

1p29 33. Each material class of similar items is presented separately in the financial statements. Items of a dissimilar nature or function are presented separately unless they are immaterial.

Offsetting

1p32 34. Assets and liabilities, and income and expenses, are not offset unless required or permitted by an IFRS. Examples of income and expenses that are required or permitted to be offset are as follows:

1p34(a) (a) Gains and losses on the disposal of non-current assets, including investments and operating assets, are reported by deducting from the proceeds on disposal the carrying amount of the asset and related selling expenses.

1p34(b) (b) Expenditure related to a provision that is recognised in accordance with IAS 37, 'Provisions, contingent liabilities and contingent assets', and reimbursed under a contractual arrangement with a third party (for example, a supplier's warranty agreement) may be netted against the related reimbursement.

1p35 (c) Gains and losses arising from a group of similar transactions are reported on a net basis (for example, foreign exchange gains and losses or gains and losses arising on financial instruments held for trading). However, such gains and losses are reported separately if they are material.

(All amounts in C thousands unless otherwise stated)

Summary

35. The disclosure requirements surrounding components of OCI can be summarised as follows:

Item	Reference	Requirement in standard	Presentation in IFRS GAAP plc
Each component of other comprehensive income recognised during the period, classified by nature and grouped into those that: – will not be reclassified subsequently to profit and loss; and – will be reclassified subsequently to profit and loss.	IAS 1p82A	Statement of comprehensive income	Statement of comprehensive income
Reclassification adjustments during the period relating to components of other comprehensive income	IAS 1p92	Statement of comprehensive income or notes	Note 29
Tax relating to each component of other comprehensive income, including reclassification adjustments	IAS 1p90	Statement of comprehensive income or notes	Note 13
Reconciliation for each component of equity, showing separately: – Profit/loss – Other comprehensive income – Transactions with owners	IAS 1p106(d)	Statement of changes in equity	Statement of changes in equity
For each component of equity, an analysis of other comprehensive income by item	IAS 1p106A	Statement of changes in equity or notes	Note 29

IFRS GAAP plc – year ended 31 December 2013

(All amounts in C thousands unless otherwise stated)

Consolidated and Parent Company balance sheets

		Note	Group As at 31 December 2013	Group As at 31 December 2012 Restated	Group As at 1 January 2012 Restated	Company As at 31 December 2013	Company As at 31 December 2012
1p10(a), 1p38, 1p113	**Assets**						
1p60, 1p66	**Non-current assets**						
1p54(a)	Property, plant and equipment	16	155,341	100,233	107,214	–	–
1p54(c)	Intangible assets	17	26,272	20,700	21,462	–	–
	Investments in subsidiaries	12	–	–	–	38,592	22,170
1p54(e), 28p38	Investments accounted for using the equity method	12	18,649	17,053	15,940	–	–
1p54(o), 1p56	Deferred income tax assets	32	3,546	3,383	2,879	–	–
1p54(d), IFRS7p8(d)	Available-for-sale financial assets	19	17,420	14,910	13,222	–	–
1p54(d), IFRS7p8(a)	Derivative financial instruments	20	395	245	187	–	–
1p54(h), IFRS7p8(c)	Trade and other receivables	21	2,322	1,352	1,106	–	–
			223,945	157,876	162,010	38,592	22,170
1p60, 1p66	**Current assets**						
1p54(g)	Inventories	22	24,700	18,182	17,273	–	–
1p54(h), IFRS7p8(c)	Trade and other receivables	21	19,765	18,330	16,599	43,711	31,296
1p54(d), IFRS7p8(d)	Available-for-sale financial assets	19	1,950	–	–	–	–
1p54(d), IFRS7p8(a)	Derivative financial instruments	20	1,069	951	980	–	–
1p54(d), IFRS7p8(a)	Financial assets at fair value through profit or loss	23	11,820	7,972	7,342	–	–
1p54(i), IFRS7p8	Cash and cash equivalents (excluding bank overdrafts)	24	17,928	34,062	22,132	3,261	6,234
			77,232	79,497	64,326	46,972	37,530
IFRS5p38, 1p54(p)	Assets of disposal group classified as held for sale	25	3,333	–	–	–	–
			80,565	79,497	64,326	46,972	37,530
	Total assets		304,510	237,373	226,336	85,564	59,700

(All amounts in C thousands unless otherwise stated)

			Group			Company	
		Note	As at 31 December 2013	As at 31 December 2012 Restated	As at 1 January 2012 Restated	As at 31 December 2013	2012
1p54(r)	**Equity and liabilities**						
	Equity attributable to owners of the parent						
1p78(e), 1p54(r)	Ordinary shares	26	**25,300**	21,000	20,000	**25,300**	21,000
1p78(e), 1p55	Share premium	26	**17,144**	10,494	10,424	**17,144**	10,494
1p78(e), 1p55	Other reserves	29	**11,612**	7,194	6,364	–	–
1p78(e), 1p55	Retained earnings	28	**74,650**	51,985	51,125	**11,299**	11,613
			128,706	90,673	87,913	**53,743**	43,107
1p54(q)	**Non-controlling interests**	12	**7,888**	1,766	1,500	–	–
	Total equity		**136,594**	92,439	89,413	**53,743**	43,107
	Liabilities						
1p60, 1p69	**Non-current liabilities**						
1p54(m), IFRS7p8(f), (g)	Borrowings	31	**115,121**	96,346	65,784	–	–
1p54(m), IFRS7p8(e)	Derivative financial instruments	20	**135**	129	130	–	–
1p54(o), 1p56	Deferred income tax liabilities	32	**12,370**	9,053	5,926	–	–
1p78(d)	Post-employment benefits	33	**5,116**	2,611	1,836	–	–
1p54(l), 1p78(d)	Provisions for other liabilities and charges	34	**316**	274	250	–	–
			133,058	108,413	73,926	–	–
1p60, 1p69	**Current liabilities**						
1p54(k), IFRS7p8(f)	Trade and other payables	30	**16,670**	12,478	11,031	**31,821**	16,593
1p54(n)	Current income tax liabilities		**2,566**	2,771	7,219	–	–
1p54(m), IFRS7p8(f)	Borrowings	31	**11,716**	18,258	42,356	–	–
1p54(m), IFRS7p8(e)	Derivative financial instruments	20	**460**	618	520	–	–
1p54(l)	Provisions for other liabilities and charges	34	**3,226**	2,396	1,871	–	–
			34,638	36,521	62,997	**31,821**	16,593
IFRS5p38, 1p54(p)	Liabilities of disposal group clasified as held for sale	25	**220**	–	–	–	–
			34,858	36,521	62,997	**31,821**	16,593
	Total liabilities		**167,916**	144,934	136,923	**31,821**	16,593
	Total equity and liabilities		**304,510**	237,373	226,336	**85,564**	59,700

The notes on pages 78 to 205 are an integral part of these consolidated financial statements.

(All amounts in C thousands unless otherwise stated)

10p17 The financial statements on pages 78 to 205 were authorised for issue by the board of directors on 26 February 2014 and were signed on its behalf.

CD Suede
Chief Executive

G Wallace
Finance Director

IFRS GAAP plc
Registered no. xxyyzz

Commentary – balance sheet

The commentary that follows explains some of the key requirements in IAS 1, 'Presentation of financial statements', that impact the balance sheet/statement of financial position.

1p10
1. IAS 1 refers to the balance sheet as the 'statement of financial position'. This title is not mandatory, so IFRS GAAP plc has elected to retain the better-known title of 'balance sheet'.

1p54, 55
2. Paragraph 54 of IAS 1 sets out the line items that are, as a minimum, required to be presented in the balance sheet. Additional line items, headings and subtotals are presented in the balance sheet when this presentation is relevant to an understanding of the entity's financial position.

1p77, 78
3. An entity discloses, either in the balance sheet or in the notes, further sub-classifications of the line items presented, classified in a manner appropriate to the entity's operations. The detail provided in sub-classifications depends on the IFRS requirements and on the size, nature and function of the amounts involved.

Current/non-current distinction

1p60
4. An entity presents current and non-current assets and current and non-current liabilities as separate classifications in its balance sheet except when a presentation based on liquidity provides information that is reliable and is more relevant. When that exception applies, all assets and liabilities are presented broadly in order of liquidity.

1p61
5. Whichever method of presentation is adopted, an entity discloses the amount expected to be recovered or settled after more than 12 months for each asset and liability line item that combines amounts expected to be recovered or settled: (a) no more than 12 months after the reporting period, and (b) more than 12 months after the reporting period.

1p66-70
6. Current assets include assets (such as inventories and trade receivables) that are sold, consumed or realised as part of the normal operating cycle even when they are not expected to be realised within 12 months after the reporting period. Some current liabilities, such as trade payables and some accruals for employee and other operating costs, are part of the working capital used in the entity's normal operating cycle. Such operating items are classified as current liabilities even if they are due to be settled more than 12 months after the reporting period.

1p68
7. The operating cycle of an entity is the time between the acquisition of assets for processing and their realisation in the form of cash or cash equivalents. When the entity's normal operating cycle is not clearly identifiable, its duration is assumed to be 12 months.

Consistency

1p45

8. The presentation and classification of items in the financial statements is retained from one period to the next unless:
   (a) it is apparent, following a significant change in the nature of the entity's operations or a review of its financial statements, that another presentation or classification would be more appropriate according to the criteria for selecting and applying accounting policies in IAS 8, 'Accounting policies, changes in accounting estimates and errors'; or
   (b) an IFRS requires a change in presentation.

Materiality and aggregation

1p29

9. Each material class of similar items is presented separately in the financial statements. Items of a dissimilar nature or function are presented separately unless they are immaterial.

Current and deferred tax assets and liabilities

1p54, 56

10. Current and deferred tax assets and liabilities are presented separately from each other and from other assets and liabilities. When a distinction is made between current and non-current assets and liabilities in the balance sheet, deferred tax assets and liabilities are presented as non-current.

Offsetting

1p32

11. Management should not offset assets and liabilities unless required or permitted to by an IFRS. Measuring assets net of valuation allowances – for example, obsolescence allowances on inventories and doubtful debt allowances on receivables – is not offsetting.

Three balance sheets required in certain circumstances

1p40A-40D

12. If an entity has applied an accounting policy retrospectively, restated items retrospectively or reclassified items in its financial statements, it provides a third balance sheet as at the beginning of the preceding period presented. However, where the retrospective change in policy or the restatement has no effect on this earliest statement of financial position, we believe that it would be sufficient for the entity merely to disclose that fact.

IFRS GAAP plc – year ended 31 December 2013

71

(All amounts in C thousands unless otherwise stated)

Consolidated statement of changes in equity[1]

			Attributable to owners of the parent						
1p109(c), 1p108, 1p109, 1p113		Notes	Share capital	Share premium	Other reserves[2]	Retained earnings	Total	Non-controlling interest	Total equity
1p106(b)	Balance as at 1 January 2012 (as previously reported)		20,000	10,424	6,263	51,456	88,143	1,263	89,406
	Effect of changes in accounting policies	43	–	–	101	(331)	(230)	237	7
	Balance as at 1 January 2012 (restated)		20,000	10,424	6,364	51,125	87,913	1,500	89,413
1p106(d)(i)	Profit for the year		–	–	–	16,304	16,304	856	17,160
1p106(d)(ii)	Other comprehensive income for the year[3]		–	–	830	(550)	280	(40)	240
1p106(a)	Total comprehensive income for the year		–	–	830	15,754	16,584	816	17,400
IFRS2p50	Value of employee services	28	–	–	–	822	822	–	822
	Tax credit relating to share option scheme	28	–	–	–	20	20	–	20
	Proceeds from shares issued	26	1,000	70	–	–	1,070	–	1,070
1p106(d)(iii)	Dividends	34	–	–	–	(15,736)	(15,736)	(550)	(16,286)
1p106(d)(iii)	Total transactions with owners, recognised directly in equity		1,000	70	–	(14,894)	(13,824)	(550)	(14,374)
	Balance as at 31 December 2012 (restated)		21,000	10,494	7,194	51,985	90,673	1,766	92,439
	Balance at 1 January 2013 (restated)		21,000	10,494	7,194	51,985	90,673	1,766	92,439
1p106(d)(i)	Profit for the year		–	–	–	31,874	31,874	2,548	34,422
1p106(d)(ii)	Other comprehensive income for the year[3]		–	–	2,249	173	2,422	252	2,674
1p106(a)	Total comprehensive income for the year		–	–	2,249	32,047	34,296	2,800	37,096

[1] A statement of changes in equity for the company is required by IAS 1. It has not been included in this set of illustrative financial statements.

[2] Individual reserves can be grouped into 'other reserves' in the statement of changes in equity if these are similar in nature and can be regarded as a component of equity. If the individual reserves are not shown in the statement of changes in equity, an analysis should be given in the notes.

[3] Companies can implement this by either (a) showing each line item of other comprehensive income separately in the above statement; or (b) by having a single-line presentation of other comprehensive income (as shown above) plus a separate note showing an analysis of each item of other comprehensive income for each component of equity.

IFRS GAAP plc – year ended 31 December 2013

(All amounts in C thousands unless otherwise stated)

		Note	Attributable to owners of the parent					Non-cont-rolling interest	Total equity
			Share capital	Share premium	Other reserves	Retained earnings	Total		
IFRS2p50	Value of employee services	28	–	–	–	690	690	–	690
	Tax credit relating to share option scheme	28	–	–	–	30	30	–	30
	Proceeds from shares issued	26	750	200	–	–	950	–	950
	Purchase of treasury shares	29	–	–	(2,564)	–	(2,564)	–	(2,564)
	Issue of ordinary shares related to business combination	26	3,550	6,450	–	–	10,000	–	10,000
	Convertible bond – equity component	29	–	–	5,433	–	5,433	–	5,433
1p106(d)(iii)	Dividends	34	–	–	–	(10,102)	(10,102)	(1,920)	(12,022)
1p106(d)(iii)	Total contributions by and distributions to owners of the parent, recognised directly in equity		4,300	6,650	2,869	(9,382)	4,437	(1,920)	2,517
1p106(d)(iii)	Non-controlling interest arising on business combination	39	–	–	–	–	–	4,542	4,542
1p106(d)(iii)	Acquisition of non-controlling interest in XYZ Group	40	–	–	(800)	–	(800)	(300)	(1,100)
1p106(d)(iii)	Sale of interest to non-controlling interest in Red Limited	40	–	–	100	–	100	1,000	1,100
1p106(d)(iii)	Total changes in ownership interests in subsidiaries that do not result in a loss of control		–	–	(700)	–	(700)	5,242	4,542
1p106(d)(iii)	Total transactions with owners, recognised directly in equity		4,300	6,650	2,169	(9,382)	3,737	3,322	7,059
	Balance as at 31 December 2013		**25,300**	**17,144**	**11,612**	**74,650**	**128,706**	**7,888**	**136,594**

The notes on pages 78 to 205 are an integral part of these consolidated financial statements.

(All amounts in C thousands unless otherwise stated)

Commentary – statement of changes in equity

The commentary that follows explains some of the key requirements in IAS 1, 'Presentation of financial statements', and other aspects that impact the statement of changes in equity.

Dividends

1p107

1. The amount of dividends recognised as distributions to owners during the period and the related amount per share are presented either in the statement of changes in equity or in the notes. Dividends cannot be displayed in the statement of comprehensive income or income statement.

Non-controlling interest

1p106

2. Information to be included in the statement of changes in equity includes:
   (a) Total comprehensive income for the period, showing separately the total amounts attributable to equity holders of the company and to non-controlling interest.
   (b) For each component of equity, the effects of retrospective application or retrospective restatement recognised in accordance with IAS 8.
   (c) For each component of equity, a reconciliation between the carrying amount at the beginning and the end of the period, separately disclosing changes resulting from:
      (i) profit or loss;
      (ii) other comprehensive income; and
      (iii) transactions with owners in their capacity as owners, showing separately contributions by and distributions to owners and changes in ownership interests in subsidiaries that do not result in loss of control.

3. For each component of equity, the analysis of other comprehensive income by item may be presented either in the statement of changes in equity or disclosed within the notes.

IFRS GAAP plc – year ended 31 December 2013

(All amounts in C thousands unless otherwise stated)

Consolidated and Parent Company statements of cash flows

1p10(d), 7p10, 18(b), 1p38, p113		Note	Group Year ended 31 December 2013	Group Year ended 31 December 2012 Restated	Company Year ended 31 December 2013	Company Year ended 31 December 2012
	Cash flows from operating activities					
	Cash generated from operations	36	74,751	41,703	(4,693)	(4,315)
7p31	Interest paid		(7,835)	(14,773)	–	–
7p35	Income tax paid		(14,909)	(10,526)	–	–
	Net cash generated from operating activities		**52,007**	**16,404**	**(4,693)**	**(4,315)**
7p21, 7p10 7p39	**Cash flows from investing activities**					
	Acquisition of subsidiary, net of cash acquired	39	(3,750)	–	(4,250)	–
7p16(a)	Purchases of property, plant and equipment	16	(9,505)	(6,042)	–	–
7p16(b)	Proceeds from sale of property, plant and equipment	36	6,354	2,979	–	–
7p16(a)	Purchases of intangible assets	17	(3,050)	(700)	–	–
7p16(c)	Purchases of available-for-sale financial assets	19	(4,887)	(1,150)	–	–
	Proceeds from disposal of available-for-sale financial assets		151	–		
7p16(e)	Loans granted to related parties	41	(1,343)	(112)	–	–
7p16(f)	Loan repayments received from related parties	41	63	98	–	–
7p16(e)	Loans granted to subsidiary undertakings		–	–	(9,851)	–
7p16(f)	Loan repayments received from subsidiary undertakings		–	–	–	1,126
7p31	Interest received		1,054	1,193	–	–
7p31	Dividends received		1,130	1,120	13,809	14,806
	Net cash used in investing activities		**(13,783)**	**(2,614)**	**(292)**	**15,932**

(All amounts in C thousands unless otherwise stated)

			Group Year ended 31 December		Company Year ended 31 December	
		Note	**2013**	2012 Restated	**2013**	2012
	Cash flows from financing activities					
7p21, 7p10						
7p17(a)	Proceeds from issuance of ordinary shares	26	**950**	1,070	**950**	1,070
7p17(b)	Purchase of treasury shares		**(2,564)**	–	**(2,564)**	–
7p17(c)	Proceeds from issuance of convertible bonds	31	**50,000**	–	**–**	–
7p17(c)	Proceeds from issuance of redeemable preference shares	31	**–**	30,000	**–**	–
7p17(c)	Proceeds from borrowings		**8,500**	18,000	**–**	–
7p17(d)	Repayments of borrowings		**(93,993)**	(34,674)	**–**	–
7p17(c)	Proceeds from loan from subsidiary undertaking		**–**	–	**13,210**	7,209
7p31	Dividends paid to owners of the parent	31	**(10,102)**	(15,736)	**(10,102)**	(15,736)
7p31	Dividends paid to holders of redeemable preference shares		**(1,950)**	(1,950)	**–**	–
	Acquisition of interest in a subsidiary		**(1,100)**	–	**–**	–
	Sale of interest in a subsidiary		**1,100**	–	**–**	–
7p31	Dividends paid to non-controlling interests		**(1,920)**	(550)	**–**	–
	Net cash used in financing activities		**(51,079)**	(3,840)	**1,494**	(7,457)
	Net (decrease)/increase in cash and cash equivalents		**(12,855)**	9,950	**(3,491)**	4,160
7p28	Cash and cash equivalents at beginning of year	24	**27,598**	17,587	**6,234**	2,074
	Exchange gains/(losses) on cash and cash equivalents		**535**	61	**–**	–
7p28	**Cash and cash equivalents at end of year**	24	**15,278**	27,598	**2,743**	6,234

The notes on pages 78 to 205 are an integral part of these consolidated financial statements.

IFRS GAAP plc – year ended 31 December 2013

(All amounts in C thousands unless otherwise stated)

Commentary – statement of cash flows

The commentary that follows explains some of the key requirements in IAS 7, 'Statement of cash flows'.

Reporting cash flows

Cash flows from operating activities

7p18
1. Cash flows from operating activities are reported using either:
   (a) the direct method, whereby major classes of gross cash receipts and gross cash payments are disclosed; or
   (b) the indirect method, whereby profit or loss is adjusted for the effects of transactions of a non-cash nature, any deferrals or accruals of past or future operating cash receipts or payments, and items of income or expense associated with investing or financing cash flows.

7p20
2. For an illustration of a statement of cash flows presented using the direct method, refer to appendix I.

Cash flows from investing and financing activities

7p21
3. Major classes of gross cash receipts and gross cash payments arising from investing and financing activities are reported separately, except to the extent that cash flows described in paragraphs 22 and 24 of IAS 7 are reported on a net basis.

Sale of property, plant and equipment held for rental to others

7p14
4. Cash flows from the sale of property, plant and equipment are normally presented as cash flows from investing activities. However, cash payments to manufacture or acquire assets that will be held for rental to others and subsequently for sale are cash flows from operating activities. The cash receipts from rents and subsequent sales of such assets are also therefore cash flows from operating activities.

Reporting on a net basis

7p22, 23
5. Cash flows arising from the following operating, investing or financing activities may be reported on a net basis:
   (a) cash receipts and payments on behalf of customers when the cash flows reflect the activities of the customer rather than those of the entity (for example, rents collected on behalf of, and paid over to, the owners of properties); and
   (b) cash receipts and payments for items in which the turnover is quick, the amounts are large, and the maturities are short (for example, advances made for, and repayment of, principal amounts relating to credit card customers).

7p24
6. Cash flows arising from each of the following activities of a financial institution may be reported on a net basis:
   (a) cash receipts and payments for the acceptance and repayment of deposits with a fixed maturity date;
   (b) the placement of deposits with, and withdrawal of deposits from, other financial institutions; and

(c) cash advances and loans made to customers and the repayment of those advances and loans.

Interest and dividends

7p31 7. Cash flows from interest and dividends received and paid are each disclosed separately. Each is classified in a consistent manner from period to period as either operating, investing or financing activities.

7p33 8. Interest paid and interest and dividends received are usually classified as operating cash flows for a financial institution. However, there is no consensus on the classification of these cash flows for other entities. Interest paid and interest and dividends received may be classified as operating cash flows because they enter into the determination of net profit or loss. Alternatively, interest paid and interest and dividends received may be classified as financing cash flows and investing cash flows respectively, because they are costs of obtaining financial resources or returns on investments.

7p34 9. Dividends paid may be classified as financing cash flows because they are a cost of obtaining financial resources. Alternatively, they may be classified as operating cash flows to assist users to determine the ability of an entity to pay dividends out of operating cash flows.

Income taxes

7p35 10. Cash flows arising from income taxes are separately disclosed and classified as cash flows from operating activities unless they can be specifically identified with financing and investing activities.

Effects of exchange rate changes

7p28 11. Unrealised gains and losses arising from changes in foreign currency exchange rates are not cash flows. However, the effect of exchange rate changes on cash and cash equivalents held or due in a foreign currency are reported in the statement of cash flows in order to reconcile cash and cash equivalents at the beginning and the end of the period. This amount is presented separately from cash flows from operating, investing and financing activities. It also includes the differences, if any, had those cash flows been reported at period-end exchange rates.

Additional recommended disclosures

7p50 12. Additional information may be relevant to users in understanding the financial position and liquidity of an entity. Disclosure of this information, together with a commentary by management, is encouraged and may include:

7p50(a) (a) The amount of undrawn borrowing facilities that may be available for future operating activities and to settle capital commitments, indicating any restrictions on the use of these facilities.

7p50(c) (b) The aggregate amount of cash flows that represent increases in operating capacity separately from those cash flows that are required to maintain operating capacity.

7p50(d) (c) The amount of the cash flows arising from the operating, investing and financing activities of each reportable segment (see IFRS 8, 'Operating segments').

IFRS GAAP plc – year ended 31 December 2013

(All amounts in C thousands unless otherwise stated)

Notes to the consolidated financial statements

1 General information

1p138(b)-(c), 1p51(a)(b) IFRS GAAP plc ('the company') and its subsidiaries (together, 'the group') manufacture, distribute and sell shoes through a network of independent retailers. The group has manufacturing plants around the world and sells mainly in countries within the UK, the US, Europe and Russia. During the year, the group acquired control of 'ABC Group', a shoe and leather goods retailer operating in the US and most western European countries.

1p138(a) The company is a public limited company, which is listed on the London Stock Exchange and incorporated and domiciled in the UK. The address of its registered office is Nice Walk Way, London.

2 Summary of significant accounting policies

> **PwC Commentary**
>
> The following note is a complete reiteration of a large number of possible accounting policies. Management should only present information that relates directly to the business and should avoid boilerplate disclosure.

1p112(a), 1p117(b), 1p119 The principal accounting policies applied in the preparation of these consolidated financial statements are set out below. These policies have been consistently applied to all the years presented, unless otherwise stated.

2.1 Basis of preparation

1p116, 1p117(a) The consolidated financial statements of IFRS GAAP plc have been prepared in accordance with International Financial Reporting Standards (IFRS) and IFRS Interpretations Committee (IFRS IC) as adopted by the European Union and the Companies Act 2006 applicable to companies reporting under IFRS. The consolidated financial statements have been prepared under the historical cost convention, as modified by the revaluation of land and buildings, available-for-sale financial assets, and financial assets and financial liabilities (including derivative instruments) at fair value through profit or loss.

The preparation of financial statements in conformity with IFRS requires the use of certain critical accounting estimates. It also requires management to exercise its judgement in the process of applying the group's accounting policies. The areas involving a higher degree of judgement or complexity, or areas where assumptions and estimates are significant to the consolidated financial statements are disclosed in note 4.

2.1.1 Going concern

UKCGC C.1.3 The group meets its day-to-day working capital requirements through its bank facilities. The current economic conditions continue to create uncertainty particularly over (a) the level of demand for the group's products; and (b) the availability of bank finance for the foreseeable future. The group's forecasts and projections, taking account of reasonably possible changes in trading performance, show that the

(All amounts in C thousands unless otherwise stated)

group should be able to operate within the level of its current facilities. After making enquiries, the directors have a reasonable expectation that the group has adequate resources to continue in operational existence for the foreseeable future. The group therefore continues to adopt the going concern basis in preparing its consolidated financial statements. Further information on the group's borrowings is given in note 31.

2.1.2 Changes in accounting policy and disclosures[1]

8p28

New and amended standards adopted by the group

The following standards have been adopted by the group for the first time for the financial year beginning on or after 1 January 2013 and have a material impact on the group:

Amendment to IAS 1, 'Financial statement presentation' regarding other comprehensive income. The main change resulting from these amendments is a requirement for entities to group items presented in 'other comprehensive income' (OCI) on the basis of whether they are potentially reclassifiable to profit or loss subsequently (reclassification adjustments).

IAS 19, 'Employee benefits' was revised in June 2011. The changes on the group's accounting policies has been as follows: to immediately recognise all past service costs; and to replace interest cost and expected return on plan assets with a net interest amount that is calculated by applying the discount rate to the net defined benefit liability (asset). See note 43 for the impact on the financial statements.

Amendment to IFRS 7, 'Financial instruments: Disclosures', on asset and liability offsetting. This amendment includes new disclosures to facilitate comparison between those entities that prepare IFRS financial statements to those that prepare financial statements in accordance with US GAAP.

IFRS 10, 'Consolidated financial statements' builds on existing principles by identifying the concept of control as the determining factor in whether an entity should be included within the consolidated financial statements of the parent company. The standard provides additional guidance to assist in the determination of control where this is difficult to assess. The standard is not mandatory for the group until 1 January 2014; however the group has decided to early adopt the standard as of 1 January 2013. See note 43 for the impact on the financial statements.

IFRS 11, 'Joint arrangements' focuses on the rights and obligations of the parties to the arrangement rather than its legal form. There are two types of joint arrangements: joint operations and joint ventures. Joint operations arise where the investors have rights to the assets and obligations for the liabilities of an arrangement. A joint operator accounts for its share of the assets, liabilities, revenue and expenses. Joint ventures arise where the investors have rights to the net assets of the arrangement; joint ventures are accounted for under the equity method. Proportional consolidation of joint arrangements is no longer permitted. The standard is not mandatory for the group until 1 January 2014; however the group has decided to early adopt the standard as of 1 January 2013. See note 43 for the impact of adoption on the financial statements.

---

[1] A detailed list of IFRSs and IFRIC interpretations effective on or after 1 January 2013 is included as Appendix III.

(All amounts in C thousands unless otherwise stated)

IFRS 12, 'Disclosures of interests in other entities' includes the disclosure requirements for all forms of interests in other entities, including joint arrangements, associates, structured entities and other off balance sheet vehicles. The standard is not mandatory for the group until 1 January 2014; however the group has decided to early adopt the standard as of 1 January 2013.

IFRS 13, 'Fair value measurement', aims to improve consistency and reduce complexity by providing a precise definition of fair value and a single source of fair value measurement and disclosure requirements for use across IFRSs. The requirements, which are largely aligned between IFRSs and US GAAP, do not extend the use of fair value accounting but provide guidance on how it should be applied where its use is already required or permitted by other standards within IFRSs.

Amendments to IAS 36, 'Impairment of assets', on the recoverable amount disclosures for non-financial assets. This amendment removed certain disclosures of the recoverable amount of CGUs which had been included in IAS 36 by the issue of IFRS 13. The amendment is not mandatory for the group until 1 January 2014, however the group has decided to early adopt the amendment as of 1 January 2013.

New standards and interpretations not yet adopted

8p30,31

A number of new standards and amendments to standards and interpretations are effective for annual periods beginning after 1 January 2013, and have not been applied in preparing these consolidated financial statement. None of these is expected to have a significant effect on the consolidated financial statements of the Group, except the following set out below:

IFRS 9, 'Financial instruments', addresses the classification, measurement and recognition of financial assets and financial liabilities. IFRS 9 was issued in November 2009 and October 2010. It replaces the parts of IAS 39 that relate to the classification and measurement of financial instruments. IFRS 9 requires financial assets to be classified into two measurement categories: those measured as at fair value and those measured at amortised cost. The determination is made at initial recognition. The classification depends on the entity's business model for managing its financial instruments and the contractual cash flow characteristics of the instrument. For financial liabilities, the standard retains most of the IAS 39 requirements. The main change is that, in cases where the fair value option is taken for financial liabilities, the part of a fair value change due to an entity's own credit risk is recorded in other comprehensive income rather than the income statement, unless this creates an accounting mismatch. The group is yet to assess IFRS 9's full impact. The Group will also consider the impact of the remaining phases of IFRS 9 when completed by the Board.

IFRIC 21, 'Levies', sets out the accounting for an obligation to pay a levy that is not income tax. The interpretation addresses what the obligating event is that gives rise to pay a levy and when should a liability be recognised. The Group is not currently subjected to significant levies so the impact on the Group is not material.

There are no other IFRSs or IFRIC interpretations that are not yet effective that would be expected to have a material impact on the Group.

2.2 Consolidation

(a) Subsidiaries

1p119	**2.2 Consolidation**
IFRS10p7, IFRS10p20, IFRS10p25	Subsidiaries are all entities (including structured entities) over which the group has control. The group controls an entity when the group is exposed to, or has rights to, variable returns from its involvement with the entity and has the ability to affect those returns through its power over the entity. Subsidiaries are fully consolidated from the date on which control is transferred to the group. They are deconsolidated from the date that control ceases.
IFRS3p5, IFRS3p37, IFRS3p39, IFRS3p18, IFRS3p19	The group applies the acquisition method to account for business combinations. The consideration transferred for the acquisition of a subsidiary is the fair values of the assets transferred, the liabilities incurred to the former owners of the acquiree and the equity interests issued by the group. The consideration transferred includes the fair value of any asset or liability resulting from a contingent consideration arrangement. Identifiable assets acquired and liabilities and contingent liabilities assumed in a business combination are measured initially at their fair values at the acquisition date. The group recognises any non-controlling interest in the acquiree on an acquisition-by-acquisition basis, either at fair value or at the non-controlling interest's proportionate share of the recognised amounts of acquiree's identifiable net assets.
IFRS3p53	Acquisition-related costs are expensed as incurred.
IFRS3p42	If the business combination is achieved in stages, the acquisition date carrying value of the acquirer's previously held equity interest in the acquiree is re-measured to fair value at the acquisition date; any gains or losses arising from such re-measurement are recognised in profit or loss.
IFRS3p58	Any contingent consideration to be transferred by the group is recognised at fair value at the acquisition date. Subsequent changes to the fair value of the contingent consideration that is deemed to be an asset or liability is recognised in accordance with IAS 39 either in profit or loss or as a change to other comprehensive income. Contingent consideration that is classified as equity is not re-measured, and its subsequent settlement is accounted for within equity.
IFRS3p32, IFRS3B63(a), 36p80	The excess of the consideration transferred, the amount of any non-controlling interest in the acquiree and the acquisition-date fair value of any previous equity interest in the acquiree over the fair value of the identifiable net assets acquired is recorded as goodwill. If the total of consideration transferred, non-controlling interest recognised and previously held interest measured is less than the fair value of the net assets of the subsidiary acquired in the case of a bargain purchase, the difference is recognised directly in the income statement (note 2.6).
	Inter-company transactions, balances and unrealised gains on transactions between group companies are eliminated. Unrealised losses are also eliminated. When necessary amounts reported by subsidiaries have been adjusted to conform with the group's accounting policies.

(b) Changes in ownership interests in subsidiaries without change of control

IFRS10p23	Transactions with non-controlling interests that do not result in loss of control are accounted for as equity transactions – that is, as transactions with the owners in their capacity as owners. The difference between fair value of any consideration paid and

the relevant share acquired of the carrying value of net assets of the subsidiary is recorded in equity. Gains or losses on disposals to non-controlling interests are also recorded in equity.

(c) Disposal of subsidiaries

When the group ceases to have control any retained interest in the entity is re-measured to its fair value at the date when control is lost, with the change in carrying amount recognised in profit or loss. The fair value is the initial carrying amount for the purposes of subsequently accounting for the retained interest as an associate, joint venture or financial asset. In addition, any amounts previously recognised in other comprehensive income in respect of that entity are accounted for as if the group had directly disposed of the related assets or liabilities. This may mean that amounts previously recognised in other comprehensive income are reclassified to profit or loss.

(d) Associates

Associates are all entities over which the group has significant influence but not control, generally accompanying a shareholding of between 20% and 50% of the voting rights. Investments in associates are accounted for using the equity method of accounting. Under the equity method, the investment is initially recognised at cost, and the carrying amount is increased or decreased to recognise the investor's share of the profit or loss of the investee after the date of acquisition. The group's investment in associates includes goodwill identified on acquisition.

If the ownership interest in an associate is reduced but significant influence is retained, only a proportionate share of the amounts previously recognised in other comprehensive income is reclassified to profit or loss where appropriate.

The group's share of post-acquisition profit or loss is recognised in the income statement, and its share of post-acquisition movements in other comprehensive income is recognised in other comprehensive income with a corresponding adjustment to the carrying amount of the investment. When the group's share of losses in an associate equals or exceeds its interest in the associate, including any other unsecured receivables, the group does not recognise further losses, unless it has incurred legal or constructive obligations or made payments on behalf of the associate.

The group determines at each reporting date whether there is any objective evidence that the investment in the associate is impaired. If this is the case, the group calculates the amount of impairment as the difference between the recoverable amount of the associate and its carrying value and recognises the amount adjacent to 'share of profit/(loss) of associates in the income statement.

Profits and losses resulting from upstream and downstream transactions between the group and its associate are recognised in the group's financial statements only to the extent of unrelated investor's interests in the associates. Unrealised losses are eliminated unless the transaction provides evidence of an impairment of the asset transferred. Accounting policies of associates have been changed where necessary to ensure consistency with the policies adopted by the group.

Dilution gains and losses arising in investments in associates are recognised in the income statement.

(All amounts in C thousands unless otherwise stated)

(e) Joint arrangements

The group has applied IFRS 11 to all joint arrangements as of 1 January 2012. Under IFRS 11 investments in joint arrangements are classified as either joint operations or joint ventures depending on the contractual rights and obligations each investor. IFRS GAAP plc has assessed the nature of its joint arrangements and determined them to be joint ventures. Joint ventures are accounted for using the equity method.

28p10

Under the equity method of accounting, interests in joint ventures are initially recognised at cost and adjusted thereafter to recognise the group's share of the post-acquisition profits or losses and movements in other comprehensive income. When the group's share of losses in a joint venture equals or exceeds its interests in the joint ventures (which includes any long-term interests that, in substance, form part of the group's net investment in the joint ventures), the group does not recognise further losses, unless it has incurred obligations or made payments on behalf of the joint ventures.

IFRS11pC2-3
28p28

Unrealised gains on transactions between the group and its joint ventures are eliminated to the extent of the group's interest in the joint ventures. Unrealised losses are also eliminated unless the transaction provides evidence of an impairment of the asset transferred. Accounting policies of the joint ventures have been changed where necessary to ensure consistency with the policies adopted by the group. The change in accounting policy has been applied as from 1 January 2012.

The effects of the change in accounting policies on the financial position, comprehensive income and the cash flows of the group at 1 January 2012 and 31 December 2012 are shown in note 43. The change in accounting policy has had no impact on earnings per share.

1p119

2.3 Segment reporting

IFRS8p5(b)

Operating segments are reported in a manner consistent with the internal reporting provided to the chief operating decision-maker. The chief operating decision-maker, who is responsible for allocating resources and assessing performance of the operating segments, has been identified as the steering committee that makes strategic decisions.

1p119

2.4 Foreign currency translation

1p119

(a) Functional and presentation currency

21p17, 21p9,
18, 1p51(d)

Items included in the financial statements of each of the group's entities are measured using the currency of the primary economic environment in which the entity operates ('the functional currency'). The consolidated financial statements are presented in 'currency' (C), which is the group's presentation currency.

1p119

(b) Transactions and balances

21p21, 28,
21p32,
39p95(a),
39p102(a)

Foreign currency transactions are translated into the functional currency using the exchange rates prevailing at the dates of the transactions or valuation where items are re-measured. Foreign exchange gains and losses resulting from the settlement of such transactions and from the translation at year-end exchange rates of monetary assets and liabilities denominated in foreign currencies are recognised in the income statement, except when deferred in other comprehensive income as qualifying cash flow hedges and qualifying net investment hedges. Foreign exchange gains and

IFRS GAAP plc – year ended 31 December 2013

84

(All amounts in C thousands unless otherwise stated)

	losses that relate to borrowings and cash and cash equivalents are presented in the income statement within 'finance income or costs'. All other foreign exchange gains and losses are presented in the income statement within 'Other (losses)/gains – net'.
39AG83	Changes in the fair value of monetary securities denominated in foreign currency classified as available for sale are analysed between translation differences resulting from changes in the amortised cost of the security and other changes in the carrying amount of the security. Translation differences related to changes in amortised cost are recognised in profit or loss, and other changes in carrying amount are recognised in other comprehensive income.
21p30	Translation differences on non-monetary financial assets and liabilities such as equities held at fair value through profit or loss are recognised in profit or loss as part of the fair value gain or loss. Translation differences on non-monetary financial assets, such as equities classified as available for sale, are included in other comprehensive income.
1p119	**(c) Group companies**
21p39	The results and financial position of all the group entities (none of which has the currency of a hyper-inflationary economy) that have a functional currency different from the presentation currency are translated into the presentation currency as follows:
21p39(a)	(a) assets and liabilities for each balance sheet presented are translated at the closing rate at the date of that balance sheet;
21p39(b)	(b) income and expenses for each income statement are translated at average exchange rates (unless this average is not a reasonable approximation of the cumulative effect of the rates prevailing on the transaction dates, in which case income and expenses are translated at the rate on the dates of the transactions); and
1p79(b), 21p39(c)	(c) all resulting exchange differences are recognised in other comprehensive income.
21p47	Goodwill and fair value adjustments arising on the acquisition of a foreign entity are treated as assets and liabilities of the foreign entity and translated at the closing rate. Exchange differences arising are recognised in other comprehensive income.
1p119	**2.5 Property, plant and equipment**
16p73(a), 16p35(b), 16p15, 16p17, 39p98(b)	Land and buildings comprise mainly factories, retail outlets and offices. Land and buildings are shown at fair value, based on valuations by external independent valuers, less subsequent depreciation for buildings. Valuations are performed with sufficient regularity to ensure that the fair value of a revalued asset does not differ materially from its carrying amount. Any accumulated depreciation at the date of revaluation is eliminated against the gross carrying amount of the asset, and the net amount is restated to the revalued amount of the asset. All other property, plant and equipment is stated at historical cost less depreciation. Historical cost includes expenditure that is directly attributable to the acquisition of the items. Cost may also include transfers from equity of any gains/losses on qualifying cash flow hedges of foreign currency purchases of property, plant and equipment.
16p12	Subsequent costs are included in the asset's carrying amount or recognised as a separate asset, as appropriate, only when it is probable that future economic benefits associated with the item will flow to the group and the cost of the item can be

(All amounts in C thousands unless otherwise stated)

measured reliably. The carrying amount of the replaced part is derecognised. All other repairs and maintenance are charged to the income statement during the financial period in which they are incurred.

16p39, 1p79(b), 16p40, 16p41 — Increases in the carrying amount arising on revaluation of land and buildings are credited to other comprehensive income and shown as other reserves in shareholders' equity. Decreases that offset previous increases of the same asset are charged in other comprehensive income and debited against other reserves directly in equity; all other decreases are charged to the income statement. Each year the difference between depreciation based on the revalued carrying amount of the asset charged to the income statement, and depreciation based on the asset's original cost is transferred from 'other reserves' to 'retained earnings'.

16p73(b), 50, 16p73(c) — Land is not depreciated. Depreciation on other assets is calculated using the straight-line method to allocate their cost or revalued amounts to their residual values over their estimated useful lives, as follows:

- Buildings — 25-40 years
- Machinery — 10-15 years
- Vehicles — 3-5 years
- Furniture, fittings and equipment — 3-8 years

16p51 — The assets' residual values and useful lives are reviewed, and adjusted if appropriate, at the end of each reporting period.

36p59 — An asset's carrying amount is written down immediately to its recoverable amount if the asset's carrying amount is greater than its estimated recoverable amount (note 2.7).

16p68, 71 — Gains and losses on disposals are determined by comparing the proceeds with the carrying amount and are recognised within 'Other (losses)/gains – net' in the income statement.

16p41, 1p79(b) — When revalued assets are sold, the amounts included in other reserves are transferred to retained earnings.

2.6 Intangible assets

1p119 — *(a) Goodwill*

IFRS3p51, 38p108(a), IFRS3p54, 36p124 — Goodwill arises on the acquisition of subsidiaries and represents the excess of the consideration transferred over IFRS GAAP plc's interest in net fair value of the net identifiable assets, liabilities and contingent liabilities of the acquiree and the fair value of the non-controlling interest in the acquiree.

For the purpose of impairment testing, goodwill acquired in a business combination is allocated to each of the CGUs, or groups of CGUs, that is expected to benefit from the synergies of the combination. Each unit or group of units to which the goodwill is allocated represents the lowest level within the entity at which the goodwill is monitored for internal management purposes. Goodwill is monitored at the operating segment level.

Goodwill impairment reviews are undertaken annually or more frequently if events or changes in circumstances indicate a potential impairment. The carrying value of goodwill is compared to the recoverable amount, which is the higher of value in use

(All amounts in C thousands unless otherwise stated)

and the fair value less costs of disposal. Any impairment is recognised immediately as an expense and is not subsequently reversed.

1p119 (b) Trademarks and licences

38p74, 38p97, 38p118(a), (b) Separately acquired trademarks and licences are shown at historical cost. Trademarks and licences acquired in a business combination are recognised at fair value at the acquisition date. Trademarks and licences have a finite useful life and are carried at cost less accumulated amortisation. Amortisation is calculated using the straight-line method to allocate the cost of trademarks and licences over their estimated useful lives of 15 to 20 years.

38p4, 38p118(a), (b) Acquired computer software licences are capitalised on the basis of the costs incurred to acquire and bring to use the specific software. These costs are amortised over their estimated useful lives of three to five years.

1p119 (c) Computer software

38p57 Costs associated with maintaining computer software programmes are recognised as an expense as incurred. Development costs that are directly attributable to the design and testing of identifiable and unique software products controlled by the group are recognised as intangible assets when the following criteria are met:

- it is technically feasible to complete the software product so that it will be available for use;
- management intends to complete the software product and use or sell it;
- there is an ability to use or sell the software product;
- it can be demonstrated how the software product will generate probable future economic benefits;
- adequate technical, financial and other resources to complete the development and to use or sell the software product are available; and
- the expenditure attributable to the software product during its development can be reliably measured.

38p66 Directly attributable costs that are capitalised as part of the software product include the software development employee costs and an appropriate portion of relevant overheads.

38p68,71 Other development expenditures that do not meet these criteria are recognised as an expense as incurred. Development costs previously recognised as an expense are not recognised as an asset in a subsequent period.

38p97, 38p118(a), (b) Computer software development costs recognised as assets are amortised over their estimated useful lives, which does not exceed three years.

1p119 **2.7 Impairment of non-financial assets**

36p9,36p10 Intangible assets that have an indefinite useful life or intangible assets not ready to use are not subject to amortisation and are tested annually for impairment. Assets that are subject to amortisation are reviewed for impairment whenever events or changes in circumstances indicate that the carrying amount may not be recoverable. An impairment loss is recognised for the amount by which the asset's carrying amount exceeds its recoverable amount. The recoverable amount is the higher of an asset's fair value less costs of disposal and value in use. For the purposes of assessing impairment, assets are grouped at the lowest levels for which there are largely independent cash inflows (cash-generating units). Prior impairments of non-financial assets (other than goodwill) are reviewed for possible reversal at each reporting date.

2.8 Non-current assets (or disposal groups) held for sale

Non-current assets (or disposal groups) are classified as assets held for sale when their carrying amount is to be recovered principally through a sale transaction and a sale is considered highly probable. They are stated at the lower of carrying amount and fair value less costs to sell.

2.9 Financial assets

2.9.1 Classification

The group classifies its financial assets in the following categories: at fair value through profit or loss, loans and receivables, and available for sale. The classification depends on the purpose for which the financial assets were acquired. Management determines the classification of its financial assets at initial recognition.

(a) Financial assets at fair value through profit or loss

Financial assets at fair value through profit or loss are financial assets held for trading. A financial asset is classified in this category if acquired principally for the purpose of selling in the short term. Derivatives are also categorised as held for trading unless they are designated as hedges. Assets in this category are classified as current assets if expected to be settled within 12 months, otherwise they are classified as non-current.

(b) Loans and receivables

Loans and receivables are non-derivative financial assets with fixed or determinable payments that are not quoted in an active market. They are included in current assets, except for maturities greater than 12 months after the end of the reporting period. These are classified as non-current assets. The group's loans and receivables comprise 'trade and other receivables' and 'cash and cash equivalents' in the balance sheet (notes 2.14 and 2.15).

(c) Available-for-sale financial assets

Available-for-sale financial assets are non-derivatives that are either designated in this category or not classified in any of the other categories. They are included in non-current assets unless the investment matures or management intends to dispose of it within 12 months of the end of the reporting period.

2.9.2 Recognition and measurement

Regular purchases and sales of financial assets are recognised on the trade-date – the date on which the group commits to purchase or sell the asset. Investments are initially recognised at fair value plus transaction costs for all financial assets not carried at fair value through profit or loss. Financial assets carried at fair value through profit or loss are initially recognised at fair value, and transaction costs are expensed in the income statement. Financial assets are derecognised when the rights to receive cash flows from the investments have expired or have been transferred and the group has transferred substantially all risks and rewards of

(All amounts in C thousands unless otherwise stated)

ownership. Available-for-sale financial assets and financial assets at fair value through profit or loss are subsequently carried at fair value. Loans and receivables are subsequently carried at amortised cost using the effective interest method.

<small>39p55(a), IFRS7 AppxB5(e)</small>

Gains or losses arising from changes in the fair value of the 'financial assets at fair value through profit or loss' category are presented in the income statement within 'Other (losses)/gains – net' in the period in which they arise. Dividend income from financial assets at fair value through profit or loss is recognised in the income statement as part of other income when the group's right to receive payments is established.

<small>39p55(b), IFRS7 AppxB5(e), 39AG83, 1p79(b)</small>

Changes in the fair value of monetary and non-monetary securities classified as available for sale are recognised in other comprehensive income.

<small>39p67</small>

When securities classified as available for sale are sold or impaired, the accumulated fair value adjustments recognised in equity are included in the income statement as 'Gains and losses from investment securities'.

Interest on available-for-sale securities calculated using the effective interest method is recognised in the income statement as part of other income. Dividends on available-for-sale equity instruments are recognised in the income statement as part of other income when the group's right to receive payments is established.

2.10 Offsetting financial instruments

<small>32p42</small>

Financial assets and liabilities are offset and the net amount reported in the balance sheet when there is a legally enforceable right to offset the recognised amounts and there is an intention to settle on a net basis or realise the asset and settle the liability simultaneously.

2.11 Impairment of financial assets

(a) Assets carried at amortised cost

<small>39p58,39p59</small>

The group assesses at the end of each reporting period whether there is objective evidence that a financial asset or group of financial assets is impaired. A financial asset or a group of financial assets is impaired and impairment losses are incurred only if there is objective evidence of impairment as a result of one or more events that occurred after the initial recognition of the asset (a 'loss event') and that loss event (or events) has an impact on the estimated future cash flows of the financial asset or group of financial assets that can be reliably estimated.

<small>IFRS7B5(f)</small>

Evidence of impairment may include indications that the debtors or a group of debtors is experiencing significant financial difficulty, default or delinquency in interest or principal payments, the probability that they will enter bankruptcy or other financial reorganisation, and where observable data indicate that there is a measurable decrease in the estimated future cash flows, such as changes in arrears or economic conditions that correlate with defaults.

<small>IFRS7p16, 39AG84</small>

For loans and receivables category, the amount of the loss is measured as the difference between the asset's carrying amount and the present value of estimated future cash flows (excluding future credit losses that have not been incurred) discounted at the financial asset's original effective interest rate. The carrying amount

(All amounts in C thousands unless otherwise stated)

of the asset is reduced and the amount of the loss is recognised in the consolidated income statement. If a loan or held-to-maturity investment has a variable interest rate, the discount rate for measuring any impairment loss is the current effective interest rate determined under the contract. As a practical expedient, the group may measure impairment on the basis of an instrument's fair value using an observable market price.

IFRS7 AppxB5(d), 39p65

If, in a subsequent period, the amount of the impairment loss decreases and the decrease can be related objectively to an event occurring after the impairment was recognised (such as an improvement in the debtor's credit rating), the reversal of the previously recognised impairment loss is recognised in the consolidated income statement.

(b) Assets classified as available for sale

39p67-70

The group assesses at the end of each reporting period whether there is objective evidence that a financial asset or a group of financial assets is impaired. For debt securities, the group uses the criteria referred to in (a) above. In the case of equity investments classified as available for sale, a significant or prolonged decline in the fair value of the security below its cost is also evidence that the assets are impaired. If any such evidence exists for available-for-sale financial assets, the cumulative loss – measured as the difference between the acquisition cost and the current fair value, less any impairment loss on that financial asset previously recognised in profit or loss – is removed from equity and recognised in profit or loss. Impairment losses recognised in the consolidated income statement on equity instruments are not reversed through the consolidated income statement. If, in a subsequent period, the fair value of a debt instrument classified as available for sale increases and the increase can be objectively related to an event occurring after the impairment loss was recognised in profit or loss, the impairment loss is reversed through the consolidated income statement.

1p119

2.12 Derivative financial instruments and hedging activities

IFRS7p21, IFRS7p22

Derivatives are initially recognised at fair value on the date a derivative contract is entered into and are subsequently re-measured at their fair value. The method of recognising the resulting gain or loss depends on whether the derivative is designated as a hedging instrument, and if so, the nature of the item being hedged. The group designates certain derivatives as either:

(a) hedges of the fair value of recognised assets or liabilities or a firm commitment (fair value hedge);
(b) hedges of a particular risk associated with a recognised asset or liability or a highly probable forecast transaction (cash flow hedge); or
(c) hedges of a net investment in a foreign operation (net investment hedge).

39p88

The group documents at the inception of the transaction the relationship between hedging instruments and hedged items, as well as its risk management objectives and strategy for undertaking various hedging transactions. The group also documents its assessment, both at hedge inception and on an ongoing basis, of whether the derivatives that are used in hedging transactions are highly effective in offsetting changes in fair values or cash flows of hedged items.

IFRS7p23, IFRS7p24

The fair values of various derivative instruments used for hedging purposes are disclosed in note 20. Movements on the hedging reserve in other comprehensive income are shown in note 29. The full fair value of a hedging derivative is classified as

(All amounts in C thousands unless otherwise stated)

a non-current asset or liability when the remaining hedged item is more than 12 months, and as a current asset or liability when the remaining maturity of the hedged item is less than 12 months. Trading derivatives are classified as a current asset or liability.

39p89 **(a) Fair value hedge**

Changes in the fair value of derivatives that are designated and qualify as fair value hedges are recorded in the income statement, together with any changes in the fair value of the hedged asset or liability that are attributable to the hedged risk. The group only applies fair value hedge accounting for hedging fixed interest risk on borrowings. The gain or loss relating to the effective portion of interest rate swaps hedging fixed rate borrowings is recognised in the income statement within 'Finance costs'. The gain or loss relating to the ineffective portion is recognised in the income statement within 'Other gains/(losses) – net'. Changes in the fair value of the hedge fixed rate borrowings attributable to interest rate risk are recognised in the income statement within 'Finance costs'.

39p92 If the hedge no longer meets the criteria for hedge accounting, the adjustment to the carrying amount of a hedged item for which the effective interest method is used is amortised to profit or loss over the period to maturity.

39p95 **(b) Cash flow hedge**

1p79(b) The effective portion of changes in the fair value of derivatives that are designated and qualify as cash flow hedges is recognised in other comprehensive income. The gain or loss relating to the ineffective portion is recognised immediately in the income statement within 'Other gains/(losses) – net'.

39p99, 39p100, 39p98(b) Amounts accumulated in equity are reclassified to profit or loss in the periods when the hedged item affects profit or loss (for example, when the forecast sale that is hedged takes place). The gain or loss relating to the effective portion of interest rate swaps hedging variable rate borrowings is recognised in the income statement within 'finance income/cost'. However, when the forecast transaction that is hedged results in the recognition of a non-financial asset (for example, inventory or fixed assets), the gains and losses previously deferred in equity are transferred from equity and included in the initial measurement of the cost of the asset. The deferred amounts are ultimately recognised in cost of goods sold in the case of inventory or in depreciation in the case of fixed assets.

39p101 When a hedging instrument expires or is sold, or when a hedge no longer meets the criteria for hedge accounting, any cumulative gain or loss existing in equity at that time remains in equity and is recognised when the forecast transaction is ultimately recognised in the income statement. When a forecast transaction is no longer expected to occur, the cumulative gain or loss that was reported in equity is immediately transferred to the income statement within 'Other gains/(losses) – net'.

39p102(a)(b) **(c) Net investment hedge**

Hedges of net investments in foreign operations are accounted for similarly to cash flow hedges.

1p79(b) Any gain or loss on the hedging instrument relating to the effective portion of the hedge is recognised in other comprehensive income. The gain or loss relating to the ineffective portion is recognised in the income statement. Gains and losses accumulated in equity are included in the income statement when the foreign operation is partially disposed of or sold.

2.13 Inventories

Inventories are stated at the lower of cost and net realisable value. Cost is determined using the first-in, first-out (FIFO) method. The cost of finished goods and work in progress comprises design costs, raw materials, direct labour, other direct costs and related production overheads (based on normal operating capacity). It excludes borrowing costs. Net realisable value is the estimated selling price in the ordinary course of business, less applicable variable selling expenses. Costs of inventories include the transfer from equity of any gains/losses on qualifying cash flow hedges for purchases of raw materials[1].

2.14 Trade receivables

Trade receivables are amounts due from customers for merchandise sold or services performed in the ordinary course of business. If collection is expected in one year or less (or in the normal operating cycle of the business if longer), they are classified as current assets. If not, they are presented as non-current assets.

Trade receivables are recognised initially at fair value and subsequently measured at amortised cost using the effective interest method, less provision for impairment.

2.15 Cash and cash equivalents

In the consolidated statement of cash flows, cash and cash equivalents includes cash in hand, deposits held at call with banks, other short-term highly liquid investments with original maturities of three months or less and bank overdrafts. In the consolidated balance sheet, bank overdrafts are shown within borrowings in current liabilities.

2.16 Share capital

Ordinary shares are classified as equity. Mandatorily redeemable preference shares are classified as liabilities (note 2.18).

Incremental costs directly attributable to the issue of new ordinary shares or options are shown in equity as a deduction, net of tax, from the proceeds.

Where any group company purchases the company's equity share capital (treasury shares), the consideration paid, including any directly attributable incremental costs (net of income taxes) is deducted from equity attributable to the company's equity holders until the shares are cancelled or reissued. Where such ordinary shares are subsequently reissued, any consideration received, net of any directly attributable incremental transaction costs and the related income tax effects, is included in equity attributable to the company's equity holders.

---

[1] Management may choose to keep these gains in equity until the acquired asset affects profit or loss. At this time, management should re-classify the gains to profit or loss.

1p119		**2.17 Trade payables**
		Trade payables are obligations to pay for goods or services that have been acquired in the ordinary course of business from suppliers. Accounts payable are classified as current liabilities if payment is due within one year or less (or in the normal operating cycle of the business if longer). If not, they are presented as non-current liabilities.
IFRS7p21, 39p43		Trade payables are recognised initially at fair value and subsequently measured at amortised cost using the effective interest method.
1p119		**2.18 Borrowings**
IFRS7p21		Borrowings are recognised initially at fair value, net of transaction costs incurred. Borrowings are subsequently carried at amortised cost; any difference between the proceeds (net of transaction costs) and the redemption value is recognised in the income statement over the period of the borrowings using the effective interest method.
39p43,39p47		Fees paid on the establishment of loan facilities are recognised as transaction costs of the loan to the extent that it is probable that some or all of the facility will be drawn down. In this case, the fee is deferred until the draw-down occurs. To the extent there is no evidence that it is probable that some or all of the facility will be drawn down, the fee is capitalised as a pre-payment for liquidity services and amortised over the period of the facility to which it relates.
32p18(a), 32p35		Preference shares, which are mandatorily redeemable on a specific date, are classified as liabilities. The dividends on these preference shares are recognised in the income statement as interest expense.
1p119		**2.19 Borrowing costs**
23p8		General and specific borrowing costs directly attributable to the acquisition, construction or production of qualifying assets, which are assets that necessarily take a substantial period of time to get ready for their intended use or sale, are added to the cost of those assets, until such time as the assets are substantially ready for their intended use or sale.
23p12		Investment income earned on the temporary investment of specific borrowings pending their expenditure on qualifying assets is deducted from the borrowing costs eligible for capitalisation.
		All other borrowing costs are recognised in profit or loss in the period in which they are incurred.
1p119		**2.20 Compound financial instruments**
32p28		Compound financial instruments issued by the group comprise convertible notes that can be converted to share capital at the option of the holder, and the number of shares to be issued does not vary with changes in their fair value.
32AG31		The liability component of a compound financial instrument is recognised initially at the fair value of a similar liability that does not have an equity conversion option. The equity component is recognised initially at the difference between the fair value of the compound financial instrument as a whole and the fair value of the liability

	component. Any directly attributable transaction costs are allocated to the liability and equity components in proportion to their initial carrying amounts.
32p36	Subsequent to initial recognition, the liability component of a compound financial instrument is measured at amortised cost using the effective interest method. The equity component of a compound financial instrument is not re-measured subsequent to initial recognition except on conversion or expiry.
1p69, 71	Borrowings are classified as current liabilities unless the group has an unconditional right to defer settlement of the liability for at least 12 months after the end of the reporting period.

1p119 2.21 Current and deferred income tax

12p58, 12p61A	The tax expense for the period comprises current and deferred tax. Tax is recognised in the income statement, except to the extent that it relates to items recognised in other comprehensive income or directly in equity. In this case, the tax is also recognised in other comprehensive income or directly in equity, respectively.
12p12, 12p46	The current income tax charge is calculated on the basis of the tax laws enacted or substantively enacted at the balance sheet date in the countries where the company and its subsidiaries operate and generate taxable income. Management periodically evaluates positions taken in tax returns with respect to situations in which applicable tax regulation is subject to interpretation. It establishes provisions where appropriate on the basis of amounts expected to be paid to the tax authorities.
12p24, 12p15, 12p47	Deferred income tax is recognised on temporary differences arising between the tax bases of assets and liabilities and their carrying amounts in the consolidated financial statements. However, deferred tax liabilities are not recognised if they arise from the initial recognition of goodwill; deferred income tax is not accounted for if it arises from initial recognition of an asset or liability in a transaction other than a business combination that at the time of the transaction affects neither accounting nor taxable profit or loss. Deferred income tax is determined using tax rates (and laws) that have been enacted or substantively enacted by the balance sheet date and are expected to apply when the related deferred income tax asset is realised or the deferred income tax liability is settled.
12p24, 12p34	Deferred income tax assets are recognised only to the extent that it is probable that future taxable profit will be available against which the temporary differences can be utilised.
12p39,	Deferred income tax liabilities are provided on taxable temporary differences arising from investments in subsidiaries, associates and joint arrangements, except for deferred income tax liability where the timing of the reversal of the temporary difference is controlled by the group and it is probable that the temporary difference will not reverse in the foreseeable future. Generally the group is unable to control the reversal of the temporary difference for associates. Only were there is an agreement in place that gives the group the ability to control the reveral of the temporary difference not recognised.
12p44	Deferred income tax assets are recognised on deductible temporary differences arising from investments in subsidiaries, associates and joint arrangements only to the extent that it is probable the temporary difference will reverse in the future and there is sufficient taxable profit available against which the temporary difference can be utilised.

IFRS GAAP plc – year ended 31 December 2013

(All amounts in C thousands unless otherwise stated)

12p74	Deferred income tax assets and liabilities are offset when there is a legally enforceable right to offset current tax assets against current tax liabilities and when the deferred income taxes assets and liabilities relate to income taxes levied by the same taxation authority on either the same taxable entity or different taxable entities where there is an intention to settle the balances on a net basis.
1p119	**2.22 Employee benefits**
	The group operates various post-employment schemes, including both defined benefit and defined contribution pension plans and post-employment medical plans.
	(a) Pension obligations
19Rp26, 19Rp27, 19Rp28	A defined contribution plan is a pension plan under which the group pays fixed contributions into a separate entity. The group has no legal or constructive obligations to pay further contributions if the fund does not hold sufficient assets to pay all employees the benefits relating to employee service in the current and prior periods. A defined benefit plan is a pension plan that is not a defined contribution plan.
19Rp30	Typically defined benefit plans define an amount of pension benefit that an employee will receive on retirement, usually dependent on one or more factors such as age, years of service and compensation.
19Rp57, 19Rp58, 19Rp59, 19Rp60, 19Rp67, 19Rp68, 19Rp83	The liability recognised in the balance sheet in respect of defined benefit pension plans is the present value of the defined benefit obligation at the end of the reporting period less the fair value of plan assets. The defined benefit obligation is calculated annually by independent actuaries using the projected unit credit method. The present value of the defined benefit obligation is determined by discounting the estimated future cash outflows using interest rates of high-quality corporate bonds that are denominated in the currency in which the benefits will be paid, and that have terms to maturity approximating to the terms of the related pension obligation. In countries where there is no deep market in such bonds, the market rates on government bonds are used.
19Rp57(d)	Actuarial gains and losses arising from experience adjustments and changes in actuarial assumptions are charged or credited to equity in other comprehensive income in the period in which they arise.
19Rp103	Past-service costs are recognised immediately in income.
19Rp51	For defined contribution plans, the group pays contributions to publicly or privately administered pension insurance plans on a mandatory, contractual or voluntary basis. The group has no further payment obligations once the contributions have been paid. The contributions are recognised as employee benefit expense when they are due. Prepaid contributions are recognised as an asset to the extent that a cash refund or a reduction in the future payments is available.
	(b) Other post-employment obligations
19Rp155	Some group companies provide post-retirement healthcare benefits to their retirees. The entitlement to these benefits is usually conditional on the employee remaining in service up to retirement age and the completion of a minimum service period. The expected costs of these benefits are accrued over the period of employment using the same accounting methodology as used for defined benefit pension plans.

Actuarial gains and losses arising from experience adjustments and changes in actuarial assumptions are charged or credited to equity in other comprehensive income in the period in which they arise. These obligations are valued annually by independent qualified actuaries.

(c) Termination benefits

19Rp159,

Termination benefits are payable when employment is terminated by the group before the normal retirement date, or whenever an employee accepts voluntary redundancy in exchange for these benefits. The group recognises termination benefits at the earlier of the following dates: (a) when the group can no longer withdraw the offer of those benefits; and (b) when the entity recognises costs for a restructuring that is within the scope of IAS 37 and involves the payment of termination benefits. In the case of an offer made to encourage voluntary redundancy, the termination benefits are measured based on the number of employees expected to accept the offer. Benefits falling due more than 12 months after the end of the reporting period are discounted to their present value.

(d) Profit-sharing and bonus plans

19Rp19

The group recognises a liability and an expense for bonuses and profit-sharing, based on a formula that takes into consideration the profit attributable to the company's shareholders after certain adjustments. The group recognises a provision where contractually obliged or where there is a past practice that has created a constructive obligation.

1p119

2.23 Share-based payments

IFRS2p15(b), IFRS2p19

The group operates a number of equity-settled, share-based compensation plans, under which the entity receives services from employees as consideration for equity instruments (options) of the group. The fair value of the employee services received in exchange for the grant of the options is recognised as an expense. The total amount to be expensed is determined by reference to the fair value of the options granted:

IFRS2p21
- including any market performance conditions (for example, an entity's share price);

IFRS2p20
- excluding the impact of any service and non-market performance vesting conditions (for example, profitability, sales growth targets and remaining an employee of the entity over a specified time period); and

IFRS2p21A
- including the impact of any non-vesting conditions (for example, the requirement for employees to save).

IFRS2p15, IFRS2p20

Non-market performance and service conditions are included in assumptions about the number of options that are expected to vest. The total expense is recognised over the vesting period, which is the period over which all of the specified vesting conditions are to be satisfied.

In addition, in some circumstances employees may provide services in advance of the grant date and therefore the grant date fair value is estimated for the purposes of recognising the expense during the period between service commencement period and grant date.

(All amounts in C thousands unless otherwise stated)

At the end of each reporting period, the group revises its estimates of the number of options that are expected to vest based on the non-market vesting conditions. It recognises the impact of the revision to original estimates, if any, in the income statement, with a corresponding adjustment to equity.

When the options are exercised, the company issues new shares. The proceeds received net of any directly attributable transaction costs are credited to share capital (nominal value) and share premium.

The grant by the company of options over its equity instruments to the employees of subsidiary undertakings in the group is treated as a capital contribution. The fair value of employee services received, measured by reference to the grant date fair value, is recognised over the vesting period as an increase to investment in subsidiary undertakings, with a corresponding credit to equity in the parent entity accounts.

The social security contributions payable in connection with the grant of the share options is considered an integral part of the grant itself, and the charge will be treated as a cash-settled transaction.

2.24 Provisions

1p119

37p14, 37p72, 37p63 Provisions for environmental restoration, restructuring costs and legal claims are recognised when: the group has a present legal or constructive obligation as a result of past events; it is probable that an outflow of resources will be required to settle the obligation; and the amount has been reliably estimated. Restructuring provisions comprise lease termination penalties and employee termination payments. Provisions are not recognised for future operating losses.

37p24 Where there are a number of similar obligations, the likelihood that an outflow will be required in settlement is determined by considering the class of obligations as a whole. A provision is recognised even if the likelihood of an outflow with respect to any one item included in the same class of obligations may be small.

37p45 Provisions are measured at the present value of the expenditures expected to be required to settle the obligation using a pre-tax rate that reflects current market assessments of the time value of money and the risks specific to the obligation. The increase in the provision due to passage of time is recognised as interest expense.

2.25 Revenue recognition

1p119

18p35(a) Revenue is measured at the fair value of the consideration received or receivable, and represents amounts receivable for goods supplied, stated net of discounts, returns and value added taxes. The group recognises revenue when the amount of revenue can be reliably measured; when it is probable that future economic benefits will flow to the entity; and when specific criteria have been met for each of the group's activities, as described below. The group bases its estimate of return on historical results, taking into consideration the type of customer, the type of transaction and the specifics of each arrangement.

18p14 *(a) Sales of goods – wholesale*

The group manufactures and sells a range of footwear products in the wholesale market. Sales of goods are recognised when a group entity has delivered products to the wholesaler, the wholesaler has full discretion over the channel and price to sell

(All amounts in C thousands unless otherwise stated)

the products, and there is no unfulfilled obligation that could affect the wholesaler's acceptance of the products. Delivery does not occur until the products have been shipped to the specified location, the risks of obsolescence and loss have been transferred to the wholesaler, and either the wholesaler has accepted the products in accordance with the sales contract, the acceptance provisions have lapsed or the group has objective evidence that all criteria for acceptance have been satisfied.

The footwear products are often sold with volume discounts, customers have a right to return faulty products in the wholesale market. Sales are recorded based on the price specified in the sales contracts, net of the estimated volume discounts and returns at the time of sale. Accumulated experience is used to estimate and provide for the discounts and returns. The volume discounts are assessed based on anticipated annual purchases. No element of financing is deemed present as the sales are made with a credit term of 60 days, which is consistent with the market practice.

18p14 (b) Sales of goods – retail

The group operates a chain of retail outlets for selling shoes and other leather products. Sales of goods are recognised when a group entity sells a product to the customer. Retail sales are usually in cash or by credit card.

It is the group's policy to sell its products to the retail customer with a right to return within 28 days. Accumulated experience is used to estimate and provide for such returns at the time of sale. The group does not operate any loyalty programmes.

18p14 (c) Internet revenue

Revenue from the provision of the sale of goods on the internet is recognised at the point that the risks and rewards of the inventory have passed to the customer, which is the point of dispatch. Transactions are settled by credit or payment card.

Provisions are made for internet credit notes based on the expected level of returns, which in turn is based upon the historical rate of returns.

18p20 (d) Sales of services

The group sells design services and transportation services to other shoe manufacturers. For sales of services, revenue is recognised in the accounting period in which the services are rendered, by reference to stage of completion of the specific transaction and assessed on the basis of the actual service provided as a proportion of the total services to be provided.

18p30(b) (e) Royalty income

Royalty income is recognised on an accruals basis in accordance with the substance of the relevant agreements.

18p30(a) **2.26 Interest income**

39p63 Interest income is recognised using the effective interest method. When a loan and receivable is impaired, the group reduces the carrying amount to its recoverable amount, being the estimated future cash flow discounted at the original effective interest rate of the instrument, and continues unwinding the discount as interest income. Interest income on impaired loan and receivables is recognised using the original effective interest rate.

2.27 Dividend income

Dividend income is recognised when the right to receive payment is established.

2.28 Leases

Leases in which a significant portion of the risks and rewards of ownership are retained by the lessor are classified as operating leases. Payments made under operating leases (net of any incentives received from the lessor) are charged to the income statement on a straight-line basis over the period of the lease.

The group leases certain property, plant and equipment. Leases of property, plant and equipment where the group has substantially all the risks and rewards of ownership are classified as finance leases. Finance leases are capitalised at the lease's commencement at the lower of the fair value of the leased property and the present value of the minimum lease payments.

Each lease payment is allocated between the liability and finance charges. The corresponding rental obligations, net of finance charges, are included in other long-term payables. The interest element of the finance cost is charged to the income statement over the lease period so as to produce a constant periodic rate of interest on the remaining balance of the liability for each period. The property, plant and equipment acquired under finance leases is depreciated over the shorter of the useful life of the asset and the lease term.

2.29 Dividend distribution

Dividend distribution to the company's shareholders is recognised as a liability in the group's financial statements in the period in which the dividends are approved by the company's shareholders.

2.30 Exceptional items

Exceptional items are disclosed separately in the financial statements where it is necessary to do so to provide further understanding of the financial performance of the group. They are material items of income or expense that have been shown separately due to the significance of their nature or amount.

Commentary – Summary of significant accounting policies

Statement of compliance with IFRS

1. An entity whose financial statements and notes comply with IFRS makes an explicit and unreserved statement of such compliance in the notes. The financial statements and notes are not described as complying with IFRS unless they comply with all the requirements of IFRS.

2. Where an entity can make the explicit and unreserved statement of compliance in respect of only:
   (a) the parent financial statements and notes, or
   (b) the consolidated financial statements and notes,
   it clearly identifies to which financial statements and notes the statement of compliance relates.

(All amounts in C thousands unless otherwise stated)

Summary of accounting policies

1p117(a) 3. A summary of significant accounting policies includes:
1p117(b)   (a) the measurement basis (or bases) used in preparing the financial statements; and
   (b) the other accounting policies used that are relevant to an understanding of the financial statements.

1p116 4. The summary may be presented as a separate component of the financial statements.

1p119 5. In deciding whether a particular accounting policy should be disclosed, management considers whether disclosure would assist users in understanding how transactions, other events and conditions are reflected in the reported financial performance and financial position. Some IFRSs specifically require disclosure of particular accounting policies, including choices made by management between different policies they allow. For example, IAS 16, 'Property, plant and equipment', requires disclosure of the measurement bases used for classes of property, plant and equipment.

Changes in accounting policies

Initial application of IFRS

8p28 6. When initial application of an IFRS:
   (a) has an effect on the current period or any prior period;
   (b) would have such an effect except that it is impracticable to determine the amount of the adjustment; or
   (c) might have an effect on future periods, an entity discloses:
      (i) the title of the IFRS;
      (ii) when applicable, that the change in accounting policy is made in accordance with its transitional provisions;
      (iii) the nature of the change in accounting policy;
      (iv) when applicable, a description of the transitional provisions;
      (v) when applicable, the transitional provisions that might have an effect on future periods;
      (vi) for the current period and each prior period presented, to the extent practicable, the amount of the adjustment:
         ■ for each financial statement line item affected;
         ■ if IAS 33, 'Earnings per share', applies to the entity, for basic and diluted earnings per share;
      (vii) the amount of the adjustment relating to periods before those presented, to the extent practicable; and
      (viii) if retrospective application required by paragraph 19(a) or (b) of IAS 8, 'Accounting policies, changes in accounting estimates and errors', is impracticable for a particular prior period, or for periods before those presented, the circumstances that led to the existence of that condition and a description of how and from when the change in accounting policy has been applied.

Financial statements of subsequent periods need not repeat these disclosures.

(All amounts in C thousands unless otherwise stated)

Voluntary change in accounting policy

8p29
7. When a voluntary change in accounting policy:
   (a) has an effect on the current period or any prior period,
   (b) would have an effect on that period except that it is impracticable to determine the amount of the adjustment, or
   (c) might have an effect on future periods,
   an entity discloses:
   (i) the nature of the change in accounting policy;
   (ii) the reasons why applying the new accounting policy provides reliable and more relevant information;
   (iii) for the current period and each prior period presented, to the extent practicable, the amount of the adjustment:
   - for each financial statement line item affected, and
   - if IAS 33 applies to the entity, for basic and diluted earnings per share;
   (iv) the amount of the adjustment relating to periods before those presented, to the extent practicable; and
   (v) if retrospective application is impracticable for a particular prior period, or for periods before those presented, the circumstances that led to the existence of that condition and a description of how and from when the change in accounting policy has been applied.

Financial statements of subsequent periods need not repeat these disclosures.

Change during interim periods

1p112(c)
8. There is no longer an explicit requirement to disclose the financial effect of a change in accounting policy that was made during the final interim period on prior interim financial reports of the current annual reporting period. However, where the impact on prior interim reporting periods is significant, an entity should consider explaining this fact and the financial effect.

IFRSs issued but not yet effective

8p30
9. When an entity has not applied a new IFRS that has been issued but is not yet effective, it discloses:
   (a) this fact; and
   (b) known or reasonably estimable information relevant to assessing the possible impact that application of the new IFRS will have on the entity's financial statements in the period of initial application.

8p31
10. An entity considers disclosing:
   (a) the title of the new IFRS;
   (b) the nature of the impending change or changes in accounting policy;
   (c) the date by which application of the IFRS is required;
   (d) the date as at which it plans to apply it initially; and
   (e) either:
   (i) a discussion of the impact that initial application of the IFRS is expected to have on the entity's financial statements, or
   (ii) if that impact is not known or reasonably estimable, a statement to that effect.

11. Our view is that disclosures in the paragraph above are not necessary in respect of standards and interpretations that are clearly not applicable to the entity (for

(All amounts in C thousands unless otherwise stated)

> example industry-specific standards) or that are not expected to have a material effect on the entity. Instead, disclosure should be given in respect of the developments that are, or could be, significant to the entity. Management will need to apply judgement in determining whether a standard is expected to have a material effect. The assessment of materiality should consider the impact both on previous transactions and financial position and on reasonably foreseeable future transactions. For pronouncements where there is an option that could have an impact on the entity, the management expectation on whether the entity will use the option should be disclosed.
>
> **Disclosures not illustrated in IFRS GAAP plc financial statements**
>
> For disclosures relating to IAS 29, 'Financial reporting in hyperinflationary economies', and IFRS 6, 'Exploration for and evaluation of mineral resources', please refer to PricewaterhouseCoopers' *IFRS disclosure checklist 2013*.

3 Financial risk management

Group

3.1 Financial risk factors

IFRS7p31   The group's activities expose it to a variety of financial risks: market risk (including currency risk, fair value interest rate risk, cash flow interest rate risk and price risk), credit risk and liquidity risk. The group's overall risk management programme focuses on the unpredictability of financial markets and seeks to minimise potential adverse effects on the group's financial performance. The group uses derivative financial instruments to hedge certain risk exposures.

Risk management is carried out by a central treasury department (group treasury) under policies approved by the board of directors. Group treasury identifies, evaluates and hedges financial risks in close co-operation with the group's operating units. The board provides written principles for overall risk management, as well as written policies covering specific areas, such as foreign exchange risk, interest rate risk, credit risk, use of derivative financial instruments and non-derivative financial instruments, and investment of excess liquidity.

(a) Market risk

(i) Foreign exchange risk

IFRS7p33(a)   The group operates internationally and is exposed to foreign exchange risk arising from various currency exposures, primarily with respect to the US dollar and the UK pound. Foreign exchange risk arises from future commercial transactions, recognised assets and liabilities and net investments in foreign operations.

IFRS7p33(b),
IFRS7p22(c)   Management has set up a policy to require group companies to manage their foreign exchange risk against their functional currency. The group companies are required to hedge their entire foreign exchange risk exposure with the group treasury. To manage their foreign exchange risk arising from future commercial transactions and recognised assets and liabilities, entities in the group use forward contracts, transacted with group treasury. Foreign exchange risk arises when future

(All amounts in C thousands unless otherwise stated)

commercial transactions or recognised assets or liabilities are denominated in a currency that is not the entity's functional currency.

IFRS7p22(c) The group treasury's risk management policy is to hedge between 75% and 100% of anticipated cash flows (mainly export sales and purchase of inventory) in each major foreign currency for the subsequent 12 months. Approximately 90% (2012: 95%) of projected sales in each major currency qualify as 'highly probable' forecast transactions for hedge accounting purposes.

IFRS7 p33(a)(b), IFRS7 p22(c) The group has certain investments in foreign operations, whose net assets are exposed to foreign currency translation risk. Currency exposure arising from the net assets of the group's foreign operations is managed primarily through borrowings denominated in the relevant foreign currencies.

IFRS7p40, IFRS7IG36 At 31 December 2013, if the currency had weakened/strengthened by 11% against the US dollar with all other variables held constant, post-tax profit for the year would have been C362 (2012: C51) higher/lower, mainly as a result of foreign exchange gains/losses on translation of US dollar-denominated trade receivables, financial assets at fair value through profit or loss, debt securities classified as available-for-sale and foreign exchange losses/gains on translation of US dollar-denominated borrowings. Profit is more sensitive to movement in currency/US dollar exchange rates in 2013 than 2012 because of the increased amount of US dollar-denominated borrowings. Similarly, the impact on equity would have been C6,850 (2012: C6,650) higher/lower due to an increase in the volume of cash flow hedging in US dollars.

At 31 December 2013, if the currency had weakened/strengthened by 4% against the UK pound with all other variables held constant, post-tax profit for the year would have been C135 (2012: C172) lower/higher, mainly as a result of foreign exchange gains/losses on translation of UK pound-denominated trade receivables, financial assets at fair value through profit or loss, debt securities classified as available-for-sale and foreign exchange losses/gains on translation of UK pound-denominated borrowings.

(ii) Price risk

IFRS7p33(a)(b) The group is exposed to equity securities price risk because of investments held by the group and classified on the consolidated balance sheet either as available-for-sale or at fair value through profit or loss. The group is not exposed to commodity price risk. To manage its price risk arising from investments in equity securities, the group diversifies its portfolio. Diversification of the portfolio is done in accordance with the limits set by the group.

The group's investments in equity of other entities that are publicly traded are included in one of the following three equity indexes: DAX equity index, Dow Jones equity index and FTSE 100 UK equity index.

IFRS7p40, IFRS7IG36 The table below summarises the impact of increases/decreases of the three equity indexes on the group's post-tax profit for the year and on equity. The analysis is based on the assumption that the equity indexes had increased/decreased by 5% with all other variables held constant and all the group's equity instruments moved according to the historical correlation with the index:

(All amounts in C thousands unless otherwise stated)

	Impact on post-tax profit in C		Impact on other components of equity in C	
	2013	2012	2013	2012
Index				
Dax	**200**	120	**290**	290
Dow Jones	**150**	120	**200**	70
FTSE 100 UK	**60**	30	**160**	150

Post-tax profit for the year would increase/decrease as a result of gains/losses on equity securities classified as at fair value through profit or loss. Other components of equity would increase/ decrease as a result of gains/losses on equity securities classified as available for sale.

(iii) Cash flow and fair value interest rate risk

IFRS7p33(a)(b), IFRSp22(c)
The group's interest rate risk arises from long-term borrowings. Borrowings issued at variable rates expose the group to cash flow interest rate risk which is partially offset by cash held at variable rates. Borrowings issued at fixed rates expose the group to fair value interest rate risk. Group policy is to maintain approximately 60% of its borrowings in fixed rate instruments. During 2013 and 2012, the group's borrowings at variable rate were denominated in the Currency and the UK pound.

IFRS7p22(b)(c)
The group analyses its interest rate exposure on a dynamic basis. Various scenarios are simulated taking into consideration refinancing, renewal of existing positions, alternative financing and hedging. Based on these scenarios, the group calculates the impact on profit and loss of a defined interest rate shift. For each simulation, the same interest rate shift is used for all currencies. The scenarios are run only for liabilities that represent the major interest-bearing positions.

Based on the simulations performed, the impact on post tax profit of a 0.1% shift would be a maximum increase of C41 (2012: C37) or decrease of C34 (2012: C29), respectively. The simulation is done on a quarterly basis to verify that the maximum loss potential is within the limit given by the management.

IFRS7p22(b)(c)
Based on the various scenarios, the group manages its cash flow interest rate risk by using floating-to-fixed interest rate swaps. Such interest rate swaps have the economic effect of converting borrowings from floating rates to fixed rates. Generally, the group raises long-term borrowings at floating rates and swaps them into fixed rates that are lower than those available if the group borrowed at fixed rates directly. Under the interest rate swaps, the group agrees with other parties to exchange, at specified intervals (primarily quarterly), the difference between fixed contract rates and floating-rate interest amounts calculated by reference to the agreed notional amounts.

IFRS7p22(b)(c)
Occasionally the group also enters into fixed-to-floating interest rate swaps to hedge the fair value interest rate risk arising where it has borrowed at fixed rates in excess of the 60% target.

IFRS7p40, IFRS7IG36
At 31 December 2013, if interest rates on Currency-denominated borrowings had been 10 basis points higher/lower with all other variables held constant, post-tax profit for the year would have been C22 (2012: C21) lower/higher, mainly as a result of higher/lower interest expense on floating rate borrowings; other components of equity would have been C5 (2012: C3) lower/ higher mainly as a result of a decrease/ increase in the fair value of fixed rate financial assets classified as available for sale.

(All amounts in C thousands unless otherwise stated)

At 31 December 2013, if interest rates on UK pound-denominated borrowings at that date had been 0.5% higher/lower with all other variables held constant, post-tax profit for the year would have been C57 (2012: C38) lower/higher, mainly as a result of higher/lower interest expense on floating rate borrowings; other components of equity would have been C6 (2012: C4) lower/higher mainly as a result of a decrease/increase in the fair value of fixed rate financial assets classified as available for sale.

(b) Credit risk

IFRS7p33(a)(b), IFRS7p34(a)

Credit risk is managed on group basis, except for credit risk relating to accounts receivable balances. Each local entity is responsible for managing and analysing the credit risk for each of their new clients before standard payment and delivery terms and conditions are offered. Credit risk arises from cash and cash equivalents, derivative financial instruments and deposits with banks and financial institutions, as well as credit exposures to wholesale and retail customers, including outstanding receivables and committed transactions. For banks and financial institutions, only independently rated parties with a minimum rating of 'A' are accepted. If wholesale customers are independently rated, these ratings are used. If there is no independent rating, risk control assesses the credit quality of the customer, taking into account its financial position, past experience and other factors. Individual risk limits are set based on internal or external ratings in accordance with limits set by the board. The utilisation of credit limits is regularly monitored. Sales to retail customers are settled in cash or using major credit cards. See notes 18(b) and 21 for further disclosure on credit risk.

No credit limits were exceeded during the reporting period, and management does not expect any losses from non-performance by these counterparties.

(c) Liquidity risk

IFRS7p33(a), (b), IFRS7p34(a)

Cash flow forecasting is performed in the operating entities of the group in and aggregated by group finance. Group finance monitors rolling forecasts of the group's liquidity requirements to ensure it has sufficient cash to meet operational needs while maintaining sufficient headroom on its undrawn committed borrowing facilities (note 31) at all times so that the group does not breach borrowing limits or covenants (where applicable) on any of its borrowing facilities. Such forecasting takes into consideration the group's debt financing plans, covenant compliance, compliance with internal balance sheet ratio targets and, if applicable external regulatory or legal requirements – for example, currency restrictions.

IFRS7p33(a), (b), IFRS7p39(c), IFRS7B11E

Surplus cash held by the operating entities over and above balance required for working capital management are transferred to the group treasury. Group treasury invests surplus cash in interest bearing current accounts, time deposits, money market deposits and marketable securities, choosing instruments with appropriate maturities or sufficient liquidity to provide sufficient headroom as determined by the above-mentioned forecasts. At the reporting date, the group held money market funds of C6,312 (2012: C934) and other liquid assets of C321 (2012: C1,400) that are expected to readily generate cash inflows for managing liquidity risk.

IFRS7p39(a)(b)

The table below analyses the group's non-derivative financial liabilities and net-settled derivative financial liabilities into relevant maturity groupings based on the remaining period at the balance sheet date to the contractual maturity date. Derivative financial liabilities are included in the analysis if their contractual maturities

(All amounts in C thousands unless otherwise stated)

are essential for an understanding of the timing of the cash flows. The amounts disclosed in the table are the contractual undiscounted cash flows.[1]

At 31 December 2013	Less than 3 month	Between 3 month and 1 year[2]	Between 1 and 2 years[2]	Between 2 and 5 years[2]	Over 5 years[2]
Borrowings (ex finance lease liabilities)	2,112	11,384	25,002	71,457	38,050
Finance lease liabilities	639	2,110	1,573	4,719	2,063
Trading and net settled derivative financial instruments (interest rate swaps)	280	–	10	116	41
Trade and other payables[3]	12,543	3,125	–	–	–
Financial guarantee contracts	21	–	–	–	–
At 31 December 2012					
Borrowings (ex finance lease liabilities)	4,061	12,197	11,575	58,679	38,103
Finance lease liabilities	697	2,506	1,790	5,370	2,891
Trading and net settled derivative financial instruments (interest rate swaps)	317	–	15	81	50
Trade and other payables[3]	9,214	2,304	–	–	–
Financial guarantee contracts	10	–	–	–	–

IFRS7B10A(a) Of the C71,457 disclosed in the 2013 borrowings time band 'Between 2 and 5 years' the company intends to repay C40,000 in the first quarter of 2014 (2012: nil).

IFRS7p39(b) The group's trading portfolio derivative instruments with a negative fair value have been included at their fair value of C 268 (2012: C298) within the less than three month time bucket. This is because the contractual maturities are not essential for an understanding of the timing of the cash flows. These contracts are managed on a net-fair value basis rather than by maturity date. Net settled derivatives comprise interest rate swaps used by the group to manage the group's interest rate profile.

IFRS7p39(b) All of the non-trading group's gross settled derivative financial instruments are in hedge relationships and are due to settle within 12 months of the balance sheet date. These contracts require undiscounted contractual cash inflows of C78,756 (2012: C83,077) and undiscounted contractual cash outflows of C78,241 (2012: C83,366).

---

[1] IFRS7 p39(a)(b) The amounts included in the table are the contractual undiscounted cash flows, except for trading derivatives, which are included at their fair value (see below). As a result, these amounts will not reconcile to the amounts disclosed on the balance sheet except for short-term payables where discounting is not applied. Entities can choose to add a reconciling column and a final total that ties into the balance sheet, if they wish.

[2] The specific time-buckets presented are not mandated by the standard but are based on a choice by management based on how the business is managed. Sufficient time buckets should be provided to give sufficient granularity to provide the reader with an understanding of the entity's liquidity.

[3] The maturity analysis applies to financial instruments only and therefore non-financial liabilities are not included.

IFRS GAAP plc – year ended 31 December 2013

(All amounts in C thousands unless otherwise stated)

1p134, 1p135, IG10

3.2 Capital management

The group's objectives when managing capital are to safeguard the group's ability to continue as a going concern in order to provide returns for shareholders and benefits for other stakeholders and to maintain an optimal capital structure to reduce the cost of capital.

In order to maintain or adjust the capital structure, the group may adjust the amount of dividends paid to shareholders, return capital to shareholders, issue new shares or sell assets to reduce debt.

Consistent with others in the industry, the group monitors capital on the basis of the gearing ratio. This ratio is calculated as net debt divided by total capital. Net debt is calculated as total borrowings (including 'current and non-current borrowings' as shown in the consolidated balance sheet) less cash and cash equivalents. Total capital is calculated as 'equity' as shown in the consolidated balance sheet plus net debt.

During 2013, the group's strategy, which was unchanged from 2012, was to maintain the gearing ratio within 40% to 50% and a BB credit rating. The BB credit rating has been maintained throughout the period. The gearing ratios at 31 December 2013 and 2012 were as follows:

	2013	2012
Total borrowings (note 31)	126,837	114,604
Less: cash and cash equivalents (note 24)	(17,928)	(34,062)
Net debt	108,909	80,542
Total equity	136,594	92,439
Total capital	**245,503**	**172,981**
Gearing ratio	**44%**	**47%**

The decrease in the gearing ratio during 2013 resulted primarily from the issue of share capital as part of the consideration for the acquisition of a subsidiary (notes 17 and 39).

3.3 Fair value estimation

The table below analyses financial instruments carried at fair value, by valuation method. The different levels have been defined as follows:

IFRS13p76
- Quoted prices (unadjusted) in active markets for identical assets or liabilities (Level 1).

IFRS13p81
- Inputs other than quoted prices included within level 1 that are observable for the asset or liability, either directly (that is, as prices) or indirectly (that is, derived from prices) (Level 2).

IFRS13p86
- Inputs for the asset or liability that are not based on observable market data (that is, unobservable inputs) (Level 3).

(All amounts in C thousands unless otherwise stated)

IFRS13p93(b) The following table presents the group's financial assets and liabilities that are measured at fair value at 31 December 2013. See note 16 for disclosures of the land and buildings that are measured at fair value and note 25 for disclosures of the disposal groups held for sale that are measured at fair value.

Assets	Level 1	Level 2	Level 3	Total
Financial assets at fair value through profit or loss				
Trading derivatives				
– Foreign exchange contracts	–	250	111	361
Trading securities				
– Real estate industry	8,522	–	–	8,522
– Retail industry	3,298	–	–	3,298
Derivatives used for hedging				
– Interest rate contracts	–	408	–	408
– Foreign exchange contracts	–	695	–	695
Available-for-sale financial assets				
Equity securities				
– Real estate industry	13,369	–	–	13,369
– Retail industry	5,366	–	–	5,366
Debt investments				
– Debentures	210	–	–	210
– Preference shares	78	–	–	78
– Debt securities with fixed interest rates	–	347	–	347
Total assets	30,843	1,700	111	32,654

Liabilities	Level 1	Level 2	Level 3	Total
Financial liabilities at fair value through profit or loss				
Trading derivatives				
– Foreign exchange contracts	–	268	–	268
Contingent consideration	–	–	1,500	1,500
Derivatives used for hedging				
– Interest rate contracts	–	147	–	147
– Foreign exchange contracts	–	180	–	180
Total liabilities	–	595	1,500	2,095

IFRS GAAP plc – year ended 31 December 2013

(All amounts in C thousands unless otherwise stated)

The following table presents the group's assets and liabilities that are measured at fair value at 31 December 2012.

Assets	Level 1	Level 2	Level 3	Total
Financial assets at fair value through profit or loss				
Trading derivatives				
– Foreign exchange contracts	–	321	–	321
Trading securities				
– Real estate industry	4,348	–	–	4,348
– Retail industry	3,624	–	–	3,624
Derivatives used for hedging				
– Interest rate contracts	–	269	–	269
– Foreign exchange contracts	–	606	–	606
Available-for-sale financial assets				
Equity securities				
– Real estate industry	8,087	–	–	8,087
– Retail industry	6,559	–	–	6,559
Debt investments				
– Debt securities with fixed interest rates	–	264	–	264
Total assets	22,618	1,460	–	24,078

Liabilities	Level 1	Level 2	Level 3	Total
Financial liabilities at fair value through profit or loss				
Trading derivatives				
– Foreign exchange contracts	–	298	–	298
Derivatives used for hedging				
– Interest rate contracts	–	132	–	132
– Foreign exchange contracts	–	317	–	317
Total liabilities	–	747	–	747

IFRS 13p93(c) There were no transfers between levels 1 and 2 during the year.

(a) Financial instruments in level 1

IFRS13 p91 The fair value of financial instruments traded in active markets is based on quoted market prices at the balance sheet date. A market is regarded as active if quoted prices are readily and regularly available from an exchange, dealer, broker, industry group, pricing service, or regulatory agency, and those prices represent actual and regularly occurring market transactions on an arm's length basis. The quoted market price used for financial assets held by the group is the current bid price. These instruments are included in Level 1. Instruments included in Level 1 comprise primarily DAX, FTSE 100 and Dow Jones equity investments classified as trading securities or available for sale.

(b) Financial instruments in level 2

IFRS13p93(d) The fair value of financial instruments that are not traded in an active market (for example, over-the-counter derivatives) is determined by using valuation techniques. These valuation techniques maximise the use of observable market data where it is available and rely as little as possible on entity specific estimates. If all significant inputs required to fair value an instrument are observable, the instrument is included in level 2.

If one or more of the significant inputs is not based on observable market data, the instrument is included in Level 3.

(All amounts in C thousands unless otherwise stated)

Specific valuation techniques used to value financial instruments include:
- Quoted market prices or dealer quotes for similar instruments;
- The fair value of interest rate swaps is calculated as the present value of the estimated future cash flows based on observable yield curves;
- The fair value of forward foreign exchange contracts is determined using forward exchange rates at the balance sheet date, with the resulting value discounted back to present value;
- Other techniques, such as discounted cash flow analysis, are used to determine fair value for the remaining financial instruments.

Note that all of the resulting fair value estimates are included in Level 2 except for certain forward foreign exchange contracts explained below.

(c) Financial instruments in level 3

IFRS13p93(e) The following table presents the changes in Level 3 instruments for the year ended 31 December 2013.

	Contingent consideration in a business combination	Trading derivatives at fair value through profit or loss	Total
Opening balance	–	–	–
Acquisition of ABC Group	1,000	–	1,000
Transfers into Level 3	–	115	115
Gains and losses recognised in profit or loss	500	(4)	496
Closing balance	1,500	111	1,611
IFRS 13p93(e)(i) Total gains or losses for the period included in profit or loss for assets held at the end of the reporting period, under 'Other gains/losses'	500	(4)	496
IFRS 13p93(f) Change in unrealised gains or losses for the period included in profit or loss for assets held at the end of the reporting period	500	(4)	496

The following table presents the changes in Level 3 instruments for the year ended 31 December 2012.

	Trading derivatives at fair value through profit or loss	Total
Opening balance	62	62
Settlements	(51)	(51)
Gains and losses recognised in profit or loss	(11)	(11)
Closing balance	–	–
IFRS 13p93(e)(i) Total gains or losses for the period included in profit or loss for assets held at the end of the reporting period, under 'Other gains/losses'	(11)	(11)
IFRS 13p93(f) Change in unrealised gains or losses for the period included in profit or loss for assets held at the end of the reporting period	–	–

IFRS GAAP plc – year ended 31 December 2013

(All amounts in C thousands unless otherwise stated)

See note 39 for disclosures of the measurement of the contingent consideration.

IFRS13 p93(h)(i) In 2013, the group transferred a held-for-trading forward foreign exchange contract from Level 2 into Level 3. This is because the counterparty for the derivative encountered significant financial difficulties, which resulted in a significant increase to the discount rate due to increased counterparty credit risk, which is not based on observable inputs.

IFRS13 p93(h)(ii) If the change in the credit default rate would be shifted by +/- 5% the impact on profit or loss would be C20.

3.4 Offsetting financial assets and financial liabilities

(a) Financial assets

IFRS p13c The following financial assets are subject to offsetting, enforceable master netting arrangements and similar agreements.

As at 31 December 2013	Gross amounts of recognised financial assets	Gross amounts of recognised financial liabilities set off in the balance sheet	Net amounts of financial assets presented in the balance sheet	Related amounts not set off in the balance sheet		Net amount
				Financial instruments	Cash collateral received	
Derivative financial assets	1,939	(475)	1,464	(701)	–	763
Cash and cash equivalents	18,953	(1,025)	17,928	(5,033)	–	12,895
Trade receivables	18,645	(580)	18,065	(92)	–	17,973
Total	**39,537**	**(2,080)**	**37,457**	**(5,826)**	**–**	**31,631**

As at 31 December 2012	Gross amounts of recognised financial assets	Gross amounts of recognised financial liabilities set off in the balance sheet	Net amounts of financial assets presented in the balance sheet	Financial instruments	Cash collateral received	Net amount
Derivative financial assets	1,801	(605)	1,196	(535)	–	661
Cash and cash equivalents	34,927	(865)	34,062	(2,905)	–	31,157
Trade receivables	17,172	(70)	17,102	(58)	–	17,044
Total	53,900	(1,540)	52,360	(3,498)	–	48,862

(All amounts in C thousands unless otherwise stated)

(b) Financial liabilities

IFRS p13c — The following financial liabilities are subject to offsetting, enforceable master netting arrangements and similar agreements

As at 31 December 2013	Gross amounts of recognised financial liabilities	Gross amounts of recognised financial assets set off in the balance sheet	Net amounts of financial liabilities presented in the balance sheet	Related amounts not set off in the balance sheet		Net amount
				Financial instruments	Cash collateral received	
Derivative financial liabilities	1,070	(475)	595	(276)	–	319
Bank overdrafts	3,675	(1,025)	2,650	–	–	2,650
Trade payables	9,563	(580)	8,983	(62)	–	8,921
Total	**14,308**	**(2,080)**	**12,228**	**(338)**	**–**	**11,890**

As at 31 December 2012	Gross amounts of recognised financial liabilities	Gross amounts of recognised financial assets set off in the balance sheet	Net amounts of financial liabilities presented in the balance sheet	Related amounts not set off in the balance sheet		Net amount
				Financial instruments	Cash collateral received	
Derivative financial liabilities	1,352	(605)	747	(182)	–	565
Bank overdrafts	7,329	(865)	6,464	(2,947)	–	3,517
Trade payables	9,565	(70)	9,495	(28)	–	9,467
Total	**18,246**	**(1,540)**	**16,706**	**(3,157)**	**–**	**13,549**

IFRS7p13C — For the financial assets and liabilities subject to enforceable master netting arrangements or similar arrangements above, each agreement between the Group and the counterparty allows for net settlement of the relevant financial assets and liabilities when both elect to settle on a net basis. In the absence of such an election, financial assets and liabilities will be settled on a gross basis, however, each party to the master netting agreement or similar agreement will have the option to settle all such amounts on a net basis in the event of default of the other party. Per the terms of each agreement, an event of default includes failure by a party to make payment when due; failure by a party to perform any obligation required by the agreement (other than payment) if such failure is not remedied within periods of 30 to 60 days after notice of such failure is given to the party; or bankruptcy.

IFRS GAAP plc – year ended 31 December 2013

(All amounts in C thousands unless otherwise stated)

> ### Commentary – disclosure of offsetting of financial assets and financial liabilities
>
> Amendments to IFRS 7, 'Disclosures – Offsetting financial assets and financial liabilities' require additional disclosures to enable users of financial statements to evaluate the effect or the potential effects of netting arrangements, including rights of set-off associated with an entity's recognised financial assets and recognised financial liabilities, on the entity's financial position. The disclosures in these amendments are required for all recognised financial instruments that are set off in accordance with paragraph 42 of IAS 32. These disclosures also apply to recognised financial instruments that are subject to an enforceable master netting arrangement or similar agreements, irrespective of whether they are set off in accordance with paragraph 42 of IAS 32 [IFRS7 paragraph 13A, B40]. The amendments do not provide a definition of "master netting arrangement" however paragraph 50 of IAS 32 identifies the following characteristics, which a master netting arrangement would have:
> – provides for a single net settlement of all financial instruments covered by the agreement in the event of default on, or termination of, any one contract.
> – used by financial institutions to provide protection against loss in the event of bankruptcy or other circumstances that result in a counterparty being unable to meet its obligations.
> – creates a right of set-off that becomes enforceable and affects the realisation or settlement of individual financial assets and financial liabilities only following a specified event of default or in other circumstances not expected to arise in the normal course of business.
>
> Because of the broad scope of the new offsetting requirements, these disclosures are relevant not only to financial institutions but also corporate entities.
>
> Per IFRS 7 paragraphs B51 and B52, entities may group the quantitative disclosures by type of financial instrument or by counterparty. The above example only illustrates the disclosures by type of financial instrument. When disclosure is provided by counterparty, amounts that are individually significant in terms of total counterparty amounts shall be separately disclosed and the remaining individually insignificant counterparty amounts shall be aggregated into one line item.

(All amounts in C thousands unless otherwise stated)

Commentary – financial risk management

Accounting standard for presentation and disclosure of financial instruments

IFRS7p3

1. IFRS 7, 'Financial instruments: Disclosures', applies to all reporting entities and to all types of financial instruments except:
   - Those interests in subsidiaries, associates and joint ventures that are accounted for under IAS 27, 'Consolidated and separate financial statements', or IAS 28, 'Investments in associates and joint ventures'. However, entities should apply IFRS 7 to an interest in a subsidiary, associate or joint venture that according to IAS 27 or IAS 28 is accounted for under IAS 39, 'Financial instruments: Recognition and measurement'. Entities should also apply IFRS 7 to all derivatives on interests in subsidiaries, associates or joint ventures unless the derivative meets the definition of an equity instrument in IAS 32.
   - Employers' rights and obligations under employee benefit plans, to which IAS 19, 'Employee benefits', applies.
   - Insurance contracts as defined in IFRS 4, 'Insurance contracts'. However, IFRS 7 applies to derivatives that are embedded in insurance contracts if IAS 39 requires the entity to account for them separately. It also applies to financial guarantee contracts if the issuer applies IAS 39 in recognising and measuring the contracts.
   - Financial instruments, contracts and obligations under share-based payment transactions to which IFRS 2, 'Share-based payment', applies, except for contracts within the scope of paragraphs 5-7 of IAS 39, which are disclosed under IFRS 7.
   - From 1 January 2009 puttable financial instruments that are required to be classified as equity instruments in accordance with paragraphs 16A and 16B or 16C and 16D of IAS 32 (revised).

Parent entity disclosures

IFRS7

2. Where applicable, all disclosure requirements outlined in IFRS 7 should be made for both the parent and consolidated entity. The relief from making parent entity disclosures, which was previously available under IAS 30, 'Disclosures in the financial statements of banks and similar financial institutions', and IAS 32, has not been retained in IFRS 7.

Classes of financial instrument

IFRS7p6, B1-B3

3. Where IFRS 7 requires disclosures by class of financial instrument, the entity groups its financial instruments into classes that are appropriate to the nature of the information disclosed and that take into account the characteristics of those financial instruments. The entity should provide sufficient information to permit reconciliation to the line items presented in the balance sheet. Guidance on classes of financial instruments and the level of required disclosures is provided in appendix B of IFRS 7.

Level of detail and selection of assumptions – information through the eyes of management

IFRS7 p34(a)

4. The disclosures in relation to an entity's financial risk management should reflect the information provided internally to key management personnel. As such, the disclosures that will be provided by an entity, their level of detail and the underlying assumptions used will vary greatly from entity to entity. The disclosures in this illustrative financial statement are only one example of the kind of information that

IFRS GAAP plc – year ended 31 December 2013

(All amounts in C thousands unless otherwise stated)

may be disclosed; the entity should consider carefully what may be appropriate in its individual circumstances.

Nature and extent of risks arising from financial instruments

IFRS7 p31, 32

5. The financial statement should include qualitative and quantitative disclosures that enable users to evaluate the nature and extent of risks arising from financial instruments to which the entity is exposed at the end of the reporting period. These risks typically include, but are not limited to, credit risk, liquidity risk and market risk.

Qualitative disclosures

IFRS7p33

6. An entity should disclose for each type of risk:
   (a) the exposures to the risk and how they arise;
   (b) the entity's objectives, policies and processes for managing the risk and the methods used to measure the risk; and
   (c) any changes in (a) or (b) from the previous period.

Quantitative disclosures

IFRS7 p34(a)(c)

7. An entity should provide for each type of risk, summary quantitative data on risk exposure at the end of the reporting period, based on information provided internally to key management personnel and any concentrations of risk. This information can be presented in narrative form. Alternatively, entities could provide the data in a table that sets out the impact of each major risk on each type of financial instruments. This table could also be a useful tool for compiling the information that should be disclosed under paragraph 34 of IFRS 7.

IFRS7 p34(b)

8. If not already provided as part of the summary quantitative data, the entity should also provide the information in paragraphs 9-15 below, unless the risk is not material.

Credit risk

IFRS7p36, 37

9. For each class of financial instrument, the entity should disclose:
   (a) the maximum exposure to credit risk and any related collateral held;
   (b) information about the credit quality of financial assets that are neither past due nor impaired;
   (c) the carrying amount of financial assets that would otherwise be past due or impaired whose terms have been renegotiated;
   (d) an analysis of the age of financial assets that are past due but not impaired; and
   (e) an analysis of financial assets that are individually determined to be impaired including the factors in determining that they are impaired.

Liquidity risk

IFRS7 p34(a), p39

10 Information about liquidity risk shall be provided by way of:
   (a) a maturity analysis for non-derivative financial liabilities (including issued financial guarantee contracts) that shows the remaining contractual maturities;
   (b) a maturity analysis for derivative financial liabilities (see paragraph 12 below for details); and
   (c) a description of how the entity manages the liquidity risk inherent in (a) and (b).

IFRS7B11F

11. In describing how liquidity risk is being managed, an entity should consider discussing whether it:

(All amounts in C thousands unless otherwise stated)

(a) has committed borrowing facilities or other lines of credit that it can access to meet liquidity needs;
(b) holds deposits at central banks to meet liquidity needs;
(c) has very diverse funding sources;
(d) has significant concentrations of liquidity risk in either its assets or its funding sources;
(e) has internal control processes and contingency plans for managing liquidity risk;
(f) has instruments that include accelerated repayment terms (for example, on the downgrade of the entity's credit rating);
(g) has instruments that could require the posting of collateral (for example, margin calls for derivatives);
(h) has instruments that allow the entity to choose whether it settles its financial liabilities by delivering cash (or another financial asset) or by delivering its own shares; and
(i) has instruments that are subject to master netting agreements.

Maturity analysis

IFRS7B11B 12. The maturity analysis for derivative financial liabilities should disclose the remaining contractual maturities if these maturities are essential for an understanding of the timing of the cash flows. For example, this will be the case for interest rate swaps in a cash flow hedge of a variable rate financial asset or liability and for all loan commitments. Where the remaining contractual maturities are not essential for an understanding of the timing of the cash flows, the expected maturities may be disclosed instead.

IFRS7p39, B11D 13. For derivative financial instruments where gross cash flows are exchanged and contractual maturities are essential to understanding, the maturity analysis should disclose the contractual amounts that are to be exchanged on a gross basis. The amount disclosed should be the amount expected to be paid in future periods, determined by reference to the conditions existing at the end of the reporting period. However, IFRS 7 does not specify whether current or forward rates should be used. We therefore recommend that entities explain which approach has been chosen. This approach should be applied consistently.

IFRS7B11 14. The specific time bands presented are not mandated by the standard but are based on what is reported internally to the key management personnel. The entity uses judgement to determine the appropriate number of time bands.

IFRS7B11D 15. If the amounts included in the maturity tables are the contractual undiscounted cash flows, these amounts will not reconcile to the amounts disclosed on the balance sheet for borrowings, derivative financial instruments and trade and other payables. Entities can choose to add a column with the carrying amounts that ties into the balance sheet and a reconciling column if they so wish, but this is not mandatory.

IFRS7B10A 16. If an outflow of cash could occur either significantly earlier than indicated or be for significantly different amounts from those indicated in the entity's disclosures about its exposure to liquidity risk, the entity should state that fact and provide quantitative information that enables users of its financial statements to evaluate the extent of this risk. This disclosure is not necessary if that information is included in the contractual maturity analysis.

(All amounts in C thousands unless otherwise stated)

Financing arrangements

IFRS7 p39(c)

17. Committed borrowing facilities are a major element of liquidity management. Entities should therefore consider providing information about their undrawn facilities. IAS 7, 'Statements of cash flows', also recommends disclosure of undrawn borrowing facilities that may be available for future operating activities and to settle capital commitments, indicating any restrictions on the use of these facilities.

Market risk

IFRS7 p40(a)(b)

18. Entities should disclose a sensitivity analysis for each type of market risk (currency, interest rate and other price risk) to which an entity is exposed at the end of the reporting period, showing how profit or loss and equity would have been affected by 'reasonably possible' changes in the relevant risk variable, as well as the methods and assumptions used in preparing such an analysis.

IFRS7 p40(c)

19. If there have been any changes in methods and assumptions from the previous period, this should be disclosed, together with the reasons for the change.

Foreign currency risk

IFRS7B23

20. Foreign currency risk can only arise on financial instruments that are denominated in a currency other than the functional currency in which they are measured. Translation related risks are therefore not included in the assessment of the entity's exposure to currency risks. Translation exposures arise from financial and non-financial items held by an entity (for example, a subsidiary) with a functional currency different from the group's presentation currency. However, foreign currency denominated inter– company receivables and payables that do not form part of a net investment in a foreign operation are included in the sensitivity analysis for foreign currency risks, because even though the balances eliminate in the consolidated balance sheet, the effect on profit or loss of their revaluation under IAS 21 is not fully eliminated.

Interest rate risk

21. Sensitivity to changes in interest rates is relevant to financial assets or financial liabilities bearing floating interest rates due to the risk that future cash flows will fluctuate. However, sensitivity will also be relevant to fixed rate financial assets and financial liabilities that are re-measured to fair value.

Fair value disclosures

Financial instruments carried at other than fair value

IFRS7p25, 29

22. An entity should disclose the fair value for each class of financial assets and financial liabilities (see paragraph 3 above) in a way that permits it to be compared with its carrying amount. Fair values do not need to be disclosed for the following:
   (a) when the carrying amount is a reasonable approximation of fair value;
   (b) investments in equity instruments (and derivatives linked to such equity instruments) that do not have a quoted market price in an active market and that are measured at cost in accordance with IAS 39 because their fair value cannot be measured reliably; and
   (c) A contract containing a discretionary participation feature (as described in IFRS 4, 'Insurance contracts') where the fair value of that feature cannot be measured reliably.

(All amounts in C thousands unless otherwise stated)

23. The information about the fair values can be provided either in a combined financial instruments note or in the individual notes. However, fair values should be separately disclosed for each class of financial instrument (see paragraph 3 above), which means that each line item in the table would have to be broken down into individual classes. For that reason, IFRS GAAP plc has chosen to provide the information in the relevant notes.

Methods and assumptions in determining fair value

IFRS13p91
24. An entity shall disclose information that helps users of its financial statements assess both of the following:
    (a) for assets and liabilities that are measured at fair value on a recurring or non-recurring basis in the statement of financial position after initial recognition, the valuation techniques and inputs used to develop those measurements.
    (b) for recurring fair value measurements using significant unobservable inputs (Level 3), the effect of the measurements on profit or loss or other comprehensive income for the period.

Financial instruments measured at cost where fair value cannot be determined reliably

IFRS7p30
25. If the fair value of investments in unquoted equity instruments, derivatives linked to such equity instruments or a contract containing a discretionary participation feature (as described in IFRS 4, 'Insurance contracts') cannot be measured reliably, the entity should disclose:
    (a) the fact that fair value information has not been disclosed because it cannot be measured reliably;
    (b) a description of the financial instruments, their carrying amount and an explanation of why fair value cannot be measured reliably;
    (c) information about the market for the instruments;
    (d) information about whether and how the entity intends to dispose of the financial instruments; and
    (e) if the instruments are subsequently derecognised, that fact, their carrying amount at the time of derecognition and the amount of gain or loss recognised.

Fair value measurements recognised in the balance sheet

IFRS13p93
26. For fair value measurements recognised in the balance sheet, the entity should also disclose for each class of financial instruments:
    (a) the level in the fair value hierarchy into which the fair value measurements are categorised;
    (b) any significant transfers between level 1 and level 2 of the fair value hierarchy and the reasons for those transfers;
    (c) for fair value measurements in level 3 of the hierarchy, a reconciliation from the beginning balances to the ending balances, showing separately changes during the period attributable to the following:
        (i) total gains or losses for the period recognised in profit or loss and the line item(s) which they are recognised, together with a description of where they are presented in the statement of comprehensive income or the income statement (as applicable);
        (ii) total gains or losses recognised in other comprehensive income;
        (iii) purchases, sales issues and settlements (each type disclosed separately); and
        (iv) transfers into or out of level 3 and the reasons for those transfers;

(d) for recurring fair value measurements categorised within Level 3 of the fair value hierarchy, the amount of the total gains or losses for the period included in profit or loss that is attributable to the change in unrealised gains or losses relating to those assets and liabilities held at the end of the reporting period, and the line item(s) in profit or loss in which those unrealised gains or losses are recognised.
(e) for recurring fair value measurements in level 3:
  (i) for all such measurements, a narrative description of the sensitivity of the fair value measurement to changes in unobservable inputs if a change in those inputs to a different amount might result in a significantly higher or lower fair value measurement. If there are interrelationships between those inputs and other unobservable inputs used in the fair value measurement, an entity shall also provide a description of those interrelationships and of how they might magnify or mitigate the effect of changes in the unobservable inputs on the fair value measurement. To comply with that disclosure requirement, the narrative description of the sensitivity to changes in unobservable inputs shall include, at a minimum, the unobservable inputs disclosed.
  (ii) for financial assets and financial liabilities, if changing one or more of the unobservable inputs to reflect reasonably possible alternative assumptions would change fair value significantly, an entity shall state that fact and disclose the effect of those changes. The entity shall disclose how the effect of a change to reflect a reasonably possible alternative assumption was calculated. For that purpose, significance shall be judged with respect to profit or loss, and total assets or total liabilities, or, when changes in fair value are recognised in other comprehensive income, total equity.

IFRS13p93(b) 27. Entities should classify fair value measurements using a fair value hierarchy that reflects the significance of the inputs used in making the measurements. The fair value hierarchy should have the following levels:
(a) Level 1: quoted prices (unadjusted) in active markets for identical assets or liabilities.
(b) Level 2: inputs other than quoted prices that are observable for the asset or liability, either directly (for example, as prices) or indirectly (for example, derived from prices).
(c) Level 3: inputs for the asset or liability that are not based on observable market data.

The appropriate level is determined on the basis of the lowest level input that is significant to the fair value measurement.

Additional information where quantitative data about risk exposure is unrepresentative

IFRS7p35, p42 28. If the quantitative data disclosed under paragraphs 7, 9, 10 and 14 above is unrepresentative of the entity's exposure to risk during the period, the entity should provide further information that is representative. If the sensitivity analyses are unrepresentative of a risk inherent in a financial instrument (for example, where the year end exposure does not reflect the exposure during the year), the entity should disclose that fact and the reason why the sensitivity analyses are unrepresentative.

4 Critical accounting estimates and judgements

Estimates and judgements are continually evaluated and are based on historical experience and other factors, including expectations of future events that are believed to be reasonable under the circumstances.

1p125

4.1 Critical accounting estimates and assumptions

The group makes estimates and assumptions concerning the future. The resulting accounting estimates will, by definition, seldom equal the related actual results. The estimates and assumptions that have a significant risk of causing a material adjustment to the carrying amounts of assets and liabilities within the next financial year are addressed below.

(a) Estimated impairment of goodwill

The group tests annually whether goodwill has suffered any impairment, in accordance with the accounting policy stated in note 2.6. The recoverable amounts of cash-generating units have been determined based on value-in-use calculations. These calculations require the use of estimates (note 17).

1p129,
36p134(f)(i)-(iii)

An impairment charge of C4,650 arose in the wholesale CGU in Step-land (included in the Russian operating segment) during the course of the 2013 year, resulting in the carrying amount of the CGU being written down to its recoverable amount. If the budgeted gross margin used in the value-in-use calculation for the wholesale CGU in Step-land had been 10% lower than management's estimates at 31 December 2013 (for example, 45.5% instead of 55.5%), the group would have recognised a further impairment of goodwill by C100 and would need to reduce the carrying value of property, plant and equipment by C300.

If the estimated cost of capital used in determining the pre-tax discount rate for the wholesale CGU in Step-land had been 1% higher than management's estimates (for example, 14.8% instead of 13.8%), the group would have recognised a further impairment against goodwill of C300.

(b) Income taxes

The group is subject to income taxes in numerous jurisdictions. Significant judgement is required in determining the worldwide provision for income taxes. There are many transactions and calculations for which the ultimate tax determination is uncertain. The group recognises liabilities for anticipated tax audit issues based on estimates of whether additional taxes will be due. Where the final tax outcome of these matters is different from the amounts that were initially recorded, such differences will impact the current and deferred income tax assets and liabilities in the period in which such determination is made.

Were the actual final outcome (on the judgement areas) of expected cash flows to differ by 10% from management's estimates, the group would need to:
- increase the income tax liability by C120 and the deferred tax liability by C230, if unfavourable; or
- decrease the income tax liability by C110 and the deferred tax liability by C215, if favourable.

(All amounts in C thousands unless otherwise stated)

(c) Fair value of derivatives and other financial instruments

IFRS13p91   The fair value of financial instruments that are not traded in an active market (for example, over-the-counter derivatives) is determined by using valuation techniques. The group uses its judgement to select a variety of methods and make assumptions that are mainly based on market conditions existing at the end of each reporting period. The group has used discounted cash flow analysis for various foreign exchange contracts that are not traded in active markets.

The carrying amount of foreign exchange contracts would be an estimated C12 lower or C15 higher were the discount rate used in the discount cash flow analysis to differ by 10% from management's estimates.

(d) Revenue recognition

The group uses the percentage-of-completion method in accounting for its fixed-price contracts to deliver design services. Use of the percentage-of-completion method requires the group to estimate the services performed to date as a proportion of the total services to be performed. Were the proportion of services performed to total services to be performed to differ by 10% from management's estimates, the amount of revenue recognised in the year would be increased by C1,175 if the proportion performed were increased, or would be decreased by C1,160 if the proportion performed were decreased.

(e) Pension benefits

The present value of the pension obligations depends on a number of factors that are determined on an actuarial basis using a number of assumptions. The assumptions used in determining the net cost (income) for pensions include the discount rate. Any changes in these assumptions will impact the carrying amount of pension obligations.

The group determines the appropriate discount rate at the end of each year. This is the interest rate that should be used to determine the present value of estimated future cash outflows expected to be required to settle the pension obligations. In determining the appropriate discount rate, the group considers the interest rates of high-quality corporate bonds that are denominated in the currency in which the benefits will be paid and that have terms to maturity approximating the terms of the related pension obligation.

Other key assumptions for pension obligations are based in part on current market conditions. Additional information is disclosed in note 33.

1p122   **4.2 Critical judgements in applying the entity's accounting policies**

(a) Revenue recognition

The group has recognised revenue amounting to C950 for sales of goods to L&Co in the UK during 2013. The buyer has the right to return the goods if their customers are dissatisfied. The group believes that, based on past experience with similar sales, the dissatisfaction rate will not exceed 3%. The group has, therefore, recognised revenue on this transaction with a corresponding provision against revenue for estimated returns. If the estimate changes by 1%, revenue will be reduced/increased by C10.

(All amounts in C thousands unless otherwise stated)

(b) Impairment of available-for-sale equity investments

The group follows the guidance of IAS 39 to determine when an available-for-sale equity investment is impaired. This determination requires significant judgement. In making this judgement, the group evaluates, among other factors, the duration and extent to which the fair value of an investment is less than its cost; and the financial health of and short-term business outlook for the investee, including factors such as industry and sector performance, changes in technology and operational and financing cash flow.

If all of the declines in fair value below cost were considered significant or prolonged, the group would suffer an additional loss of C1,300 in its 2013 financial statements, being the transfer of the accumulated fair value adjustments recognised in equity on the impaired available-for-sale financial assets to the income statement.

(c) Consolidation of entities in which the group holds less than 50%.

Management consider that the group has de facto control of Delta Inc even though it has less than 50% of the voting rights. The group is the majority shareholder of Delta Inc with a 40% equity interest, while all other shareholders individually own less than 1% of its equity shares. There is no history of other shareholders forming a group to exercise their votes collectively.

(d) Investment in Alpha Limited

Management has assessed the level of influence that the Group has on Alpha Limited and determined that it has significant influence even though the share holding is below 20% because of the board representation and contractual terms. Consequently, this investment has been classified as an associate.

(e) Joint arrangements

IFRS GAAP plc holds 50% of the voting rights of its joint arrangement. The group has joint control over this arrangement as under the contractual agreements, unanimous consent is required from all parties to the agreements for all relevant activities.

The group's joint arrangement is structured as a limited company and provides the group and the parties to the agreements with rights to the net assets of the limited company under the arrangements. Therefore, this arrangement is classified as a joint venture.

5 Segment information

IFRS8p22(a) The strategic steering committee is the group's chief operating decision-maker. Management has determined the operating segments based on the information reviewed by the strategic steering committee for the purposes of allocating resources and assessing performance.

IFRS8p22(a)(b) The strategic steering committee considers the business from both a geographic and product perspective. Geographically, management considers the performance in the UK, US, China, Russia and Europe. From a product perspective, management separately considers the wholesale and retail activities in these geographies. The group's retail activities are only in the UK and US. The wholesale segments derive their revenue primarily from the manufacture and wholesale sale of the group's own

IFRS GAAP plc – year ended 31 December 2013

(All amounts in C thousands unless otherwise stated)

brand of shoes, Footsy Tootsy. The UK and US retail segments derive their revenue from retail sales of shoe and leather goods including the group's own brand and other major retail shoe brands.

IFRS8p22(a) Although the China segment does not meet the quantitative thresholds required by IFRS 8 for reportable segments, management has concluded that this segment should be reported, as it is closely monitored by the strategic steering committee as a potential growth region and is expected to materially contribute to group revenue in the future.

IFRS8p18 During 2012, US retail did not qualify as a reportable operating segment. However, with the acquisition in 2013 of ABC Group (see note 39), retail qualifies as a reportable operating segment, the comparatives have been restated.

IFRS8p16 All other segments primarily relate to the sale of design services and goods transportation services to other shoe manufacturers in the UK and Europe and wholesale shoe revenue from the Central American region. These activities are excluded from the reportable operating segments, as these activities are not reviewed by the strategic steering committee.

IFRS8p28 The strategic steering committee assesses the performance of the operating segments based on a measure of adjusted EBITDA. This measurement basis excludes discontinued operations and the effects of non-recurring expenditure from the operating segments such as restructuring costs, legal expenses and goodwill impairments when the impairment is the result of an isolated, non-recurring event. The measure also excludes the effects of equity-settled share-based payments and unrealised gains/losses on financial instruments. Interest income and expenditure are not allocated to segments, as this type of activity is driven by the central treasury function, which manages the cash position of the group.

Revenue

IFRS8p27(a) Sales between segments are carried out at arm's length. The revenue from external parties reported to the strategic steering committee is measured in a manner consistent with that in the income statement.

	Year ended 31 December 2013			Year ended 31 December 2012 Restated		
	Total segment revenue	Inter-segment revenue	Revenue from external customers	Total segment revenue	Inter-segment revenue	Revenue from external customers
UK wholesale	46,638	(11,403)	**35,235**	42,284	(11,457)	30,827
UK retail	43,257	–	**43,257**	31,682	–	31,682
US wholesale	28,820	(7,364)	**21,456**	18,990	(6,798)	12,192
US retail	42,672	–	**42,672**	2,390	–	2,390
Russia wholesale	26,273	(5,255)	**21,018**	8,778	(1,756)	7,022
China wholesale	5,818	(1,164)	**4,654**	3,209	(642)	2,567
Europe wholesale	40,273	(8,055)	**32,218**	26,223	(5,245)	20,978
All other segments	13,155	(2,631)	**10,524**	5,724	(1,022)	4,702
Total	**246,906**	**(35,872)**	**211,034**	**139,280**	**(26,920)**	**112,360**

(All amounts in C thousands unless otherwise stated)

IFRS8p28(b) **EBITDA**

	Year ended 31 December 2013	Year ended 31 December 2012 Restated
	Adjusted EBITDA	Adjusted EBITDA
UK wholesale	**17,298**	17,183
UK retail	**9,550**	800
US wholesale	**9,146**	10,369
US retail	**9,686**	1,298
Russia wholesale	**12,322**	3,471
China wholesale	**2,323**	1,506
Europe wholesale	**16,003**	10,755
All other segments	**3,504**	1,682
Total adjusted EBITDA	**79,832**	47,064
Depreciation	**(17,754)**	(9,662)
Amortisation	**(800)**	(565)
Restructuring costs	**(1,986)**	–
Legal expenses	**(737)**	(855)
Goodwill impairment	**(4,650)**	–
Unrealised financial instrument gains	**102**	101
Share options granted to directors and employees	**(690)**	(822)
Finance costs – net	**(6,443)**	(10,588)
Other	**2,059**	1,037
Profit before tax and discontinued operations	**48,933**	25,710

IFRS GAAP plc – year ended 31 December 2013

(All amounts in C thousands unless otherwise stated)

IFRS8p23 **Other profit and loss disclosures**[1]

	Year ended 31 December 2013				
	Depreciation and amortisation	Goodwill impairment	Restructuring costs	Income tax expense	Share of profit from associates
UK wholesale	(3,226)	–	–	(2,550)	200
UK retail	(3,830)	–	–	(2,780)	–
US wholesale	(1,894)	–	–	(1,395)	–
US retail	(3,789)	–	–	(3,040)	–
Russia wholesale	(2,454)	(4,650)	(1,986)	(1,591)	–
China wholesale	(386)	–	–	(365)	–
Europe wholesale	(2,706)	–	–	(2,490)	–
All other segments	(269)	–	–	(400)	15
Total	**(18,554)**	**(4,650)**	**(1,986)**	**(14,611)**	**215**

	Year ended 31 December 2012 Restated				
	Depreciation and amortisation	Goodwill impairment	Restructuring costs	Income tax expense	Share of profit from associates
UK wholesale	(3,801)	–	–	(2,772)	155
UK retail	(201)	–	–	(650)	–
US wholesale	(2,448)	–	–	(1,407)	–
US retail	(199)	–	–	(489)	–
Russia wholesale	(453)	–	–	(509)	–
China wholesale	(286)	–	–	(150)	–
Europe wholesale	(2,701)	–	–	(2,201)	–
All other segments	(138)	–	–	(492)	(10)
Total	(10,227)	–	–	(8,670)	145

See note 17 for details of the impairment of goodwill of C4,650 in the Russian operating segment in 2013 relating to the decision to reduce manufacturing output. There has been no further impact on the measurement of the group's assets and liabilities. There was no impairment charge or restructuring costs recognised in 2012.

IFRS8p27(f) Due to the European operations utilising excess capacity in certain Russian assets that are geographically close to the European region, a portion of the depreciation charge of C197 (2012: C50) relating to the Russian assets has been allocated to the European segment to take account of this.

---

[1] Paragraph 23 of IFRS 8 requires disclosures of interest revenue and expense even if not included in the measure of segment profit and loss. This disclosure has not been included in the illustrative because these balances are not allocated to the segments.

(All amounts in C thousands unless otherwise stated)

IFRS8p23,
IFRS8p24,
IFRS8p28(c)

Assets[1]

	Year ended 31 December 2013			Year ended 31 December 2012 Restated		
	Total assets	Investments in associates and joint ventures	Additions to non-current assets[2]	Total assets	Investments in associates and joint ventures	Additions to non-current assets[2]
UK wholesale	46,957	–	–	43,320	–	–
UK retail	46,197	–	35,543	9,580	–	47
US wholesale	27,313	–	–	32,967	–	–
US retail	45,529	–	39,817	8,550	–	46
Russia	22,659	–	–	5,067	–	–
China	6,226	–	11,380	20,899	–	2,971
Europe	47,912	18,649	1,222	40,259	17,053	2,543
All other segments	22,184	–	278	49,270	–	1,135
Total	**264,977**	**18,649**	**88,240**	**209,912**	**17,053**	**6,742**
Unallocated						
Deferred tax	3,546			3,383		
Available-for-sale financial assets	19,370			14,910		
Financial assets at fair value through profit and loss	11,820			7,972		
Derivative financial instruments	1,464			1,196		
Assets of disposal group classified as held for sale	3,333					
Total assets per the balance sheet	**304,510**			**237,373**		

IFRS8p27(c) The amounts provided to the strategic steering committee with respect to total assets are measured in a manner consistent with that of the financial statements. These assets are allocated based on the operations of the segment and the physical location of the asset.

Investment in shares (classified as available-for-sale financial assets or financial assets at fair value through profit or loss) held by the group are not considered to be segment assets but rather are managed by the treasury function. The measure of assets reviewed by the CODM does not include assets held for sale. The group's interest-bearing liabilities are not considered to be segment liabilities but rather are managed by the treasury function.

---

[1] The measure of assets has been disclosed for each reportable segment as is regularly provided to the chief operating decision-maker. If the chief operating decision-maker reviews a measure of liabilities, this should also be disclosed.

[2] Additions to non-current assets excludes other than financial instruments and deferred tax assets.

IFRS GAAP plc – year ended 31 December 2013

(All amounts in C thousands unless otherwise stated)

Entity-wide information

IFRS8p32 Breakdown of the revenue from all services is as follows:

	2013	2012 Restated
Analysis of revenue by category:		
– Sales of goods	**202,884**	104,495
– Revenue from services	**8,000**	7,800
– Royalty income	**150**	65
Total	**211,034**	112,360

IFRS8p33(a) The group is domiciled in the UK. The result of its revenue from external customers in the UK is C50,697 (2012: C48,951), and the total of revenue from external customers from other countries is C160,337 (2012: C63,409). The breakdown of the major component of the total of revenue from external customers from other countries is disclosed above.

IFRS8p33(b) The total of non-current assets other than financial instruments and deferred tax assets (there are no employment benefit assets and rights arising under insurance contracts) located in the UK is C49,696 (2012: C39,567), and the total of such non-current assets located in other countries is C146,762 (2012: C93,299).

IFRS8p34 Revenues of approximately C32,023 (2012: C28,034) are derived from a single external customer. These revenues are attributable to the US retail and UK wholesale segments.

6 Exceptional items

Items that are material either because of their size or their nature, or that are non-recurring are considered as exceptional items and are presented within the line items to which they best relate. During the year, the exceptional items as detailed below have been included in cost of sales in the income statement.

An analysis of the amount presented as exceptional item in these financial statements is given below.

	2013	2012
Operating items:		
– Inventory write-down	3,117	–

The inventory write-down of C3,117 relates to leather accessories that have been destroyed by fire in an accident. This amount is included within cost of sales in the income statement.

(All amounts in C thousands unless otherwise stated)

7 Other income

	Group	2013	2012
	Gain on re-measuring to fair value the existing interest in ABC Group on acquisition of control (note 39)	850	–
18p35(b)(v)	Dividend income on available-for-sale financial assets	1,100	883
18p35(b)(v)	Dividend income on financial assets at fair value through profit or loss	800	310
	Investment income	2,750	1,193
	Insurance reimbursement	–	66
	Total	**2,750**	**1,259**

The insurance reimbursement relates to the excess of insurance proceeds over the carrying values of goods damaged.

8 Other (losses)/gains – net

	Group	2013	2012
IFRS7p20(a)(i)	Financial assets at fair value through profit or loss (note 23):		
	– Fair value losses	(508)	(238)
	– Fair value gains	593	–
IFRS7p20(a)(i)	Foreign exchange forward contracts:		
	– Held for trading	86	88
21p52(a)	– Net foreign exchange (losses)/gains (note 15)	(277)	200
IFRS7p24(a)	Ineffectiveness on fair value hedges (note 20)	(1)	(1)
IFRS7p24(b)	Ineffectiveness on cash flow hedges (note 20)	17	14
	Total	**(90)**	**63**

9 Expenses

9(a) Expenses by nature

		Group		Company	
		2013	2012 Restated	2013	2012
1p104	Changes in inventories of finished goods and work in progress	6,950	(2,300)	–	–
1p104	Raw material and consumables used	53,302	31,845	–	–
1p104	Employee benefit expense (note 10)	40,310	15,577	4,574	4,190
1p104	Depreciation, amortisation and impairment charges (notes 16 and 17)	23,204	10,227	–	–
1p104	Transportation expenses	8,584	6,236	–	–
1p104	Advertising costs	14,265	6,662	–	–
1p104	Operating lease payments (note 16)	10,604	8,500	–	–
1p104	Other expenses	2,781	1,659	–	–
	Total cost of sales, distribution costs and administrative expenses	**160,000**	**78,406**	**4,574**	**4,190**

IFRS GAAP plc – year ended 31 December 2013

(All amounts in C thousands unless otherwise stated)

9(b) Auditor remuneration

Tech 04/11 **Services provided by the company's auditor and its associates[1]**

SI 2008/489 as amended by SI 2011/2198

During the year the group (including its overseas subsidiaries) obtained the following services from the company's auditor and its associates:

Group	2013	2012
Fees payable to company's auditor and its associates for the audit of parent company and consolidated financial statements	738	625
Fees payable to company's auditor and its associates for other services:		
– The audit of company's subsidiaries	901	543
– Audit-related assurance services	312	154
– Tax advisory services	35	52
– Tax compliance service	72	91
	2,058	1,465

	2013	2012
Fees in respect of the IFRS GAAP plc pension scheme:		
– Audit	1,204	931
– Audit-related assurance services	123	–
	1,327	931

10 Employees

10(a) Employee benefit expense

		Group		Company	
		2013	2012 Restated	2013	2012
19Rp171	Wages and salaries, including restructuring costs C799 (2012: nil) and other termination benefits C1,600 (2012: nil) (note 35 and note 41)	28,363	10,041	2,824	2,486
	Social security costs	9,369	3,802	1,160	1,087
IFRS2p51(a)	Share options granted to directors and employees (notes 27 and 28)	690	822	518	617
19Rp53	Pension costs – defined contribution plans	756	232	72	–
19Rp141	Pension costs – defined benefit plans (note 33)	948	561	–	–
19Rp141	Other post-employment benefits (note 33)	184	119	–	–
		40,310	15,577	4,574	4,190

---

[1] The annual report should outline how the directors ensure that the independence of the group's auditors has not been compromised by the provision of non-audit services. For listed companies, guidance on independence is included in the UK Corporate Governance Code. This disclosure may be given as part of the corporate governance statement or disclosure in the annual report [CGC C3.8].

(All amounts in C thousands unless otherwise stated)

10(b) Average number of people employed

	Group	2013	2012 Restated
DV	Number of employees	535	210
CA06 s411(1)	Average number of people (including executive directors) employed:		
	Wholesale	257	95
	Retail	178	75
	Administration	100	40
	Total average headcount	**535**	**210**

Company

The average number of administration staff employed by the company during the year, including executive directors was C50 (2012: C48).

11 Finance income and costs

	Group	2013	2012 Restated
IFRS7p20(b)	Interest expense:		
	– Bank borrowings	(5,317)	(10,646)
	– Dividend on redeemable preference shares (note 31)	(1,950)	(1,950)
	– Convertible bond (note 31)	(3,083)	–
	– Finance lease liabilities	(547)	(646)
37p84(e)	– Provisions: unwinding of discount (note 21 and 35)	(47)	(39)
21p52(a)	Net foreign exchange gains on financing activities (note 15)	2,594	996
	Fair value gains on financial instruments:		
IFRS7p23(d)	– Interest rate swaps: cash flow hedges, transfer from equity	102	88
IFRS7p24(a)(i)	– Interest rate swaps: fair value hedges	16	31
IFRS7p24(a)(ii)	Fair value adjustment of bank borrowings attributable to interest rate risk	(16)	(31)
	Total finance costs	(8,248)	(12,197)
	Less: amounts capitalised on qualifying assets	75	–
	Finance costs	**(8,173)**	**(12,197)**
	Finance income:		
	– Interest income on short-term bank deposits	550	489
IFRS7p20(b)	– Interest income on available-for-sale financial assets	963	984
IFRS7p20(b)	– Interest income on loans to related parties (note 41)	217	136
	Finance income	**1,730**	**1,609**
	Net finance costs	**(6,443)**	**(10,588)**

(All amounts in C thousands unless otherwise stated)

12 Investments

The amounts recognised in the balance sheet are as follows:

	2013	2012 Restated
Associates	13,373	13,244
Joint ventures	5,276	3,809
At 31 December	**18,649**	**17,053**

The amounts recognised in the income statement are as follows:

	2013	2012 Restated
Associates	215	145
Joint ventures	1,467	877
At 31 December	**1,682**	**1,022**

12(a) Investment in associates

IFRS 12p21(a) Set out below are the associates of the group as at 31 December 2013, which, in the opinion of the directors, are material to the group. The associates as listed below have share capital consisting solely of ordinary shares, which are held directly by the group; the country of incorporation or registration is also their principal place of business.

Nature of investment in associates 2013 and 2012:

Name of entity	Place of business/ country of incorporation	% of ownership interest	Nature of the relationship	Measurement method
Alpha Limited	Cyprus	18	Note 1	Equity
Beta SA	Greece	30	Note 2	Equity

Note 1: Alpha Limited provides products and services to the footware industry. Alpha is a strategic partnership for the group, providing access to new customers and markets in Europe.

Note 2: Beta SA manufactures parts for the footware industry and distributes its products globally. Beta SA is strategic for the group's growth in the European market and provides the group with access to expertise in efficient manufacturing processes for its footware business and access to key fashion trends.

IFRS 12p21(b)(iii) As at 31 December 2013, the fair value of the groups interest in Beta SA, which is listed on the Euro Money Stock Exchange, was C13,513 (2012: C12,873) and the carrying amount of the group's interest was C11,997 (2012: C11,240).

Alpha Limited is a private company and there is no quoted market price available for its shares.

IFRS12p23(b) There are no contingent liabilities relating to the group's interest in the associates

IFRS GAAP plc – year ended 31 December 2013

(All amounts in C thousands unless otherwise stated)

Summarised financial information for associates

Set out below are the summarised financial information for Alpha Limited and Beta SA which are accounted for using the equity method.

Summarised balance sheet

		Alpha Limited		Beta SA		Total	
		As at 31 December		As at 31 December		As at 31 December	
		2013	2012	2013	2012	2013	2012
	Current						
IFRS12pB13(a)	Cash and cash equivalents	1,170	804	5,171	8,296	6,341	9,100
IFRS12p B12(b)(i)	Other current assets (excluding cash)	2,433	2,635	7,981	9,722	10,414	12,357
IFRS12p B12(b)(i)	Total current assets	3,603	3,439	13,152	18,018	16,755	21,457
IFRS12pB13(b)	Financial liabiliites (excluding trade payables)	(808)	(558)	(8,375)	(8,050)	(9,183)	(8,608)
IFRS12p B12(b)(iii)	Other current liabilities (including trade payables)	(2,817)	(2,635)	(6,017)	(14,255)	(8,834)	(16,890)
IFRS12p B12(b)(iii)	Total current liabilities	(3,625)	(3,193)	(14,392)	(22,305)	(18,017)	(25,498)
	Non-current						
IFRS12p B12(b)(ii)	Assets	13,340	14,751	53,201	54,143	66,541	68,894
IFRS12p B13(c)	Financial liabilities	(4,941)	(3,647)	(9,689)	(8,040)	(14,630)	(11,687)
IFRS12p B12(b)(iv)	Other liabilities	(733)	(217)	(2,282)	(4,349)	(3,015)	(4,566)
	Total non-current liabiliites	(5,674)	(3,864)	(11,971)	(12,389)	(17,645)	(16,253)
DV	**Net assets**	**7,644**	11,133	**39,990**	37,467	**47,634**	48,600

IFRS GAAP plc – year ended 31 December 2013

(All amounts in C thousands unless otherwise stated)

Summarised statement of comprehensive income

		Alpha Limited		Beta SA		Total	
		For period ended 31 December		For period ended 31 December		For period ended 31 December	
		2013	2012	2013	2012	2013	2012
IFRS12p B12(b)(v)	Revenue	11,023	15,012	26,158	23,880	37,181	38,892
IFRS12p B13(d)	Depreciation and amortisation	(2,576)	(1,864)	(3,950)	(3,376)	(6,526)	(5,240)
IFRS12p B13(e)	Interest income[1]	–	–	–	–	–	–
IFRS12p B13(e)(f)	Interest expense	(1,075)	(735)	(1,094)	(1,303)	(2,169)	(2,038)
IFRS12p B12(b)(vi)	Profit or loss from continuing operations	(3,531)	(2,230)	3,443	2,109	(88)	(121)
IFRS12p B13(g)	Income tax expense	175	208	(713)	(412)	(538)	(204)
IFRS12p B12(b)(vi)	Post-tax profit from continuing operations	(3,356)	(2,022)	2,730	1,697	(626)	(325)
IFRS12p B12(b)(vii)	Post-tax profit from discontinued operations[1]	–	–	–	–	–	–
IFRS12p B12(b)(viii)	Other comprehensive income	–	–	(40)	(47)	(40)	(47)
IFRS12p B12(b)(ix)	Total comprehensive income	(3,356)	(2,022)	2,690	1,650	(666)	(372)
IFRS12pb12(a)	Dividends received from associate[1]	–	–	–	–	–	–

IFRS12pB14 The information above reflects the amounts presented in the financial statements of the associates (and not IFRS GAAP plc's share of those amounts) adjusted for differences in accounting policies between the group and the associates.

Commentary – summarised financial information

Summarised financial information is required for the group's interest in material associates; however, IFRS GAAP plc has provided the total amounts voluntarily.

---

[1] Some of the line items above have a nil balance but have still been included for illustrative purposes only.

(All amounts in C thousands unless otherwise stated)

Reconciliation of summarised financial information

IFRS12 pB14(b)

Reconciliation of the summarised financial information presented to the carrying amount of its interest in associates

	Alpha Limited		Beta SA		Total	
Summarised financial information	**2013**	2012	**2013**	2012	**2013**	2012
Opening net assets 1 January	**11,133**	12,977	**37,467**	35,573	**48,600**	48,550
Profit/(loss) for the period	(3,356)	(2,022)	2,730	1,697	(626)	(325)
Other comprehensive income	–	–	(40)	(47)	(40)	(47)
Foreign exchange differences	(133)	178	(167)	243	(300)	421
Closing net assets	**7,644**	**11,133**	**39,990**	**37,466**	**47,634**	**48,599**
Interest in associates (18%; 30%)	1,376	2,004	11,997	11,240	13,373	13,244
Goodwill[1]	–	–	–	–	–	–
Carrying value	**1,376**	**2,004**	**11,997**	**11,240**	**13,373**	**13,244**

12(b) Investment in joint venture

	2013	2012
At 1 January	**3,809**	**2,932**
Share of profit	1,467	877
Other comprehensive income[1]	–	–
At 31 December	**5,276**	**3,809**

IFRS 12p21(a) The joint venture listed below has share capital consisting solely of ordinary shares, which is held directly by the group.

Nature of investment in joint ventures 2013 and 2012

Name of entity	Place of business/country of incorporation	% of ownership interest	Nature of the relationship	Measurement method
Gamma Ltd	United Kingdom	50	Note 1	Equity

Note 1: Gamma Ltd provides products and services to the footware industry in the UK. Gamma Ltd is a strategic partnership for the group, providing access to new technology and processes for its footware business.

IFRS 12p21(b)(iii) Gamma Ltd is a private company and there is no quoted market price available for its shares.

---

[1] Some of the line items above have a nil balance but have still been included for illustrative purposes only.

IFRS GAAP plc – year ended 31 December 2013

(All amounts in C thousands unless otherwise stated)

> **Commentary – fair value of interest in joint venture**
>
> Where there is a quoted market price for an entity's investment in a joint venture, the fair value of that interest should be disclosed.

Commitments and contingent liabilities in respect of joint ventures

IFRS12p23(a) The group has the following commitments relating to its joint ventures.

	2013	2012
Commitment to provide funding if called	100	100

IFRS12p23(b) There are no contingent liabilities relating to the group's interest in the joint venture. Gamma Ltd has a contingent liability relating to an unresolved legal case relating to a contract dispute with a customer. As the case is at an early stage in proceedings it is not possible to determine the likelihood or amount of any settlement should Gamma Ltd not be successful.

Summarised financial information for joint ventures

IFRS12p21(b)(ii) Set out below are the summarised financial information for Gamma Ltd which is accounted for using the equity method.

Summarised balance sheet

		As at 31 December	
		2013	2012
	Current		
IFRS12pB13(a)	Cash and cash equivalents	1,180	780
IFRS12p B12(b)(i)	Other current assets (excluding cash)	7,368	4,776
IFRS12p B12(b)(i)	Total current assets	8,548	5,556
IFRS12p B13(b)	Financial liabiliites (excluding trade payables)	(1,104)	(1,094)
IFRS12p B12(b)(iii)	Other current liabilities (including trade payables)	(890)	(726)
IFRS12p B12(b)(iii)	Total current liabilities	(1,994)	(1,820)
	Non-current		
IFRS12p B12(b)(ii)	Assets	11,016	9,786
IFRS12p B13(c)	Financial liabilities	(6,442)	(5,508)
IFRS12p B12(b)(iv)	Other liabilities	(576)	(396)
	Total non-current liabilities	(7,018)	(5,904)
DV	**Net assets**	10,552	7,618

(All amounts in C thousands unless otherwise stated)

	Summarised statement of comprehensive income	For period ended 31 December	
		2013	2012
IFRS12p B12(b)(v)	Revenue	23,620	23,158
IFRS12pB13(d)	Depreciation and amortisation		
IFRS12pB13(e)	Interest income	206	648
IFRS12p B13(f)	Interest expense	(1,760)	(2,302)
IFRS12p B12(b)(vi)	Profit or loss from continuing operations	5,750	5,206
IFRS12p B13(g)	Income tax expense	(2,816)	(3,452)
IFRS12p B12(b)(vi)	Post-tax profit from continuing operations	2,934	1,754
IFRS12p B12(b)(vii)	Post-tax profit from discontinued operations[1]	–	–
IFRS12p B12(b)(viii)	Other comprehensive income[1]	–	–
IFRS12p B12(b)(ix)	Total comprehensive income	2,934	1,754
IFRS12pb12(a)	Dividends received from joint venture or associate[1]	–	–

IFRS12pB14 The information above reflects the amounts presented in the financial statements of the joint venture adjusted for differences in accounting policies between the group and the joint venture (and not IFRS GAAP plc's share of those amounts).

Reconciliation of summarised financial information

IFRS12 pB14(b) Reconciliation of the summarised financial information presented to the carrying amount of its interest in the joint venture.

Summarised financial information	2013	2012
Opening net assets 1 January	7,618	5,864
Profit/(loss) for the period	2,934	1,754
Other comprehensive income[1]	–	–
Closing net assets	10,552	7,618
Interest in joint venture @50%	5,276	3,809
Goodwill[1]	–	–
Carrying value	5,276	3,809

[1] Some of the line items above have a nil balance but have still been included for illustrative purposes only.

IFRS GAAP plc – year ended 31 December 2013

(All amounts in C thousands unless otherwise stated)

12(c) Principal subsidiaries

The group had the following principal subsidiaries at 31 December 2013

	Name	Country of incorporation and place of business	Nature of business	Proportion of ordinary shares directly held by parent (%)	Proportion of ordinary shares held by the group (%)	Proportion of ordinary shares held by non-controlling interests (%)	Proportion of preference shares held by the group (%)
IFRS12p10(a), 12(a-c)							
SI 2008/410 - 4 Sch 1(1)-(3), 16(1)-(3) SI 2008/410 - 4 Sch17	Treasury Limited	UK	Head office financing company	100	100	–	–
	A Limited	UK	Intermediate holding company	–	100	–	100
	O Limited	UK	Shoe manufacturer and wholesaler	–	85	15	–
	Shoe Limited	UK	Shoe and leather goods retailer	–	100	–	–
	L Limited	UK	Logistics company	100	100	–	–
	D Limited	UK	Design services	100	100	–	–
	Delta Inc	US	Shoe and leather goods retailer	–	40	60	–
	ABC Group	US	Shoe and leather goods retailer	72	72	28	–
	M GbmH	Germany	Shoe manufacturer and wholesaler	–	100	–	–
	L SARL	France	Logistics company	–	100	–	–
	E GbmH	Germany	Design services	–	100	–	–
	C Group	China	Shoe manufacturer and wholesaler	–	100	–	–
	R Group	Russia	Shoe manufacturer and wholesaler	–	100	–	–

All subsidiary undertakings are included in the consolidation. The proportion of the voting rights in the subsidiary undertakings held directly by the parent company do

(All amounts in C thousands unless otherwise stated)

not differ from the proportion of ordinary shares held. The parent company further does not have any shareholdings in the preference shares of subsidiary undertakings included in the group.

The directors consider that to give full particulars of all subsidiary undertakings would led to a statement of excessive length. A full list of subsidiary undertakings, joint ventures and associates at 31 December 2013 will be annexed to the company's next annual return.

Commentary – Disclosure of related undertakings

Where the directors consider that to give the full particulars of all subsidiary undertakings under section 409 of the Companies Act 2006 would lead to a statement of excessive length, section 410 allows for only the principal subsidiaries to be disclosed. If advantage is taken of this exemption, there must be included in the notes a statement that the exemption has been taken and that the full information will be annexed to the company's next annual return.

IFRS12 p12 (f) The total non-controlling interest for the period is C7,888, of which C5,327 is for ABC Group and C2,466 is attributed to Delta Inc. The non-controlling interest in respect of O Limited is not material.

Significant restrictions

IFRS12p 10(b)(i) Cash and short-term deposits of C1,394 are held in China and are subject to local exchange control regulations. These local exchange control regulations provide for restrictions on exporting capital from the country, other than through normal dividends.

Summarised financial information on subsidiaries with material non-controlling interests

IFRS12p12(g), B10(b) Set out below are the summarised financial information for each subsidiary that has non-controlling interests that are material to the group.

See note 40 for transactions with non-controlling interests.

Summarised balance sheet

	Delta Inc		ABC Group	
	As at 31 December		As at 31 December	
	2013	2012	2013	2012
Current				
Assets	5,890	4,828	16,935	14,742
Liabilities	(3,009)	(2,457)	(4,514)	(3,686)
Total current net assets	2,881	2,371	12,421	11,056
Non-current				
Assets	3,672	2,357	10,008	8,536
Liabilities	(2,565)	(1,161)	(3,848)	(1,742)
Total non-current net assets	1,107	1,196	6,160	6,794
Net assets	3,988	3,567	18,581	17,850

IFRS GAAP plc – year ended 31 December 2013

(All amounts in C thousands unless otherwise stated)

Summarised income statement

	Delta Inc		ABC Group	
	For period ended 31 December		For period ended 31 December	
	2013	2012	2013	2012
Revenue	19,602	17,883	29,403	26,825
Profit before income tax	4,218	3,007	6,327	6,611
Income tax expense/income	(1,692)	(1,411)	(2,838)	(2,667)
Post-tax profit from continuing operations	2,526	1,596	3,489	3,944
Post-tax profit from discontinued operations	–	–	23	19
Other comprehensive income	369	(203)	554	495
Total comprehensive income	2,895	1,393	4,066	4,458
Total comprehensive income allocated to non-controlling interests	1,737	836	1,138	–
Dividends paid to non-controlling interests	1,770	550	150	–

Summarised cash flows

	Delta Inc	ABC Group
	31 December 2013	31 December 2013
Cash flows from operating activities		
Cash generated from operations	6,854	6,586
Interest paid	(134)	(86)
Income tax paid	(1,534)	(2,748)
Net cash generated from operating activities	5,186	3,752
Net cash used in investing activities	(1,218)	(1,225)
Net cash used in financing activities	(3,502)	(478)
Net (decrease)/increase in cash and cash equivalents	466	2,049
Cash, cash equivalents and bank overdrafts at beginning of year	576	1,576
Exchange gains/(losses) on cash and cash equivalents	(56)	38
Cash and cash equivalents at end of year	986	3,663

IFRS12pB11 — The information above is the amount before inter-company eliminations.

27p16

12(d) Investment in subsidiaries

Company	2013	2012
Shares in group undertakings		
Beginning of year	22,170	21,964
Additions in year (note 39)	16,050	–
Capital contribution relating to share based payment	372	206
End of year	38,592	22,170

(All amounts in C thousands unless otherwise stated)

Investments in group undertakings are recorded at cost, which is the fair value of the consideration paid.

DV The capital contribution relating to share based payment relates to 1,210 share options granted by the company to employees of subsidiary undertakings in the group. Refer to note 27 for further details on the group's share option schemes.

13 Income tax expense

	Group	2013	2012 Restated
	Current tax:		
12p80(a)	Current tax on profits for the year	14,082	6,035
12p80(b)	Adjustments in respect of prior years	150	–
	Total current tax	**14,232**	**6,035**
	Deferred tax (note 32):		
12p80(c)	Origination and reversal of temporary differences	476	2,635
12p80(d)	Impact of change in the Euravian tax rate[1]	(97)	–
	Total deferred tax	**379**	**2,635**
	Income tax expense	**14,611**	**8,670**

12p81(c) The tax on the group's profit before tax differs from the theoretical amount that would arise using the weighted average tax rate applicable to profits of the consolidated entities as follows:

	2013	2012 Restated
Profit before tax	**48,933**	**25,710**
Tax calculated at domestic tax rates applicable to profits in the respective countries	16,148	7,713
Tax effects of:		
– Associates results reported net of tax	57	(44)
– Income not subject to tax	(1,072)	(212)
– Expenses not deductible for tax purposes	845	866
– Utilisation of previously unrecognised tax losses	(1,450)	–
– Tax losses for which no deferred income tax asset was recognised	30	347
Re-measurement of deferred tax – change in Euravian tax rate	(97)	–
Adjustment in respect of prior years	150	–
Tax charge	**14,611**	**8,670**

12p81(d) The weighted average applicable tax rate was 33% (2012: 30%). The increase is caused by a change in the profitability of the group's subsidiaries in the respective countries partially offset by the impact of the reduction in the Euravian tax rate (see below).

---

[1] The impact of change in Euravian tax rate is shown for illustrative purposes.

IFRS GAAP plc – year ended 31 December 2013

(All amounts in C thousands unless otherwise stated)

12p81(d) During the year, as a result of the change in the Euravian corporation tax rate from 30% to 28% that was substantively enacted on 26 June 2013 and that will be effective from 1 April 2014, the relevant deferred tax balances have been re-measured. Deferred tax expected to reverse in the year to 31 December 2013 has been measured using the effective rate that will apply in Euravia for the period (28.5%).[1]

1p125,10p21 Further reductions to the Euravian tax rate have been announced. The changes, which are expected to be enacted separately each year, propose to reduce the rate by 1% per annum to 24% by 1 April 2018. The changes had not been substantively enacted at the balance sheet date and, therefore, are not recognised in these financial statements.[2]

12p81(ab) The tax (charge)/credit relating to components of other comprehensive income is as follows:

		2013		
		Before tax	Tax (charge) /credit	After tax
	Fair value gains:			
1p90	– Land and buildings	1,005	(250)	755
1p90	– Available-for-sale financial assets	560	(198)	362
1p90	Share of other comprehensive income of associates	(86)	–	(86)
1p90	Remeasurements of post employment benefit liabilities	119	(36)	83
1p90	Impact of change in the Euravian tax rate on deferred tax[3]	–	(10)	(10)
1p90	Cash flow hedges	97	(33)	64
1p90	Net investment hedge	(45)	–	(45)
1p90	Currency translation differences	2,401	–	2,401
IFRS3p59	Reclassification of revaluation of previously held interest in ABC Group	(850)	–	(850)
	Other comprehensive income	**3,201**	**(527)**	**2,674**
	Current tax[4]		–	
	Deferred tax (note 32)		(527)	
			(527)	

---

[1] If the effect of the proposed changes is material, disclosure should be given of the effect of the changes, either as disclosure of events after the reporting period or as future material adjustment to the carrying amounts of assets and liabilities. This disclosure does not need to be tailored or reconciled to the income statement.
[2] Disclosure in respect of the impact of change in Euravian tax rate is shown for illustrative purposes. UK companies will need to consider the impact of any tax rate changes which have been announced but not substantively enacted at the balance sheet date.
[3] The impact of change in Euravian tax rate is shown for illustrative purposes.
[4] There are no current tax items relating to other comprehensive income in these financial statements, but the line item is shown for illustrative purposes.

(All amounts in C thousands unless otherwise stated)

		2012 Restated		
		Before tax	Tax (charge) /credit	After tax
	Fair value gains:			
1p90	– Land and buildings	1,133	(374)	759
1p90	– Available-for-sale financial assets	973	(61)	912
1p90	Share of other comprehensive income of associates	91	–	91
1p90	Remeasurements of post employment benefit liabilities	(910)	273	(637)
1p90	Impact of change in the Euravian tax rate on deferred tax[1]	–	–	–
1p90	Cash flow hedges	(3)	–	(3)
1p90	Net investment hedge	40	–	40
1p90	Currency translation differences	(922)	–	(922)
IFRS3p59	Reclassification of revaluation of previously held interest in ABC Group	–	–	–
	Other comprehensive income	**402**	**(162)**	**240**
	Current tax[2]		–	
	Deferred tax (note 32)		(162)	
			(162)	

12p81(a) The income tax (charged)/credited directly to equity during the year is as follows:

	2013	2012
Current tax[3]		
Share option scheme	–	–
Deferred tax[4]		
Share option scheme	30	20
Convertible bond – equity component[5] (note 29)	(2,328)	–
	(2,298)	**20**

In addition, deferred income tax of C49 (2012: C43) was transferred from other reserves (note 29) to retained earnings (note 28). This represents deferred tax on the difference between the actual depreciation on buildings and the equivalent depreciation based on the historical cost of buildings.

---

[1] The impact of change in Euravian tax rate is shown for illustrative purposes.
[2] There are no current tax items relating to other comprehensive income in these financial statements, but the line item is shown for illustrative purposes.
[3] IAS 12 requires disclosure of current tax charged/credited directly to equity, in addition to deferred tax. There are no current tax items shown directly in equity in these financial statements, but the line item is shown for illustrative purposes.
[4] UK companies with 31 December 2013 year ends will need to consider the impact of the reduction in tax rates to 21% from 1 April 2014 in the Finance Act 2013.
[5] It is assumed that the tax base on the convertible bond is not split between the debt and equity elements. If the tax base were split, this would impact the deferred tax position.

IFRS GAAP plc – year ended 31 December 2013

(All amounts in C thousands unless otherwise stated)

14 Earnings per share

(a) Basic

Basic earnings per share is calculated by dividing the profit attributable to equity holders of the company by the weighted average number of ordinary shares in issue during the year excluding ordinary shares purchased by the company and held as treasury shares (note 26).

		2013	2012 Restated
33p70(a)	Profit from continuing operations attributable to owners of the parent	31,774	16,184
	Profit from discontinued operations attributable to owners of the parent	100	120
	Total	31,874	16,304
33p70(b)	Weighted average number of ordinary shares in issue (thousands)	23,454	20,500

(b) Diluted

Diluted earnings per share is calculated by adjusting the weighted average number of ordinary shares outstanding to assume conversion of all dilutive potential ordinary shares. The company has two categories of dilutive potential ordinary shares: convertible debt and share options. The convertible debt is assumed to have been converted into ordinary shares, and the net profit is adjusted to eliminate the interest expense less the tax effect. For the share options, a calculation is done to determine the number of shares that could have been acquired at fair value (determined as the average annual market share price of the company's shares) based on the monetary value of the subscription rights attached to outstanding share options. The number of shares calculated as above is compared with the number of shares that would have been issued assuming the exercise of the share options.

		2013	2012 Restated
	Earnings		
	Profit from continuing operations attributable to owners of the parent	31,774	16,184
	Interest expense on convertible debt (net of tax)	2,158	–
33p70(a)	Profit used to determine diluted earnings per share	33,932	16,184
	Profit from discontinued operations attributable to owners of the parent	100	120
		34,032	16,304
	Weighted average number of ordinary shares in issue (thousands)	23,454	20,500
	Adjustment for:		
	– Assumed conversion of convertible debt (thousands)	3,300	–
	– Share options (thousands)	1,213	1,329
33p70(b)	Weighted average number of ordinary shares for diluted earnings per share (thousands)	27,967	21,829

IFRS GAAP plc – year ended 31 December 2013

143

(All amounts in C thousands unless otherwise stated)

15 Net foreign exchange gains/(losses)

21p52(a) The exchange differences charged/credited to the income statement are included as follows:

Group	2013	2012 Restated
Other (losses)/gains – net (note 8)	(277)	200
Net finance costs (note 11)	2,594	996
Total	**2,317**	**1,196**

16 Property, plant and equipment

	Group	Land and buildings	Vehicles and machinery	Furniture, fittings and equipment	Construction in progress	Total
1p78(a)						
16p73(d)	At 1 January 2012 (Restated)					
	Cost or valuation	39,664	71,072	20,025	–	130,761
	Accumulated depreciation	(2,333)	(17,524)	(3,690)	–	(23,547)
	Net book amount	**37,331**	**53,548**	**16,335**	**–**	**107,214**
16p73(e)	Year ended 31 December 2012 (Restated)					
	Opening net book amount	37,331	53,548	16,335	–	107,214
16p73(e)(viii)	Exchange differences	(381)	(703)	(423)	–	(1,507)
16p73(e)(iv)	Revaluation surplus (note 29)	1,133	–	–	–	1,133
16p73(e)(i)	Additions	1,588	2,970	1,484	–	6,042
16p73(e)(ix)	Disposals (note 36)	–	(2,607)	(380)	–	(2,987)
16p73(e)(vii)	Depreciation charge (note 9)	(636)	(4,186)	(4,840)	–	(9,662)
	Closing net book amount	**39,035**	**49,022**	**12,176**	**–**	**100,233**
16p73(d)	At 31 December 2012 (Restated)					
	Cost or valuation	42,004	70,732	20,706	–	133,442
	Accumulated depreciation	(2,969)	(21,710)	(8,530)	–	(33,209)
	Net book amount	**39,035**	**49,022**	**12,176**	**–**	**100,233**
	Year ended 31 December 2013					
16p73(e)	Opening net book amount	39,035	49,022	12,176	–	100,233
16p73(e)(viii)	Exchange differences	846	1,280	342	–	2,468
16p73(e)(iv)	Revaluation surplus (note 29)	1,005	–	–	–	1,005
16p73(e)(iii)	Acquisition of subsidiary (note 39)	49,072	5,513	13,199	–	67,784
16p73(e)(i)	Additions	4,421	427	2,202	2,455	9,505
16p73(e)(ix)	Disposals (note 36)	(2,000)	(3,729)	(608)	–	(6,337)
	Transfers	1,245	–	–	(1,245)	–
16p73(e)(vii)	Depreciation charge (note 9)	(3,545)	(4,768)	(9,441)	–	(17,754)
IFRS5p38	Transferred to disposal group classified as held for sale	(341)	(1,222)	–	–	(1,563)
	Closing net book amount	**89,738**	**46,523**	**17,870**	**1,210**	**155,341**
16p73(d)	At 31 December 2013					
	Cost or valuation	96,593	74,223	35,841	1,210	207,867
	Accumulated depreciation	(6,855)	(27,700)	(17,971)	–	(52,526)
	Net book amount	**89,738**	**46,523**	**17,870**	**1,210**	**155,341**

IFRS GAAP plc – year ended 31 December 2013

(All amounts in C thousands unless otherwise stated)

Ref	
DV	Property, plant and equipment transferred to the disposal group classified as held-for-sale amounts to C1,563 and relates to assets that are used by Shoes Limited (part of the UK wholesale segment). See note 25 for further details regarding the disposal group held for sale.
DV, 1p104	Depreciation expense of C8,054 (2012: C5,252) has been charged in 'cost of sales', C5,568 (2012: C2,410) in 'distribution costs' and C4,132 (2012: C2,000) in 'administrative expenses'.
17p35(c)	Lease rentals amounting to C1,172 (2012: C895) and C9,432 (2012: C7,605) relating to the lease of machinery and property, respectively, are included in the income statement (note 9(a)).
	Construction work in progress as at 31 December, 2013 mainly comprises new shoe manufacturing equipment being constructed in the UK.
23p26	During the year, the group has capitalised borrowing costs amounting to C75 (2012: nil) on qualifying assets. Borrowing costs were capitalised at the weighted average rate of its general borrowings of 7.5%.
16p77(e)	If land and buildings were stated on the historical cost basis, the amounts would be as follows:

	2013	2012
Cost	93,079	37,684
Accumulated depreciation	(6,131)	(2,197)
Net book amount	**86,948**	**35,487**

Ref	
16p74(a)	Bank borrowings are secured on land and buildings for the value of C37,680 (2012: C51,306) (note 31).
17p31(a)	Vehicles and machinery includes the following amounts where the group is a lessee under a finance lease:

	2013	2012
Cost-capitalised finance lease	13,996	14,074
Accumulated depreciation	(5,150)	(3,926)
Net book amount	**8,846**	**10,148**

Ref	
17p31(e)	The group leases various vehicles and machinery under non-cancellable finance lease agreements. The lease terms are between 3 and 15 years, and ownership of the assets lies within the group.

Fair values of land and buildings

Ref	
16p77(a)-(b)	An independent valuation of the group's land and buildings was performed by valuers to determine the fair value of the land and buildings as at 31 December 2013 and 2012. The revaluation surplus net of applicable deferred income taxes was credited to other comprehensive income and is shown in 'other reserves' in shareholders equity (note 29). The following table analyses the non-financial assets carried at fair value, by valuation method. The different levels have been defined as follows: – Quoted prices (unadjusted) in active markets for identical assets or liabilities (Level 1).

(All amounts in C thousands unless otherwise stated)

- Inputs other than quoted prices included within level 1 that are observable for the asset or liability, either directly (that is, as prices) or indirectly (that is, derived from prices) (Level 2).
- Inputs for the asset or liability that are not based on observable market data (that is, unobservable inputs) (Level 3).

		Fair value measurements at 31 December 2013 using		
IFRS 13p93(a), (b)		Quoted prices in active markets for identical assets (Level 1)	Significant other observable inputs (Level 2)	Significant unobservable inputs (Level 3)
	Recurring fair value measurements			
	Land and buildings			
	– Office buildings – UK	–	7,428	–
	– Retail units – UK	–	19,027	–
	– Retail units – US	–	14,200	–
	– Manufacturing sites – UK	–	–	25,392
	– Manufacturing sites – Asia Pacific	–	–	23,691

IFRS 13p93(c) There were no transfers between levels 1 and 2 during the year.

Valuation techniques used to derive level 2 fair values

IFRS 13p93(d) Level 2 fair values of land and retail units have been derived using the sales comparison approach. Sales prices of comparable land and buildings in close proximity are adjusted for differences in key attributes such as property size. The most significant input into this valuation approach is price per square foot.

IFRS 13p93(e) **Fair value measurements using significant unobservable inputs (Level 3)**

		Manufacturing sites – UK	Manufacturing sites – Asia Pacific
	Opening balance	24,562	18,327
	Transfers to/ (from) Level 3	–	3,434
	Additions	1,489	1,651
	Disposals	(1,100)	–
IFRS 13p93(e)(i)	Gains and losses recognised in other comprehensive income	441	279
	Closing balance	25,392	23,691

The Group commenced redevelopment of a factory in China during the year. The redevelopment will greatly expand the transport infrastructure of the factory, and is expected to be completed in 2014. Prior to redevelopment, this property was valued using the sales comparison approach, which resulted in a level 2 fair value. Upon redevelopment, the Group had to revise its valuation technique for the property under construction. The revised valuation technique uses significant unobservable inputs. Accordingly, the fair value was reclassified to level 3.

(All amounts in C thousands unless otherwise stated)

The revised valuation technique uses the sales comparison approach to derive the fair value of the completed property. The following were then deducted from the fair value of the completed property:
- estimated construction and other costs to completion that would be incurred by a market participant; and
- estimated profit margin that a market participant would require to hold and develop the property to completion, based on the state of the property as at 31 December 2013.

IFRS13p 93(c),(e)(iv)

The group's policy is to recognise transfers into and transfers out of fair value hierarchy levels as of the date of the event or change in circumstances that caused the transfer.

IFRS13 p93g

Valuation processes of the group

IFRS13 IE 65

The group's finance department includes a team that performs the valuations of land and buildings required for financial reporting purposes, including level 3 fair values. This team reports directly to the chief financial officer (CFO) and the audit committee (AC). Discussions of valuation processes and results are held between the CFO, AC and the valuation team at least once every quarter, in line with the group's quarterly reporting dates.

On an annual basis, the group engages external, independent and qualified valuers to determine the fair value of the group's land and buildings. As at 31 December 2013, the fair values of the land and buildings have been determined by XYZ Property Surveyors Limited.

The external valuations of the level 3 land and buildings have been performed using a sales comparison approach, similar to the level 2 land and buildings. However for manufacturing sites there have been a limited number of similar sales in the local market and the valuations have been performed using unobservable inputs. The external valuers, in discussion with the group's internal valuation team, has determined these inputs based on the size, age and condition of the land and buildings, the state of the local economy and comparable prices in the corresponding national economy.

The group has also valued land and buildings in China which is undergoing significant development of the transport infrastructure. The valuation has been performed using an adjusted sales comparison approach. The fair value of the completed land and buildings has been derived from observable sales prices of similar land and buildings in the local market. The estimated costs of completion, including a reasonable profit margin a market participant would require, has then been deducted to give estimate of the current fair value of the land and buildings.

(All amounts in C thousands unless otherwise stated)

IFRS 13p93(d),(h)(i)	Information about fair value measurements using significant unobservable inputs (Level 3)					
	Description	Fair value at 31 December 2013	Valuation technique(s)	Unobservable inputs[1]	Range of unobservable inputs (probability – weighted average)	Relationship of unobservable inputs to fair value
	Manufacturing sites – UK	25,392	Sales comparison approach	Price per square metre	C350-C470 (C400)	The higher the price per square metre, the higher the fair value
	Manufacturing sites – Asia Pacific	19,098	Sales comparison approach	Price per square metre	C235-C390 (C330)	The higher the price per square metre, the higher the fair value
		4,593	Adjusted sales comparison approach	Estimated costs to completion	C2,780,000-C3,220,000 (C2,900,000)	The higher the estimated costs, the lower the fair value.
				Estimated profit margin required to hold and develop property to completion	10%-15% (14%) of property value	The higher the profit margin required, the lower the fair value.

17 Intangible assets

	Group Cost	Goodwill	Trademarks and licences	Internally generated software development costs	Total
38p118(c)	At 1 January 2012 (Restated)	12,546	8,301	1,455	22,302
38p118(e)(vii)	Exchange differences	(546)	(306)	(45)	(897)
38p118(e)(i)	Additions	–	700	–	700
	As at 31 December 2012 (Restated)	12,000	8,695	1,410	22,105
38p118(e)(vii)	Exchange differences	341	96	134	571
38p118(e)(i)	Additions	–	684	2,366	3,050
38p118(e)(i)	Acquisition of subsidiary (note 39)	4,501	4,000	–	8,501
IFRS5p38	Transferred to disposal group classified as held for sale	(100)	(1,000)	–	(1,100)
	As at 31 December 2013	16,742	12,475	3,910	33,127
	Accumulated amortisation and impairment				
38p118(c)	At 1 January 2012	–	(330)	(510)	(840)
38p118(e)(vi)	Amortisation charge (note 9)	–	(365)	(200)	(565)
	As at 31 December 2012 (Restated)	–	(695)	(710)	(1,405)
38p118(e)(iv)	Impairment charge (note 9)	(4,650)	–	–	(4,650)
38p118(e)(vi)	Amortisation charge (note 9)	–	(680)	(120)	(800)
	As at 31 December 2013	**(4,650)**	**(1,375)**	**(830)**	**(6,855)**
	Net book value				
38p118(c)	Cost	12,000	8,695	1,410	22,105
38p118(c)	Accumulated amortisation and impairment	–	(695)	(710)	(1,405)
	As at 31 December 2012 (Restated)	12,000	8,000	700	20,700
38p118(c)	Cost	16,742	12,475	3,910	33,127
38p118(c)	Accumulated amortisation and impairment	(4,650)	(1,375)	(830)	(6,855)
	As at 31 December 2013	**12,092**	**11,100**	**3,080**	**26,272**

36p126(a)   The carrying amount of the Russia wholesale segment has been reduced to its recoverable amount through recognition of an impairment loss against goodwill. This loss has been included in 'cost of sales' in the income statement.

38p118(d)   Amortisation of C40 (2012: C100) is included in 'cost of sales' in the income statement; C680 (2012: C365) in 'distribution costs'; and C80 (2012: C100) in 'administrative expenses'.

DV   The trademark transferred to the disposal group classified as held for sale relates to the Shoes Limited trademark (part of the wholesale segment), which was previously recognised by the group on the acquisition of the entity in 2007. A further net book amount of C100 transferred to the disposal group relates to goodwill. See note 25 for further details regarding the disposal group held for sale.

IFRS GAAP plc – year ended 31 December 2013

149

(All amounts in C thousands unless otherwise stated)

Impairment tests for goodwill

36p130(d) Management reviews the business performance based on geography and type of business. It has identified UK, US, China, Russia and Europe as the main geographies. There are both retail and wholesale segments in the UK and the US. In all other geographies, the group has only wholesale business. Goodwill is monitored by the management at the operating segment level. The following is a summary of goodwill allocation for each operating segment:

36p134(a)

2013	Opening	Addition	Disposal	Impairment	Other adjustments	Closing
UK wholesale	6,075	–	(100)	–	215	6,190
UK retail	15	–	–	–	5	20
US wholesale	115	–	–	–	15	130
US retail	30	3,597	–	–	(55)	3,572
Europe wholesale	770	904	–	–	100	1,774
Russia wholesale	4,695	–	–	(4,650)	5	50
China wholesale	100	–	–	–	46	146
All other segments	200	–	–	–	10	210
Total	**12,000**	**4,501**	**(100)**	**(4,650)**	**341**	**12,092**

2012 (Restated)	Opening	Addition	Disposal	Impairment	Other adjustments	Closing
UK wholesale	6,370	–	–	–	(295)	6,075
UK retail	20	–	–	–	(5)	15
US wholesale	125	–	–	–	(10)	115
US retail	131	–	–	–	(101)	30
Europe wholesale	705	–	–	–	65	770
Russia wholesale	4,750	–	–	–	(55)	4,695
China wholesale	175	–	–	–	(75)	100
All other segments	270	–	–	–	(70)	200
Total	**12,546**	**–**	**–**	**–**	**(546)**	**12,000**

During 2012, US retail did not qualify as a reportable operating segment. However, with the acquisition in 2013 of ABC Group (note 39), US retail qualifies as a separate reportable segment, the comparatives have therefore been restated to be consistent.

36p130(e), 36p134(c), 36p134(d)(iii) The recoverable amount of all CGUs has been determined based on value-in-use calculations. These calculations use pre-tax cash flow projections based on financial budgets approved by management covering a five-year period. Cash flows beyond the five-year period are extrapolated using the estimated growth rates stated below. The growth rate does not exceed the long-term average growth rate for the shoe business in which the CGU operates.

IFRS GAAP plc – year ended 31 December 2013

150

(All amounts in C thousands unless otherwise stated)

		UK whole-sale	UK retail	US whole-sale	US retail	Europe whole-sale	Russia whole-sale	China whole-sale	All other segments
36p134(d)(i)	The key assumptions used for value-in-use calculations in 2013 are as follows:[1]								
36p134(d)	Compound annual volume growth[2]	3.5%	4.3%	3.8%	4.1%	5.4%	6.2%	8.7%	4.4%
36p134(d)(iv)	Long term growth rate[3]	1.8%	2.1%	1.8%	2.3%	1.8%	2.0%	3.0%	3.9%
36p134(d)(v), 130(g)	Discount rate[4]	12.5%	13.0%	12.0%	12.5%	12.7%	13.8%	14.0%	14.8%
36p134(c)	Recoverable amount of the CGU						22,659		

		UK whole-sale	UK retail	US whole-sale	US retail	Europe whole-sale	Russia whole-sale	China whole-sale	All other segments
36p134(d)(i)	The key assumptions used for value-in-use calculations in 2012 are as follows:								
36p134(d)	Compound annual volume growth rate[2]	3.4%	4.5%	3.9%	4.1%	5.4%	5.8%	8.9%	3.8%
36p134 (d)(iv)	Long term growth rate[3]	2.0%	2.3%	2.0%	2.5%	2.0%	2.5%	3.5%	3.3%
36p134(d)(v), 36p130(g)	Discount rate[4]	12.0%	12.3%	11.5%	12.5%	12.1%	13.5%	14.5%	13.0%

Commentary – disclosure of recoverable amount

IFRS 13 amended IAS 36 paragraph 134 (c) to include the disclosure of the recoverable amount for CGUs with significant carrying amounts of goodwill. However the IASB indicated that this was not their intention and published an amendment to IAS 36 in May 2013 to remove the disclosure requirements. Disclosure of the recoverable amount will still be required for CGUs for which there has been an impairment loss during the period. The amendment is effective for annual periods starting on or after 1 January 2014, early adoption is permitted. IFRS plc has early adopted the amendment.

---

[1] Disclosure of long-term growth rates and discount rates is required. Other key assumptions are required to be disclosed and quantified where a reasonably possible change in the key assumption would remove any remaining headroom in the impairment calculation. Otherwise the additional disclosures are encouraged but not required.
[2] Compound annual volume growth rate in the initial five-year period
[3] Weighted average growth rate used to extrapolate cash flows beyond the budget period.
[4] Pre-tax discount rate applied to the cash flow projections.

(All amounts in C thousands unless otherwise stated)

> At the time of publication of these illustrative financial statements the EU had not endorsed the amendment. It is anticipated that the EU will endorse the amendment by 31 December 2013 and early adoption will be available, and therefore its effect has been included in these illustrative financial statements. If the EU does not endorse the amendment, or early adoption is not available, entities should disclose the recoverable amount for all CGUs.

36p134(d)(ii) These assumptions have been used for the analysis of each CGU within the operating segment.

36p134(d)(ii) Management determined compound annual volume growth rate for each CGU covering over the five-year forecast period to be a key assumption. The volume of sales in each period is the main driver for revenue and costs. The compound annual volume growth rate is based on past performance and management's expectations of market development. The long term growth rates used are consistent with the forecasts included in industry reports. The discount rates used are pre-tax and reflect specific risks relating to the relevant operating segments.

36p130(a) The impairment charge arose in a wholesale CGU in Step-land (included in the Russian operating segment) following a decision in early 2013 to reduce the manufacturing output allocated to these operations (note 35). This was a result of a redefinition of the group's allocation of manufacturing volumes across all CGUs in order to benefit from advantageous market conditions. Following this decision, the group reassessed the depreciation policies of its property, plant and equipment in this country and estimated that their useful lives would not be affected. No class of asset other than goodwill was impaired. The pre-tax discount rate used in the previous years for the wholesale CGU in Step-land was 13.5%.

36p134(f) In European Wholesale, the recoverable amount calculated based on value in use exceeded carrying value by C705. A compound annual volume growth rate of 1.5%, a fall in long term growth rate to 1.6% or a rise in discount rate to 14.9% would remove the remaining headroom.

IFRS GAAP plc – year ended 31 December 2013

(All amounts in C thousands unless otherwise stated)

18 Financial instruments

18(a) Financial instruments by category

IFRS7p6

Group	Loans and receivables	Assets at fair value through profit and loss	Derivatives used for hedging	Available for sale	Total
31 December 2013					
Assets as per balance sheet					
Available-for-sale financial assets	–	–	–	19,370	19,370
Derivative financial instruments	–	361	1,103	–	1,464
Trade and other receivables excluding pre-payments[1]	20,837	–	–	–	20,837
Financial assets at fair value through profit or loss	–	11,820	–	–	11,820
Cash and cash equivalents	17,928	–	–	–	17,928
Total	**38,765**	**12,181**	**1,103**	**19,370**	**71,419**

Group	Liabilities at fair value through profit and loss	Derivatives used for hedging	Other financial liabilities at amortised cost	Total
Liabilities as per balance sheet				
Borrowings (excluding finance lease liabilities)	–	–	117,839	117,839
Finance lease liabilities[2]	–	–	8,998	8,998
Derivative financial instruments	268	327	–	595
Trade and other payables excluding non-financial liabilities[3]	–	–	15,668	15,668
Total	**268**	**327**	**142,505**	**143,100**

Group	Loans and receivables	Assets at fair value through profit and loss	Derivatives used for hedging	Available for sale	Total
31 December 2012 (Restated)					
Assets as per balance sheet					
Available-for-sale financial assets	–	–	–	14,910	14,910
Derivative financial instruments	–	321	875	–	1,196
Trade and other receivables excluding pre-payments[1]	18,576	–	–	–	18,576
Financial assets at fair value through profit or loss	–	7,972	–	–	7,972
Cash and cash equivalents	34,062	–	–	–	34,062
Total	**52,638**	**8,293**	**875**	**14,910**	**76,716**

[1] Pre-payments are excluded from the trade and other receivables balance, as this analysis is required only for financial instruments.

[2] The categories in this disclosure are determined by IAS 39. Finance leases are mostly outside the scope of IAS 39, but they remain within the scope of IFRS 7. Therefore finance leases have been shown separately.

[3] Non-financial liabilities are excluded from the trade payables balance, as this analysis is required only for financial instruments.

(All amounts in C thousands unless otherwise stated)

Group	Liabilities at fair value through profit and loss	Derivatives used for hedging	Other financial liabilities at amortised cost	Total
Liabilities as per balance sheet				
Borrowings (excluding finance lease liabilities)	–	–	104,006	104,006
Finance lease liabilities[1]	–	–	10,598	10,598
Derivative financial instruments	298	449	–	747
Trade and other payables excluding non-financial liabilities	–	–	11,518	11,518
Total	**298**	**449**	**126,122**	**126,869**

	31 December 2013				
Company	Loans and receivables	Assets at fair value through profit and loss	Derivatives used for hedging	Available-for-sale	Total
Assets as per balance sheet					
Trade and other receivables	43,711	–	–	–	43,711
Cash and cash equivalents	3,261	–	–	–	3,261
Total	**46,972**	**–**	**–**	**–**	**46,972**

	31 December 2012				
Company	Loans and receivables	Assets at fair value through profit and loss	Derivatives used for hedging	Available-for-sale	Total
Assets as per balance sheet					
Trade and other receivables	31,296	–	–	–	31,296
Cash and cash equivalents	6,234	–	–	–	6,234
Total	**37,530**	**–**	**–**	**–**	**37,530**

[1] The categories in this disclosure are determined by IAS 39. Finance leases are mostly outside the scope of IAS 39, but they remain within the scope of IFRS 7. Therefore finance leases have been shown separately.

(All amounts in C thousands unless otherwise stated)

18(b) Credit quality of financial assets

IFRS7p36(c) The credit quality of financial assets that are neither past due nor impaired can be assessed by reference to external credit ratings (if available) or to historical information about counterparty default rates:

	Group	2013	2012 Restated
	Trade receivables		
	Counterparties with external credit rating (Moody's)		
	A	5,895	5,757
	BB	3,200	3,980
	BBB	1,500	1,830
		10,595	11,567
	Counterparties without external credit rating:		
	Group 1	750	555
	Group 2	4,832	3,596
	Group 3	1,770	1,312
		7,352	5,463
	Total unimpaired trade receivables	**17,947**	**17,030**
	Cash at bank and short-term bank deposits[1]		
	AAA	8,790	15,890
	AA	5,300	7,840
	A	3,038	9,832
		17,128	33,562
DV	**Available-for-sale debt securities**		
	AA	347	264
		347	264
DV	**Derivative financial assets**		
	AAA	1,046	826
	AA	418	370
		1,464	1,196
	Loans to related parties		
	Group 2	2,501	1,301
	Group 3	167	87
		2,668	1,388

Group 1 – new customers/related parties (less than 6 months).
Group 2 – existing customers/related parties (more than 6 months) with no defaults in the past.
Group 3 – existing customers/related parties (more than 6 months) with some defaults in the past. All defaults were fully recovered.

None of the loans to related parties is past due but not impaired.

---

[1] The rest of the balance sheet item 'cash and cash equivalents' is cash in hand.

IFRS GAAP plc – year ended 31 December 2013

(All amounts in C thousands unless otherwise stated)

19 Available-for-sale financial assets

	Group	2013	2012
	At 1 January	14,910	13,222
	Exchange differences	646	(435)
	Acquisition of subsidiary (note 39)	473	–
	Additions	4,887	1,150
	Disposals	(106)	–
	Transfer on account of acquisition of control	(1,150)	–
	Net gains/(losses) transfer from equity (note 29)	(980)	(152)
1p79(b)	Net gains/(losses) transfer to equity (note 29)	690	1,125
	At 31 December	19,370	14,910
1p66,1p69	Less non-current portion	(17,420)	(14,910)
1p66,1p69	Current portion	1,950	–

IFRS7p20(a)(ii) The group removed profits of C217 (2012: C187) and losses C87 (2012: C35) from equity into the income statement. Losses in the amount of C55 (2012: C20) were due to impairments.

Available-for-sale financial assets include the following:

IFRS7p31, 34

	2013	2012
Listed securities:		
Equity securities – UK	8,335	8,300
Equity securities – Europe	5,850	2,086
Equity securities – US	4,550	4,260
Debentures with fixed interest of 6.5% and maturity date of 27 August 2015	210	–
Non cumulative 9% non-redeemable preference shares	78	–
Unlisted securities:		
Debt securities with fixed interest ranging from 6.3% to 6.5% and maturity dates between July 2014 and May 2016	347	264
Total	19,370	14,910

IFRS7p34(c) Available-for-sale financial assets are denominated in the following currencies:

	2013	2012
UK pound	8,335	8,300
Euro	5,850	2,086
US dollar	4,550	4,260
Other currencies	635	264
Total	19,370	14,910

IFRS7p27 The fair values of unlisted securities are based on cash flows discounted using a rate based on the market interest rate and the risk premium specific to the unlisted securities (2013: 6%; 2012: 5.8%).

IFRS7p36(a) The maximum exposure to credit risk at the reporting date is the carrying value of the debt securities classified as available for sale.

IFRS7p36(c) None of these financial assets is either past due or impaired.

IFRS GAAP plc – year ended 31 December 2013

(All amounts in C thousands unless otherwise stated)

20 Derivative financial instruments

		2013		2012	
Group		Assets	Liabilities	Assets	Liabilities
IFRS7p22(a)(b) Interest rate swaps – cash flow hedge		351	110	220	121
IFRS7p22(a)(b) Interest rate swaps – fair value hedges		57	37	49	11
IFRS7p22(a)(b) Forward foreign exchange contracts – cash flow hedges		695	180	606	317
Forward foreign exchange contracts – held-for-trading		361	268	321	298
Total		**1,464**	**595**	**1,196**	**747**
1p66, p69 Less non-current portion:					
Interest rate swaps – cash flow hedges		345	100	200	120
Interest rate swaps – fair value hedges		50	35	45	9
		395	135	245	129
1p66, p69 **Current portion**		**1,069**	**460**	**951**	**618**

Trading derivatives are classified as a current asset or liability. The full fair value of a hedging derivative is classified as a non-current asset or liability if the remaining maturity of the hedged item is more than 12 months and, as a current asset or liability, if the maturity of the hedged item is less than 12 months.

IFRS7p24 The ineffective portion recognised in the profit or loss that arises from fair value hedges amounts to a loss of C1 (2012: loss of C1) (note 8). The ineffective portion recognised in the profit or loss that arises from cash flow hedges amounts to a gain of C17 (2012: a gain of C14) (note 8). There was no ineffectiveness to be recorded from net investment in foreign entity hedges.

(a) Forward foreign exchange contracts

IFRS7p31 The notional principal amounts of the outstanding forward foreign exchange contracts at 31 December 2013 were C92,370 (2012: C89,689).

IFRS7p23(a), 39p100, 1p79(b) The hedged highly probable forecast transactions denominated in foreign currency are expected to occur at various dates during the next 12 months. Gains and losses recognised in the hedging reserve in equity (note 29) on forward foreign exchange contracts as of 31 December 2013 are recognised in the income statement in the period or periods during which the hedged forecast transaction affects the income statement. This is generally within 12 months of the end of the reporting period unless the gain or loss is included in the initial amount recognised for the purchase of fixed assets, in which case recognition is over the lifetime of the asset (5 to 10 years).

(b) Interest rate swaps

IFRS7p31 The notional principal amounts of the outstanding interest rate swap contracts at 31 December 2013 were C4,314 (2012: C3,839).

IFRS7p23(a), 1p79(b) At 31 December 2013, the fixed interest rates vary from 6.9% to 7.4% (2012: 6.7% to 7.2%), and the main floating rates are EURIBOR and LIBOR. Gains and losses recognised in the hedging reserve in equity (note 29) on interest rate swap contracts as of 31 December 2013 will be continuously released to the income statement within finance cost until the repayment of the bank borrowings (note 31).

(All amounts in C thousands unless otherwise stated)

(c) Hedge of net investment in foreign entity

IFRS7p22, 1p79(b) — A proportion of the group's US dollar-denominated borrowing amounting to C321 (2012: C321) is designated as a hedge of the net investment in the group's US subsidiary. The fair value of the borrowing at 31 December 2013 was C370 (2012: C279). The foreign exchange loss of C45 (2012: gain of C40) on translation of the borrowing to currency at the end of the reporting period is recognised in other comprehensive income.

IFRS7p36(a) — The maximum exposure to credit risk at the reporting date is the fair value of the derivative assets in the balance sheet.

21 Trade and other receivables

		Group		Company	
		2013	2012 Restated	2013	2012
IFRS7p36, 1p77	Trade receivables	18,174	17,172	–	–
	Less: provision for impairment of trade receivables	(109)	(70)	–	–
1p78(b)	Trade receivables - net	18,065	17,102	–	–
1p78(b)	Prepayments	1,250	1,106	–	–
24p18(b), 1p78(b)	Receivables from related parties (note 41)	104	86	43,711	31,296
24p18(b),	Loans to related parties (note 41)	2,668	1,388	–	–
		22,087	19,682	43,711	31,296
1p78(b),1p66	Less non-current portion: loans to related parties	(2,322)	(1,352)	–	–
1p66	**Current portion**	**19,765**	**18,330**	**43,711**	**31,296**

All non-current receivables are due within five years from the end of the reporting period.

The fair values of trade and other receivables are as follows:

IFRS7p25

	Group		Company	
	2013	2012 Restated	2013	2012
Trade receivables	18,065	17,102	–	–
Receivables from related parties	104	86	43,711	31,296
Loans to related parties	2,722	1,398	–	–
	20,891	18,586	43,711	31,296

IFRS13p93(b),(d), IFRS13p97 — The fair values of loans to related parties are based on cash flows discounted using a rate based on the borrowings rate of 7.5% (2012: 7.2%). The discount rate equals to LIBOR plus appropriate credit rating. The fair values are within level 2 of the fair value hierarchy.

IFRS GAAP plc – year ended 31 December 2013

(All amounts in C thousands unless otherwise stated)

24p18(b)(i) The effective interest rates on non-current receivables were as follows:

	2013	2012
Loans to related parties (note 41)	6.5-7%	6.5-7%

IFRS7p14 Certain European subsidiaries of the group transferred receivable balances amounting to C1,014 to a bank in exchange for cash during the year ended 31 December 2013. The transaction has been accounted for as a collateralised borrowing (note 31). In case the entities default under the loan agreement, the bank has the right to receive the cash flows from the receivables transferred. Without default, the entities will collect the receivables and allocate new receivables as collateral.

DV As of 31 December 2013, trade receivables of C17,670 (2012: C16,823) were fully performing.

IFRS7p37(a) As of 31 December 2013, trade receivables of C277 (2012: C207) were past due but not impaired. These relate to a number of independent customers for whom there is no recent history of default. The ageing analysis of these trade receivables is as follows:

	2013	2012 Restated
Up to 3 months	177	108
3 to 6 months	100	99
	277	207

IFRS7p37(b) As of 31 December 2013, trade receivables of C227 (2012: C142) were impaired. The amount of the provision was C109 as of 31 December 2013 (2012: C70). The individually impaired receivables mainly relate to wholesalers, which are in unexpectedly difficult economic situations. It was assessed that a portion of the receivables is expected to be recovered. The ageing of these receivables is as follows:

	2013	2012 Restated
3 to 6 months	177	108
Over 6 months	50	34
	227	142

The carrying amounts of the group's trade and other receivables are denominated in the following currencies:

	2013	2012 Restated
UK pound	9,846	8,669
Euros	5,987	6,365
US dollar	6,098	4,500
Other currencies	156	148
	22,087	19,682

(All amounts in C thousands unless otherwise stated)

IFRS7p16   Movements on the group provision for impairment of trade receivables are as follows:

	2013	2012 Restated
At 1 January	70	38
Provision for receivables impairment	74	61
Receivables written off during the year as uncollectible	(28)	(23)
Unused amounts reversed	(10)	(8)
Unwind of discount	3	2
At 31 December	**109**	**70**

IFRS7p20(e) applies to "Provision for receivables impairment" row.

The creation and release of provision for impaired receivables have been included in 'other expenses' in the income statement (note 9a). Unwind of discount is included in 'finance costs' in the income statement (note 11). Amounts charged to the allowance account are generally written off, when there is no expectation of recovering additional cash.

IFRS7p16   The other classes within trade and other receivables do not contain impaired assets.

IFRS7p36(a)   The maximum exposure to credit risk at the reporting date is the carrying value of each class of receivables mentioned above. The group does not hold any collateral as security.

Company

IFRS7p25   The fair value of trade and other receivables is as follows:

	Company	
	2013	2012
Receivables from related parties	43,711	31,296
	43,711	31,296

DV   As of 31 December 2013, company receivables from related parties of C14,120 (2012: 16,279) were fully performing.

IFRS7p37(a), IFRS7p36(c)   As of 31 December 2013, receivables of C27,027 (2012: C15,017) were past due but not impaired. These relate to subsidiary undertakings for which there is no history of default. The ageing analysis of these trade receivables is as follows:

	2013	2012
3 to 6 months	27,027	15,017
	27,027	15,017

IFRS7p31, 34(c)   The carrying amounts of the company's receivables are denominated in the following currencies:

	2013	2012
UK pound	43,711	31,296
	43,711	31,296

22 Inventories

	Group	2013	2012 Restated
2p36(b), 1p78(c)	Raw materials	7,622	7,612
	Work in progress	1,810	1,796
	Finished goods[1]	15,268	8,774
		24,700	18,182

2p36(d), p38 — The cost of inventories recognised as an expense and included in 'cost of sales' amounted to C60,252 (2012:C29,545).

2p36(f-g) — The group reversed C603 of a previous inventory write-down in July 2013. The group has sold all the goods that were written down to an independent retailer in Australia at original cost. The amount reversed has been included in 'cost of sales' in the income statement.

23 Financial assets at fair value through profit or loss

	Group	2013	2012
IFRS7p8(a), p31, p34(c)	Listed securities – held for trading		
	– Equity securities – UK	5,850	3,560
	– Equity securities – Europe	4,250	3,540
	– Equity securities – US	1,720	872
		11,820	7,972

7p15 — Financial assets at fair value through profit or loss are presented within 'operating activities' as part of changes in working capital in the statement of cash flows (note 36).

IFRS7p20 — Changes in fair values of financial assets at fair value through profit or loss are recorded in 'other (losses)/gains – net' in the income statement (note 8).

IFRS13p91 — The fair value of all equity securities is based on their current bid prices in an active market.

24 Cash and cash equivalents

	Group		Company	
	2013	2012 Restated	2013	2012
Cash at bank and in hand	8,398	28,648	3,261	6,234
Short-term bank deposits	9,530	5,414	–	–
Cash and cash equivalents (excluding bank overdrafts)	17,928	34,062	3,261	6,234

[1] Separate disclosure of finished goods at fair value less cost to sell is required, where applicable.

(All amounts in C thousands unless otherwise stated)

7p45 Cash and cash equivalents include the following for the purposes of the statement of cash flows:

	Group		Company	
	2013	2012 Restated	2013	2012
Cash and cash equivalents	17,928	34,062	3,261	6,234
Bank overdrafts (note 31)	(2,650)	(6,464)	–	–
Cash and cash equivalents	15,278	27,598	3,261	6,234

7p8 applies to the Bank overdrafts row.

25 Non-current assets held for sale and discontinued operations

Group

IFRS5p41 (a)(b)(d) The assets and liabilities related to Shoes Limited (part of the UK wholesale segment) have been presented as held for sale following the approval of the group's management and shareholders on 23 September 2013 to sell Shoes Limited in the UK. The completion date for the transaction is expected by May 2014.

	2013	2012
Operating cash flows[1]	300	190
Investing cash flows[1]	(103)	(20)
Financing cash flows[1]	(295)	(66)
Total cash flows	**(98)**	**104**

(IFRS5p33(c) applies to each of the three cash flow lines.)

IFRS5p38 *(a) Assets of disposal group classified as held for sale*

	2013	2012
Property, plant and equipment	1,563	–
Goodwill	100	–
Other intangible assets	1,000	–
Inventory	442	–
Other current assets	228	–
Total	**3,333**	**–**

IFRS5p38 *(b) Liabilities of disposal group classified as held for sale*

	2013	2012
Trade and other payables	104	–
Other current liabilities	20	–
Provisions	96	–
Total	**220**	**–**

---

[1] Under this approach, the entity presents the statement of cash flows as if no discontinued operation has occurred and makes the required IFRS5p33 disclosures in the notes. It would also be acceptable to present the three categories separately on the face of the statement of cash flows and present the line-by-line breakdown of the categories, either in the notes or on the face of the statement of cash flows. It would not be acceptable to present all cash flows from discontinued operations in one line either as investing or operating activity.

IFRS GAAP plc – year ended 31 December 2013

(All amounts in C thousands unless otherwise stated)

IFRS13p 93(a),(b),(d)	In accordance with IFRS 5, the assets and liabilities held for sale were written down to their fair value less costs to sell of C3,113,000. This is a non-recurring fair value which has been measured using observable inputs, being the prices for recent sales of similar businesses, and is therefore within level 2 of the fair value hierarchy. The fair value has been measured by calculating the ratio of transaction price to annual revenue for the similar businesses and applying the average to Shoes Limited.

IFRS5p33(b) Analysis of the result of discontinued operations,[1] and the result recognised on the re-measurement of assets or disposal group is as follows:[2]

		2013	2012
	Revenue	1,200	1,150
	Expenses	(960)	(950)
	Profit before tax of discontinued operations	240	200
12p81(h)(ii)	Tax	(96)	(80)
	Profit after tax of discontinued operations	144	120
	Pre-tax gain/(loss) recognised on the re-measurement of assets of disposal group	(73)	–
12p81(h)(ii)	Tax	29	–
	After tax gain/(loss) recognised on the re-measurement of assets of disposal group	(44)	–
	Profit for the year from discontinued operations	100	120

26 Share capital and premium

		Number of shares (thousands)	Ordinary shares	Share premium	Total
1p79	At 1 January 2012	20,000	20,000	10,424	30,424
	Employee share option scheme:				
1p106(d)(iii)	– Proceeds from shares issued	1,000	1,000	70	1,070
	At 31 December 2012	21,000	21,000	10,494	31,494
	Employee share option scheme:				
1p106(d)(iii)	– Proceeds from shares issued	750	750	200	950
IFRS3p B64(f)(iv)	Acquisition of subsidiary (note 39)	3,550	3,550	6,450	10,000
1p79(a)	**At 31 December 2013**	25,300	25,300	17,144	42,444

1p79(a) The company acquired 875,000 of its own shares through purchases on the EuroMoney stock exchange on 18 April 2013. The total amount paid to acquire the shares, net of income tax, was C2,564. The shares are held as 'treasury shares'.[3] The company has the right to re-issue these shares at a later date. All shares issued by the company were fully paid.

---

[1] IFRS 5 requires the separate presentation of any cumulative income or expense recognised in other comprehensive income relating to a non-current asset (or disposal group) classified as held for sale. There are no items recognised in equity relating to the disposal group classified as held-for-sale.

[2] These disclosures can also be given in the primary financial statements.

[3] Treasury shares should be accounted for in accordance with local company law and practice. Treasury shares may be disclosed separately on the balance sheet or deducted from retained earnings or a specific reserve. Depending on local company law, the company could have the right to resell the treasury shares.

(All amounts in C thousands unless otherwise stated)

The group issued 3,550,000 shares on 1 March 2013 14% of the total ordinary share capital issued) to the shareholders of ABC Group as part of the purchase consideration for 70% of its ordinary share capital. The ordinary shares issued have the same rights as the other shares in issue. The fair value of the shares issued amounted to C10,050 (C2.83 per share). The related transaction costs amounting to C50 have been netted off with the deemed proceeds.

27 Share-based payments

IFRS2p45(a) Share options are granted to directors and to selected employees. The exercise price of the granted options is equal to the market price of the shares less 15% on the date of the grant. Options are conditional on the employee completing three years' service (the vesting period). The options are exercisable starting three years from the grant date, subject to the group achieving its target growth in earnings per share over the period of inflation plus 4%, the options have a contractual option term of five years. The group has no legal or constructive obligation to repurchase or settle the options in cash.

Movements in the number of share options outstanding and their related weighted average exercise prices are as follows:

		2013		2012	
		Average exercise price in C per share option	Options (thousands)	Average exercise price in C per share option	Options (thousands)
IFRS2p45(b)(i)	At 1 January	1.73	4,744	1.29	4,150
IFRS2p45(b)(ii)	Granted	2.95	964	2.38	1,827
IFRS2p 45(b)(iii)	Forfeited	2.30	(125)	0.80	(33)
IFRS2p 45(b)(iv)	Exercised	1.28	(750)	1.08	(1,000)
IFRS2p45(b)(v)	Expired	0.00	–	2.00	(200)
IFRS2p 45(b)(vi)	At 31 December	2.03	4,833	1.73	4,744

IFRS2p45 (b)(vii), IFRS2p45(c)

Out of the 4,833,000 outstanding options (2012: 4,744,000 options), 1,875,000 options (2012: 1,400,000) were exercisable. Options exercised in 2013 resulted in 750,000 shares (2012: 1,000,000 shares) being issued at a weighted average price of C1.28 each (2012: C1.08 each). The related weighted average share price at the time of exercise was C2.85 (2012: C2.65) per share. The related transaction costs amounting to C10 (2012: C10) have been netted off with the proceeds received.

(All amounts in C thousands unless otherwise stated)

IFRS2p45(d) Share options outstanding at the end of the year have the following expiry date and exercise prices:

Grant-vest	Expiry date – 1 July	Exercise price in C per share options	Share options (thousands) 2013	2012
2008-11	2013	1.10	–	500
2009-12	2014	1.20	800	900
2010-13	2015	1.35	1,075	1,250
2011-14	2016	2.00	217	267
2012-15	2017	2.38	1,777	1,827
2013-16	2018	2.95	964	–
			4,833	4,744

IFRS2p46, p47(a) The weighted average fair value of options granted during the period determined using the Black-Scholes valuation model was C0.86 per option (2012: C0.66). The significant inputs into the model were weighted average share price of C3.47 (2012: C2.80) at the grant date, exercise price shown above, volatility of 30% (2012: 27%), dividend yield of 4.3% (2012: 3.5%), an expected option life of three years (2012: 3 years) and an annual risk-free interest rate of 5% (2012: 4%). The volatility measured at the standard deviation of continuously compounded share returns is based on statistical analysis of daily share prices over the last three years. See note 10(a) for the total expense recognised in the income statement for share options granted to directors and employees.

28 Retained earnings

		Group	Company
1p106(d)	At 1 January 2012 (Restated)	51,125	16,036
	Profit for the year	16,304	10,491
1p106(d)	Dividends paid relating to 2011	(15736)	(15,736)
IFRS2p50	Value of employee services[1]	822	822
16p41	Depreciation transfer on land and buildings net of tax	87	–
12p68C	Tax credit relating to share option scheme	20	–
19Rp120(c)	Remeasurements of post employment benefit liabilities net of tax	(637)	–
	At 31 December 2012 (Restated)	51,985	11,613
1p106(d)	At 1 January 2013	51,985	11,613
	Profit for the year	31,874	9,098
1p106(d)	Dividends paid relating to 2012	(10,102)	(10,102)
IFRS2p50	Value of employee services[1]	690	690
16p41	Depreciation transfer on land and buildings net of tax	80	–
	Revaluation transfer on disposal of land and buildings	20	–
12p68C	Tax credit relating to share option scheme	30	–
19Rp120(c)	Remeasurements of post employment benefit liabilities net of tax	83	–
12p81(a),(b)	Impact of change in Euravian tax rate on deferred tax	(10)	–
	At 31 December 2013	74,650	11,299

[1] The credit entry to equity in respect of the IFRS 2 charge should be recorded in accordance with local company law and practice. This may be a specific reserve, retained earnings or share capital.

(All amounts in C thousands unless otherwise stated)

29 Other reserves

	Group	Note	Convertible bond	Land and buildings revaluation[1]	Hedging	Treasury shares	Available-for-sale investments	Translation	Transactions with non-controlling interests	Total
	At 1 January 2012 (Restated)		–	1,152	65	–	1,320	3,827	–	6,364
16p39, 12p61A, 12p81(ae)	Revaluation of land and buildings – gross	16	–	1,133	–	–	–	–	–	1,133
12p61A, 12p81(ae)	Revaluation of land and buildings – tax	13	–	(374)	–	–	–	–	–	(374)
16p41	Depreciation transfer – gross		–	(130)	–	–	–	–	–	(130)
12p61A, 12p81(ae)	Depreciation transfer – tax		–	43	–	–	–	–	–	43
16p39, IFRS7p20(a)(ii)	Revaluation of AFS – gross		–	–	–	–	1,125	–	–	1,125
16p39, IFRS7p20(a)(ii)	Revaluation transfer AFS – gross	19	–	–	–	–	(152)	–	–	(152)
12p61A, 12p81(ae)	Revaluation of AFS – tax	13	–	–	–	–	(61)	–	–	(61)
28p39	Revaluation – associates	12	–	–	–	–	(14)	–	–	(14)
IFRS7p23(c)	Cash flow hedge: – Fair value gains in year		–	–	300	–	–	–	–	300
12p61,81(ae)	– Tax on fair value gains	13	–	–	(101)	–	–	–	–	(101)
IFRS7p23(d)	– Transfers to sales		–	–	(236)	–	–	–	–	(236)
12p61A, 81(ae)	– Tax on transfer to sales		–	–	79	–	–	–	–	79
IFRS7p23(e)	– Transfers to inventory		–	–	(67)	–	–	–	–	(67)
12p61, 12p81(ae)	– Tax on transfer to inventory	13	–	–	22	–	–	–	–	22
39p102(a)	Net investment hedge	20	–	–	–	–	–	40	–	40
21p52(b)	Currency translation differences – Group		–	–	–	–	–	(882)	–	(882)
28p39	Currency translation differences – Associates	12	–	–	–	–	–	105	–	105
	At 31 December 2012 (Restated)		–	1,824	62	–	2,218	3,090	–	7,194
16p39, 12p61A, 12p81(ae)	Revaluation of land and buildings – gross	16	–	1,005	–	–	–	–	–	1,005
12p61A, 12p81(ae)	Revaluation of land and buildings- tax	13	–	(250)	–	–	–	–	–	(250)
16p41	Depreciation transfer – gross		–	(129)	–	–	–	–	–	(129)

[1] An entity should disclose in its financial statements whether there are any restrictions on the distribution of the 'land and buildings' fair value reserve to the equity holders of the company (IAS16p77(f)).

(All amounts in C thousands unless otherwise stated)

	Group	Note	Convertible bond	Land and buildings revaluation	Hedging	Treasury shares	Available-for-sale investments	Translation	Transactions with non-controlling interests	Total
12p61A, 12p81(ae)	Depreciation transfer – tax		–	49	–	–	–	–	–	49
	Disposal of land and buildings		–	(20)	–	–	–	–	–	(20)
16p39, IFRS7p20(a)(ii)	Revaluation of AFS – gross	19	–	–	–	–	690	–	–	690
16p39, IFRS7p20(a)(ii)	Revaluation transfer AFS – gross	19	–	–	–	–	(130)	–	–	(130)
12p61A, 12p81(ae)	Revaluation of AFS – tax	13	–	–	–	–	(198)	–	–	(198)
28p39	Revaluation – associates	12	–	–	–	–	(12)	–	–	(12)
IFRS7p23(c)	Cash flow hedge: – Fair value gains in year		–	–	368	–	–	–	–	368
12p61,81(ae)	– Tax on fair value gains	13	–	–	(123)	–	–	–	–	(123)
IFRS7p23(d)	– Transfers to sales		–	–	(120)	–	–	–	–	(120)
12p61A, 81(ae)	– Tax on transfers to sales	13	–	–	40	–	–	–	–	40
IFRS7p23(e)	– Transfers to inventory		–	–	(151)	–	–	–	–	(151)
12p61, 12p81(ae)	– Tax on transfers to inventory	13	–	–	50	–	–	–	–	50
39p102(a)	Net investment hedge	20	–	–	–	–	–	(45)	–	(45)
21p52(b)	Currency translation differences – Group		–	–	–	–	–	2,149	–	2,149
28p39	Currency translation differences – Associates	12	–	–	–	–	–	(74)	–	(74)
28p39	Convertible bond – equity component	31	7,761	–	–	–	–	–	–	7,761
12p61A, 12p81(ae)	Tax on convertible bond[1]	13	(2,328)	–	–	–	–	–	–	(2,328)
	Purchase of treasury shares		–	–	–	(2,564)	–	–	–	(2,564)
1p106(d)(iii)	Acquisition of non-controlling interest in XYZ Group		–	–	–	–	–	–	(800)	(800)
1p106(d)(iii)	Decrease in ownership interest in Red Limited		–	–	–	–	–	–	100	100
IFRS3p59	Reclassification of revaluation of previously held interest in ABC Group		–	–	–	–	(850)	–	–	(850)
	At 31 December 2013		**5,433**	**2,479**	**126**	**(2,564)**	**1,718**	**5,120**	**(700)**	**11,612**

[1] Temporary taxable difference for the liability component of the convertible bond in accordance with paragraph 23 of IAS 12. It is assumed that the tax base on the convertible bond is not split between the debt and equity elements. If the tax base were split, this would impact the deferred tax position.

(All amounts in C thousands unless otherwise stated)

Other comprehensive income, net of tax

	Group	Other reserves	Retained earnings	Total	Non-controlling interests	Total other comprehensive income
DV	**31 December 2013**					
	Items that will not be reclassified to profit or loss					
16p39	Gains on revaluation of land and buildings	755	–	755	–	755
19p93A	Remeasurement of post employment benefit obligations	–	83	83	–	83
DV		755	83	838	–	838
DV	**Items that may be subsequently reclassified to profit or loss**					
	Change in value of available-for-sale financial assets	362	–	362	–	362
IFRS3p59	Reclassification of revaluation of previously held interest in ABC Group	(850)	–	(850)	–	(850)
	Share of other comprehensive income of associates	(86)	–	(86)	–	(86)
	Impact of change in Euravian tax rate on deferred tax	–	(10)	(10)	–	(10)
	Cash flow hedges	64	–	64	–	64
39p102(a)	Net investment hedge	(45)	–	(45)	–	(45)
21p52(b)	Currency translation differences	2,149	–	2,149	252	2,401
	Depreciation on land and buildings	(100)	100	–	–	–
DV		1,494	90	1,584	252	1,836
	Total	**2,249**	**173**	**2,422**	**252**	**2,674**
DV	**31 December 2012 (Restated)**					
	Items that will not be reclassified to profit or loss					
16p39	Gains on revaluation of land and buildings	759	–	759	–	759
19p93A	Remeasurement of post employment benefit obligations	–	(637)	(637)	–	(637)
DV		759	(637)	122	–	122
DV	**Items that may be subsequently reclassified to profit or loss**					
	Change in value of available-for-sale financial assets	912	–	912	–	912
28p39	Share of other comprehensive income of associates	91	–	91	–	91
	Cash flow hedges	(3)	–	(3)	–	(3)
39p102(a)	Net investment hedge	40	–	40	–	40
21p52(b)	Currency translation differences	(882)	–	(882)	(40)	(922)
	Depreciation on land and buildings	(87)	87	–	–	–
DV		71	87	158	(40)	118
	Total	**830**	**(550)**	**280**	**(40)**	**240**

IFRS GAAP plc – year ended 31 December 2013

(All amounts in C thousands unless otherwise stated)

> **1p106A** **PwC Commentary**
>
> Entities are allowed to show the disaggregation of changes in each component of equity arising from transactions recognised in other comprehensive income in either the statement of changes in equity or in the notes. In these illustrative financial statements, we present this information in the notes.

30 Trade and other payables

			Group		Company	
		Note	2013	2012 Restated	2013	2012
1p77	Trade payables		8,983	9,495	–	–
24p18	Amounts due to related parties	41	3,202	1,195	30,162	16,452
	Social security and other taxes		1,502	960	21	16
	Other liabilities – contingent consideration	39	1,500	–	1,500	–
	Accrued expenses		1,483	828	138	125
			16,670	12,478	31,821	16,593

31 Borrowings

Group	2013	2012 Restated
Non-current		
Bank borrowings	32,193	40,244
Convertible bond	42,822	–
Debentures and other loans	3,300	18,092
Redeemable preference shares	30,000	30,000
Finance lease liabilities	6,806	8,010
	115,121	96,346
Current		
Bank overdraft (note 24)	2,650	6,464
Collaterised borrowings	1,014	–
Bank borrowings	3,368	4,598
Debentures and other loans	2,492	4,608
Finance lease liabilities	2,192	2,588
	11,716	18,258
Total borrowings	126,837	114,604

(a) Bank borrowings

IFRS7p31 Bank borrowings mature until 2017 and bear average coupons of 7.5% annually (2012: 7.4% annually).

IFRS7p14 Total borrowings include secured liabilities (bank and collateralised borrowings) of C37,680 (2012: C51,306). Bank borrowings are secured by the land and buildings of the group (note 16). Collaterised borrowings are secured by trade receivables (note 21).

IFRS7p31 The exposure of the group's borrowings to interest rate changes and the contractual re-pricing dates at the end of the reporting period are as follows:

	2013	2012 Restated
6 months or less	10,496	16,748
6-12 months	36,713	29,100
1-5 years	47,722	38,555
Over 5 years	31,906	30,201
	126,837	114,604

The carrying amounts and fair value of the non-current borrowings are as follows:

IFRS7p25

	Carrying amount		Fair value	
	2013	2012 Restated	2013	2012 Restated
Bank borrowings	32,193	40,244	32,590	39,960
Redeemable preference shares	30,000	30,000	28,450	28,850
Debentures and other loans	3,300	18,092	3,240	17,730
Convertible bond	42,822	–	42,752	–
Finance lease liabilities	6,806	8,010	6,205	7,990
Total	115,121	96,346	113,237	94,530

IFRS13p93(b), (d), IFRS13p97, IFRS7p25

The fair value of current borrowings equals their carrying amount, as the impact of discounting is not significant. The fair values are based on cash flows discounted using a rate based on the borrowing rate of 7.5% (2012: 7.2%) and are within level 2 of the fair value hierarchy.

IFRS7p31, IFRS7p34(c)

The carrying amounts of the group's borrowings are denominated in the following currencies:

	2013	2012 Restated
UK pound	80,100	80,200
Euro	28,353	16,142
US dollar	17,998	17,898
Other currencies	386	364
Total	126,837	114,604

7p50(a) DV

The group has the following undrawn borrowing facilities:

	2013	2012 Restated
Floating rate:		
Expiring within one year	6,150	4,100
Expiring beyond one year	14,000	8,400
Fixed rate:		
Expiring within one year	18,750	12,500
Total	38,900	25,000

(All amounts in C thousands unless otherwise stated)

IFRS7p17, 1p79(b)

The facilities expiring within one year are annual facilities subject to review at various dates during 2013. The other facilities have been arranged to help finance the proposed expansion of the group's activities in Europe.

(b) Convertible bonds

32p28, 32p31, 1p79(b)

The company issued 500,000 5.0% convertible bonds at a par value of C50 million[1] on 2 January 2013. The bonds mature five years from the issue date at their nominal value of C50 million or can be converted into shares at the holder's option at the maturity date at the rate of 33 shares per C5,000. The values of the liability component and the equity conversion component were determined at issuance of the bond.

The convertible bond recognised in the balance sheet is calculated as follows:

	2013	2012
Face value of convertible bond issued on 2 January 2013	50,000	–
Equity component (note 29)	(7,761)	–
Liability component on initial recognition at 2 January 2013	42,239	–
Interest expense (note 11)	3,083	–
Interest paid	(2,500)	–
Liability component at 31 December 2013	**42,822**	**–**

12AppxBEx4

IFRS13p93(b), (d), IFRS13p97

The fair value of the liability component of the convertible bond at 31 December 2013 amounted to C42,617. The fair value is calculated using cash flows discounted at a rate based on the borrowings rate of 7.5% and are within level 2 of the fair value hierarchy.

(c) Redeemable preference shares

32p15, 32p18(a)

The group issued 30 million cumulative redeemable preference shares with a par value of C1 per share on 4 January 2012. The shares are mandatorily redeemable at their par value on 4 January 2016, and pay dividends at 6.5% annually.

10p21

On 1 February 2014, the group issued C6,777 6.5% US dollar bonds to finance its expansion programme and working capital requirements in the US. The bonds are repayable on 31 December 2017.

(d) Finance lease liabilities

Lease liabilities are effectively secured as the rights to the leased asset revert to the lessor in the event of default.

17p31(b)

	2013	2012
Gross finance lease liabilities– minimum lease payments:		
No later than 1 year	2,749	3,203
Later than 1 year and no later than 5 years	6,292	7,160
Later than 5 years	2,063	2,891
	11,104	13,254
Future finance charges on finance lease liabilities	(2,106)	(2,656)
Present value of finance lease liabilities	**8,998**	**10,598**

[1] This amount is not in C thousands.

(All amounts in C thousands unless otherwise stated)

17p31(b) The present value of finance lease liabilities is as follows:

	2013	2012
No later than 1 year	**2,192**	2,588
Later than 1 year and no later than 5 years	**4,900**	5,287
Later than 5 years	**1,906**	2,723
	8,998	10,598

32 Deferred income tax

The analysis of deferred tax assets and deferred tax liabilities is as follows:

Group	2013	2012 Restated
Deferred tax assets:		
– Deferred tax assets to be recovered after more than 12 months	**(2,899)**	(3,319)
– Deferred tax asset to be recovered within 12 months	**(647)**	(64)
	(3,546)	(3,383)
Deferred tax liabilities:		
– Deferred tax liability to be recovered after more than 12 months	**10,743**	8,016
– Deferred tax liability to be recovered within 12 months	**1,627**	1,037
	12,370	9,053
Deferred tax liabilities (net)	**8,824**	5,670

1p61 (applies to Deferred tax assets section)

The gross movement on the deferred income tax account is as follows:

	2013	2012 Restated
At 1 January	5,670	3,047
Exchange differences	(2,003)	(154)
Acquisition of subsidiary (note 39)	1,953	–
Income statement charge (note 13)	379	2,635
Tax charge /(credit) relating to components of other comprehensive income (note 13)	527	162
Tax charged/(credited) directly to equity (note 13)	2,298	(20)
At 31 December	**8,824**	5,670

(All amounts in C thousands unless otherwise stated)

12p81(g)(i)(ii) The movement in deferred income tax assets and liabilities during the year, without taking into consideration the offsetting of balances within the same tax jurisdiction, is as follows:

Deferred tax liabilities	Accelerated tax depreciation	Fair value gains	Convertible bond	Other	Total
At 1 January 2012 (Restated)	6,412	413	–	284	7,109
Charged/(credited) to the income statement	1,786	–	–	799	2,585
Charged/(credited) to other comprehensive income	–	435	–	–	435
Exchange difference	(100)	–	–	(54)	(154)
At 31 December 2012 (Restated)	8,098	848	–	1,029	9,975
Charged/(credited) to the income statement	425	–	(193)	388	620
Charged/(credited)/charged to other comprehensive income	–	448	–	43	491
Charged directly to equity	–	–	2,328	–	2,328
Acquisition of subsidiary	553	1,125	–	275	1,953
Exchange difference	(333)	(600)	–	(350)	(1,283)
At 31 December 2013	8,743	1,821	2,135	1,385	14,084

12p81(g)(ii) applies to rows "Charged/(credited) to the income statement"; 12p81(e) to OCI rows; 12p81(a) to equity rows; 12p81(g)(i) to balance rows.

Deferred tax assets	Retirement benefit obligation	Provisions	Impairment losses	Tax losses	Other	Total
At 1 January 2012 (Restated)	(428)	(997)	(732)	(1,532)	(373)	(4,062)
Charged/(credited) to the income statement	–	181	–	–	(131)	50
Charged/(credited) to other comprehensive income	(273)	–	–	–	–	(273)
Charged/(credited) directly to equity	–	–	–	–	(20)	(20)
Exchange difference	–	–	–	–	–	–
At 31 December 2012 (Restated)	(701)	(816)	(732)	(1,532)	(524)	(4,305)
Charged/(credited) to the income statement	–	(538)	(322)	750	(131)	(241)
Charged/(credited) to other comprehensive income	36	–	–	–	–	36
Charged/(credited) directly to equity	–	–	–	–	(30)	(30)
Exchange difference	(150)	(280)	(210)	–	(80)	(720)
At 31 December 2012	(815)	(1,634)	(1,264)	(782)	(765)	(5,260)

12p81(e) Deferred income tax assets are recognised for tax loss carry-forwards to the extent that the realisation of the related tax benefit through future taxable profits is probable. The group did not recognise deferred income tax assets of C333 (2012: C1,588) in respect of losses amounting to C1,000 (2012: C5,294) that can be carried forward

(All amounts in C thousands unless otherwise stated)

against future taxable income. Losses amounting to C900 (2012: C5,294) and C100 (2012: nil) expire in 2014 and 2015 respectively.

12p81(f) Deferred income tax liabilities of C3,141 (2012: C2,016) have not been recognised for the withholding tax and other taxes that would be payable on the unremitted earnings of certain subsidiaries. Such amounts are permanently reinvested. Unremitted earnings totalled C30,671 at 31 December 2013 (2012: C23,294).

33 Post-employment benefits

Group

The table below outlines where the group's post-employment amounts and activity are included in the financial statements.

	2013	2012 Restated
Balance sheet obligations for:		
– Defined pension benefits	3,684	1,900
– Post-employment medical benefits	1,432	711
Liability in the balance sheet	**5,116**	**2,611**
Income statement charge included in operating profit for[1]:		
– Defined pension benefits	948	561
– Post-employment medical benefits	184	119
	1,132	680
Remeasurements for:		
– Defined pension benefits	(84)	717
– Post-employment medical benefits	(35)	193
	(119)	910

33(a) Defined benefit pension plans

DV, 19Rp136, 19Rp138, 19Rp139

The group operates defined benefit pension plans in the UK and US under broadly similar regulatory frameworks. All of the plans are final salary pension plans, which provide benefits to members in the form of a guaranteed level of pension payable for life. The level of benefits provided depends on members' length of service and their salary in the final years leading up to retirement. In the UK plans, pensions in payment are generally updated in line with the retail price index, whereas in the US plans, pensions generally do not receive inflationary increases once in payment. With the exception of this inflationary risk in the UK, the plans face broadly similar risks, as described below. The majority of benefit payments are from trustee-administered funds; however, there are also a number of unfunded plans where the company meets the benefit payment obligation as it falls due. Plan assets held in trusts are governed by local regulations and practice in each country, as is the nature of the relationship between the group and the trustees (or equivalent) and their composition. Responsibility for governance of the plans – including investment decisions and contribution schedules – lies jointly with the company and the board of trustees. The board of trustees must be composed of representatives of the company and plan participants in accordance with the plan's regulations.

---

[1] The income statement charge included within operating profit includes current service cost, interest cost, past service costs and gains and losses on settlement and curtailment.

IFRS GAAP plc – year ended 31 December 2013

(All amounts in C thousands unless otherwise stated)

19Rp140(a) The amounts recognised in the balance sheet are determined as follows:

	2013	2012 Restated
Present value of funded obligations	**6,155**	2,943
Fair value of plan assets	**(5,211)**	(2,797)
Deficit of funded plans	**944**	146
Present value of unfunded obligations	**2,426**	1,549
Total deficit of defined benefit pension plans	**3,370**	1,695
Impact of minimum funding requirement/asset ceiling	**314**	205
Liability in the balance sheet	**3,684**	**1,900**

19Rp140(a), 141(a-h) The movement in the defined benefit obligation over the year is as follows:

	Present value of obligation	Fair value of plan assets	Total	Impact of minimum funding requirement/ asset ceiling	Total
At 1 January 2012 (Restated)	3,479	(2,264)	1,215	120	1,335
Current service cost	498	–	498	–	498
Interest expense/(income)	214	(156)	58	5	63
	712	(156)	556	5	561
Remeasurements:					
– Return on plan assets, excluding amounts included in interest expense/(income)	–	(85)	(85)	–	(85)
– (Gain)/loss from change in demographic assumptions	20	–	20	–	20
– (Gain)/loss from change in financial assumptions	61	–	61	–	61
– Experience (gains)/losses	641	–	641	–	641
– Change in asset ceiling, excluding amounts included in interest expense	0	–	–	80	80
	722	(85)	637	80	717
Exchange differences	(324)	22	(302)	–	(302)
Contributions:					
– Employers	–	(411)	(411)	–	(411)
– Plan participants	30	(30)	–	–	–
Payments from plans:					
– Benefit payments	(127)	127	–	–	–
At 31 December 2012 (Restated)	4,492	(2,797)	1,695	205	1,900

(All amounts in C thousands unless otherwise stated)

	Present value of obligation	Fair value of plan assets	Total	Impact of minimum funding requirement/ asset ceiling	Total
At 1 January 2013	4,492	(2,797)	1,695	205	1,900
Current service cost	751	–	751	–	751
Interest expense/(income)	431	(308)	123	9	132
Past service cost and gains and losses on settlements	65	–	65	–	65
	1,247	(308)	939	9	948
Remeasurements:					
– Return on plan assets, excluding amounts included in interest expense/(income)	–	(187)	(187)	–	(187)
– (Gain)/loss from change in demographic assumptions	32	–	32	–	32
– (Gain)/loss from change in financial assumptions	121	–	121	–	121
– Experience (gains)/losses	(150)	–	(150)	–	(150)
– Change in asset ceiling, excluding amounts included in interest expense	–	–	–	100	100
	3	(187)	(184)	100	(84)
Exchange differences	(61)	(25)	(86)	–	(86)
Contributions:					
– Employers	–	(908)	(908)	–	(908)
– Plan participants	55	(55)	–	–	–
Payments from plans:					
– Benefit payments	(566)	566	–	–	–
– Settlements	(280)	280	–	–	–
Acquired in a business combination	3,691	(1,777)	1,914	–	1,914
At 31 December 2013	8,581	(5,211)	3,370	314	3,684

19Rp141 One of our US plans has a surplus that is not recognised on the basis that future economic benefits are not available to the entity in the form of a reduction in future contributions or a cash refund.

19Rp139 (c) In connection with the closure of a factory, a curtailment loss was incurred and a settlement arrangement agreed with the plan trustees, effective December 30, 2012, which settled all retirement benefit plan obligations relating to the employees of that factory.

IFRS GAAP plc – year ended 31 December 2013

(All amounts in C thousands unless otherwise stated)

DV   The defined benefit obligation and plan assets are composed by country as follows:

	2013			2012 Restated		
	UK	US	Total	UK	US	Total
Present value of obligation	4,366	4,215	8,581	3,442	1,050	4,492
Fair value of plan assets	(3,109)	(2,102)	(5,211)	(2,403)	(394)	(2,797)
	1,257	2,113	3,370	1,039	656	1,695
Impact of minimum funding requirement/asset ceiling	–	314	314	–	205	205
Total	1,257	2,427	3,684	1,039	861	1,900

As at the last valuation date, the present value of the defined benefit obligation was comprised of approximately C3,120 relating to active employees, C3,900 relating to deferred members and C1,560 relating to members in retirement.

19Rp144   The significant actuarial assumptions were as follows:

	2013		2012	
	UK	US	UK	US
Discount rate	5.1%	5.2%	5.5%	5.6%
Inflation	3.0%	4.0%	3.5%	4.2%
Salary growth rate	4.0%	4.5%	4.5%	4.0%
Pension growth rate	3.0%	2.8%	3.1%	2.7%

Assumptions regarding future mortality are set based on actuarial advice in accordance with published statistics and experience in each territory. These assumptions translate into an average life expectancy in years for a pensioner retiring at age 65:

	2013		2012	
	UK	US	UK	US
Retiring at the end of the reporting period:				
– Male	22	20	22	20
– Female	25	24	25	24
Retiring 20 years after the end of the reporting period				
– Male	24	23	24	23
– Female	27	26	27	26

(All amounts in C thousands unless otherwise stated)

19Rp145(a) The sensitivity of the defined benefit obligation to changes in the weighted principal assumptions is:

	Impact on defined benefit obligation		
	Change in assumption	Increase in assumption	Decrease in assumption
Discount rate	0.50%	Decrease by 8.2%	Increase by 9.0%
Salary growth rate	0.50%	Increase by 1.8%	Decrease by 1.7%
Pension growth rate	0.25%	Increase by 4.7%	Decrease by 4.4%
		Increase by 1 year in assumption	Decrease by 1 year in assumption
Life expectancy		Increase by 2.8%	Decrease by 2.9%

19Rp145(b) The above sensitivity analyses are based on a change in an assumption while holding all other assumptions constant. In practice, this is unlikely to occur, and changes in some of the assumptions may be correlated. When calculating the sensitivity of the defined benefit obligation to significant actuarial assumptions the same method (present value of the defined benefit obligation calculated with the projected unit credit method at the end of the reporting period) has been applied as when calculating the pension liability recognised within the statement of financial position.

19Rp145(c) The methods and types of assumptions used in preparing the sensitivity analysis did not change compared to the previous period.

33(b) Post-employment medical benefits

DV, 19Rp144 The group operates a number of post-employment medical benefit schemes, principally in the US. The majority of these plans are unfunded. The method of accounting, significant assumptions and the frequency of valuations are similar to those used for defined benefit pension schemes set out above with the addition of actuarial assumptions relating to the long-term increase in healthcare costs of 8.0% a year (2012:7.6%) and claim rates of 6% (2012: 5.2%).

19Rp140(a) The amounts recognised in the balance sheet are determined as follows:

	2013	2012 Restated
Present value of funded obligations	727	350
Fair value of plan assets	(605)	(294)
Deficit of the funded plans	122	56
Present value of unfunded obligations	1,310	655
Liability in the balance sheet	**1,432**	**711**

(All amounts in C thousands unless otherwise stated)

19Rp140(a), 141(a-h) The movement in the defined benefit liability over the year is as follows:

	Present value of obligation	Fair value of plan assets	Total
At 1 January 2012 (Restated)	708	(207)	501
Current service cost	107	–	107
Interest expense/(income)	25	(13)	12
	132	(13)	119
Remeasurements:			
– Return on plan assets, excluding amounts included in interest expense/(income)	–	(11)	(11)
– (Gain)/loss from change in demographic assumptions	3	–	3
– (Gain)/loss from change in financial assumptions	7	–	7
– Experience (gains)/losses	194	–	194
	204	(11)	193
Exchange differences	(31)	2	(29)
Contributions/premiums paid:			
– Employers	–	(73)	(73)
Payments from plans:			
– Benefit payments	(8)	8	–
At 31 December 2012 (Restated)	1,005	(294)	711
At 1 January 2013	1,005	(294)	711
Current service cost	153	–	153
Interest expense/(income)	49	(18)	31
	202	(18)	184
Remeasurements:			
– Return on plan assets, excluding amounts included in interest expense/(income)	–	(33)	(33)
– (Gain)/loss from change in demographic assumptions	4	–	4
– (Gain)/loss from change in financial assumptions	10	–	10
– Experience (gains)/losses	(16)	–	(16)
	(2)	(33)	(35)
Exchange differences	37	(5)	32
Contributions/premiums paid:			
– Employers	–	(185)	(185)
Payments from plans:			
– Benefit payments	(7)	7	–
Acquired in a business combination (note 39)	802	(77)	725
At 31 December 2013	**2,037**	**(605)**	**1,432**

33(c) Post-employment benefits (pension and medical)

19Rp142 Plan assets are comprised as follows:

	2013				2012			
	Quoted	Unquoted	**Total**	%	Quoted	Unquoted	Total	%
Equity instruments			**1,824**	**31%**			1,216	39%
Information technology	502	–	502		994	–	994	
Energy	557	–	557		–	–	–	
Manufacturing	746	–	746		194	–	194	
Other	–	19	19		–	28	28	
Debt instruments			**2,161**	**37%**			571	18%
Government	916	–	916		321	–	321	
Corporate bonds (Investment grade)	900	–	900		99	–	99	
Corporate bonds (Non-investment grade)	68	277	345		41	110	151	
Property			**1,047**	**18%**			943	31%
in US	–	800	800		–	697	697	
in UK	–	247	247		–	246	246	
Qualifying insurance policies	–	496	**496**	**9%**	–	190	190	6%
Cash and cash equivalents	177	–	**177**	**3%**	94	–	94	3%
Investment funds	111	–	**111**	**2%**	77	–	77	2%
Total	**3,977**	**1,839**	**5,816**	**100%**	**1,820**	**1,271**	**3,091**	**100%**

19Rp143 Pension and medical plan assets include the company's ordinary shares with a fair value of C136 (2012: C126) and US real estate occupied by the group with a fair value of C612 (2012: C609).

19Rp139(b) Through its defined benefit pension plans and post-employment medical plans, the group is exposed to a number of risks, the most significant of which are detailed below:

Asset volatility — The plan liabilities are calculated using a discount rate set with reference to corporate bond yields; if plan assets underperform this yield, this will create a deficit. Both the UK and US plans hold a significant proportion of equities, which are expected to outperform corporate bonds in the long-term while providing volatility and risk in the short-term.

As the plans mature, the group intends to reduce the level of investment risk by investing more in assets that better match the liabilities. The first stage of this process was completed in FY12 with the sale of a number of equity holdings and purchase of a mixture of government and corporate bonds. The government bonds represent investments in UK and US government securities only. The corporate bonds are global securities with an emphasis on the UK and US.

However, the group believes that due to the long-term nature of the plan liabilities and the strength of the supporting group, a level of continuing equity investment is an appropriate element of the group's long term strategy to manage the plans efficiently. See below for more details on the group's asset-liability matching strategy.

Changes in bond yields — A decrease in corporate bond yields will increase plan liabilities, although this will be partially offset by an increase in the value of the plans' bond holdings.

(All amounts in C thousands unless otherwise stated)

	Inflation risk	The some of the group pension obligations are linked to inflation, and higher inflation will lead to higher liabilities (although, in most cases, caps on the level of inflationary increases are in place to protect the plan against extreme inflation). The majority of the plan's assets are either unaffected by (fixed interest bonds) or loosely correlated with (equities) inflation, meaning that an increase in inflation will also increase the deficit.
		In the US plans, the pensions in payment are not linked to inflation, so this is a less material risk.
	Life expectancy	The majority of the plans' obligations are to provide benefits for the life of the member, so increases in life expectancy will result in an increase in the plans' liabilities. This is particularly significant in the UK plan, where inflationary increases result in higher sensitivity to changes in life expectancy.
19Rp146		In case of the funded plans, the group ensures that the investment positions are managed within an asset-liability matching (ALM) framework that has been developed to achieve long-term investments that are in line with the obligations under the pension schemes. Within this framework, the Group's ALM objective is to match assets to the pension obligations by investing in long-term fixed interest securities with maturites that match the benefit payments as they fall due and in the appropriate currency. The company actively monitors how the duration and the expected yield of the investments are matching the expected cash outflows arising from the pension obligations. The group has not changed the processes used to manage its risks from previous periods. The group does not use derivatives to manage its risk. Investments are well diversified, such that the failure of any single investment would not have a material impact on the overall level of assets. A large portion of assets in 2013 consists of equities and bonds, although the group also invests in property, bonds, cash and investment (hedge) funds. The group believes that equities offer the best returns over the long term with an acceptable level of risk. The majority of equities are in a globally diversified portfolio of international blue chip entities, with a target of 60% of equities held in the UK and Europe, 30% in the US and the remainder in emerging markets.
19Rp147(a)		The group has agreed that it will aim to eliminate the pension plan deficit over the next nine years. Funding levels are monitored on an annual basis and the current agreed contribution rate is 14% of pensionable salaries in the UK and 12% in the US. The next triennial valuation is due to be completed as at 31 December 2014. The group considers that the contribution rates set at the last valuation date are sufficient to eliminate the deficit over the agreed period and that regular contributions, which are based on service costs, will not increase significantly.
19Rp147(b)		Expected contributions to post-employment benefit plans for the year ending 31 December 2014 are C1,150.
19Rp147(c)		The weighted average duration of the defined benefit obligation is 25.2 years.

IFRS GAAP plc – year ended 31 December 2013

181

(All amounts in C thousands unless otherwise stated)

19Rp147(c) Expected maturity analysis of undiscounted pension and post-employment medical benefits:

At 31 December 2013	Less than a year	Between 1-2 years	Between 2-5 years	Over 5 years	Total
Pension benefits	628	927	2,004	21,947	25,506
Post-employment medical benefits	127	174	714	4,975	5,990
Total	**755**	**1,101**	**2,718**	**26,922**	**31,496**

34 Dividends per share

Group

1p107,
1p137(a),
10p12

The dividends paid in 2013 and 2012 were C10,102 (C0.48 per share) and C15,736 (C0.78 per share) respectively. A dividend in respect of the year ended 31 December 2013 of C0.51 per share, amounting to a total dividend of C12,945, is to be proposed at the annual general meeting on 30 April 2014. These financial statements do not reflect this dividend payable.

35 Provisions for other liabilities and charges

	Group	Environ-mental restoration	Restruc-turing	Legal claims	Profit-sharing and bonuses	Contingent liability arising on a business combination	Total
1p78(d)							
37p84(a)	At 1 January 2013 (restated)	842	–	828	1,000	–	2,670
	Charged/(credited) to the income statement:						
37p84(b)	– Additional provisions	316	1,986	2,405	500	–	5,207
	– On acquisition of ABC Group	–	–	–	–	1,000	1,000
37p84(d)	– Unused amounts reversed	(15)	–	(15)	(10)	–	(40)
37p84(e)	– Unwinding of discount	40	–	–	–	4	44
37p84(c)	Used during year	(233)	(886)	(3,059)	(990)	–	(5,168)
	Exchange differences	(7)	–	(68)	–	–	(75)
IFRS5p38	Transferred to disposal group classified as held for sale	(96)	–	–	–	–	(96)
37p84(a)	**At 31 December 2013**	**847**	**1,100**	**91**	**500**	**1,004**	**3,542**

	Analysis of total provisions:	2013	2012 Restated
1p69	Non-current	316	274
1p69	Current	3,226	2,396
	Total	**3,542**	**2,670**

(All amounts in C thousands unless otherwise stated)

(a) Environmental restoration

37p85(a(-(c) The group uses various chemicals in working with leather. A provision is recognised for the present value of costs to be incurred for the restoration of the manufacturing sites. It is expected that C531 will be used during 2014 and C316 during 2015. Total expected costs to be incurred are C880 (2012: C760).

DV The provision transferred to the disposal group classified as held for sale amounts to C96 and relates to an environmental restoration provision for Shoes Limited (part of the UK wholesale segment). See note 25 for further details regarding the disposal group held for sale.

(b) Restructuring

37p85(a)-(c) The reduction of the volumes assigned to manufacturing operations in Step-land (a subsidiary) will result in the reduction of a total of 155 jobs at two factories. An agreement was reached with the local union representatives, which specifies the number of staff involved and the voluntary redundancy compensation package offered by the group, as well as amounts payable to those made redundant, before the financial year-end. The estimated staff restructuring costs to be incurred are C799 at 31 December 2013 (note 10a). Other direct costs attributable to the restructuring, including lease termination, are C1,187. These costs were fully provided for in 2013. The provision of C1,100 at 31 December 2013 is expected to be fully utilised during the first half of 2014.

36p130 A goodwill impairment charge of C4,650 was recognised in the cash-generating unit relating to Step-land as a result of this restructuring (note 17).

(c) Legal claims

37p85(a)-(c) The amounts represent a provision for certain legal claims brought against the group by customers of the US wholesale segment. The provision charge is recognised in profit or loss within 'administrative expenses'. The balance at 31 December 2013 is expected to be utilised in the first half of 2014. In the directors' opinion, after taking appropriate legal advice, the outcome of these legal claims will not give rise to any significant loss beyond the amounts provided at 31 December 2013.

(d) Profit-sharing and bonuses

19p8(c),10, DV, 37p85(a)-(c) The provision for profit-sharing and bonuses is payable within three months of the finalisation of the audited financial statements.

(e) Recognised contingent liability

19p8(c),10, DV, 37p85(a)-(c) A contingent liability of C1,000 has been recognised on the acquisition of ABC Group for a pending lawsuit in which the entity is a defendant. The claim has arisen from a customer alleging defects on products supplied to them. It is expected that the courts will have reached a decision on this case by the end of 2014. The potential undiscounted amount of all future payments that the group could be required to make if there was an adverse decision related to the lawsuit is estimated to be between C500 and C1,500. As of 31 December 2013, there has been no change in the amount recognised (except for the unwinding of the discount of C4) for the liability at 31 March 2013, as there has been no change in the probability of the outcome of the lawsuit.

(All amounts in C thousands unless otherwise stated)

IFRS3B64(g) The selling shareholders of ABC Group have contractually agreed to indemnify IFRS GAAP plc for the claim that may become payable in respect of the above-mentioned lawsuit. An indemnification asset of C1,000, equivalent to the fair value of the indemnified liability, has been recognised by the group. The indemnification asset is deducted from consideration transferred for the business combination. As is the case with the indemnified liability, there has been no change in the amount recognised for the indemnification asset as at 31 December 2013, as there has been no change in the range of outcomes or assumptions used to develop the estimate of the liability.

36 Cash generated from operations

		Group		Company	
		2013	2012 Restated	**2013**	2012
7p18(b), 7p20	Profit before income tax including discontinued operations	**49,100**	25,837	**9,098**	10,491
	Adjustments for:				
	– Depreciation (note 16)	**17,754**	9,662	–	–
	– Amortisation (note 17)	**800**	565	–	–
	– Goodwill impairment charge (note 17)	**4,650**	–	–	–
	– (Profit)/loss on disposal of property, plant and equipment	**(17)**	8	–	–
	– Share-based payment	**690**	822	–	–
	– Post-employment benefits	**39**	196		
	– Fair value gains on derivative financial instruments (note 8)	**(86)**	(88)	–	–
	– Fair value (gains)/losses on financial assets at fair value through profit or loss (note 8)	**(85)**	238	–	–
	– Dividend income on available-for-sale financial assets (note 7)	**(1,100)**	(883)	**(13,809)**	(14,806)
	– Dividend income on financial assets at fair value through profit or loss (note 7)	**(800)**	(310)	–	–
	– Provision for restructuring cost	**1,100**	–		
	– Inventory write-down (note 6)	**3,117**	–		
	– Finance costs – net (note 11)	**6,443**	10,588	–	–
	– Share of loss/(profit) from joint ventures and associates (note 12)	**(1,682)**	(1,022)	–	–
	– Foreign exchange losses/(gains) on operating activities (note 8)	**277**	(200		
	Gains on revaluation of available-for-sale investments (note 7)	**(850)**	–	–	–
	Changes in working capital (excluding the effects of acquisition and exchange differences on consolidation):				
	– Inventories	**(3,073)**	(966)	–	–
	– Trade and other receivables	**1,203**	(2,429)	–	–
	– Financial assets at fair value through profit or loss	**(3,883)**	(858)	–	–
	– Trade and other payables	**1,154**	543	**18**	–
	Cash generated from operations	**74,751**	**41,703**	**(4,693)**	**(4,315)**

(All amounts in C thousands unless otherwise stated)

In the statement of cash flows, proceeds from sale of property, plant and equipment comprise:

Group	2013	2012
Net book amount (note 16)	6,337	2,987
Profit/(loss) on disposal of property, plant and equipment	17	(8)
Proceeds from disposal of property, plant and equipment	**6,354**	**2,979**

7p43

Non-cash transactions

The principal non-cash transaction is the issue of shares as consideration for the acquisition discussed in note 39.

37 Contingencies

Group

37p86

Since 2011, the Group has been defending an action brought by an environment agency in Europe. The group has disclaimed the liability.

No provision in relation to this claim has been recognised in these consolidated financial statements, as legal advice indicates that it is not probable that a significant liability will arise. Further claims for which provisions have been made are reflected in note 35.

38 Commitments

(a) Capital commitments

Capital expenditure contracted for at the end of the reporting period but not yet incurred is as follows:

	Group	2013	2012 Restated
16p74(c)	Property, plant and equipment	3,593	3,667
38p122(e)	Intangible assets	460	474
	Total	**4,053**	**4,141**

(b) Operating lease commitments – group company as lessee

17p35(d)

The group leases various retail outlets, offices and warehouses under non-cancellable operating lease agreements. The lease terms are between 5 and 10 years, and the majority of lease agreements are renewable at the end of the lease period at market rate.

17p35(d)

The group also leases various plant and machinery under cancellable operating lease agreements. The group is required to give a six-month notice for the termination of these agreements. The lease expenditure charged to the income statement during the year is disclosed in note 9.

(All amounts in C thousands unless otherwise stated)

17p35(a) The future aggregate minimum lease payments under non-cancellable operating leases are as follows:

Group	2013	2012 Restated
No later than 1 year	11,664	10,604
Later than 1 year and no later than 5 years	45,651	45,651
Later than 5 years	15,710	27,374
Total	**73,025**	**83,629**

39 Business combinations

IFRS3B64(a)(d) On 30 June 2012, the group acquired 15% of the share capital of ABC Group for C1,150. On 1 March 2013, the group acquired a further 56.73% of the share capital and obtained control of ABC Group, a shoe and leather goods retailer operating in the US and a wholesaler operating in most western European countries.

IFRS3B64(e) As a result of the acquisition, the group is expected to increase its presence in these markets. It also expects to reduce costs through economies of scale. The goodwill of C4,501 arising from the acquisition is attributable to acquired customer base and economies of scale expected from combining the operations of the group and ABC Group. None of the goodwill recognised is expected to be deductible for income tax purposes.

IFRS3B64(k) The following table summarises the consideration paid for ABC group, the fair value of assets acquired, liabilities assumed and the non-controlling interest at the acquisition date.

	Consideration at 1 March 2013	
IFRS3B64(f)(i), IFRS3B64(f)(iv)	Cash	4,050
IFRS3B64(f)(iii)	Equity instruments (3.55m ordinary shares)	10,000
IFRS3B64(g)(i)	Contingent consideration	1,000
IFRS3B64(f)	**Total consideration transferred**	**15,050**
	Indemnification asset	(1,000)
IFRS3B64(p)(i)	Fair value of equity interest in ABC Group held before the business combination	2,000
	Total consideration	**16,050**

IFRS GAAP plc – year ended 31 December 2013

(All amounts in C thousands unless otherwise stated)

IFRS3B64(i)	**Recognised amounts of identifiable assets acquired and liabilities assumed**	
	Cash and cash equivalents	300
	Property, plant and equipment (note 16)	67,784
	Trademarks (included in intangibles) (note 17)	2,500
	Licences (included in intangibles) (note 17)	1,500
	Available-for-sale financial assets (note 19)	473
	Inventories	459
	Trade and other receivables	585
	Trade and other payables	(11,409)
	Retirement benefit obligations:	
	– Pensions (note 33)	(1,914)
	– Other post-retirement obligations (note 33)	(725)
	Borrowings	(40,509)
	Contingent liability	(1,000)
	Deferred tax liabilities (note 32)	(1,953)
	Total identifiable net assets	**16,091**
IFRS3B64(o)(i)	Non-controlling interest	(4,542)
	Goodwill	4,501
	Total	**16,050**

IFRS3B64(m) — Acquisition-related costs of C200 have been charged to administrative expenses in the consolidated income statement for the year ended 31 December 2013.

IFRS3B 64 (f)(iv), IFRSB64(m) — The fair value of the 3,550 thousand ordinary shares issued as part of the consideration paid for ABC Group (C10,050) was based on the published share price on 1 March 2013. Issuance costs totalling C50 have been netted against the deemed proceeds.

IFRS3B 64(f)(iii), IFRS3B64(g), IFRS3B67(b) — The contingent consideration arrangement requires the group to pay, in cash, to the former owners of ABC Group, 10% of the average profit of ABC Group for three years from 2013 – 2015, in excess of C7,500, up to a maximum undiscounted amount of C2,500.

The potential undiscounted amount of all future payments that the group could be required to make under this arrangement is between C0 and C2,500.

The fair value of the contingent consideration arrangement of C1,000 was estimated by applying the income approach. The fair value estimates are based on a discount rate of 8% and assumed probability-adjusted profit in ABC Group of C10,000 to C20,000. This is a level 3 fair value measurement.

As of 31 December 2013, there was an increase of C500 recognised in the income statement for the contingent consideration arrangement, as the assumed probability-adjusted profit in ABC Group was recalculated to be approximately C20,000-30,000.

IFRS3B64(h) — The fair value of trade and other receivables is C585 and includes trade receivables with a fair value of C510. The gross contractual amount for trade receivables due is C960, of which C450 is expected to be uncollectible.

IFRS3B67(a) — The fair value of the acquired identifiable intangible assets of C4,000 (including trademarks and licences) is provisional pending receipt of the final valuations for those assets.

(All amounts in C thousands unless otherwise stated)

IFRS3B64(j), **IFRS3B67(c),** **37p84, 37p85**	A contingent liability of C1,000 has been recognised for a pending lawsuit in which ABC Group is a defendant. The claim has arisen from a customer alleging defects on products supplied to them. It is expected that the courts will have reached a decision on this case by the end of 2014. The potential undiscounted amount of all future payments that the group could be required to make if there was an adverse decision related to the lawsuit is estimated to be between C500 and C1,500. As of 31 December 2013, there has been no change in the amount recognised (except for unwinding of the discount C4) for the liability at 1 March 2013, as there has been no change in the range of outcomes or assumptions used to develop the estimates.
IFRS3B64(g), **IFRS3p57**	The selling shareholders of ABC Group have contractually agreed to indemnify IFRS GAAP plc for the claim that may become payable in respect of the above-mentioned lawsuit. An indemnification asset of C1,000, equivalent to the fair value of the indemnified liability, has been recognised by the group. The indemnification asset is deducted from consideration transferred for the business combination. As is the case with the indemnified liability, there has been no change in the amount recognised for the indemnification asset as at 31 December 2013, as there has been no change in the range of outcomes or assumptions used to develop the estimate of the liability.
IFRS3B64(o)	The fair value of the non-controlling interest in ABC Group, an unlisted company, was estimated by using the purchase price paid for acquisition of 55% stake in ABC group. This purchase price was adjusted for the lack of control and lack of marketability that market participants would consider when estimating the fair value of the non-controlling interest in ABC Group.
IFRS3B64(p)(ii)	The group recognised a gain of C850 as a result of measuring at fair value its 15% equity interest in ABC Group held before the business combination. The gain is included in other income in the group's statement of comprehensive income for the year ended 31 December 2013.
IFRS3B64(q)(i)	The revenue included in the consolidated statement of comprehensive income since 1 March 2013 contributed by ABC Group was C44,709. ABC Group also contributed profit of C12,762 over the same period.
IFRS3B64(q)(ii)	Had ABC Group been consolidated from 1 January 2013, the consolidated statement of income would show pro-forma revenue[1] of C220,345 and profit of C35,565.

---

[1] The information on combined revenue and profit does not represent actual results for the year and is therefore labelled as pro-forma.

IFRS GAAP plc – year ended 31 December 2013

40 Transactions with non-controlling interests

(a) Acquisition of additional interest in a subsidiary

IFRS12p18

On 21 April 2013, the company acquired the remaining 5% of the issued shares of XYZ group for a purchase consideration of C1,100. The group now holds 100% of the equity share capital of XYZ group. The carrying amount of the non-controlling interests in XYZ group on the date of acquisition was C300. The group derecognised non-controlling interests of C300 and recorded a decrease in equity attributable to owners of the parent of C800. The effect of changes in the ownership interest of XYZ group on the equity attributable to owners of the company during the year is summarised as follows:

	2013	2012
Carrying amount of non-controlling interests acquired	300	–
Consideration paid to non-controlling interests	(1,100)	–
Excess of consideration paid recognised in parent's equity	**(800)**	**–**

(b) Disposal of interest in a subsidiary without loss of control

IFRS12p18

On 5 September 2013, the company disposed of a 10% interest out of the 80% interest held in Red Limited at a consideration of C1,100. The carrying amount of the non-controlling interests in Red Limited on the date of disposal was C2,000 (representing 20% interest). This resulted in an increase in non-controlling interests of C1,000 and an increase in equity attributable to owners of the parent of C100. The effect of changes in the ownership interest of Red Limited on the equity attributable to owners of the company during the year is summarised as follows:

	31 December 2013	31 December 2012
Carrying amount of non-controlling interests disposed of	(1,000)	–
Consideration received from non-controlling interests	1,100	–
Increase in parent's equity	**100**	**–**

There were no transactions with non-controlling interests in 2012.

IFRS12p18

(c) Effects of transactions with non-controlling interests on the equity attributable to owners of the parent for the year ended 31 December 2013

	31 December 2013
Changes in equity attributable to shareholders of the company arising from:	
– Acquisition of additional interests in a subsidiary	(800)
– Disposal of interests in a subsidiary without loss of control	100
Net effect on parent's equity	**(700)**

41 Related parties

Group

1p138(c), 24p13

The group is controlled by M Limited (incorporated in the UK), which owns 57% of the company's shares. The remaining 43% of the shares are widely held. The group's ultimate parent is G Limited (incorporated in the UK). The group's ultimate controlling party is Mr Wong.

24p18, p19, p24

The following transactions were carried out with related parties:

24p18(a)

(a) Sales of goods and services

	2013	2012
Sale of goods:		
– Associates	1,002	204
– Associates of G Limited	121	87
Sales of services:		
– Ultimate parent (legal and administration services)	67	127
– Close family members of the ultimate controlling party (design services)	100	104
Total	**1,290**	**522**

Goods are sold based on the price lists in force and terms that would be available to third parties[1]. Sales of services are negotiated with related parties on a cost-plus basis, allowing a margin ranging from 15% to 30% (2012: 10% to 18%).

(b) Purchases of goods and services

24p18(a)

	2013	2012
Purchase of goods:		
– Associates	3,054	3,058
Purchase of services:		
– Entity controlled by key management personnel	83	70
– Immediate parent (management services)	295	268
Total	**3,432**	**3,396**

24p23

Goods and services are bought from associates and an entity controlled by key management personnel on normal commercial terms and conditions. The entity controlled by key management personnel is a firm belonging to Mr Chamois, a non-executive director of the company. Management services are bought from the immediate parent on a cost-plus basis, allowing a margin ranging from 15% to 30% (2012: 10% to 24%).

24p17

(c) Key management compensation

Key management includes directors (executive and non-executive), members of the Executive Committee, the Company Secretary and the Head of Internal Audit. The compensation paid or payable to key management for employee services is shown below:

---

[1] Management should disclose that related-party transactions were made on an arm's length basis only when such terms can be substantiated (24p23).

IFRS GAAP plc – year ended 31 December 2013

(All amounts in C thousands unless otherwise stated)

		2013	2012
24p17(a)	Salaries and other short-term employee benefits	2,200	1890
24p17(d)	Termination benefits	1,600	–
24p17(b)	Post-employment benefits	123	85
24p17(c)	Other long-term benefits	26	22
24p17(e)	Share-based payments	150	107
	Total	**4,099**	**2,104**

24p18(b)	In addition to the above amounts, the Group is committed to pay the members of the Executive Committee up to C1,250 in the event of a change in control of the Group.

CA06 s412 *(d) Directors*

		2013	2012
SI 2008/410, 5 Sch 1(1)(a)	Aggregate emoluments	860	661
SI 2008/410,5 Sch 1 (1)(b)	Aggregate gains made on the exercise of share options	311	157
SI 2008/410,5 Sch 1 (1)(c)	Aggregate amounts receivable under long-term incentive schemes	211	239
SI 2008/410, 5 Sch 1(1)(d)	Company contributions to money purchase pension scheme	72	0
	Total	**1,454**	**1,057**

24p18(b), 1p77 *(e) Year-end balances arising from sales/purchases of goods/services*

	2013	2012
Receivables from related parties (note 21):		
– Associates	26	32
– Associates of G Limited	24	8
– Ultimate parent	50	40
– Close family members of key management personnel	4	6
Payables to related parties (note 30):		
– Immediate parent	200	190
– Associates	2,902	1,005
– Entity controlled by key management personnel	100	–

The receivables from related parties arise mainly from sale transactions and are due two months after the date of sales. The receivables are unsecured in nature and bear no interest. No provisions are held against receivables from related parties (2012: nil).

The payables to related parties arise mainly from purchase transactions and are due two months after the date of purchase. The payables bear no interest.

IFRS GAAP plc – year ended 31 December 2013

(All amounts in C thousands unless otherwise stated)

24p18, 1p77   (f) Loans to related parties

	2013	2012
Loans to key management of the company (and their families)[1]:		
At 1 January	196	168
Loans advanced during year	343	62
Loan repayments received	(49)	(34)
Interest charged	30	16
Interest received	(30)	(16)
At 31 December	**490**	**196**
Loans to associates:		
At 1 January	1,192	1,206
Loans advanced during year	1,000	50
Loan repayments received	(14)	(64)
Interest charged	187	120
Interest received	(187)	(120)
At 31 December	**2,178**	**1,192**
Total loans to related parties:		
At 1 January	1,388	1,374
Loans advanced during year	1,343	112
Loan repayments received	(63)	(98)
Interest charged (note 11)	217	136
Interest received	(217)	(136)
At 31 December (note 21)	**2,668**	**1,388**

24p18(b)(i)   The loans advanced to key management have the following terms and conditions:

Name of key management	Amount of loan	Term	Interest rate
2013			
Mr Brown	173	Repayable monthly over 2 years	6.3%
Mr White	170	Repayable monthly over 2 years	6.3%
2012			
Mr Black	20	Repayable monthly over 2 years	6.5%
Mr White	42	Repayable monthly over 1 year	6.5%

IFRS7p15   Certain loans advanced to associates during the year amounting to C1,500 (2012: C500) are collateralised by shares in listed companies. The fair value of these shares was C65 at the end of the reporting period (2012: C590).

The loans to associates are due on 1 January 2014 and carry interest at 7.0% (2012:8%). The fair values and the effective interest rates of loans to associates are disclosed in note 21.

24p18(c)   No provision was required in 2013 (2012: nil) for the loans made to key management personnel and associates

---

[1] None of the loans made to members of key management has been made to directors.

(All amounts in C thousands unless otherwise stated)

24p19(a)	**Company**	
	The following transactions with subsidiaries occurred in the year.	

		2013	2012
24p18(a)	Dividends received	**13,809**	14,806

24p18(a), 24p18(b)   Treasury Limited, an indirect subsidiary of the company provided the company with additional cash funding of C13,210 on 1 March 2013. The funding was used to partially finance the acquisition of 'ABC Group', which resulted in a C4,250 cash outflow and the acquisition of 875,000 of the company's own shares on 18 April 2013 which resulted in a cash outflow of C2,564. No interest is repayable on the outstanding loan of C29,662 as at 31 December 2013 (2012:C16,452) from Treasury Limited, which is repayable on demand. See note 31.

24p18(a)-(b)   Short-term cash financing is provided to subsidiary undertakings in the group. The monies advanced are generally repayable within 3 months. The outstanding receivable balance is C43,711 as at 31 December 2013 (2012:C31,296). See note 21 for further details.

No purchase or sales transactions were entered into between the company and subsidiary undertakings.

42 Events after the reporting period

(a) Business combinations

10p21, IFRS B64(a)-(d)   The group acquired 100% of the share capital of K&Co, a group of companies specialising in the manufacture of shoes for extreme sports, for a cash consideration of C5,950 on 1 February 2014.

Details of net assets acquired and goodwill are as follows:

		On acquisition
IFRS3B64(f)(i)	Purchase consideration:	
	– Cash paid	5,950
IFRS3B64(m)	– Direct cost relating to acquisition – charged in the income statement	150
7p40(a)	Total purchase consideration	5,950
	Fair value of assets acquired (see below)	(5,145)
	Goodwill	**805**

IFRS3B64(e)   The above goodwill is attributable to K&Co's strong position and profitability in trading in the niche market for extreme sports equipment.

(All amounts in C thousands unless otherwise stated)

IFRS3B64(i) The assets and liabilities arising from the acquisition, provisionally determined, are as follows:

	Fair value
Cash and cash equivalents	195
Property, plant and equipment	31,580
Trademarks	1,000
Licences	700
Customer relationships	1,850
Favourable lease agreements	800
Inventories	995
Trade and other receivables	855
Trade and other payables	(9,646)
Retirement benefit obligations	(1,425)
Borrowings	(19,259)
Deferred tax liabilities	(2,500)
Net assets acquired	**5,145**

(b) Associates

10p21 The group acquired 40% of the share capital of L&Co, a group of companies specialising in the manufacture of leisure shoes, for a cash consideration of C2,050 on 25 January 2014.

Details of net assets acquired and goodwill are as follows:

	On acquisition
Purchase consideration:	
– Cash paid	2,050
– Direct cost relating to acquisition	70
Total purchase consideration	2,120
Share of fair value of net assets acquired (see below)	(2,000)
Goodwill	**120**

DV The goodwill is attributable to L&Co's strong position and profitability in trading in the market of leisure shoes and to its workforce, which cannot be separately recognised as an intangible asset.

DV The assets and liabilities arising from the acquisition, provisionally determined, are as follows:

	Fair value
Contractual customer relationships	380
Property, plant and equipment	3,200
Inventory	500
Cash	220
Trade creditors	(420)
Borrowings	(1,880)
Net assets acquired	**2,000**

IFRS GAAP plc – year ended 31 December 2013

(All amounts in C thousands unless otherwise stated)

(c) Equity transactions

<small>10p21, 33p71(e), 10p21, 10p22(f)</small>

On 1 January 2014, 1,200 thousand share options were granted to directors and employees with an exercise price set at the market share prices less 15% on that date of C3.13 per share (share price: C3.68) (expiry date: 31 December 2017).

The company re-issued 500,000 treasury shares for a total consideration of C1,500 on 15 January 2014.

(d) Borrowings

<small>10p21</small>

On 1 February 2014, the group issued C6,777 6.5% US dollar bonds to finance its expansion programme and working capital requirements in the US. The bonds are repayable on 31 December 2017.

43 Changes in accounting policies

IFRS GAAP plc adopted IFRS 10, 'Consolidated financial statements', IFRS 11, 'Joint arrangements', IFRS 12, 'Disclosure of interests in other entities', and consequential amendments to IAS 28, 'Investments in associates and joint ventures' and IAS 27, 'Separate financial statements', on 1 January 2012. The group has also adopted IAS 19 (revised 2011), 'Employee benefits' on 1 January 2012. The new accounting policies has had the following impact on the financial statements.

(a) Consolidation of entities in which the group holds less than 50%

The group is the largest shareholder of Delta Inc with a 40% equity interest, while all other shareholders individually own less than 1% of its equity shares. There is no history of other shareholders forming a group to exercise their votes collectively. Based on the absolute size of the group's shareholding and the relative size of the other shareholdings, management have concluded that the group has sufficiently dominant voting interest to have the power to direct the relevant activities of the entity. As a result the entity has been fully consolidated into these financial statements. Previously Delta Inc was classified as an associate of the group and accounted for using the equity method.

(b) Joint ventures accounted for using the equity method

The group has joint control over Gamma Limited by virtue of its 50% share in the equity shares of the company and the requirement for unanimous consent by all parites over decisions related to the relevant activities of the arrangement. The investment has been classified as a joint venture under IFRS 11 and therefore the equity method of accounting has been used in the consolidated financial statements. Prior to the adoption of IFRS 11, the group's interest in Gamma Limited was proportionately consolidated.

The group recognised its investment in the joint venture at the beginning of the earliest period presented (1 January 2012), as the total of the carrying amounts of the assets and liabilities previously proportionately consolidated by the group. This is the deemed cost of the group's investment in the joint venture for applying equity accounting.

(All amounts in C thousands unless otherwise stated)

> (c) Adoption of IAS 19 (revised 2011)
>
> The revised employee benefit standard introduces changes to the recognition, measurement, presentation and disclosure of post-employment benefits. The standard also requires net interest expense / income to be calculated as the product of the net defined benefit liability / asset and the discount rate as determined at the beginning of the year. The effect of this is to remove the previous concept of recognising an expected return on plan assets.
>
> The effects of the changes to the accounting policies is shown in the following tables.

IFRS GAAP plc – year ended 31 December 2013

(All amounts in C thousands unless otherwise stated)

Impact of change in accounting policy on consolidated balance sheet

		As at 31 December 2013	Consoli-dation of Delta Inc	Equity accounting for Gamma Limited	Adopt IAS 19 (revised 2011)	As at 31 December 2013 as presented
8p28	**Assets**					
	Non-current assets					
	Property, plant and equipment	153,590	6,351	(4,600)	–	155,341
	Intangible assets	25,339	1,841	(908)	–	26,272
	Investments accounted for using the equity method	18,542	(5,169)	5,276	–	18,649
	Deferred income tax asset	3,520	–	–	26	3,546
	Available-for-sale financial assets	17,420	–	–	–	17,420
	Derivative financial instruments	395	–	–	–	395
	Trade and other receivables	2,322	–	–	–	2,322
		221,128	3,023	(232)	26	223,945
	Current assets					
	Inventories	25,058	1,471	(1,829)	–	24,700
	Trade and other receivables	19,490	2,130	(1,855)	–	19,765
	Available-for-sale financial assets	1,950	–	–	–	1,950
	Derivative financial instruments	1,069	–	–	–	1,069
	Financial assets at fair value through profit or loss	11,820	–	–	–	11,820
	Cash and cash equivalents (excluding bank overdrafts)	17,549	969	(590)	–	17,928
		76,936	4,570	(4,274)	–	77,232
	Assets of disposal group	3,333	–	–	–	3,333
		80,269	4,570	(4,274)	–	80,565
	Total assets	301,397	7,593	(4,506)	26	304,510

(All amounts in C thousands unless otherwise stated)

As at 31 December 2012 (previously stated)	Consolidation of Delta Inc	Equity accounting for Gamma Limited	Adopt IAS 19 (revised 2011)	As at 31 December 2012 (restated)	As at 1 January 2012 (previously stated)	Consolidation of Delta Inc	Equity accounting for Gamma Limited	Adopt IAS 19 (revised 2011)	As at 1 January 2012 (restated)
98,399	5,844	(4,010)	–	100,233	106,750	3,924	(3,460)	–	107,214
19,763	1,820	(883)	–	20,700	20,576	1,744	(858)	–	21,462
17,979	(4,735)	3,809	–	17,053	16,834	(3,826)	2,932	–	15,940
3,321	–	–	62	3,383	2,832	–	–	47	2,879
14,910	–	–	–	14,910	13,222	–	–	–	13,222
245	–	–	–	245	187	–	–	–	187
1,352	–	–	–	1,352	1,106	–	–	–	1,106
155,969	2,929	(1,084)	62	157,876	161,507	1,842	(1,386)	47	162,010
17,845	1,607	(1,270)	–	18,182	16,751	1,447	(925)	–	17,273
17,237	2,211	(1,118)	–	18,330	15,709	1,573	(683)	–	16,599
–	–	–	–	–	–	–	–	–	–
951	–	–	–	951	980	–	–	–	980
7,972	–	–	–	7,972	7,342	–	–	–	7,342
34,130	322	(390)	–	34,062	22,090	234	(192)	–	22,132
78,135	4,140	(2,778)	–	79,497	62,872	3,254	(1,800)	–	64,326
–	–	–	–	–	–	–	–	–	–
78,135	4,140	(2,778)	–	79,497	62,872	3,254	(1,800)	–	64,326
234,104	7,069	(3,862)	62	237,373	224,379	5,096	(3,186)	47	226,336

IFRS GAAP plc – year ended 31 December 2013

(All amounts in C thousands unless otherwise stated)

	As at 31 December 2013	Consolidation of Delta Inc	Equity accounting for Gamma Limited	Adopt IAS 19 (revised 2011)	As at 31 December 2013 as presented
Equity and liabilities					
Equity attributable to equity holders of the company					
Ordinary shares	25,300	–	–	–	25,300
Share premium	17,144	–	–	–	17,144
Other reserves	11,435	–	–	177	11,612
Retained earnings	75,282	–	–	(632)	74,650
	129,161	–	–	(455)	128,706
Non-controlling interests	6,846	1,042	–	–	7,888
Total equity	136,007	1,042	–	(455)	136,594
Liabilities					
Non-current liabilities					
Borrowings	114,730	3,812	(3,421)	–	115,121
Derivative financial instruments	135	–	–	–	135
Deferred income tax liabilities	12,370	–	–	–	12,370
Retirement benefit obligations	4,635	–	–	481	5,116
Provisions for other liabilities and charges	339	65	(88)	–	316
	132,209	3,877	(3,509)	481	133,058
Current liabilities					
Trade and other payables	16,121	870	(321)	–	16,670
Current income tax liabilities	2,125	540	(99)	–	2,566
Borrowings	11,810	458	(552)	–	11,716
Derivative financial instruments	460	–	–	–	460
Provisions for other liabilities and charges	2,445	806	(25)	–	3,226
	32,961	2,674	(997)	–	34,638
Liabilities of disposal group	220	–	–	–	220
	33,181	2,674	(997)	–	34,858
Total liabilities	165,390	6,551	(4,506)	481	167,916
Total equity and liabilities	301,397	7,593	(4,506)	26	304,510

(All amounts in C thousands unless otherwise stated)

As at 31 December 2012 (previously stated)	Consoli- dation of Delta Inc	Equity accounting for Gamma Limited	Adopt IAS 19 (revised 2011)	As at 31 December 2012 (restated)	As at 1 January 2012 (previously stated)	Consoli- dation of Delta Inc	Equity accounting for Gamma Limited	Adopt IAS 19 (revised 2011)	As at 1 January 2012 (restated)
21,000	–	–	–	21,000	20,000	–	–	–	20,000
10,494	–	–	–	10,494	10,424	–	–	–	10,424
7,005	–	–	189	7,194	6,263	–	–	101	6,364
52,490	–	–	(505)	51,985	51,456	–	–	(331)	51,125
90,989	–	–	(316)	90,673	88,143	–	–	(230)	87,913
984	782	–	–	1,766	1,263	237	–	–	1,500
91,973	782	–	(316)	92,439	89,406	237	–	(230)	89,413
95,682	3,518	(2,854)	–	96,346	66,315	1,801	(2,332)	–	65,784
129	–	–	–	129	130	–	–	–	130
9,053	–	–	–	9,053	5,926	–	–	–	5,926
2,233	–	–	378	2,611	1,559	–	–	277	1,836
353	19	(98)	–	274	184	77	(11)	–	250
107,450	3,537	(2,952)	378	108,413	74,114	1,878	(2,343)	277	73,926
11,964	755	(241)	–	12,478	10,568	650	(187)	–	11,031
2,232	632	(93)	–	2,771	6,765	543	(89)	–	7,219
17,889	916	(547)	–	18,258	41,903	995	(542)	–	42,356
618	–	–	–	618	520	–	–	–	520
1,978	447	(29)	–	2,396	1,103	793	(25)	–	1,871
34,681	2,750	(910)	–	36,521	60,859	2,981	(843)	–	62,997
–	–	–	–	–	–	–	–	–	–
34,681	2,750	(910)	–	36,521	60,859	2,981	(843)	–	62,997
142,131	6,287	(3,862)	378	144,934	134,973	4,859	(3,186)	277	136,923
234,104	7,069	(3,862)	62	237,373	224,379	5,096	(3,186)	47	226,336

IFRS GAAP plc – year ended 31 December 2013

Impact of change in accounting policy on the consolidated income statement

8p28

	For period ended 31 December 2013	Consolidation of Delta Inc	Equity accounting for Gamma Limited	Adopt IAS 19 (revised 2011)	For period ended 31 December 2013 as presented
Continuing operations					
Revenue	206,085	16,759	(11,810)	–	211,034
Cost of sales	(70,977)	(11,797)	5,408	–	(77,366)
Gross profit	135,108	4,962	(6,402)	–	133,668
Distribution costs	(52,054)	(1,354)	879	–	(52,529)
Administrative expenses	(29,231)	(2,535)	1,871	(210)	(30,105)
Other income	2,750	–	–	–	2,750
Other (losses)/gains- net	(90)	–	–	–	(90)
Operating profit	56,483	1,073	(3,652)	(210)	53,694
Finance income	1,796	37	(103)	–	1,730
Finance costs	(8,578)	(475)	880	–	(8,173)
Finance costs–net	(6,782)	(438)	777	–	(6,443)
Share of profit of investments accounted for using the equity method	389	(174)	1467	–	1,682
Profit before income tax	50,090	461	(1,408)	(210)	48,933
Income tax expense	(15,881)	(201)	1408	63	(14,611)
Profit for the year from continuing operations	34,209	260	–	(147)	34,322
Discontinued operations					
Profit for the year from discontinued operations (attributable to equity holders of the company)	100	–	–	–	100
Profit for the year	34,309	260	–	(147)	34,422

(All amounts in C thousands unless otherwise stated)

For period ended 31 December 2012	Consolidation of Delta Inc	Equity accounting for Gamma Limited	Adopt IAS 19 (revised 2011)	For period ended 31 December 2012 (Restated)
106,693	17,246	(11,579)	–	112,360
(40,373)	(11,896)	5,587	–	(46,682)
66,320	5,350	(5,992)	–	65,678
(20,795)	(1,421)	1,003	–	(21,213)
(9,896)	(2,089)	1,559	(85)	(10,511)
1,259	–	–	–	1,259
63	–	–	–	63
36,951	1,840	(3,430)	(85)	35,276
1,891	42	(324)	–	1,609
(12,933)	(415)	1151	–	(12,197)
(11,042)	(373)	827	–	(10,588)
509	(364)	877	–	1,022
26,418	1,103	(1,726)	(85)	25,710
(9,864)	(558)	1726	26	(8,670)
16,554	545	–	(59)	17,040
120	–	–	–	120
16,674	545	–	(59)	17,160

IFRS GAAP plc – year ended 31 December 2013

Impact of change in accounting policy on the consolidated statement of comprehensive income

	For period ended 31 December 2013	Consolidation of Delta Inc	Equity accounting for Gamma Limited	Adopt IAS 19 (revised 2011)	For period ended 31 December 2013 as presented
Profit for the year	34,309	260	–	(147)	34,422
Other comprehensive income:					
Items that will not be reclassified to profit or loss					
Gains on revaluation of land and buildings	755	–	–	–	755
Remeasurements of post employment benefit obligations	0	–	–	83	83
	755	–	–	83	838
Items that may be subsequently reclassified to profit or loss					
Change in value of available-for-sale financial assets	362	–	–	–	362
Reclassification of revaluation of previously held interest in ABC Group	(850)	–	–	–	(850)
Share of other comprehensive income of associates	(86)	–	–	–	(86)
Impact of change in Euravian tax rate on deferred tax	(10)	–	–	–	(10)
Cash flow hedges	64	–	–	–	64
Net investment hedge	(45)	–	–	–	(45)
Currency translation differences	2,413	–	–	(12)	2,401
	1,848	–	–	(12)	1,836
Other comprehensive income for the year, net of tax	2,603	–	–	71	2,674
Total comprehensive income for the year	36,912	260	–	(76)	37,096
Attributable to:					
– Owners of the parent	34,372	–	–	(76)	34,296
– Non-controlling interests	2,540	260	–	–	2,800
Total comprehensive income for the year	36,912	260	–	(76)	37,096
Total comprehensive income attributable to equity shareholders arises from:					
– Continuing operations	34,272	–	–	(76)	34,196
– Discontinued operations	100	–	–	–	100
	34,372	–	–	(76)	34,296

(All amounts in C thousands unless otherwise stated)

For period ended 31 December 2012	Consolidation of Delta Inc	Equity accounting for Gamma Limited	Adopt IAS 19 (revised 2011)	For period ended 31 December 2012 (Restated)
16,674	545	–	(59)	17,160
759	–	–	–	759
(494)	–	–	(143)	(637)
265	–	–	(143)	122
912	–	–	–	912
–	–	–	–	–
91	–	–	–	91
–	–	–	–	–
(3)	–	–	–	(3)
40	–	–	–	40
(1,111)	–	–	189	(922)
(71)	–	–	189	118
194	–	–	46	240
16,868	545	–	(13)	17,400
16,597	–	–	(13)	16,584
271	545	–	–	816
16,868	545	–	(13)	17,400
16,477	–	–	(13)	16,464
120	–	–	–	120
16,597	–	–	(13)	16,584

IFRS GAAP plc – year ended 31 December 2013

Impact of change in accounting policy on the consolidated statement of cash flows

	For period ended 31 December 2013	Consolidation of Delta Inc	Equity accounting for Gamma Limited	Adopt IAS 19 (revised 2011)	For period ended 31 December 2013 as presented
Cash flows from operating activities					
Cash generated from operations	76,652	1,522	(3,423)	–	74,751
Interest paid	(8,187)	(483)	835	–	(7,835)
Income tax paid	(16,044)	(186)	1,321	–	(14,909)
Net cash generated from operating activities	52,421	853	(1,267)	–	52,007
Cash flows from investing activities					
Acquisition of subsidiary, net of cash acquired	(3,750)	–	–	–	(3,750)
Purchases of property, plant and equipment	(9,021)	(1,363)	879	–	(9,505)
Proceeds from sale of property, plant and equipment	6,296	90	(32)	–	6,354
Purchases of intangible assets	(2,990)	(165)	105	–	(3,050)
Purchases of available-for-sale financial assets	(4,887)	–	–	–	(4,887)
Proceeds from disposal of available-for-sale financial assets	151	–	–	–	151
Loans granted to related parties	(1,343)	–	–	–	(1,343)
Loan repayments received from related parties	63	–	–	–	63
Interest received	1,077	72	(95)	–	1,054
Dividends received	1,130	–	–	–	1,130
Net cash used in investing activities	(13,274)	(1,366)	857	–	(13,783)

(All amounts in C thousands unless otherwise stated)

For period ended 31 December 2012	Consolidation of Delta Inc	Equity accounting for Gamma Limited	Adopt IAS 19 (revised 2011)	For period ended 31 December 2012 (Restated)
42,453	1,925	(2,675)	–	41,703
(15,437)	(381)	1,045	–	(14,773)
(11,639)	(358)	1,471	–	(10,526)
15,377	1,186	(159)	–	16,404
–	–	–	–	–
(4,915)	(2,033)	906	–	(6,042)
2,910	193	(124)	–	2,979
(928)	107	121	–	(700)
(1,150)	–	–	–	(1,150)
–	–	–	–	–
(112)	–	–	–	(112)
98	–	–	–	98
1,371	29	(207)	–	1,193
1,120	–	–	–	1,120
(1,606)	(1,704)	696	–	(2,614)

IFRS GAAP plc – year ended 31 December 2013

203

(All amounts in C thousands unless otherwise stated)

	For period ended 31 December 2013	Consolidation of Delta Inc	Equity accounting for Gamma Limited	Adopt IAS 19 (revised 2011)	For period ended 31 December 2013 as presented
Cash flows from financing activities					
Proceeds from issuance of ordinary shares	950	–	–	–	950
Purchase of treasury shares	(2,564)	–	–	–	(2,564)
Proceeds from issuance of convertible bonds	50,000	–	–	–	50,000
Proceeds from issuance of redeemable preference shares	–	–	–	–	–
Proceeds from borrowings	9,500	–	(1,000)	–	8,500
Repayments of borrowings	(94,429)	(253)	689	–	(93,993)
Dividends paid to owners of the parent	(10,102)	–	–	–	(10,102)
Dividends paid to holders of redeemable preference shares	(1,950)	–	–	–	(1,950)
Acquisition of interest in a subsidiary	(1,100)	–	–	–	(1,100)
Sale of interest in a subsidiary	1,100	–	–	–	1,100
Dividends paid to non-controlling interests	(1,920)	–	–	–	(1,920)
Net cash used in financing activities	(50,515)	(253)	(311)	–	(51,079)
Net (decrease)/ increase in cash and cash equivalents	(11,368)	(766)	(721)	–	(12,855)
Cash and cash equivalents at beginning of year	27,666	322	(390)	–	27,598
Exchange gains/(losses) on cash and cash equivalents	(1,399)	1,413	521	–	535
Cash and cash equivalent at end of year	14,899	969	(590)	–	15,278

(All amounts in C thousands unless otherwise stated)

For period ended 31 December 2012	Consolidation of Delta Inc	Equity accounting for Gamma Limited	Adopt IAS 19 (revised 2011)	For period ended 31 December 2012 (Restated)
1,070	–	–	–	1,070
–	–	–	–	–
–	–	–	–	–
30,000	–	–	–	30,000
16,536	2,214	(750)	–	18,000
(34,737)	(245)	308	–	(34,674)
(15,736)	–	–	–	(15,736)
(1,950)	–	–	–	(1,950)
–	–	–	–	–
–	–	–	–	–
(550)	–	–	–	(550)
(5,367)	1,969	(442)	–	(3,840)
8,404	1,451	95	–	9,950
17,545	234	(192)	–	17,587
1,717	(1,363)	(293)	–	61
27,666	322	(390)	–	27,598

IFRS GAAP plc – year ended 31 December 2013

(All amounts in C thousands unless otherwise stated)

Impact of change in accounting policy on the statement of changes in equity

	Attributable to owners of the parent					Non-controlling interest	Total equity
	Share capital	Share premium	Other reserves	Retained earnings	Total		
Balance as at 1 January 2012 as previously reported	20,000	10,424	6,263	51,456	88,143	1,263	89,406
Effect of changes in accounting policies	–	–	101	(331)	(230)	237	7
Balance as at 1 January 2012 as restated	20,000	10,424	6,364	51,125	87,913	1,500	89,413
Profit for the year as previously reported	–	–	–	16,363	16,363	311	16,674
Effect of changes in accounting policies	–	–	–	(59)	(59)	545	486
Profit for the year as restated	–	–	–	16,304	16,304	856	17,160
Other comprehensive income for the year as previously reported	–	–	784	(550)	234	(40)	194
Effect of changes in accounting policies	–	–	46	–	46	–	46
Other comprehensive income for the year as restated	–	–	830	(550)	280	(40)	240
Total comprehensive income for the year as previously reported	–	–	784	15,813	16,597	271	16,868
Effect of changes in accounting policies	–	–	46	(59)	(13)	545	532
Total comprehensive income for the year	–	–	830	15,754	16,584	816	17,400
Value of employee services[1]	–	–	–	822	822	–	822
Tax credit relating to share option scheme[1]	–	–	–	20	20	–	20
Proceeds from shares issued[1]	1,000	70	–	–	1,070	–	1,070
Dividends[1]	–	–	–	(15,736)	(15,736)	(550)	(16,286)
Total contributions by and distributions to owners of the parent, recognised directly in equity[1]	1,000	70	–	(14,894)	(13,824)	(550)	(14,374)
Balance as at 31 December 2012 as previously reported	21,000	10,494	7,047	52,375	90,916	984	91,900
Effect of changes in accounting policies	–	–	147	(390)	(243)	782	539
Balance as at 31 December 2012	21,000	10,494	7,194	51,985	90,673	1,766	92,439

[1] There is no impact on these financial statement line items for the change in the accounting policies.

Appendix I – Alternative presentation of primary statements

> This appendix is independent of the illustrative financial statements in the main body of IFRS GAAP plc. The figures do not have any correlation with those in the main body and hence should not be compared.

Consolidated statement of cash flows – direct method

IAS 7 encourages the use of the 'direct method' for the presentation of cash flows from operating activities. The presentation of cash flows from operating activities using the direct method in accordance with IAS 7p18 is as follows:

Consolidated statement of cash flows

1p113, 7p10

		Year ended 31 December	
		2013	2012 Restated
7p18(a)	**Cash flows from operating activities**		
	Cash receipts from customers	212,847	114,451
	Cash paid to suppliers and employees	(156,613)	(72,675)
	Cash generated from operations	56,234	41,776
	Interest paid	(7,835)	(14,773)
	Income taxes paid	(16,909)	(10,526)
	Net cash flows from operating activities	31,490	16,477
7p21,7p10	**Cash flows from investing activities**		
7p39	Acquisition of subsidiary, net of cash acquired	(3,950)	–
7p16(a)	Purchases of property, plant and equipment	(9,755)	(6,042)
7p16(b)	Proceeds from sale of property, plant and equipment	6,354	2,979
7p16(a)	Purchases of intangible assets	(3,050)	(700)
7p16(c)	Purchases of available-for-sale financial assets	(2,781)	(1,126)
7p16(e)	Loans granted to associates	(1,000)	(50)
7p16(f)	Loan repayments received from associates	14	64
7p31	Interest received	1,054	1,193
7p31	Dividends received	1,130	1,120
	Net cash used in investing activities	(11,984)	(2,562)
7p21,7p10	**Cash flows from financing activities**		
7p17(a)	Proceeds from issuance of ordinary shares	950	1,070
7p17(b)	Purchase of treasury shares	(2,564)	–
7p17(c)	Proceeds from issuance of convertible bond	50,000	–
7p17(c)	Proceeds from issuance of redeemable preference shares	–	30,000
7p17(c)	Proceeds from borrowings	8,500	18,000
7p17(d)	Repayments of borrowings	(78,117)	(34,674)
7p31	Dividends paid to owners of the parent	(10,102)	(15,736)
7p31	Dividends paid to holders of redeemable preference shares	(1,950)	(1,950)
7p31	Dividends paid to non-controlling interests	(1,920)	(550)
	Net cash used in financing activities	(35,203)	(3,840)
	Net (decrease)/increase in cash, cash equivalents and bank overdrafts	(15,697)	10,075
7p28	Cash, cash equivalents and bank overdrafts at beginning of the year	27,598	17,587
	Exchange gains/(losses) on cash, cash equivalents and bank overdrafts	535	(64)
7p28	**Cash, cash equivalents and bank overdrafts at end of the year**	**12,436**	**27,598**

The notes on pages 78 to 205 are an integral part of these consolidated financial statements.

IFRS GAAP plc – year ended 31 December 2013

(All amounts in C thousands unless otherwise stated)

Consolidated statement of comprehensive income – single statement, showing expenses by function

		Year ended 31 December	
1p10(b),10A		**2013**	**2012** Restated
	Continuing operations		
1p82(a)	Revenue	211,034	112,360
1p99, 1p103	Cost of sales	(77,366)	(46,682)
1p103	**Gross profit**	**133,668**	**65,678**
1p99, 1p103	Distribution costs	(52,529)	(21,213)
1p99, 1p103	Administrative expenses	(30,105)	(10,511)
1p99, 1p103	Other income	2,750	1,259
1p85	Other (losses)/gains – net	(90)	63
1p85	**Operating profit**	**53,694**	**35,276**
1p85	Finance income	1,730	1,609
1p82(b)	Finance cost	(8,173)	(12,197)
1p85	Finance costs – net	(6,443)	(10,588)
1p82(c)	Share of profit of invesments accounted for using the equity method	1,682	1,022
1p85	**Profit before income tax**	**48,933**	**25,710**
1p82(d),12p77	Income tax expense	(14,611)	(8,670)
1p85	**Profit for the year from continuing operations**	**34,322**	**17,040**
IFRS5p33(a)	**Discontinued operations:**		
	Profit for the year from discontinued operations	100	120
1p81A(a)	**Profit for the year**	**34,422**	**17,160**
	Other comprehensive income:		
1p82A	**Items that will not be reclassified to profit or loss**		
16p39	Gains on revaluation of land and buildings	755	759
19p93B	Remeasurements of post employment benefit obligations	83	(637)
		838	122
1p82A	**Items that may be subsequently reclassified to profit or loss**		
IFRS7p20(a)(ii)	Change in value of available-for-sale financial assets	362	912
IFRS3p59	Reclassification of revaluation of previously held interest in ABC Group	(850)	–
1p85	Impact of change in the Euravian tax rate on deferred tax	(10)	–
IFRS7p23(c)	Cash flow hedges	64	(3)
1p85	Net investment hedge	(45)	40
21p52(b)	Currency translation differences	2,401	(922)
1p82A	Share of other comprehensive income of associates	(86)	91
		1,836	118
	Other comprehensive income for the year, net of tax	2,674	240
1p81A(c)	**Total comprehensive income for the year**	**37,096**	**17,400**
	Profit attributable to:		
1p81B(a)(ii)	Owners of the parent	31,874	16,304
1p81B(a)(i), IFRS12p12(e)	Non-controlling interests	2,548	856
		34,422	17,160

(All amounts in C thousands unless otherwise stated)

		Year ended 31 December	
		2013	2012 Restated
	Total comprehensive income attributable to:		
1p81B(b)(ii)	Equity holders of the company	**34,296**	16,584
1p81B(b)(i)	Non-controlling interest	**2,800**	816
		37,096	17,400
	Total comprehensive income attributable to equity shareholders arises from:		
	Continuing operations	**34,196**	16,464
IFRS5p33(d)	Discontinued operations	**100**	120
		34,296	16,584

Earnings per share from continuing and discontinued operations to the equity holders of the parent during the year (expressed in C per share)

		2013	2012
	Basic earnings per share		
33p66	From continuing operations	**1.35**	0.79
33p68	From discontinued operations	**0.01**	0.01
		1.36	0.8
	Diluted earnings per share[1]		
33p66	From continuing operations	**1.21**	0.74
33p68	From discontinued operations	**0.01**	0.01
		1.22	0.75

The notes on pages 78 to 205 are an integral part of these consolidated financial statements.

---

[1] EPS for discontinued operations may be given in the notes to the accounts instead of the face of the income statement. The income tax effect has been presented on an aggregate basis; therefore an additional note disclosure resents the income tax effect of each component. Alternatively, this information could be presented within the statement of comprehensive income.

IFRS GAAP plc – year ended 31 December 2013

(All amounts in C thousands unless otherwise stated)

Appendix II – Areas not illustrated in financial statements of IFRS GAAP plc

1. Biological assets

Note 1 – General information

1p138(b), 41p46(a)

The group is engaged in the business of farming sheep primarily for sale to meat processors. The group is also engaged in the business of growing and managing palm oil plantations for the sale of palm oil. The group earns ancillary income from various agricultural produce, such as wool.

Note 2 – Accounting policies

Basis of preparation

1p117(a)

The consolidated financial statements have been prepared under the historical cost convention, as modified by the revaluation of land and buildings, available-for-sale financial assets, financial assets and financial liabilities (including derivative financial instruments at fair value through profit or loss) and certain biological assets.

1p119 **Biological assets**

41p41

Biological assets comprise sheep and palm oil plantations.

IFRS13p93(d)

Sheep are measured at fair value less cost to sell, based on market prices at auction of livestock of similar age, breed and genetic merit with adjustments, where necessary, to reflect the differences.

IFRS13p93(d)

The fair value of oil palms excludes the land upon which the trees are planted or the fixed assets utilised in the upkeep of planted areas. The biological process starts with preparation of land for planting seedlings and ends with the harvesting of crops in the form of fresh fruit bunches ('FFB'). Thereafter, crude palm oil and palm kernel oil is extracted from FFB. Consistently with this process, the fair value of oil palms is determined using a discounted cash flow model, by reference to the estimated FFB crop harvest over the full remaining productive life of the trees of up to 20 years, applying an estimated produce value for transfer to the manufacturing process and allowing for upkeep, harvesting costs and an appropriate allocation of overheads. The estimated produce value is derived from a long term forecast of crude palm oil prices to determine the present value of expected future cash flows over the next 20 years. The estimated FFB crop harvest used to derive the fair value is derived by applying palm oil yield to plantation size.

41p54(a),(b)

Costs to sell include the incremental selling costs, including auctioneers' fees and commission paid to brokers and dealers.

Changes in fair value of livestock and palm oil plantations are recognised in the income statement.

Farming costs such as feeding, labour costs, pasture maintenance, veterinary services and sheering are expensed as incurred. The cost of purchase of sheep plus transportation charges are capitalised as part of biological assets.

Note 3 – Estimates and judgements – Biological assets

IFRS13p93(d) In measuring the fair value of sheep and palm oil plantations various management estimates and judgements are required:

(a) Sheep

Estimates and judgements in determining the fair value of sheep relate to the market prices, average weight and quality of animals and mortality rates.

Market price of sheep is obtained from the weekly auctions at the local market. The quality of livestock sold at the local market is considered to approximate the group's breeding and slaughter livestock.

The sheep grow at different rates and there can be a considerable spread in the quality and weight of animals and that affects the price achieved. An average weight is assumed for the slaughter sheep livestock that are not yet at marketable weight.

(b) Palm oil plantations

Estimates and judgements in determining the fair value of palm oil plantations relate to determining the palm oil yield, the long term crude palm oil price, palm kernel oil price and the discount rates.

Consolidated income statement (extracts)

	Note	2013	2012
Revenue	4	**26,240**	27,548
41p40 Change in fair value of biological assets	5	**23,480**	19,028
Cost of sales of livestock and palm oil	5	**(23,180)**	(24,348)

Consolidated balance sheet (extracts)

	Note	2013	2012
1p68			
Assets			
1p60 **Non-current assets**			
1p54(f) Biological assets	5	**37,500**	25,940
1p60 **Current assets**			
1p54(f) Biological assets	5	**4,300**	5,760

Note 4 – Revenue (extract)

	Note	2013	2012
Sale of livestock and palm oil	5	**23,740**	25,198
Sale of wool		**2,500**	2,350
Total revenue		**26,240**	27,548

IFRS GAAP plc – year ended 31 December 2013

(All amounts in C thousands unless otherwise stated)

Note 5 – Biological assets

		2013	2012
41p50	At 1 January	31,700	32,420
41p50(b)	Increase due to purchases	10,280	4,600
41p50(a)	Livestock losses	(480)	(350)
41p50(a)	Change in fair value due to biological transformation	21,950	17,930
41p50(a)	Change in fair value of livestock due to price changes	1,530	1,448
41p50(d)	Transfer of harvested FFB to inventory	(18,450)	(19,450)
41p50(c)	Decrease due to sales	(4,730)	(4,898)
	At 31 December	**41,800**	**31,700**
41p43, p45	Sheep – at fair value less cost to sell:		
	– Mature	4,300	5,760
	– Immature	8,200	5,690
		12,500	11,450
	Palm oil plantation		
	– Mature – at fair value less cost to sell	29,300	20,250
		29,300	20,250
	At 31 December	**41,800**	**31,700**

41p46(b) As at 31 December the group had 6,500 sheep and 2,600,000 hectares palm oil plantations (2012: 5,397 sheep and 2,170,000 hectares of palm oil plantations). During the year the group sold 3,123 sheep (2012: 4,098 sheep) and 550,000 kgs of palm oil (2012: 545,000 kgs of palm oil).

41p43 Sheep for slaughter are classified as immature until they are ready for slaughter.

Selling expenses of C560 (2012:C850) were incurred during the year.

Livestock are classified as current assets if they are to be sold within one year. Harvested FFB are transferred to inventory at fair value when harvested.

IFRS13p93(a-b) The following table presents the group's biological assets that are measured at fair value at 31 December 2013.

	Level 1	Level 2	Level 3	Total
Sheep				
– Mature	–	4,300	–	4,300
– Immature	–	8,200	–	8,200
Palm oil plantation				
– Mature	–	–	29,300	29,300

IFRS13p93(c) There were no transfers between any levels during the year.

IFRS GAAP plc – year ended 31 December 2013

212

(All amounts in C thousands unless otherwise stated)

The movement in the fair value of the assets within level 3 of the hierarchy is as follows:

	Palm oil plantation
Opening balance	20,250
Increases due to expenditure to planted areas	4,309
Decreases due to harvest	(14,115)
Gain in profit or loss arising from biological transformation	18,856
Closing balance	**29,300**

IFRS 13p93(e)(i) Total gains or losses for the period included in profit or loss for assets held at the end of the reporting period, under 'Change in fair value of biological assets'	18,856
IFRS 13p93(f) Change in unrealised gains or losses for the period included in profit or loss for assets held at the end of the reporting period	16,532

IFRS13p 93(d),(h)(i) The following unobservable inputs were used to measure the group's palm oil plantation:

Description	Fair value at 31 December 2013	Valuation technique(s)	Unobservable inputs	Range of unobservable inputs (probability – weighted average)	Relationship of unobservable inputs to fair value
Palm oil plantation	6,815	Discounted cash flows	Palm oil yield – tonnes per hectare	20-30 (24) per year	The higher the palm oil yield, the higher the fair value
			Crude palm oil price	US$ 800-1100 (900) per tonne	The higher the market price, the higher the fair value.
			Palm Kernel Oil price	US$ 1000-1200 (1050) per tonne	
			Discount rate	9%-11% (10.5%)	The higher the discount rate, the lower the fair value.

41p49(c)

Note 6 – Financial risk management strategies

The group is exposed to risks arising from environmental and climatic changes, commodity prices and financing risks.

The group's geographic spread of farms allows a high degree of mitigation against adverse climatic conditions such as droughts and floods and disease outbreaks. The group has strong environmental policies and procedures in place to comply with environmental and other laws.

The group is exposed to risks arising from fluctuations in the price and sales volume of sheep. Where possible, the group enters into supply contracts for sheep to ensure sales volumes can be met by meat processing companies. The group has long-term contracts in place for supply of palm oil to its major customers.

(All amounts in C thousands unless otherwise stated)

The seasonal nature of the sheep farming business requires a high level of cash flow in the second half of the year. The group actively manages the working capital requirements and has secured sufficient credit facilities sufficient to meet the cash flow requirements.

41p49(b)
Note 7 – Commitments

The group has entered into a contract to acquire 250 breeding sheep at 31 December 2013 for C1,250 (2012: nil).

2. Construction contracts

Note – Accounting policies

11p3
A construction contract is defined by IAS 11, 'Construction contracts', as a contract specifically negotiated for the construction of an asset.

11p22
When the outcome of a construction contract can be estimated reliably and it is probable that the contract will be profitable, contract revenue is recognised over the period of the contract by reference to the stage of completion. Contract costs are recognised as expenses by reference to the stage of completion of the contract activity at the end of the reporting period. When it is probable that total contract costs will exceed total contract revenue, the expected loss is recognised as an expense immediately.

When the outcome of a construction contract cannot be estimated reliably, contract revenue is recognised only to the extent of contract costs incurred that are likely to be recoverable.

Variations in contract work, claims and incentive payments are included in contract revenue to the extent that may have been agreed with the customer and are capable of being reliably measured.

The group uses the 'percentage-of-completion method 'to determine the appropriate amount to recognise in a given period. The stage of completion is measured by reference to the contract costs incurred up to the end of the reporting period as a percentage of total estimated costs for each contract. Costs incurred in the year in connection with future activity on a contract are excluded from contract costs in determining the stage of completion.

On the balance sheet, the group reports the net contract position for each contract as either an asset or a liability. A contract represents an asset where costs incurred plus recognised profits (less recognised losses) exceed progress billings; a contract represents a liability where the opposite is the case.

(All amounts in C thousands unless otherwise stated)

	Consolidated balance sheet (extracts)			
		Note	2013	2012
1p60	**Current assets**			
1p54(h)	Trade and other receivables	12	23,303	20,374
1p60	**Current liabilities**			
1p54(k)	Trade and other payables	21	17,667	13,733

	Consolidated income statement (extracts)			
		Note	2013	2012
11p39(a)	Contract revenue		58,115	39,212
11p16	Contract costs		(54,729)	(37,084)
1p103	Gross profit		3,386	2,128
1p103	Selling and marketing costs		(386)	(128)
1p103	Administrative expenses		(500)	(400)

Note – Trade and other receivables (extract)[1]

		2013	2012
IFRS7p36, 1p78(b)	Trade receivables	18,174	16,944
	Less: Provision for impairment of receivables	(109)	(70)
	Trade receivables – net	18,065	16,874
11p42(a)	Amounts due from customers for contract work	1,216	920
	Prepayments	1,300	1,146
1p77, 24p18	Receivables from related parties (note 41)	54	46
1p77, 24p18	Loans to related parties (note 41)	2,668	1,388
	Total	**23,303**	**20,374**

Note – Trade and other payables (extract)[2]

		2013	2012
1p77	Trade payables	10,983	9,495
24p18	Amounts due to related parties (note 41)	2,202	1,195
11p42(b)	Amounts due to customers for contract work	997	1,255
	Social security and other taxes	2,002	960
	Accrued expenses	1,483	828
	Total	**17,667**	**13,733**

Note – Construction contracts

		2013	2012
11p40(a)	The aggregate costs incurred and recognised profits (less recognised losses) to date	69,804	56,028
	Less: Progress billings	(69,585)	(56,383)
	Net balance sheet position for ongoing contracts	**219**	**(355)**

---

[1] At 31 December 2013, trade and other receivables include retentions of C232 (2012: 132) related to construction contracts in progress.

[2] At 31 December 2013, trade and other payables include customer advances of C142 (2012: C355) related to construction contracts in progress.

IFRS GAAP plc – year ended 31 December 2013

(All amounts in C thousands unless otherwise stated)

3. Oil and gas exploration assets

IFRS6p24

Note – Accounting policies

Oil and natural gas exploration and evaluation expenditures are accounted for using the 'successful efforts' method of accounting. Costs are accumulated on a field-by-field basis. Geological and geophysical costs are expensed as incurred. Costs directly associated with an exploration well, and exploration and property leasehold acquisition costs, are capitalised until the determination of reserves is evaluated. If it is determined that commercial discovery has not been achieved, these costs are charged to expense.

Capitalisation is made within property, plant and equipment or intangible assets according to the nature of the expenditure.

Once commercial reserves are found, exploration and evaluation assets are tested for impairment and transferred to development tangible and intangible assets. No depreciation and/or amortisation is charged during the exploration and evaluation phase.

(a) Development tangible and intangible assets

Expenditure on the construction, installation or completion of infrastructure facilities such as platforms, pipelines and the drilling of commercially proven development wells, is capitalised within property, plant and equipment and intangible assets according to nature. When development is completed on a specific field, it is transferred to production or intangible assets. No depreciation or amortisation is charged during the exploration and evaluation phase.

(b) Oil and gas production assets

Oil and gas production properties are aggregated exploration and evaluation tangible assets, and development expenditures associated with the production of proved reserves.

(c) Depreciation/amortisation

Expenditure on the construction, installation or completion of infrastructure facilities such as platforms, pipelines and the drilling of commercially proven development wells, is capitalised within property, plant and equipment and intangible assets according to nature. When development is completed on a specific field, it is transferred to production or intangible assets. No depreciation or amortisation is charged during the exploration and evaluation phase.

Oil and gas properties intangible assets are depreciated or amortised using the unit-of-production method. Unit-of-production rates are based on proved developed reserves, which are oil, gas and other mineral reserves estimated to be recovered from existing facilities using current operating methods. Oil and gas volumes are considered produced once they have been measured through meters at custody transfer or sales transaction points at the outlet valve on the field storage tank.

(d) Impairment – exploration and evaluation assets

Exploration and evaluation assets are tested for impairment when reclassified to development tangible or intangible assets, or whenever facts and circumstances indicate impairment. An impairment loss is recognised for the amount by which the exploration and evaluation assets' carrying amount exceeds their recoverable amount. The recoverable amount is the higher of the exploration and evaluation assets' fair value less costs to sell and their value in use.

(e) Impairment – proved oil and gas production properties and intangible assets

Proven oil and gas properties and intangible assets are reviewed for impairment whenever events or changes in circumstances indicate that the carrying amount may not be recoverable. An impairment loss is recognised for the amount by which the asset's carrying amount exceeds its recoverable amount. The recoverable amount is the higher of an asset's fair value less costs to sell and value in use. For the purposes of assessing impairment, assets are grouped at the lowest levels for which there are separately identifiable cash flows.

Note – Property, plant and equipment[1]

	Capitalised exploration and evaluation expenditure	Capitalised development expenditure	Production assets	Other businesses and corporate assets	Total
At 1 January 2013					
Cost	218	12,450	58,720	3,951	75,339
Accumulated amortisation and impairment	(33)	–	(5,100)	(77)	(5,210)
Net book amount	185	12,450	53,620	3,874	70,129
Year ended 31 December 2013					
Opening net book amount	185	12,450	53,620	3,874	70,129
Exchange differences	17	346	1,182	325	1,870
Acquisitions	–	386	125	4	515
Additions	45	1,526	5,530	95	7,196
Transfers	(9)	(958)	1,712	–	745
Disposals	(12)	(1,687)	–	–	(1,699)
Depreciation charge	–	–	(725)	(42)	(767)
Impairment charge	(7)	(36)	(250)	(3)	(296)
Closing net book amount	**219**	**12,027**	**61,194**	**4,253**	**(1,063)**
At 31 December 2013					
Cost	264	12,027	67,019	4,330	83,640
Accumulated amortisation and impairment	(45)	–	(5,825)	(77)	(5,947)
Net book amount	**219**	**12,027**	**61,194**	**4,253**	**77,693**

[1] For the purpose of this illustrative appendix, comparatives for the year ended 31 December 2012 are not disclosed, although they are required by IAS 1.

IFRS GAAP plc – year ended 31 December 2013

(All amounts in C thousands unless otherwise stated)

Note – Intangible assets[1]

	Capitalised exploration and evaluation expenditure	Capitalised development expenditure	Production assets	Goodwill	Other	Total
At 1 January 2013						
Cost	5,192	750	3,412	9,475	545	19,374
Accumulated amortisation and impairment	(924)	–	(852)	(75)	(19)	(1,870)
Net book amount	4,268	750	2,560	9,400	526	17,504
Year ended 31 December 2013						
Opening net book amount	4,268	750	2,560	9,400	526	17,504
Exchange differences	152	8	195	423	28	806
Acquisitions	26	32	5	–	5	68
Additions	381	8	15	–	86	490
Transfers to production	(548)	(302)	105	–	–	(745)
Disposals	–	(28)	(15)	–	–	(43)
Amortisation charge	–	–	(98)	–	(42)	(140)
Impairment charge	(45)	–	–	(175)	(5)	(225)
Closing net book amount	**4,234**	**468**	**2,767**	**9,648**	**598**	**17,715**
At 31 December 2013						
Cost	5,203	468	3,717	9,898	659	19,945
Accumulated amortisation and impairment	(969)	–	(950)	(250)	(61)	(2,230)
Net book amount	**4,234**	**468**	**2,767**	**9,648**	**598**	**17,715**

Assets and liabilities related to the exploration and evaluation of mineral resources other than those presented above are as follows:

	2013	2012
Receivables from joint venture partners	**25**	22
Payable to subcontractors and operators	**32**	34

Exploration and evaluation activities have led to total expenses of C5,900 (2012: C5,700), of which C5,200 (2012: C4,300) are impairment charges to write off costs of unsuccessful exploration activities.

In 2013, the disposal of a 16.67% interest in an offshore exploration stage 'Field X' resulted in post-tax profits on sale of C3000 (2012: nil).

Cash payments of C41,500 (2012: C39,500) have been incurred related to exploration and evaluation activities. The cash proceeds due to the disposal of the interest in Field X were C8,000 (2012: nil).

---

[1] For the purpose of this illustrative appendix, comparatives for the year ended 31 December 2012 are not disclosed, although they are required by IAS 1.

(All amounts in C thousands unless otherwise stated)

4. Leases: Accounting by lessor

17p4　A lease is an agreement whereby the lessor conveys to the lessee in return for a payment, or series of payments, the right to use an asset for an agreed period of time.

Note – Accounting policies

1p119　When assets are leased out under a finance lease, the present value of the lease payments is recognised as a receivable. The difference between the gross receivable and the present value of the receivable is recognised as unearned finance income.

> **Commentary**
>
> Additional disclosure is required of the following for a lease:
> (a) reconciliation between the gross investment in the lease and the present value of the minimum lease payments receivable at the end of the reposting period. An entity discloses the gross investment in the lease and the present value of the minimum lease payments receivable at the end of the reporting periods:
>   (i) not later than one year;
>   (ii) later than one year and not later than five years; and
>   (iii) later than five years;
> (b) unearned finance income;
> (c) the unguaranteed residual values accruing to the benefit of the lessor;
> (d) the accumulated allowance for uncollectible minimum lease payments receivable;
> (e) contingent rents recognised as income in the period; and
> (f) a general description of the lessor's material leasing arrangements.

　The method for allocating gross earnings to accounting periods is referred to a as the 'actuarial method'. The actuarial method allocates rentals between finance income and repayment of capital in each accounting period in such a way that finance income will emerge as a constant rate of return on the lessor's net investment in the lease.

17p49　When assets are leased out under an operating lease, the asset is included in the balance sheet based on the nature of the asset.

17p50　Lease income on operating leases is recognised over the term of the lease on a straight-line basis.

IFRS GAAP plc – year ended 31 December 2013

(All amounts in C thousands unless otherwise stated)

Note – Property, plant and equipment

The category of vehicles and equipment includes vehicles leased by the group to third parties under operating leases with the following carrying amounts:

17p57		2013	2012
	Cost	70,234	83,824
	Accumulated depreciation at 1 January	(14,818)	(9,800)
	Depreciation charge for the year	(5,058)	(3,700)
	Net book amount	**50,358**	**70,324**

Note – Trade and other receivables

		2013	2012
1p78(b)	**Non-current receivables**		
17p47(a)	Finance leases – gross receivables	1,810	630
17p47(b)	Unearned finance income	(222)	(98)
		1,588	532
1p78(b)	**Current receivables**		
17p47(a)	Finance leases – gross receivables	1,336	316
17p47(b)	Unearned finance income	(140)	(38)
		1,196	278
1p78(b) 17p47(a)	Gross receivables from finance leases:		
	– No later than 1 year	1,336	316
	– Later than 1 year and no later than 5 years	1,810	630
	– Later than 5 years	–	–
		3,146	946
1p78(b), 17p47(b)	Unearned future finance income on finance leases	(362)	(136)
	Net investment in finance leases	**2,784**	**810**

1p78(b)	The net investment in finance leases may be analysed as follows:		
17p47(a)	No later than 1 year	1,196	278
	Later than 1 year and no later than 5 years	1,588	532
	Later than 5 years	–	–
		2,784	810

Note – Operating leases

17p56(a) Operating leases rental receivables – group company as lessor

The future minimum lease payments receivable under non-cancellable operating leases are as follows:

	2013	2012
No later than 1 year	12,920	12,920
Later than 1 year and no later than 5 years	41,800	41,800
Later than 5 years	840	10,840
	55,560	65,560

17p56(b)	Contingent-based rents recognised in the income statement were C235 (2012: C40).
17p56(c)	The company leases vehicles under various agreements which terminate between 2013 and 2017. The agreements do not include an extension option.

5. Government grants

Note – Accounting policies

Government grants

20p39(a), p12	Grants from the government are recognised at their fair value where there is a reasonable assurance that the grant will be received and the group will comply with all attached conditions.
	Government grants relating to costs are deferred and recognised in the income statement over the period necessary to match them with the costs that they are intended to compensate.
	Government grants relating to property, plant and equipment are included in non-current liabilities as deferred government grants and are credited to the income statement on a straight- line basis over the expected lives of the related assets.

Note – Other (losses)/gains

20p39(b-c)	The group obtained and recognised as income a government grant of C100 (2012: nil) to compensate for losses caused by flooding incurred in the previous year. The group is obliged not to reduce its average number of employees over the next three years under the terms of this government grant.
	The group benefits from government assistance for promoting in international markets products made in the UK; such assistance includes marketing research and similar services provided by various UK government agencies free of charge.

6. Revenue recognition: multiple arrangements

Note – Accounting policies

The group offers certain arrangements whereby a customer can purchase a personal computer together with a two-year servicing agreement. Where such multiple-element arrangements exist, the amount of revenue allocated to each element is based upon the relative fair values of the various elements. The fair values of each element are determined based on the current market price of each of the elements when sold separately. The revenue relating to the computer is recognised when risks and rewards of the computer are transferred to the customer which occurs on delivery. Revenue relating to the service element is recognised on a straight-line basis over the service period.

(All amounts in C thousands unless otherwise stated)

7. Customer loyalty programmes

Note – Accounting policy

The Group operates a loyalty programme where customers accumulate points for purchases made which entitle them to discounts on future purchases. The reward points are recognised as a separately identifiable component of the initial sale transaction, by allocating the fair value of the consideration received between the award points and the other components of the sale such that the reward points are initially recognised as deferred income at their fair value. Revenue from the reward points is recognised when the points are redeemed. Breakage is recognised as reward points are redeemed based upon expected redemption rates. Reward points expire 12 months after the initial sale.

Note – Current liabilities – Other liabilities

	Group	
	2013	2012
Deferred revenue: customer loyalty programme	395	370

8. Put option arrangement

The potential cash payments related to put options issued by the group over the equity of subsidiary companies are accounted for as financial liabilities when such options may only be settled other than by exchange of a fixed amount of cash or another financial asset for a fixed number of shares in the subsidiary. The amount that may become payable under the option on exercise is initially recognised at fair value within borrowings with a corresponding charge directly to equity. The charge to equity is recognised separately as written put options over non-controlling interests, adjacent to non-controlling interests in the net assets of consolidated subsidiaries.

The group recognises the cost of writing such put options, determined as the excess of the fair value of the option over any consideration received, as a financing cost. Such options are subsequently measured at amortised cost, using the effective interest rate method, in order to accrete the liability up to the amount payable under the option at the date at which it first becomes exercisable. The charge arising is recorded as a financing cost. In the event that the option expires unexercised, the liability is derecognised with a corresponding adjustment to equity.

9. Foreign currency translations – disposal of foreign operation and partial disposal

21p48, 48A-C   On the disposal of a foreign operation (that is, a disposal of the group's entire interest in a foreign operation, or a disposal involving loss of control over a subsidiary that includes a foreign operation, a disposal involving loss of joint control over a jointly controlled entity that includes a foreign operation, or a disposal involving loss of significant influence over an associate that includes a foreign operation), all of the exchange differences accumulated in equity in respect of that operation attributable to the equity holders of the company are reclassified to profit or loss.

(All amounts in C thousands unless otherwise stated)

In the case of a partial disposal that does not result in the group losing control over a subsidiary that includes a foreign operation, the proportionate share of accumulated exchange differences are re-attributed to non-controlling interests and are not recognised in profit or loss. For all other partial disposals (that is, reductions in the group's ownership interest in associates or jointly controlled entities that do not result in the group losing significant influence or joint control) the proportionate share of the accumulated exchange difference is reclassified to profit or loss.

10. Share-based payments – modification and cancellation

IFRS2p27

If the terms of an equity-settled award are modified, at a minimum an expense is recognised as if the terms had not been modified. An additional expense is recognised for any modification that increases the total fair value of the share-based payment arrangement, or is otherwise beneficial to the employee, as measured at the date of modification.

IFRS2 p28(a),(c)

If an equity-settled award is cancelled, it is treated as if it had vested on the date of cancellation, and any expense not yet recognised for the award is recognised immediately. However, if a new award is substituted for the cancelled award, and designated as a replacement award on the date that it is granted, the cancelled and new award are treated as if they were a modification of the original award, as described in the previous paragraph.

If an equity award is cancelled by forfeiture, when the vesting conditions (other than market conditions) have not been met, any expense not yet recognised for that award, as at the date of forfeiture, is treated as if it had never been recognised. At the same time, any expense previously recognised on such cancelled equity awards are reversed from the accounts effective as at the date of forfeiture.

The dilutive effect, if any, of outstanding options is reflected as additional share dilution in the computation of earnings per share.

(All amounts in C thousands unless otherwise stated)

Appendix III – New standards and amendments

This appendix details (a) new standards and amendments effective for the first time for periods beginning on or after 1 January 2013 and (b) forthcoming requirements – that is, new standards and amendments issued and effective after 1 January 2013.

New standards and amendments

Below is a list of standards/interpretations that have been issued and are effective for periods beginning on or after 1 January 2013.

Topic	Key requirements	Effective date
Amendment to IFRS 1, 'First time adoption', on hyperinflation and fixed dates	The first amendment replaces references to a fixed date of '1 January 2004' with 'the date of transition to IFRSs', thus eliminating the need for companies adopting IFRSs for the first time to restate derecognition transactions that occurred before the date of transition to IFRSs. The second amendment provides guidance on how an entity should resume presenting financial statements in accordance with IFRSs after a period when the entity was unable to comply with IFRSs because its functional currency was subject to severe hyperinflation.	1 July 2011 (EU endorsed from 1 January 2013, although early adoption is permitted)
Amendment to IAS 12, 'Income taxes', on deferred tax	Currently IAS 12, 'Income taxes', requires an entity to measure the deferred tax relating to an asset depending on whether the entity expects to recover the carrying amount of the asset through use or sale. It can be difficult and subjective to assess whether recovery will be through use or through sale when the asset is measured using the fair value model in IAS 40 Investment Property. Hence this amendment introduces an exception to the existing principle for the measurement of deferred tax assets or liabilities arising on investment property measured at fair value. As a result of the amendments, SIC 21, 'Income taxes- recovery of revalued non-depreciable assets', would no longer apply to investment properties carried at fair value. The amendments also incorporate into IAS 12 the remaining guidance previously contained in SIC 21, which is accordingly withdrawn.	1 January 2012 (EU endorsed from 1 January 2013, although early adoption is permitted)
Amendment to IAS 1, 'Financial statement presentation', regarding other comprehensive income	The main change resulting from these amendments is a requirement for entities to group items presented in 'other comprehensive income' (OCI) on the basis of whether they are potentially reclassifiable to profit or loss subsequently (reclassification adjustments). The amendments do not address which items are presented in OCI.	1 July 2012
Amendment to IAS 19, 'Employee benefits'	These amendments eliminate the corridor approach and calculate finance costs on a net funding basis.	1 January 2013
Amendment to IFRS 1, 'First time adoption', on government loans	This amendment addresses how a first-time adopter would account for a government loan with a below-market rate of interest when transitioning to IFRS. It also adds an exception to the retrospective application of IFRS, which provides the same relief to first-time adopters granted to existing preparers of IFRS financial statements when the requirement was incorporated into IAS 20 in 2008.	1 January 2013

IFRS GAAP plc – year ended 31 December 2013

224

(All amounts in C thousands unless otherwise stated)

Topic	Key requirements	Effective date
Amendment to IFRS 7, 'Financial instruments: Disclosures', on asset and liability offsetting	This amendment includes new disclosures to facilitate comparison between those entities that prepare IFRS financial statements to those that prepare financial statements in accordance with US GAAP.	1 January 2013
Amendment to IFRSs 10, 11 and 12 on transition guidance	These amendments provide additional transition relief to IFRSs 10, 11 and 12, limiting the requirement to provide adjusted comparative information to only the preceding comparative period. For disclosures related to unconsolidated structured entities, the amendments will remove the requirement to present comparative information for periods before IFRS 12 is first applied.	1 January 2013
Annual improvements 2011	These annual improvements, address six issues in the 2009-2011 reporting cycle. It includes changes to: • IFRS 1, 'First time adoption' • IAS 1, 'Financial statement presentation' • IAS 16, 'Property plant and equipment' • IAS 32, 'Financial instruments; Presentation' • IAS 34, 'Interim financial reporting'	1 January 2013
IFRS 10, 'Consolidated financial statements'	The objective of IFRS 10 is to establish principles for the presentation and preparation of consolidated financial statements when an entity controls one or more other entity (an entity that controls one or more other entities) to present consolidated financial statements. It defines the principle of control, and establishes controls as the basis for consolidation. It sets out how to apply the principle of control to identify whether an investor controls an investee and therefore must consolidate the investee. It also sets out the accounting requirements for the preparation of consolidated financial statements.	1 January 2013 (EU endorsed from 1 January 2014, although early adoption is permitted)
IFRS 11, 'Joint arrangements'	IFRS 11 is a more realistic reflection of joint arrangements by focusing on the rights and obligations of the arrangement rather than its legal form. There are two types of joint arrangement: joint operations and joint ventures. Joint operations arise where a joint operator has rights to the assets and obligations relating to the arrangement and therefore accounts for its interest in assets, liabilities, revenue and expenses. Joint ventures arise where the joint operator has rights to the net assets of the arrangement and therefore equity accounts for its interest. Proportional consolidation of joint ventures is no longer allowed.	1 January 2013 (EU endorsed from 1 January 2014, although early adoption is permitted)
IFRS 12, 'Disclosures of interests in other entities'	IFRS 12 includes the disclosure requirements for all forms of interests in other entities, including joint arrangements, associates, special purpose vehicles and other off balance sheet vehicles.	1 January 2013 (EU endorsed from 1 January 2014, although early adoption is permitted)
IFRS 13, 'Fair value measurement'	IFRS 13 aims to improve consistency and reduce complexity by providing a precise definition of fair value and a single source of fair value measurement and disclosure requirements for use across IFRSs. The requirements, which are largely aligned between IFRS and US GAAP, do not extend the use of fair value accounting but provide guidance on how it should be applied where its use is already required or permitted by other standards within IFRSs or US GAAP.	1 January 2013

(All amounts in C thousands unless otherwise stated)

Topic	Key requirements	Effective date
IAS 27 (revised 2011), 'Separate financial statements'	IAS 27 (revised 2011) includes the provisions on separate financial statements that are left after the control provisions of IAS 27 have been included in the new IFRS 10.	1 January 2013 (EU endorsed from 1 January 2014, although early adoption is permitted)
IAS 28 (revised 2011), 'Associates and joint ventures'	IAS 28 (revised 2011) includes the requirements for joint ventures, as well as associates, to be equity accounted following the issue of IFRS 11.	1 January 2013 (EU endorsed from 1 January 2014, although early adoption is permitted)
IFRIC 20, 'Stripping costs in the production phase of a surface mine'	This interpretation sets out the accounting for overburden waste removal (stripping) costs in the production phase of a mine. The interpretation may require mining entities reporting under IFRS to write off existing stripping assets to opening retained earnings if the assets cannot be attributed to an identifiable component of an ore body.	1 January 2013

Forthcoming requirements

Below is a list of standards/interpretations that have been issued and are effective for periods after 1 January 2013.

Topic	Key requirements	Effective date
Amendment to IAS 32, 'Financial instruments: Presentation', on asset and liability offsetting	These amendments are to the application guidance in IAS 32, 'Financial instruments: Presentation', and clarify some of the requirements for offsetting financial assets and financial liabilities on the balance sheet.	1 January 2014
Amendments to IFRS 10, 12 and IAS 27 on consolidation for investment entities	These amendments mean that many funds and similar entities will be exempt from consolidating most of their subsidiaries. Instead, they will measure them at fair value through profit or loss. The amendments give an exception to entities that meet an 'investment entity' definition and which display particular characteristics. Changes have also been made IFRS 12 to introduce disclosures that an investment entity needs to make.	1 January 2014 (not EU endorsed at the time of going to print)
Amendment to IAS 36, 'Impairment of assets' on recoverable amount disclosures	This amendment addresses the disclosure of information about the recoverable amount of impaired assets if that amount is based on fair value less costs of disposal.	1 January 2014 (not EU endorsed at the time of going to print)
Financial Instruments: Recognition and Measurement Amendment to IAS 39 'Novation of derivatives'	This amendment provides relief from discontinuing hedge accounting when novation ot a hedging instrument to a central counter party meets specified criteria.	1 January 2014 (not EU endorsed at time of going to print)

(All amounts in C thousands unless otherwise stated)

Topic	Key requirements	Effective date
IFRIC 21, 'Levies'	This is an interpretation of IAS 37, 'Provisions, contingent liabilities and contingent assets'. IAS 37 sets out criteria for the recognition of a liability, one of which is the requirement for the entity to have a present obligation as a result of a past event (known as an obligating event). The interpretation clarifies that the obligating event that gives rise to a liability to pay a levy is the activity described in the relevant legislation that triggers the payment of the levy.	1 January 2014 (not EU endorsed at the time of going to print)
IFRS 9, 'Financial instruments'	IFRS 9 is the first standard issued as part of a wider project to replace IAS 39. IFRS 9 retains but simplifies the mixed measurement model and establishes two primary measurement categories for financial assets: amortised cost and fair value. The basis of classification depends on the entity's business model and the contractual cash flow characteristics of the financial asset. The guidance in IAS 39 on impairment of financial assets and hedge accounting continues to apply.	See Appendix IV

(All amounts in C thousands unless otherwise stated)

Appendix IV – IFRS 9, 'Financial instruments'

PwC commentary – IFRS 9

IFRS9p7.2.14 As part of the Limited Amendments to IFRS 9 project, the IASB tentatively decided at the July 2013 board meeting to defer the mandatory effective date of IFRS 9. The IASB agreed that the mandatory effective date should no longer be annual periods beginning on or after 1 January 2015 but rather be left open pending the finalisation of the impairment and classification and measurement requirements. As a result of these decisions and the changes being proposed to IFRS 9, the transitional guidance will change.

IFRS 9 is currently still available for early application. If the entity adopts IFRS 9 (2010) for annual periods on or after 1 January 2013, it provides the disclosures required by IFRS 7 as amended in December 2011 and does not need to restate prior periods.

For an entity considering adopting IFRS 9, an example of the disclosures relating to the implementation of IFRS 9 are included as Appendix VI to PwC's 'Illustrative IFRS consolidated financial statements for 2012 year ends".

Note that the IFRS 9 appendix VI disclosures in the "Illustrative IFRS consolidated financial statements for 2012 year ends" have not been updated for changes in IFRS standards, in particular IFRSs 10, 11, 12 and 13 and the amendments to IAS 1 and IAS 19.

GAAP UK Group Limited – Year ended 31 December 2013

Example annual report under UK GAAP

Introduction

The example annual report that follows includes the consolidated financial statements of the GAAP UK Group Limited. The annual report has been prepared to show the disclosures and format that might be expected for a group of its size that prepares its financial statements in accordance with Schedule 1 and Schedule 6 to SI 2008/410 and subsequent Statutory Instruments.

> Significant changes to this illustrative annual report include:
> - The Strategic report requirements and related amendments to the Directors' report for private companies
> - Updated illustrative Auditor's report for private companies.

GAAP UK Group Limited is a fictional, large private company that is incorporated in the UK. As part of a large private group, it has voluntarily adopted certain standards, such as FRS 22, 'Earnings per share'. It is not required to include a directors' remuneration report or corporate governance report.

Disclosures that are voluntary have been indicated by 'DV' in the margin. GAAP UK Group Limited has a number of UK and overseas investments, including subsidiaries and joint ventures. We acknowledge that GAAP UK Group Limited is not listed and perhaps would not adopt all the following standards; however, we have followed this course of action to show the disclosures necessary for those companies that do. GAAP UK Group Limited has adopted FRS 26 and the disclosure requirements of FRS 25, FRS 23 and FRS 29.

GAAP UK Group Limited is required to prepare a Strategic Report. It has prepared this on the basis of a private company. We have included an overview and the principles from the FRC Exposure Draft 'Guidance on the Strategic Report'. The Strategic report is intended to replace the operating and financial review. Guidance on an operating and financial review was given in the ASB's statement of best practice, 'Reporting statement: Operating and financial review (OFR)'. It is expected that, in due course, the FRC guidance will replace the ASB Reporting statement.

Guidance and information

References to source material are given in the left-hand margin. PwC guidance is presented in *italics*.

GAAP UK Group Limited – Year ended 31 December 2013

If you require further guidance on the UK law and accounting requirements affecting companies' financial statements, PwC's *Manual of accounting – UK GAAP 2012* may be of assistance.

This annual report does not show all conceivable disclosures. It should not therefore be used as a checklist. Neither is it a substitute for exercising judgement as to the fairness of presentation. These financial statements include many of the disclosure requirements contained in Financial Reporting Standards, Statements of Standard Accounting Practice, Urgent Issues Task Force Abstracts and Company Law applicable on or after 1 January 2013.

The suggested disclosure throughout is intended for guidance only and is not necessarily applicable to all groups or all companies. The names of the undertakings included in the annual report are used for illustration only; any resemblance to any existing undertaking is not intended.

Abbreviations

SI 2008/410 1 Sch 6	=	Statutory Instrument [year/number], Schedule [number], paragraph number.
s417	=	Companies Act 2006, section number.
APB 2002/2	=	Auditing Practices Board Bulletin, number.
DV	=	Disclosure voluntary.
FRS 3 p14	=	Financial Reporting Standard [number], paragraph number.
ISA (UK&I) 720 p11	=	International Standard on Auditing (UK and Ireland) [number], paragraph number.
SI 1996/189	=	Statutory Instrument [year/number].
SSAP 9 p14	=	Statement of Standard Accounting Practice [number], paragraph number.
UITF 38 p8	=	Urgent Issues Task Force Abstract [number], paragraph number.
Tech 24/03	=	Technical release [number], issued by the Institute of Chartered Accountants in England and Wales.

GAAP UK Group Limited

Example annual report for the year ended 31 December 2013

GAAP UK Group Limited – Year ended 31 December 2013

Contents

Strategic Report	1
Appendix I – Financial Reporting Council – Exposure Draft: Guidance on the Strategic Report – Overview and Principles	3
Directors' report	6
Independent auditors' report to the members of GAAP UK Group Limited	10
Consolidated profit and loss account	13
Statement of group total recognised gains and losses	15
Note of group historical cost profits and losses	15
Reconciliation of movements in group shareholders' funds	15
Balance sheets	16
Consolidated cash flow statement	18
Notes to the financial statements	19

Strategic report

Strategic report for the year ended 31 December 2013[1]

CA06 s414A The directors present their strategic report on the group for the year ended 31 December 2013.

Review of the business

The report should include a review of the business containing:

CA06 s414C(2)(a)
- a fair review of the business of the company; and

CA06 s414C(2)(b)
- a description of the principal risks and uncertainties facing the company.

Where non-GAAP numbers are disclosed, it should be clear that these differ from the GAAP numbers; the equivalent GAAP number should be disclosed; and there should be a reconciliation between the GAAP and non- GAAP numbers, together with relevant comment. This disclosure may be necessary to ensure that the annual report is fair, balanced and understandable

CA06 s414C(3) The review is a balanced and comprehensive analysis of:

- the development and performance of the business of the company during the financial year; and
- the position of the company at the end of the year,

consistent with the size and complexity of the business.

CA06 s414C(4) The review must, to the extent necessary for an understanding of the development, performance or position of the business of the company, include:

CA06 s414C(4)(a)
- analysis using financial key performance indicators; and

CA06 s414C(2)(b)
- where appropriate, analysis using other key performance indicators, including information relating to environmental matters and employee matters.

CA06 S414C(6) Note: For medium sized companies, where these indicators relate to non-financial information, disclosure is not required

General

CA06 s414C(11); SI 2008/410 7 Sch 1A. Disclosure may include any matters that are directors' report disclosure requirements but considered by the directors to be of strategic importance to the company. (If this is the case, the directors' report includes a cross-reference to the relevant information in the strategic report.)

CA06 s414C(12) The report must, where appropriate, include references to, and additional explanations of, amounts included in the financial statements of the company.

CA06 s414C(14) The report need not disclose any information about impending developments or matters in the course of negotiation if, in the opinion of the directors, such disclosure would be seriously prejudicial to the interests of the company.

---

[1] A small company is entitled to exemption from preparing a strategic report if it is entitled to prepare accounts in accordance with the small companies regime or it would be so entitled but for being or having been a member of an ineligible group. [CA06s414B].

CA06 s414D(1) By order of the board

CA06 s414D(1) AB Smith

    Company Secretary[1]

    26 February 2014

---

[1] The strategic report has to be signed by the company secretary or a director after it has been approved by the board of directors. The copy of the strategic report that is delivered to the Registrar of Companies must be manually signed by the company secretary or a director.

Appendix I – Financial Reporting Council – Exposure Draft: Guidance on the Strategic Report – Overview and Principles

In August 2013 the Financial Reporting Council (FRC) issued an "Exposure Draft: Guidance on the Strategic Report" (ED) to provide non-mandatory guidance to preparers. The existing guidance on the business review (the part of the directors' report that the strategic report will replace) is the Accounting Standards Board's (ASB) "Reporting Statement: Operating and Financial Review" (RS). At the time of writing, the FRC exposure draft is open for comment.

FRC ED Intro (vii) The draft guidance aims to be:

(a) principles-based;
(b) shorter and more streamlined than the RS;
(c) mindful of recent developments in narrative reporting best practice; and
(d) aligned with the requirements in the UK Corporate Governance Code.

The Accounting Council, in providing advice to the FRC on issuing the exposure draft, noted that the final guidance will replace the ASB's Reporting Statement. We provide illustrative disclosure requirements of the RS in Appendix II "Operating and financial review" as this is current guidance until it is replaced by new FRC guidance.

The exposure draft is structured into various sections with each section identifying –

- main principles or content elements; and
- supporting guidance including summary of legal requirements and where applicable, examples and linkage examples.

In this appendix we summarise the principles identified in the exposure draft.

Scope

FRC ED 2.1 The draft guidance has been written with quoted companies in mind. It may also serve as best practice guidance for other entities preparing strategic reports.

Purpose of the annual report

FRC ED 3.4 The purpose of the annual report is to provide shareholders with relevant information that is useful for making resource allocation decisions and assessing management's stewardship.

FRC ED 3.8 The annual report as a whole should be fair, balanced and understandable

Placement of information in the annual report

FRC ED 3.10 The placement of information in the annual report should facilitate the communication of the information contained within it.

Strategic reports and materiality

FRC ED 5.1 Information is material if its omission from or misrepresentation in the strategic report might reasonably be expected to influence the economic decisions shareholders make on the basis of the annual report as a whole. Such information should be included in the strategic report.

Conversely, the inclusion of immaterial information can obscure key messages and impair the understandability of information provided in the strategic report. Immaterial information should be exclude from the strategic report.

The purpose of the strategic report

FRC ED 6.1 The strategic report should provide shareholders of the company with the ability to assess how the directors have performed their duty to promote the success of the company for their collective benefit.

FRC ED 6.6 The strategic report should be fair[1], balanced[2] and understandable[3].

FRC ED 6.11 The strategic report should be concise.

FRC ED 6.16 Where appropriate, information in the strategic report should have a forward-looking orientation.

FRC ED 6.19 The strategic report should provide information that is entity-specific.

FRC ED 6.21 The strategic report should highlight relationships and interdependencies (linkages) between information presented in different parts of the annual report.

FRC ED 6.26 The structure and presentation of the strategic report should be reviewed annually to ensure that it continues to meet its objectives in an efficient and effective manner.

The content elements of the strategic report

FRC ED 6.31 The strategic report should include a description of the entity's principal objectives and its strategies for achieving those objectives[4].

FRC ED 6.37 The strategic report should include a description of the entity's business model[5].

FRC ED 6.42 To the extent necessary for an understanding of the development, performance or position of the entity's business, the strategic report should include the main trends and factors likely to affect the future development, performance or position of the business.[6]

FRC ED 6.49 The strategic report should include a description of the principal risks and uncertainties facing the entity[7], together with an explanation of how they are managed or mitigated.

FRC ED 6.55 The analysis in the strategic report should include the financial and non-financial key performance indicators (KPIs)[8] utilised by the directors to measure progress towards achieving a particular objective or strategy.

FRC ED 6.60 The strategic report should provide an analysis of the development and performance of the business in the financial year and of its position at the end of that year.[9]

FRC ED 6.64 To the extent necessary for an understanding of the development, performance or position of the entity's business, the strategic report should include information about:

(a) environmental matters (including the impact of the business of the entity in the environment)[10];

---

[1] Companies Act 2006 Section 414C(2)(a).
[2] Companies Act 2006 Section 414C(3).
[3] 2012 UK Corporate Governance Code C.1.1.
[4] Companies Act 2006 Section 414C(8)(a).
[5] Companies Act 2006 section 414C(8)(b).
[6] Companies Act 2006 Section 414C(7)(a).
[7] Companies Act 2006 Section 414C(2)(b).
[8] Companies Act 2006 Section 414C94).
[9] Companies Act 2006 Section 414C(2)(a) and (3).
[10] Companies Act 2006 Section 414C(7)(b)(i).

(b) the entity's employees[1]; and
(c) social, community and human rights issues[2].

FRC ED 6.68 The strategic report should provide a breakdown showing, as at the end of the financial year[3]:

(a) the number of persons of each sex who are directors of the company;
(b) the number of persons of each sex who were senior managers of the entity (other than persons falling within sub-paragraph (a)); and
(c) the number of persons of each sex who were employees of the entity.

FRC ED 6.72 To the extent that they are matters which are considered to be of strategic importance to the entity, the strategic report should also include information which would otherwise be disclosed in the directors report[4].

---

[1] Companies Act 2006 Section 414C(7)(b)(ii).
[2] Companies Act 2006 Section 414C(7)(b)(iii).
[3] Companies Act 2006 Section 414C(8)(c).
[4] Companies Act 2006 Section 414C(11).

Directors' report

CA06 s415(2) **Directors' report for the year ended 31 December 2013**

CA06 s415(1) The directors present their report and the audited financial statements for the year ended 31 December 2013.

SI 2008/410 Reg 10 Notes:
The directors' report must also comply with the relevant requirements of Schedule 7 to SI 2008/410.

Various matters listed below may be included in the chairman's statement, or the notes to the financial statements provided there is a cross-reference in the directors' report to where the matter may be found.

Branches outside the UK

CA06 Sch 7(1)(d) There must be an indication of the existence of branches (as defined in paragraph 7(1)(d) of Schedule 7 to SI 2008/410) outside the UK. (The disclosure of existence of branches outside the UK is only needed for those in the UK).

Future developments

SI 2008/410 7 Sch 7(1)(b) The directors' report must contain an indication of the likely future developments in the company's/group's business.

Note: This disclosure is likely to be relevant to the Strategic report. It could be included in the Strategic report and incorporated into the directotrs' report by cross reference.

Dividends

CA06 s416(3) Disclosure of the recommended dividend is required.

Research and development

SI 2008/410 7 Sch 7(1)(c) (see also SSAP 13 p30, 31 for notes to financial statements) Provide an indication of the group's research and development activities.

DV Comment on the profit and loss account charge for year (which must be separately disclosed in the notes to financial statements).

Donations

SI 2008/410 7 Sch 3 If the company, and/or any of its subsidiaries, made any donations to a registered political party or other political organisation in the EU (including the UK), any independent election candidate, or incurred EU political expenditure exceeding £2,000 in aggregate in the financial year, disclose:

- EU donations – name of political party and total amount given per party, by the company and each subsidiary that has donated individually.
- EU political expenditure – total amount incurred in the financial year, by the company and each subsidiary that has incurred such expenditure individually.

SI 2008/410 7 Sch 4 Total contributions to non-EU political parties must be disclosed, for the group as a whole in aggregate. (There is no threshold for this disclosure.)

Financial instruments

SI 2008/410 7 Sch 6 Where material for the assessment of the assets, liabilities, financial position and profit or loss of the group, the directors' report must contain an indication of:

- the financial risk management objectives and policies of the entity, including the policy for hedging each major type of forecasted transaction for which hedge accounting is used; and
- the exposure of the entity to price risk, credit risk, liquidity risk and cash flow risk.

Post balance sheet events

SI 2008/410 7 Sch 7(1)(a), (see also FRS 21, p19-22 regarding disclosure in the notes) The directors' report must include particulars of any important events affecting the company or group since the year end.

Directors

CA06 s416(1)(a) Provide the names of all persons who were directors during any part of the period.

DV Include changes in directors since the end of the financial year and the dates of any appointments and/or resignations of directors occurring during the financial year.

DV Include information regarding the retirement of directors at the AGM and whether they offer themselves for election.

Directors' qualifying third party and pension scheme indemnity provisions

CA06 s236(1–5) Disclose whether:

(a) at the time the report is approved, any qualifying third-party indemnity provision or qualifying pension scheme indemnity provision (whether made by the company or otherwise) is in place for the benefit of one or more of the directors or one or more directors of an associated company; or

(b) at any time during the year, any such provision was in force for the benefit of one or more persons who were then directors or directors of an associated company.

Employees

SI 2008/410 7 Sch 11(1) The requirements below only apply if the company employed on average 250 or more employees in the UK each week during the financial year.

SI 2008/410 7 Sch 11(3) A statement is required describing the action that has been taken during the period to introduce, maintain or develop arrangements aimed at involving UK employees in the company's affairs. This statement must discuss the group's policy on:

- systematic provision of relevant information to employees;
- regular consultation with employees or their representatives so that the employees' views may be taken into account in making decisions that are likely to affect their interests;
- encouragement of employees' participation in the group's performance by employee share schemes or other means; and
- achieving awareness on the part of all employees of the financial and economic factors affecting the group's performance.

SI 2008/410 7 Sch 10(3) A statement must be included as to the UK policy for giving full and fair consideration to applications for employment that disabled people make to the company, the policy for employment, training, career development and promotion of disabled people and for the continuing employment and training of employees who have become disabled while employed by the company.

Health and safety

DV

This includes areas such as:

- Policy on health and safety.
- Risks faced by employees and controls in place.
- Health and safety goals and progress towards their achievement.
- The total cost of occupational injuries and illnesses suffered by staff in the reporting period.

Corporate social responsibility

DV

This includes areas such as:

- Whether the board takes regular account of the significance of social, environmental and ethical (SEE) matters to the group.
- Whether the board has identified and assessed the significant risks to the group's short- and long-term value arising from SEE matters, as well as the opportunities to enhance value that may arise from an appropriate response.
- Whether the board has received adequate training and information to make this assessment.
- Information on the SEE-related risks and opportunities identified and how they may impact the business.
- Whether the group has effective systems for managing significant risks which, where relevant, incorporate performance management systems and appropriate remuneration incentives.
- A description of the policies and procedures in place for managing short- and long-term risks arising from SEE matters (or, if there are none, that this is the case and the reason for this) and information about the group's level of compliance with these policies and procedures.
- A description of how the disclosures in respect of SEE matters are verified.

Statement of directors' responsibilities

The directors are responsible for preparing the annual report and the financial statements in accordance with applicable law and regulations.

Company law requires the directors to prepare financial statements for each financial year. Under that law, the directors have prepared the group and parent company financial statements in accordance with United Kingdom Generally Accepted Accounting Practice (United Kingdom Accounting Standards and applicable law). Under company law, the directors must not approve the financial statements unless they are satisfied that they give a true and fair view of the state of affairs of the group and the company, and of the profit or loss of the group for that period. In preparing these financial statements, the directors are required to:

- select suitable accounting policies and then apply them consistently;
- make judgements and accounting estimates that are reasonable and prudent;
- state whether applicable UK Accounting Standards have been followed, subject to any material departures disclosed and explained in the financial statements; and
- prepare the financial statements on the going concern basis unless it is inappropriate to presume that the company will continue in business

The directors are responsible for keeping adequate accounting records that are sufficient to show and explain the company's transactions, disclose with reasonable accuracy at any time the financial position of the company and the group, and enable them to ensure that the financial statements comply with the Companies Act 2006. They are also responsible for safeguarding the assets of the company and the group and hence for taking reasonable steps for the prevention and detection of fraud and other irregularities.

Statement of disclosure of information to auditors

CA06 s418(2) The report must contain a statement to the effect that, in the case of each of the persons who are directors at the time when the report is approved:

(a) as far as the director is aware, there is no relevant audit information of which the company's auditor is unaware; and

(b) he/she has taken all the steps that he ought to have taken as a director in order to make himself/herself aware of any relevant audit information and to establish that the company's auditor is aware of that information.

Independent auditors

DV (see also CA 06 s489(1), (2)) The auditors, PricewaterhouseCoopers LLP, have indicated their willingness to continue in office, and a resolution that they be reappointed will be proposed at the annual general meeting.

CA06 s419(1) By order of the board.

CA06 s419(1) AB Smith
Company secretary
26 February 2014

Notes:

CA06 s419(1) (a) The directors' report must be signed by the company secretary or a director after it has been approved by the board of directors.

(b) The copy of the strategic report and directors' report that is delivered to the Registrar of Companies must be manually signed by the company secretary or a director.

Note: Where the financial statements are published on a website, the statement of directors' responsibilities may also include a statement that:

- the directors are responsible for the maintenance and integrity of the web site; and
- legislation in the UK concerning the preparation and dissemination of financial statements may differ from legislation in other jurisdictions.

Independent auditors' report to the members of GAAP UK Group Limited

> **Warning:** This audit report format was current at the date of going to press. However it may not be the most up-to-date version. It should not be used without checking that it is the appropriate version

Report on the financial statements

Our opinion

In our opinion:

- The financial statements give a true and fair view of the state of the Group's and of the Parent Company's affairs as at 31 December 2013 and of the Group's profit and cash flows for the year then ended;
- The financial statements have been properly prepared in accordance with United Kingdom Generally Accepted Accounting Practice; and
- The financial statements have been prepared in accordance with the requirements of the Companies Act 2006.

This opinion is to be read in the context of what we say below.

What we have audited

The Group financial statements and Parent Company financial statements (the "financial statements"), which are prepared by GAAP UK Group Limited, comprise:

- the Group and Parent Company balance sheets as at 31 December 2013;
- the Group profit and loss account for the year then ended;
- the Group statement of cash flows for the year then ended;
- the Group and Parent Company reconciliation of movements in shareholders' funds for the year then ended; and
- the notes to the financial statements, which include a summary of significant accounting policies and other explanatory information.

The financial reporting framework that has been applied in the preparation of the financial statements is applicable law and United Kingdom Accounting Standards (United Kingdom Generally Accepted Accounting Practice).

In applying the financial reporting framework, the directors have made a number of subjective judgements, for example in respect of significant accounting estimates. In making such estimates, they have made assumptions and considered future events.

What an audit of financial statements involves

We conducted our audit in accordance with International Standards on Auditing (UK and Ireland) (ISAs (UK & Ireland)). An audit involves obtaining evidence about the amounts and disclosures in the financial statements sufficient to give reasonable assurance that the financial statements are free from material misstatement, whether caused by fraud or error. This includes an assessment of:

- whether the accounting policies are appropriate to the Group's and Parent Company's circumstances and have been consistently applied and adequately disclosed;
- the reasonableness of significant accounting estimates made by the directors; and
- the overall presentation of the financial statements.

In addition, we read all the financial and non-financial information in the Annual Report to identify material inconsistencies with the audited financial statements and to identify any information that is apparently materially incorrect based on, or materially inconsistent with, the knowledge acquired by us in the course of performing the audit. If we become aware of any apparent material misstatements or inconsistencies we consider the implications for our report.

Opinion on matter prescribed by the Companies Act 2006

In our opinion the information given in the Strategic Report and the Directors' Report for the financial year for which the financial statements are prepared is consistent with the financial statements.

Other matters on which we are required to report by exception

Adequacy of accounting records and information and explanations received

Under the Companies Act 2006 we are required to report to you if, in our opinion:

- we have not received all the information and explanations we require for our audit; or
- adequate accounting records have not been kept by the Parent Company, or returns adequate for our audit have not been received from branches not visited by us; or
- the Parent Company financial statements are not in agreement with the accounting records and returns.

We have no exceptions to report arising from this responsibility.

Directors' remuneration

Under the Companies Act 2006 we are required to report if, in our opinion, certain disclosures of directors' remuneration specified by law have not been made.

We have no exceptions to report arising from this responsibility.

Other information in the Annual Report

Under ISAs (UK & Ireland), we are required to report to you if, in our opinion, information in the Annual Report is:

- materially inconsistent with the information in the audited financial statements; or
- apparently materially incorrect based on, or materially inconsistent with, our knowledge of the Group and Parent Company acquired in the course of performing our audit; or
- is otherwise misleading.

We have no exceptions to report arising from this responsibility.

Responsibilities for the financial statements and the audit

Our responsibilities and those of the directors

As explained more fully in the Directors' Responsibilities Statement set out on page 8, the directors are responsible for the preparation of the Group and Parent Company financial statements and for being satisfied that they give a true and fair view.

Our responsibility is to audit and express an opinion on the Group and Parent Company financial statements in accordance with applicable law and ISAs (UK & Ireland). Those standards require us to comply with the Auditing Practices Board's Ethical Standards for Auditors.

This report, including the opinions, has been prepared for and only for the Company's members as a body in accordance with Chapter 3 of Part 16 of the Companies Act 2006 and for no other purpose. We do not, in giving these opinions, accept or assume responsibility for any other purpose or to any other person to whom this report is shown or into whose hands it may come save where expressly agreed by our prior consent in writing.

John Smith (Senior Statutory Auditor)
for and on behalf of PricewaterhouseCoopers LLP
Chartered Accountants and Statutory Auditors
London
26 February 2014

GAAP UK Group Limited – Year ended 31 December 2013

Consolidated profit and loss account

			2013		2012	
FRS 28 p6, CA06 s403(2)						
CA06 s404(1)) SI 2008/410 1 Sch Formats		Note	£m	£m	£m	£m
FRS 9 p21	Turnover (including share of joint ventures)					
FRS 3 p14,30	Continuing operations:					
FRS 3 p16	Existing		532.8		368.8	
FRS 6 p23,28	Acquisitions					
	– Newsub plc		689.8		–	
	– other		51.6		–	
			–	1,274.2	–	368.8
FRS 3 p17	Discontinued operations		–	25.6	–	117.0
		2	–	1,299.8	–	485.8
FRS 9 p21, 27	Less: share of joint ventures' turnover					
	Continuing operations:					
	– existing		(9.1)		(9.9)	
	– acquisitions		(29.8)	(38.9)	–	(9.9)
SI 2008/410 1 Sch Formats	**Group turnover**	3	–	**1,260.9**	–	475.9
SI 2008/410 1 Sch Formats	Cost of sales	3	–	(1,083.9)	–	(342.4)
SI 2008/410 1 Sch Formats	Gross profit	3	–	177.0	–	133.5
SI 2008/410 1Sch 3	Net operating expenses	3	–	(70.8)	–	(30.1)
	Operating profit					
FRS 3 p14,30	Continuing operations		82.2		76.3	
	Acquisitions (after £40.2m (2012 £nil) goodwill amortisation)					
FRS 6 p28	– Newsub plc		21.6		–	
	– other		0.2		–	
			–	104.0	–	76.3
FRS 3 p17	Discontinued operations		–	2.2	–	27.1
FRS 3 p14	**Group operating profit**	3	–	**106.2**	–	103.4
SI 2008/410 6 Sch 20(3)	Share of operating profit in joint ventures (after £0.9m (2012: £nil) goodwill amortisation)		–	2.8	–	1.2

GAAP UK Group Limited – Year ended 31 December 2013

		Note	2013 £m	2013 £m	2012 £m	2012 £m
	Total operating profit: group and share of joint ventures					
	Profit on sale of subsidiary	2	–	109.0	–	104.6
FRS 3 p20	– Discontinued operations	5	–	6.3	–	–
SI 2008/410 1 Sch Formats	Net interest (payable)/receivable					
	– Group	3a	(11.3)	–	3.6	–
FRS 9 p21, 27	– Joint ventures	3a	0.7	(10.6)	–	3.6
FRS 17 App (ii) p6 FRS 12 p48	Other finance income	3b	–	4.0	–	4.0
SI 2008/410 1 Sch 3	**Profit on ordinary activities before taxation**		–	108.7	–	112.2
SI 2008/410 1 Sch Formats, FRS 16 p17	Tax on profit on ordinary activities	6	–	(82.8)	–	(48.8)
SI 2008/410 1 Sch Formats	**Profit on ordinary activities after taxation**		–	25.9	–	63.4
SI 2008/410 6Sch 17 FRS 2 p36	Equity non-controlling interests		–	(0.5)	–	(0.2)
SI 2008/410 1 Sch Formats	**Profit for the financial year**	25	–	25.4	–	63.2
FRS 22 p66, DV	Earnings per share expressed in pence per share	7				
	– Basic				2.23p	7.17p
	– Diluted				2.22p	7.03p
	Earnings per share from continuing operations expressed in pence per share	7				
	– Basic				1.55p	6.60p
	– Diluted				1.54p	6.48p

Statement of group total recognised gains and losses

Notes:

(a) If the group has no recognised gains or losses other than its profit or loss for the period, a statement to this effect must be given immediately below the profit and loss account.

(b) Where an associate or joint venture has gains and losses reported in its STRGL, or has such gains and losses when its financial statements are restated on to the investor's GAAP, the investor's share of such gains and losses must be included in the investor's consolidated STRGL. The amounts must be shown separately under each heading, if material, either in the statement or in a note referred to in the statement.

Note of group historical cost profits and losses

For the year ended 31 December	2013 £m	2012 £m
Reported profit on ordinary activities before taxation	108.7	112.2
Realisation of property revaluation gains of previous years	0.1	0.1
Difference between historical cost depreciation charge and the actual depreciation charge of the year calculated on the revalued amount	0.1	–
Historical cost profit on ordinary activities before taxation	**108.9**	**112.3**
Historical cost profit for the year retained after taxation and minority interests	**25.6**	**63.3**

Note: The above note is only required if the difference is material. The difference is unlikely to be material in this example, but is shown for illustrative purposes.

Reconciliation of movements in group shareholders' funds

For the year ended 31 December	Note	2013 £m	2012 £m
Profit for the financial year		25.4	63.2
Dividends		(23.7)	(15.7)
Other recognised gains and losses relating to the year (shown in STRGL)		(42.7)	10.7
Proceeds of ordinary shares issued for cash	21	2.6	4.7
Purchase of own shares	25	–	(23.1)
Nominal value of ordinary shares issued for the acquisition of Newsub plc	21	4.8	–
Premium (net of issue expenses) on ordinary shares issued for the acquisition of Newsub plc	27	913.6	–
Goodwill recycled on disposal of subsidiary	32	3.9	–
Adjustment in respect of employee share schemes	25	3.2	1.4
Net change in shareholders' funds		**887.1**	**41.2**
Opening shareholders' funds		167.0	125.8
Closing shareholders' funds		**1,054.1**	**167.0**

Balance sheets

At 31 December 2013

		Note	Group 2013 £m	Group 2012 £m	Company 2013 £m	Company 2012 £m
	Fixed assets					
	Intangible assets	8	1,078.7	–	–	–
	Tangible assets	9	406.8	91.3	11.5	9.7
	Financial assets					
	– Derivative financial instruments	19	12.1	4.9	–	–
	– Available for sale investments	14	523.1	410.0	–	–
	Investment in subsidiary undertakings	10	–	–	419.2	98.5
	Interests in joint ventures	10				
	– share of gross assets		105.6	7.2	–	–
	– share of gross liabilities		(96.7)	(5.4)	–	–
	– goodwill arising on acquisition		7.6	–	–	–
			16.5	1.8	–	–
			2,037.2	508.0	430.7	108.2
	Current assets					
	Stock	11	33.8	17.0	–	–
	Financial assets					
	– Derivative financial instruments	19	8.6	2.2	–	–
	– Current asset investments	13	25.3	55.3	–	48.7
	– Debtors	15	290.6	109.6	68.3	101.0
	– Cash at bank and in hand		74.8	40.5	7.0	0.5
			433.1	224.6	75.3	150.2
	Creditors – Amounts falling due within one year	16	(401.2)	(136.7)	(99.8)	(68.3)
	Net current assets/(liabilities)		31.9	87.9	(24.5)	81.9
	Total assets less current liabilities		2,069.1	595.9	406.2	190.1
	Creditors – Amounts falling due after more than one year	17	(865.5)	(427.9)	(240.5)	(17.0)
	Provisions for liabilities	20	(163.0)	(22.2)	(0.1)	(0.5)
	Net assets excluding pension asset		1,040.6	145.8	165.6	172.6
	Pension asset	34	15.0	22.0	–	–
	Net assets including pension asset		1,055.6	167.8	165.6	172.6

GAAP UK Group Limited – Year ended 31 December 2013

			Group		Company	
			2013	2012	**2013**	2012
		Note	**£m**	£m	**£m**	£m
SI 2008/410 1 Sch Formats	**Capital and reserves**					
SI 2008/410 1 Sch Formats	Called up share capital	21	**13.8**	8.9	**13.8**	8.9
SI 2008/410 1 Sch Formats	Share premium account	23	**10.8**	8.3	**10.8**	8.3
SI 2008/410 1 Sch Formats	Revaluation reserve	24	**7.5**	2.5	**2.3**	0.8
SI 2008/410 1 Sch Formats	Other reserves	27	**964.2**	5.8	**–**	–
SI 2008/410 1 Sch Formats	Profit and loss reserve	25	**57.8**	141.5	**138.7**	154.6
	Total shareholders' funds		**1,054.1**	167.0	**165.6**	172.6
FRS 2 p35, SI 2008/410 6Sch 17 (2)	Minority interests		**1.5**	0.8	**–**	–
	Capital employed		**1,055.6**	167.8	**165.6**	172.6

FRS 21 p17
CA06 s414

The financial statements on pages 19 to 73 were approved by the board of directors on 26 February 2014 and were signed on its behalf by:

CD Jones
Director

GAAP UK Group Limited
Registered number. xxyyzz

GAAP UK Group Limited – Year ended 31 December 2013

Consolidated cash flow statement

			2013		2012	
		Note	£m	£m	£m	£m
FRS 1 p7	**Net cash inflow from operating activities**	28	–	189.4	–	116.6
FRS 1 p7	Dividends received from joint ventures		–	0.1	–	0.2
FRS 1 p7	**Returns on investments and servicing of finance**					
FRS 1 p14(a)	Interest received		4.8		4.1	
FRS 1 p15(a)	Interest paid		(25.7)		(1.1)	
FRS 1 p15(b)	Issue costs of new bank loan		(5.3)		–	
FRS 1 p15(c)	Interest element of finance lease payments		(1.0)		–	
FRS 1 p15(e)	Dividends paid to minority interests		(0.1)		(0.1)	
FRS 1 p15(d)	Preference share dividends paid to shareholders		(0.1)		(0.1)	
	Net cash (outflow)/inflow from returns on investments and servicing of finance		–	(27.4)	–	2.8
FRS 1 p7	**Taxation**		–	(24.7)	–	(37.2)
FRS 1 p7	**Capital expenditure and financial investment**					
FRS 1 p21(a)	Purchase of tangible fixed assets		(106.1)		(34.5)	
FRS 1 p20(a)	Sale of tangible fixed assets		4.2		6.7	
	Net cash outflow for capital expenditure and financial investment		–	(101.9)	–	(27.8)
FRS 1 p7	**Acquisitions**					
FRS 6 p33, FRS 1 p24(a)	Purchase of subsidiary undertakings	31	(307.2)		(23.6)	
FRS 1 p24(a)	Net overdrafts acquired with subsidiary undertakings	32	(15.1)		–	
	Net cash outflow for acquisitions		–	(322.3)	–	(23.6)
FRS 1 p7	**Equity dividends paid to shareholders**		–	(23.7)	–	(15.7)
	Net cash (outflow)/inflow before use of liquid resources and financing		–	(310.5)	–	15.3
FRS 1 p7,52	**Management of liquid resources**	29	91.7		(21.9)	
FRS 1 p27,28	Reduction/(increase) in short-term deposits with banks					
FRS 1 p28	Purchase of current asset investments	14	(100.0)		(400.0)	
	Net cash outflow from management of liquid resources		–	(8.3)	–	(421.9)
FRS 1 p7	**Financing**					
FRS 1 p30(a)	Issue of ordinary share capital	23	2.6		4.7	
FRS 1 p31(c)	Purchase of own shares		–		(23.1)	
FRS 1 p31(d)	Expenses of share issue to acquire Newsub plc	29	(1.4)		–	
FRS 1 p31(b)	Capital element of finance lease payments	31	(10.8)		–	
FRS 1 p31(b)	Increase in borrowings	31	276.5		421.1	
	Net cash inflow from financing		–	266.9	–	402.7
	Decrease in net cash		–	(51.9)	–	(3.9)
FRS 1 p33	**Reconciliation to net (debt)/cash**					
	Net cash at 1 January	29	–	33.2	–	39.0
	Decrease in net cash		–	(51.9)	–	(3.9)
	Borrowings net of short-term deposits acquired with subsidiaries		–	(57.1)	–	–
	Movement in liquid resources		–	8.3	–	421.9
	Movement in borrowings		–	(260.4)	–	(421.1)
FRS 1 p33(c)	Other non-cash changes		–	(2.1)	–	(3.0)
FRS 1 p33(d)	Exchange adjustments		–	44.5	–	0.3
	Net (debt)/cash at 31 December	29	–	(285.5)	–	33.2

Notes to the financial statements

1 Accounting policies

SI 2008/410 (1), FRS 18,58 — The group financial statements have been prepared under the provision of the Large and Medium-sized Companies and Groups (Accounts and Reports) Regulations 2008 (SI 2008/410) and applicable accounting standards.

The principal accounting policies applied in the preparation of these financial statements are set out below. These policies have been consistently applied to all the years presented unless otherwise stated. The financial statements are prepared under the historical cost convention modified to include the revaluation of certain financial assets and liabilities.

Note: Company disclosures should be given where appropriate. These have not been included in these financial statements.

CA06 s464 — *Note:*
'Accounting standards' refers to those issued by bodies prescribed by regulations. The International Accounting Standards Board and the Accounting Standards Board are the only bodies so prescribed. Financial statements drawn up under UK GAAP should therefore only be prepared in accordance with the UK SSAPs and FRSs.

SI 2008/410 1 Sch (44), FRS 18 p55(a),56 — The accounting policies used for dealing with items that are judged material or critical in the context of the company's financial statements should be disclosed.

Where an accounting policy is prescribed by and fully described in an accounting standard, UITF Abstract or company's legislation, a succinct description of the policy should be given. Where an accounting policy is not prescribed by an accounting standard, a UITF Abstract or companies legislation, or an option permitted therein is used, a fuller description should be provided.

FRS 18 p55(b), 57 — A description should be given of those estimation techniques adopted that are significant — that is, where the range of reasonable amounts is so large that the use of a different amount from within the range could materially affect the view shown by the financial statements.

FRS 18 p58 — Where a company falls within the scope of a SORP, the financial statements should state the name of the SORP and whether or not the company has complied with it. Where there is a departure from the SORP, further disclosure is required.

SI 2008/410 6 Sch

Consolidation

- FRS 6 p21 — Basis of consolidation.
- FRS 2 p23 — Inclusion of all subsidiaries.
- FRS 9 p20,26 — Equity accounting for associates and gross equity accounting for joint ventures.
- FRS 2 p40 — Uniform accounting policies for group.
- FRS 2 p39 — Elimination of profits or losses on intra-group transactions.
- FRS 9 p31(b) — Elimination of investor's shares of profits or losses on transactions with amounts and joint ventures.

CA06 s474

Turnover

- FRS 5 AppG — Basis of income recognition and measurement for each principal income stream.
- UITF 26 — Barter transactions.

GAAP UK Group Limited – Year ended 31 December 2013

	Foreign currencies
SI 2008/410 1Sch 70	
FRS 23 p23	■ Basis of translating foreign currency assets and liabilities.
FRS 23 p44	■ Basis of translating results of foreign subsidiaries.
	■ Treatment of exchange differences arising on the retranslation of opening net investments in subsidiary companies and translation of results (if at an average rate).
	■ Translation of all other exchange differences.
FRS 23 p53	■ Functional currency if different from presentation currency and reason why.
FRS 23 p54	■ Any change in the functional currency and reason why.
FRS 24 p39(b)	■ Method adopted for dealing with results of foreign subsidiaries operating in hyperinflationary economies.

Capitalisation of finance costs and interest

FRS 15 p31, IAS 18 p56	■ Whether interest is capitalised or not.
	■ If capitalised, basis of capitalisation of interest and other finance costs.

Tangible fixed assets

FRS 15	
FRS 18 p55(a), 56	■ Whether carried at cost or revalued amount.
FRS 15 p 42	■ Basis and frequency of revaluations.
UITF 24, UITF 29	■ What is included in cost.
FRS 15 p 100(a)	■ Methods of depreciation (for example, straight line or reducing balance).
FRS 15 p100(b)	■ Useful economic lives/depreciation rates.
FRS 15 p100(d), FRS 18 p55(d)	■ The reason for any change in the depreciation method, useful lives or residual values, if the effect is material.

Goodwill and intangible assets

FRS 10, UITF 27	
FRS 10 p52	■ The method used to value intangible assets.
FRS 10 p55	■ The methods and periods of amortisation of goodwill and intangibles and the reasons for choosing those periods.
FRS 10 p71	■ Treatment of goodwill on disposal, including previously eliminated goodwill.
FRS 10 p56,57, FRS 18 p55(a)	■ The reason for any change in the amortisation method or period, if the effect is material.
FRS 10 p58	■ Where the period of amortisation exceeds 20 years, the grounds for rebutting the 20 year presumption.
UITF 27, 5	Where estimates of the useful economic lives of goodwill or intangible assets are revised, the carrying value should be amortised over the revised remaining useful economic life. This requirement applies equally where the presumption of a 20-year life has previously been rebutted as it does to other revisions of estimates of the useful economic lives of goodwill and intangible assets.
FRS 10 p64	■ Where negative goodwill exceeds the fair values of the non-monetary assets, the source of the excess negative goodwill and the periods in which it is being written back.

Investment properties

SSAP 19 p11	■ Basis of inclusion in the balance sheet.
SSAP 19 p13	■ Treatment of changes in value.

Research and development

SSAP 13 p30
- Classification of expenditure.
- Treatment of expenditure.

FRS 11 Impairment of fixed assets and goodwill

FRS 11 p14
- Basis for determining impairment write-down, by reference to higher of net realisable value and value in use.

FRS 11 p41
- Use of discounting in determining value in use.

FRS 11 p45
- Basis for using risk-free discount rate and method for adjusting cash flows for risk, where applicable.

FRS 11 p63
- Treatment of impairment write-down on revalued assets.

SSAP 4 p17 Government grants

SSAP 4 p28(a)
- Treatment of capital grants.
- Treatment of revenue based grants.
- Period over which the grants are credited to the profit and loss account.

FRS 29 p21 Accounting for financial assets

FRS 26 p14, 15, 39, 43, 45-47
- Basis of recognition and measurements (cost or valuation).

FRS 26 p58
- Recognition of impairments.

FRS 29appB5(a)-(f)
- For financial assets designated as at fair value through profit or loss:
    (i) the nature of the financial assets or financial liabilities the entity has designated as at fair value through profit or loss;
    (ii) the criteria for so designating such financial assets or financial liabilities on initial recognition; and
    (iii) how the entity has satisfied the conditions in paragraphs 9, 11A or 12 of FRS 26 for such designation. For instruments designated in accordance with paragraph (b)(i) of the definition of a financial asset or financial liability at fair value through profit or loss in FRS 26, that disclosure includes a narrative description of the circumstances underlying the measurement or recognition inconsistency that would otherwise arise. For instruments designated in accordance with paragraph (b)(ii) of the definition of a financial asset or financial liability at fair value through profit or loss in FRS 26, that disclosure includes a narrative description of how designation at fair value through profit or loss is consistent with the entity's documented risk management or investment strategy.
- the criteria for designating financial assets as available for sale;
- when an allowance account is used to reduce the carrying amount of financial assets impaired by credit losses:
    (i) the criteria for determining when the carrying amount of impaired financial assets is reduced directly (or, in the case of a reversal of a write-down, increased directly) and when the allowance account is used; and
    (ii) the criteria for writing off amounts charged to the allowance account against the carrying amount of impaired financial assets.
- how net gains or net losses on each category of financial instrument are determined, for example, whether the net gains or net losses on items at fair value through profit or loss include interest or dividend income;
- the criteria the entity uses to determine that there is objective evidence that an impairment loss has occurred;

	■ when the terms of financial assets that would otherwise be past due or impaired have been re-negotiated, the accounting policy for financial assets that are the subject of re- negotiated terms;
FRS 29p27(a)	■ methods and, where a valuation technique is used, assumptions applied in determining fair values for each class of financial assets or financial liabilities; and
FRS 26 p9	■ how assets are classified.

FRS 29p21

Derivative financial instruments and hedging activities

FRS 18 p14
FRS 29p21

Derivatives are initially accounted for and measured at fair value on the date a derivative contract is entered into and subsequently measured at fair value. The gain or loss on re-measurement is taken to the profit or loss account except where the derivative is a designated cash flow hedging instrument. The accounting treatment of derivatives classified as hedges depends on their designation, which occurs on the date that the derivative contract is committed to. The group designates derivatives as:

FRS 26 p86(a) ■ A hedge of the fair value of an asset or liability ('fair value hedge').
FRS 26 p86(b) ■ A hedge of the income/cost of a highly probable forecasted transaction or commitment ('cash flow hedge').
FRS 26 p86(c) ■ A hedge of a net investment in a foreign operation.

FRS 29p23,24

In order to qualify for hedge accounting, the group is required to document in advance the relationship between the item being hedged and the hedging instrument. The group is also required to document and demonstrate an assessment of the relationship between the hedged item and the hedging instrument, which shows that the hedge will be highly effective on an on-going basis. This effectiveness testing is re-performed at each period end to ensure that the hedge remains highly effective.

FRS 26 p89

Gains or losses on fair value hedges that are regarded as highly effective are recorded in the profit and loss account with the gain or loss on the hedged item attributable to the hedged risk.

FRS 26 p95
FRS 26 p97-98

Gains or losses on cash flow hedges that are regarded as highly effective are recognised in equity. Where the forecast transaction results in a financial asset or financial liability, only gains or losses previously recognised in equity are reclassified to profit or loss in the same period as the asset or liability affects profit or loss. Where the forecasted transaction or commitment results in a non-financial asset or a non-financial liability, any gains or losses previously deferred in equity are included in the cost of the related asset or liability. If the forecasted transaction or commitment results in future income or expenditure, gains or losses deferred in equity are transferred to the profit and loss account in the same period as the underlying income or expenditure. The ineffective portions of the gain or loss on the hedging instrument are recognised in profit or loss.

FRS 26 p101

For the portion of hedges deemed ineffective or transactions that do not qualify for hedge accounting under FRS 26, any change in assets or liabilities is recognised immediately in the profit and loss account. Where a hedge no longer meets the effectiveness criteria, any gains or losses deferred in equity are only transferred to the profit and loss account when the committed or forecasted transaction is recognised in the profit and loss account. However, where an entity applied cash flow hedge accounting for a forecasted or committed transaction that is no longer expected to occur, the cumulative gain or loss that has been recorded in equity is transferred to the profit and loss account. When a hedging instrument expires or is sold, any cumulative gain or loss existing in equity at that time remains in equity and is recognised when the forecast transaction is ultimately recognised in the profit and loss account.

GAAP UK Group Limited – Year ended 31 December 2013

FRS 26 p102	Where the group hedges net investments in foreign operations through currency borrowings, the gains or losses on the translation of the borrowings are recognised in equity. If the group uses derivatives as the hedging instrument, the effective portion of the hedge is recognised in equity, with any ineffective portion being recognised in the profit and loss account. The group has not separated out the interest element of the fair value of the forward currency contract. Gains and losses accumulated in equity are included in the profit and loss account when the foreign operation is disposed of.

SSAP 9 p32 **Stocks, work in progress and long-term contracts**

SSAP 9 p32, 4 Sch 27
- Basis of amount stated at in the balance sheet (for example, lower of cost and NRV, FIFO).
- Methods of valuation (for example, average price, FIFO).
- Basis for inclusion of overheads.
- Basis of provision for obsolete, slow moving and defective stocks.
- Method of ascertaining turnover and attributable profit for long-term contracts.

FRS 29p21, **Trade debtors**

FRS 29appBp5(d)(f)
- When an allowance account is used to reduce the carrying amount of financial assets impaired by credit losses:
  (i) the criteria for determining when the carrying amount of impaired financial assets is reduced directly (or, in the case of a reversal of a write-down, increased directly) and when the allowance account is used; and
  (ii) the criteria for writing off amounts charged to the allowance account against the carrying amount of impaired financial assets.
- The criteria the entity uses to determine that there is objective evidence that an impairment loss has occurred.

FRS 26 p43, 46(a), 59
- When a financial asset or financial liability is recognised initially, an entity measures it at its fair value plus, in the case of a financial asset or financial liability not at fair value through profit or loss, transaction costs that are directly attributable to the acquisition or issue of the financial asset or financial liability.

FRS 29p21 **Trade creditors**

FRS 26p43, 47
- When a financial liability is recognised initially, an entity measures it at its fair value plus, in the case of a financial asset or financial liability not at fair value through profit or loss, transaction costs that are directly attributable to the acquisition or issue of the financial asset or financial liability.
- After initial recognition, an entity measures all financial liabilities at amortised cost using the effective interest method.

FRS 29p21 **Borrowings**

FRS 26p43, 47
FRS 25p18(a), 28, 33, FRS 29p27(a)
- When a financial liability is recognised initially, an entity measures it at its fair value plus, in the case of a financial liability not at fair value through profit or loss, transaction costs that are directly attributable to the acquisition or issue of the financial asset or financial liability.
- After initial recognition, an entity measures all financial liabilities at amortised cost using the effective interest method.
- The substance of a financial instrument, rather than its legal form, governs its classification on the entity's balance sheet.
- The issuer of a non-derivative financial instrument evaluates the terms of the financial instrument to determine whether it contains both a liability and an equity component. Such components are classified separately as financial liabilities, financial assets or equity instruments in accordance with paragraph 15 of FRS 25.

Own equity instruments

- If an entity reacquires its own equity instruments, those instruments ('treasury shares') are deducted from equity. No gain or loss is recognised in profit or loss on the purchase, sale, issue or cancellation of an entity's own equity instruments. Such treasury shares may be acquired and held by the entity or by other members of the consolidated group. Consideration paid or received is recognised directly in equity.
- The methods and, when a valuation technique is used, the assumptions applied in determining fair values of each class of financial assets or financial liabilities. For example, if applicable, an entity discloses information about the assumptions relating to prepayment rates, rates of estimated credit losses, and interest rates or discount rates.

Leases

SSAP 21 p57 As lessee:

- Basis of recognition of fixed assets held under finance leases in the balance sheet.
- Depreciation policy for assets held under finance leases.
- Treatment of the interest element of finance lease rental obligations.
- Treatment of payments for operating leases.

UITF 28 p14
- Treatment of incentives to take on operating leases (for example, rent free periods).

SSAP 21 p60 As lessor:

- Policy for operating leases.
- Policy for finance leases.
- Policy for finance lease income.
- Treatment of the costs of assets acquired for the purpose of letting under finance lease.

UITF 28 p15
- Treatment of lease incentives.

Leases include hire purchase contracts which have characteristics similar to operating or finance leases.

FRS 12 ### Provisions

FRS 12 p14
- Basis of accounting for each class of provision.
- Extent of use of discounting.

FRS 17, UITF 35 ### Pensions and post retirement benefits

- Type of scheme – defined contribution or defined benefit.
- For defined benefit schemes – valuation frequency and method.
- Method of charging to profit and loss account.
- Treatment of actuarial gains and losses for defined benefit schemes.
- Funding policy.

FRS 16
FRS 19
UITF 19
FRS 19 p61
Taxation including deferred tax

- Basis of charge for taxation.
- Policy adopted for providing for deferred taxation.
- Policy adopted regarding discounting.

Share-based payment

FRS 20, UITF 32, UITF 25, UITF 38

- Basis of accounting.
- Basis of accounting for employee share ownership plans (ESOPs).
- Basis of recognition and measurement of the cost of share-based payments.
- Basis of accounting for employer NICs on employee share schemes.

Treasury shares

FRS 25 p33

- Basis of accounting.

Financial risk management

FRS 29 p31 The group's activities expose it to a variety of financial risks: market risk (including currency risk, fair value interest rate risk, cash flow interest rate risk and price risk), credit risk and liquidity risk. The group's overall risk management programme focuses on the unpredictability of financial markets and seeks to minimise potential adverse effects on the group's financial performance. The group uses derivative financial instruments to hedge certain risk exposures.

Risk management is carried out by a central treasury department (group treasury) under policies approved by the Board of Directors. Group treasury identifies, evaluates and hedges financial risks in close co-operation with the group's operating units. The Board provides written principles for overall risk management, as well as written policies covering specific areas, such as foreign exchange risk, interest rate risk, and credit risk, use of derivative financial instruments and non-derivative financial instruments, and investment of excess liquidity.

(a) Market risk

(i) Foreign exchange risk

FRS 29 p33(a) The group operates internationally and is exposed to foreign exchange risk arising from various currency exposures, primarily with respect to the US dollar and the euro. Foreign exchange risk arises from future commercial transactions, recognised assets and liabilities and net investments in foreign operations.

FRS 29 p33(b), FRS 29 p22(c) The management has a policy that requires group companies to manage their foreign exchange risk against their functional currency. The group companies are required to hedge their entire foreign exchange risk exposure with the group treasury. To manage their foreign exchange risk arising from future commercial transactions and recognised assets and liabilities, entities in the group use forward contracts, transacted with group treasury. Foreign exchange risk arises when future commercial transactions or recognised assets or liabilities are denominated in a currency that is not the entity's functional currency.

FRS 26 p73 The group treasury's risk management policy is to hedge between 75% and 100% of anticipated cash flows (mainly export sales and purchase of inventory) in each major foreign currency for the next 12 months. Approximately 90% (2012: 95%) of projected sales in each major currency qualify as 'highly probable' forecast transactions for hedge accounting purposes.

FRS 29 p33(a)(b) FRS 29 p22(c) For segment reporting purposes, each subsidiary designates contracts with group treasury as fair value hedges or cash flow hedges, as appropriate. External foreign exchange contracts are designated at group level as hedges of foreign exchange risk on specific assets, liabilities or future transactions on a gross basis.

| FRS 29 p40, IG36 | The group has certain investments in foreign operations, whose net assets are exposed to foreign currency translation risk. Currency exposure arising from the net assets of the group's foreign operations is managed primarily through borrowings denominated in the relevant foreign currencies. |

At 31 December 2013, if the pound had weakened/strengthened by 11% against the euro with all other variables held constant, post-tax profit for the year would have been £251,000 (2012: £220,000) higher/lower, mainly as a result of foreign exchange gains/losses on translation of euro-denominated trade receivables, financial assets at fair value through profit or loss and debt securities classified as available for sale. Equity would have been £1,913,000 (2012: £932,000) lower/higher, arising mainly from foreign exchange losses/gains on translation of euro-denominated borrowings designated as a hedge of the net investment in subsidiaries. The impact on equity in net investment hedges is netted by a corresponding credit/charge resulting from the translation of the hedged net investment. Equity is more sensitive to movement in pound/euro exchange rate in 2013 than 2012 because of the increased amount of euro-denominated borrowings designated as a hedge of the net investment and anticipated cash flows hedged in a cash flow hedge.

At 31 December 2013, if the pound had weakened/strengthened by 4% against the US dollar with all other variables held constant, post-tax profit for the year would have been £135,000 (2012: £172,000) lower/higher, mainly as a result of foreign exchange gains/losses on translation of US dollar-denominated trade receivables, financial assets at fair value through profit or loss, debt securities classified as available for sale and foreign exchange losses/gains on translation of US dollar-denominated borrowings.

(ii) Price risk

FRS 29 p33(a)(b) The group is exposed to equity securities price risk because of investments held by the group and classified on the consolidated balance sheet either as available for sale or at fair value through profit or loss. The group is not exposed to commodity price risk. To manage its price risk arising from investments in equity securities, the group diversifies its portfolio. Diversification of the portfolio is done in accordance with the limits set by the group.

The group's equity investments are publicly traded and are included in the FTSE-100.

FRS 29 p40, IG36 The table below summarises the impact of increases/decreases of the FTSE 100 on the group's post-tax profit for the year and on equity. The analysis is based on the assumption that the equity indexes had increased/decreased by 5% with all other variables held constant and all the group's equity instruments moved according to the historical correlation with the index:

	Impact on post-tax profit £m		Impact on equity £m	
	2013	2012	2013	2012
FTSE-100 UK	–	–	23	19

Post-tax profit for the year would increase/decrease as a result of gains/losses on equity securities classified as at fair value through profit or loss. Equity would increase/decrease as a result of gains/losses on equity securities classified as available for sale.

(b) Credit risk

Credit risk is managed on a group basis. Credit risk arises from cash and cash equivalents, derivative financial instruments and deposits with banks and financial institutions, as well as credit exposures to wholesale and retail customers, including outstanding receivables and committed transactions. For banks and financial institutions, only independently rated parties with a minimum rating of 'A' are accepted. If wholesale customers are independently rated, these ratings are used. Otherwise, if there is no independent rating, risk control assesses the credit quality of the customer taking into account its financial position, past experience and other factors. Individual risk limits are set based on internal or external ratings in accordance with limits set by the Board. The utilisation of credit limits is regularly monitored. Sales to retail customers are settled in cash or using major credit cards.

The below table shows the credit rating and the utilisation of the credit facilities of the six major counterparties at the balance sheet date.

Counterparty	Rating	31 December 2013		31 December 2012	
		Credit facility £m	Utilised £m	Credit facility £m	Utilised £m
Bank A	AAA	750	739	450	414
Bank B	AA	60	53	30	25
Bank C	A	40	34	20	17
		850	826	500	456
Wholesaler Q	A	64	26	62	9
Wholesaler T	BBB	18	17	31	2
Wholesaler Z	BB	9	4	11	1
		91	47	104	12

No credit limits were exceeded during the reporting period, and management does not expect any losses from non-performance by these counterparties.

(c) Liquidity risk

Prudent liquidity risk management includes maintaining sufficient cash and marketable securities, the availability of funding from an adequate amount of committed credit facilities and the ability to close out market positions. Due to the dynamic nature of the underlying businesses, group treasury maintains flexibility in funding by maintaining availability under committed credit lines.

Management monitors the group's liquidity reserves defined as follows:

Liquidity reserve as of 31 December 2013

	December 2013 £m	September 2013 £m	June 2013 £m	March 2013 £m	December 2012 £m
Cash at bank and on hand	74.8	84.7	106.1	73.5	40.5
Unused portion of committed long-term credit lines	212.0	207.0	196.0	224.0	253.0
Liquidity reserve	286.8	291.7	302.1	297.5	293.5

Cash flow forecasting is performed in the operating entities of the group in and aggregated by group finance. Group finance monitors rolling forecasts of the group's liquidity requirements to ensure it has sufficient cash to meet operational needs while

GAAP UK Group Limited – Year ended 31 December 2013

28

maintaining sufficient headroom on its undrawn committed borrowing facilities (note 19) at all times so that the group does not breach borrowing limits or covenants (where applicable) on any of its borrowing facilities. Such forecasting takes into consideration the group's debt financing plans, covenant compliance, compliance with internal balance sheet ratio targets and, if applicable external regulatory or legal requirements – for example, currency restrictions.

FRS 29 p33, 39(c)
FRS 29 B11E

Surplus cash held by the operating entities, over and above balance required for working capital management are transferred to the group treasury. The group treasury invests surplus cash in interest-bearing current accounts, time deposits, money market deposits and marketable securities, choosing instruments with appropriate maturities or sufficient liquidity to provide sufficient head-room as determined by the above-mentioned forecasts.

FRS 29 p39(a)(b)

The table below analyses the group's non-derivative financial liabilities and net-settled derivative financial liabilities into relevant maturity groupings based on the remaining period at the balance sheet date to the contractual maturity date. Derivative financial liabilities are included in the analysis if their contractual maturities are essential for an understanding of the timing of the cash flows. The amounts disclosed in the table are the contractual undiscounted cash flows.

At 31 December 2013	Less than 1 month £m	Between 1 and 3 months £m	Between 3 and 12 months £m	Between 1 and 2 years £m	Between 2 and 5 years £m	Over 5 years £m
Bank borrowings	11.5	21.9	54.2	188.4	192.6	642.0
Trade and other payables (including net settled derivatives)	103.6	41.1	154.2	50.2	2.7	3.0
At 31 December 2012						
Bank borrowings	11.7	8.7	21.2	164.1	74.3	219.6
Trade and other payables (including net settled derivatives)	31.2	25.2	27.9	5.0	2.7	3.9

FRS 29 p39(a) AppxB15

The table below analyses the group's derivative financial instruments that will be settled on a gross basis into relevant maturity groupings based on the remaining period at the balance sheet to the contractual maturity date. The amounts disclosed in the table are the contractual undiscounted cash flows.

At 31 December 2013	Less than 1 month £m	Between 1 and 3 months £m	Between 3 and 12 months £m	Between 1 and 2 years £m	Between 2 and 5 years £m	Over 5 Years £m
Forward foreign exchange contracts – Cash flow hedges:						
– Outflow	940.1	836.7	1,082.7	–	–	–
– Inflow	942.3	835.2	1,086.4	–	–	–
At 31 December 2012						
Forward foreign exchange contracts – Cash flow hedges:						
– Outflow	287.1	321.4	198.2	–	–	–
– Inflow	287.2	323.2	195.2	–	–	–

(d) Cash flow and fair value interest rate risk

As the group has no significant interest-bearing assets, the group's income and operating cash flows are substantially independent of changes in market interest rates.

The group's interest rate risk arises from long-term borrowings. Borrowings issued at variable rates expose the group to cash flow interest rate risk. Borrowings issued at fixed rates expose the group to fair value interest rate risk. Group policy is to maintain approximately 60% of its borrowings in fixed rate instruments. During 2013 and 2012, the group's borrowings at variable rate were denominated in the pound and the euro.

The group analyses its interest rate exposure on a dynamic basis. Various scenarios are simulated taking into consideration refinancing, renewal of existing positions, alternative financing and hedging. Based on these scenarios, the group calculates the impact on profit and loss of a defined interest rate shift. For each simulation, the same interest rate shift is used for all currencies. The scenarios are run only for liabilities that represent the major interest bearing positions.

Based on the simulations performed, the impact on profit or loss of a 10 basis point shift would be a maximum increase of £41,000 (2012: £37,000) or decrease of £34,000 (2012: £29,000), respectively. The simulation is done on a quarterly basis to verify that the maximum loss potential is within the limit given by the management.

Based on the various scenarios, the group manages its cash flow interest rate risk by using floating-to-fixed interest rate swaps. Such interest rate swaps have the economic effect of converting borrowings from floating rates to fixed rates. Generally, the group raises long-term borrowings at floating rates and swaps them into fixed rates that are lower than those available if the group borrowed at fixed rates directly. Under the interest rate swaps, the group agrees with other parties to exchange, at specified intervals (primarily quarterly), the difference between fixed contract rates and floating-rate interest amounts calculated by reference to the agreed notional amounts.

Occasionally the group also enters into fixed-to-floating interest rate swaps to hedge the fair value interest rate risk arising where it has borrowed at fixed rates in excess of the 60% target.

At 31 December 2013, if interest rates on pound-denominated borrowings at that date had been 10 basis points higher/lower with all other variables held constant, post-tax profit for the year would have been £22,000 (2012: £21,000) lower/higher, mainly as a result of higher/lower interest expense on floating rate borrowings; equity would have been £5,000 (2012: £3,000) lower/higher mainly as a result of a decrease/increase in the fair value of fixed rate financial assets classified as available for sale. At 31 December 2013, if interest rates on UK pound-denominated borrowings at that date had been 50 basis points higher/lower with all other variables held constant, post-tax profit for the year would have been £57,000 (2012: £38,000) lower/higher, mainly as a result of higher/lower interest expense on floating rate borrowings; equity would have been £6,000 (2012: £4,000) lower/higher mainly as a result of a decrease/ increase in the fair value of fixed rate financial assets classified as available for sale.

(e) Capital risk management

The group's objectives when managing capital are to safeguard the group's ability to continue as a going concern in order to provide returns for shareholders and benefits for other stakeholders and to maintain an optimal capital structure to reduce the cost of capital.

GAAP UK Group Limited – Year ended 31 December 2013

In order to maintain or adjust the capital structure, the group may adjust the amount of dividends paid to shareholders, return capital to shareholders, issue new shares or sell assets to reduce debt.

Consistent with others in the industry, the group monitors capital on the basis of the gearing ratio. This ratio is calculated as net debt divided by total capital. Net debt is calculated as total borrowings (including borrowings and trade and other payables, as shown in the consolidated balance sheet) less cash and cash equivalents. Total capital is calculated as equity, as shown in the consolidated balance sheet, plus net debt.

During 2013, the group's strategy, which was unchanged from 2012, was to maintain a gearing ratio over 40% and a BB credit rating. The gearing ratio has been over 40% and the BB rating maintained throughout the year. The gearing ratios at 31 December 2013 and at 31 December 2012 were as follows:

	2013 £m	2012 £m
Total borrowings	908.7	459.6
Less: cash at banks and in hand	(74.8)	(40.5)
Net debt	833.9	419.1
Total equity	1,055.6	167.8
Total capital	**1,889.5**	**586.9**
Gearing ratio	**44%**	**71%**

The decrease in the gearing ratio during 2013 resulted primarily from the issue of shares for the acquisition of Newsub plc (see note 32).

(f) Fair value estimation

The following table presents the group's assets and liabilities that are measured at fair value at 31 December 2013.

FRS 29p27B(a)

	Level 1 £m	Level 2 £m	Level 3 £m	Total balance £m
Assets				
Financial assets at fair value through profit or loss				
– Trading derivatives	–	4.9	–	4.9
Derivatives used for hedging	–	15.8	–	15.8
Available-for-sale financial assets				
– Equity securities	459.3	–	–	459.3
– Debt investments	39.2	–	24.6	63.8
Total assets	**498.5**	**20.7**	**24.6**	**543.8**
Liabilities				
Financial liabilities at fair value through profit or loss				
– Trading derivatives	–	2.2	–	2.2
Derivatives used for hedging	–	13.6	–	13.6
Total liabilities	–	**15.8**	–	**15.8**

GAAP UK Group Limited – Year ended 31 December 2013

The following table presents the group's assets and liabilities that are measured at fair value at 31 December 2012.

FRS 29p27B(a)

	Level 1 £m	Level 2 £m	Level 3 £m	Total balance £m
Assets				
Financial assets at fair value through profit or loss				
– Trading derivatives	–	3.1	–	3.1
Derivatives used for hedging	–	4.0	–	4.0
Available-for-sale financial assets				
– Equity securities	377.0	–	–	377.0
– Debt investments	21.1	–	11.9	33.0
Total assets	**398.1**	**7.1**	**11.9**	**417.1**
Liabilities				
Financial liabilities at fair value through profit or loss				
– Trading derivatives	–	3.3	–	3.3
Derivatives used for hedging	–	13.8	–	13.8
Total liabilities	**–**	**17.1**	**–**	**17.1**

The fair value of financial instruments traded in active markets is based on quoted market prices at the balance sheet date. A market is regarded as active if quoted prices are readily and regularly available from an exchange, dealer, broker, industry group, pricing service, or regulatory agency, and those prices represent actual and regularly occurring market transactions on an arm's length basis. The quoted market price used for financial assets held by the group is the current bid price. These instruments are included in Level 1. Instruments included in Level 1 comprise FTSE 100 equity investments classified as available for sale.

FRS 29p27

The fair value of financial instruments that are not traded in an active market (for example, over-the-counter derivatives) is determined by using valuation techniques. These valuation techniques maximise the use of observable market data where it is available and rely as little as possible on entity specific estimates. If all significant inputs required to fair value an instrument are observable, the instrument is included in Level 2.

If one or more of the significant inputs is not based on observable market data, the instrument would be included in Level 3.

The following table presents the changes in Level 3 instruments for the year ended 31 December 2013.

FRS 29p27B(c)

	Available for sale – Unlisted debt securities Total balance £m
Opening balance	11.9
Transfers into Level 3	–
Additions	9.7
Gains and losses recognised in the statement of total recognised gains and losses	3
Closing balance	**24.6**

GAAP UK Group Limited – Year ended 31 December 2013

The following table presents the changes in Level 3 instruments for the year ended 31 December 2012.

	Available for sale – Unlisted debt securities Total balance £m
FRS 29p27B(c)	
Opening balance	–
Additions	11.9
Gains and losses recognised in the statement of total recognised gains and losses	–
Closing balance	**11.9**

SSAP 25 p35-48

2 Group segment reporting

	Turnover		Profit before tax	
	2013 £m	2012 £m	2013 £m	2012 £m
Geographical analysis				
UK	576.9	207.2	34.6	39.7
Continental Europe				
– Group	243.1	98.8	28.8	28.8
– Joint ventures[1]	38.9	9.9	2.8	1.2
North America	344.7	91.6	11.0	10.4
Asia Pacific and Africa	96.2	78.3	31.8	24.5
	1,299.8	485.8	109.0	104.6
Profit on sale of subsidiary – UK			6.3	–
Net finance (cost)/income			(6.6)	7.6
Total				
– Group[2]	1,260.9	475.9	105.2	111.0
– Joint ventures	38.9	9.9	3.5	1.2
	1,299.8	485.8	108.7	112.2
Business analysis				
Food products	404.4	175.1	38.8	37.7
Personnel services	125.7	3.3	(15.4)	0.3
Retail services	113.8	113.3	35.8	36.2
Distribution services				
– Group	259.3	11.9	15.9	4.6
– Joint ventures[1]	38.9	9.9	2.8	1.2
Property services	154.3	84.9	18.8	18.0
Healthcare	203.4	87.4	12.3	6.6
	1,299.8	485.8	109.0	104.6

SI 2008/410 1Sch 68(2)

FRS 9 p21, 27 SSAP 25 p36

SSAP 25 p34

FRS 9 p21, 27

SI 2008/410 1Sch 68(1))

FRS 9 p21 SSAP 25 p36

SSAP 25 p34 Analyses by business are based on the group's management structure. Turnover between segments is immaterial. Geographical analysis is based on the country in which the order is received. It would not be materially different if based on the country in which the customer is located.

Notes:

SSAP 25 p36

1 The group's share of the profit before taxation and net assets of its joint ventures and associates should be separately disclosed on a segmental basis if any exceed 20% of the relevant total.

2 Where non-statutory profit measures are shown, the statutory profit measure should be also shown.

	Net assets	2013 £m	2012 £m
SSAP 25 p34(c)	**Geographical analysis**		
	UK	465.3	77.1
	Continental Europe:		
FRS 9 p21, 27, SSAP 25 p26	– Group	354.0	34.5
	– Joint ventures	16.5	1.8
	North America	505.7	17.0
	Asia Pacific and Africa	29.9	20.2
		1,371.4	150.6
SSAP 25 p37	Central	518.1	439.3
	Net debt excluding liquid resources (note 30)	(833.9)	(422.1)
	Total	**1,055.6**	**167.8**
	Attributable to:		
FRS 9 p21, 27	– Group	1,039.1	166.0
	– Joint ventures	16.5	1.8
		1,055.6	167.8
SSAP 25 p34(c)	**Business analysis**		
	Food products	199.2	62.2
	Personnel service	644.7	0.1
	Retail services	16.0	33.2
	Distribution services		
FRS 9 p21 SSAP 25 p26	– Group	420.1	46.1
	– Joint ventures	16.5	1.8
	Property services	37.3	10.1
	Healthcare	37.6	(2.9)
		1,371.4	150.6
SSAP 25 p37	Central	518.1	439.3
	Net debt excluding liquid resources (note 30)	(833.9)	(422.1)
	Total	**1,055.6**	**167.8**

SSAP 25 p37 Central net assets comprise assets, partially offset by liabilities that cannot practicably be divided between the segments. These liabilities and assets are:

	2013 £m	2012 £m
AFS investment	539.0	410.0
Other central current assets	39.3	68.7
Corporation tax payable	(60.2)	(29.4)
	518.1	439.3

GAAP UK Group Limited – Year ended 31 December 2013

FRS 3 p15,53 The above business analyses of turnover, profit before tax and net assets in 2013
FRS 6 p28   includes contributions from Newsub plc:

Geographical analysis	Turnover £m	Profit £m	Net operating assets £m
UK	300.6	12.7	57.2
Continental Europe			
– Group	120.2	5.6	24.8
– Joint ventures	29.8	1.1	6.6
North America	234.0	4.7	20.1
Asia Pacific and Africa	5.2	0.3	21.7
	689.8	24.4	130.4
Net interest (including £0.7m in joint ventures)	–	(17.4)	–
Total	**689.8**	**8.8**	**130.4**
Attributable to:			
– Group	660.0	7.3	123.8
– Joint ventures	29.8	1.5	6.6
	689.8	8.8	130.4

Business analysis	Turnover £m	Profit £m	Net operating assets £m
Food products	214.7	14.0	31.1
Personnel services	121.7	(8.4)	18.1
Distribution services			
– Group	190.9	10.1	75.4
– Joint ventures	29.8	2.2	6.6
Property services	66.9	(0.7)	0.4
Healthcare	65.8	7.2	(1.2)
	689.8	24.4	130.4
Net interest (including £0.7m in joint ventures)	–	(17.4)	–
Total	**689.8**	**8.8**	**130.4**

FRS 3 p53 The segment analysis of turnover, profit before tax and net assets for the UK and Food Products includes £25.6m (2012: £117.0m) turnover, £2.2m (2012: £6.2m) profit before tax and £5.3m of net assets at 31 December 2012 in respect of H Limited, which was sold during the year.

GAAP UK Group Limited – Year ended 31 December 2013

3 Cost of sales, gross profit, distribution costs and administrative expenses

		2013				2012		
FRS 3 p14		Continuing £m	Acquisitions £m	Discontinued £m	Total £m	Continuing £m	Discontinued £m	Total £m
	Turnover	523.7	711.6	25.6	1,260.9	358.9	117.0	475.9
	Cost of sales	408.4	613.5	(18.3)	(1,040.2)	(259.5)	(82.9)	(342.4)
	Exceptional cost of sales	–	3.5	–	(3.5)	–	–	–
FRS 10 App 1 p16	Goodwill amortisation	–	40.2	–	(40.2)	–	–	–
	Total cost of sales	408.4	657.2	(18.3)	(1,083.9)	(259.5)	(82.9)	(342.4)
	Gross profit	**115.3**	**54.4**	**7.3**	**177.0**	**99.4**	**34.1**	**133.5**
SI 2008/410 1 Sch Formats	Distribution costs	9.1	4.7	–	13.8			
SI 2008/410 1 Sch Formats	Administrative expenses	26.5	18.8	5.1	50.4	25.1	7.0	32.1
FRS 6 p31	Exceptional acquisition reorganisation costs	–	9.1	–	9.1	–	–	–
SI 2008/410 1 Sch Formats	Total administrative expenses	35.6	32.6	5.1	73.3	25.1	7.0	32.1
SI 2008/410 1 Sch	Less: other operating income – Royalties	(2.5)	–	–	(2.5)	(2.0)	–	(2.0)
	Net operating expenses	33.1	32.6	5.1	70.8	23.1	7.0	30.1
	Group operating profit	**82.2**	**21.8**	**2.2**	**106.2**	**76.3**	**27.1**	**103.4**

3(a) Interest and similar items

		2013 £m	2012 £m
SI 2008/410 1 Sch 66 (1)	Interest payable on bank loans and overdrafts	(16.4)	(1.3)
	Amortisation of issue costs of bank loan	(1.1)	–
SI 2008/410 1 Sch 66(2)	Interest payable on other loans	(5.2)	(0.1)
SSAP 21 p53	Interest payable on finance leases	(1.2)	–
	Preference share dividends paid: 7p per £1 share	(0.1)	–
SI 2008/410 1 Sch Formats	Group interest and similar charges payable	(24.0)	(1.4)
FRS 9 p21	Share of joint venture interest payable	(0.5)	–
	Total interest and similar charges payable	(24.5)	(1.4)
SI 2008/410 1 Sch Formats	Group interest receivable	12.7	5.0
FRS 9 p21, 27	Share of joint venture interest receivable	1.2	–
SI 2008/410 1Sch Formats, FRS 29 p20(b)	Total interest receivable and similar income	13.9	5.0
	Net interest (payable)/receivable and similar items	(10.6)	3.6

		2013	2012

SI 2008/410 1Sch 27(3), FRS 15 p31 — *Note: If the group capitalises interest or other finance cost into assets, the total finance cost for the year should be shown in the above table and the amount capitalised shown as a deduction in arriving at the net amount shown in the profit and loss account. In addition, the rate of capitalisation should be given.*

3(b) Other finance income

		2013 £m	2012 £m
FRS 12 p48	Unwinding of discounts in provisions (note 20)	(0.4)	–
FRS 17 App(ii) p6	Other finance income (note 34)	4.4	4.0
		4.0	4.0

4 Profit on ordinary activities before taxation

		2013 £m	2012 £m
	Profit on ordinary activities before taxation is stated after charging/(crediting):		
SI 2008/410 1 Sch Formats	Staff costs (note 33)	626.9	237.0
FRS 15 p100	Depreciation of tangible fixed assets		
	– Owned assets	68.5	22.9
SSAP 21 p50	– Under finance leases	2.6	–
	Amortisation of goodwill		
FRS 10 p53	– Subsidiaries	40.2	–
FRS 9 p27	– Joint ventures	0.9	–
FRS 3 p19	Loss/(profit) on disposal of fixed assets	6.6	(1.3)
SSAP 21 p55	Hire of machinery and equipment	12.2	1.2
SSAP 21 p55	Other operating lease rentals	5.2	5.6
FRS 29 p20(e)	Trade debtors impairment	21.8	18.4
FRS 3 p19	Costs of product remediation (see below)	3.5	–
FRS 6 p31, SI 2008/410 1 Sch 69(3), FRS 3 p19	Costs incurred in reorganising acquired businesses (see below)	9.1	–
FRS 23 p 52(a)	Net exchange differences on foreign currency borrowings less deposits	5.4	2.3
SI 2008/410 55(2)	Net fair value gains on open forward foreign exchange contracts	4.1	–

Services provided by the company's auditors and its associates

SI 2008/489, as amended by SI 2011/2198 ICAEW Tech 04/11

During the year the group (including its overseas subsidiaries) obtained the following services from the company's auditor and its associates:

	2013 £m	2012 £m
Fees payable to company's auditor and its associates for the audit of parent company and consolidated financial statements	0.7	0.6
Fees payable to the company's auditors and its associates for other services:		
The audit of company's subsidiaries	0.8	0.4
Audit-related assurance services	0.3	–
Tax compliance services	0.1	0.1
Tax advisory services	0.1	0.1
	2.0	1.2
Fees in respect of the GAAP UK Group Limited pension scheme:		
Audit	0.2	0.2
Audit-related assurance services	0.1	–
	0.3	0.2

SI 2008/489, as amended by SI 2011/2198

The requirements in the Companies (Disclosure of Auditor Remuneration and Liability Limitation Agreements) Regulations 2008 (SI2008/489 as amended by SI 2011/2198) on disclosure of auditor remuneration, apply to all financial statements with the following exceptions:

PwC commentary

Where a parent company is required to (and does) prepare consolidated financial statements, there is no requirement to disclose, in addition to the group audit fee, the audit fee for the company.

Large companies disclose the audit fee receivable by the auditor and its associates; small and medium-sized companies disclose the audit fee receivable by the auditor only.

The disclosures in respect of fees for 'Other services' are not required to be given by:

- small or medium companies or groups (reduced disclosure requirements apply);
- subsidiary companies in their individual financial statements, whose parents are required to, and do, prepare consolidated financial statements in accordance with the Companies Act 2006 and the subsidiary company is included in the consolidation; or
- parent companies in their individual financial statements, where the company is required to, and does, prepare consolidated financial statements in accordance with the Companies Act 2006.

The disclosure in respect of fees for 'Other services' provided by a distant associate of the company's auditor are not required if the total remuneration receivable for all of those services supplied by that associate does not exceed £10,000 or, if higher, 1% of the total audit remuneration received by the company's auditor in the most recent financial year of the auditor.

GAAP UK Group Limited – Year ended 31 December 2013

The statutory requirements in relation to auditors' remuneration are supported by guidance published by the ICAEW in Tech 04/11, 'Disclosure of Auditor Remuneration', which also provides example disclosures.

Disclosure is required in the parent company's group and individual financial statements in respect of fees paid in the following categories:

- fees payable to the company's auditor and its associates for the audit of the parent and consolidated financial statements; and
- fees payable to the company's auditor and its associates from the company and its associates for other services including:
  - audit of accounts of any associate of the company ;
  - audit-related assurance services;
  - taxation compliance services;
  - all other taxation advisory services;
  - internal audit services;
  - all other assurance services;
  - services relating to corporate finance transactions entered into or proposed to be entered into by or on behalf of the company or any of its associates; and
  - all other non-audit services.

Separate disclosure is required of:

- fees in respect of the company and its subsidiaries; and
- fees in respect of company pension schemes.

The 'company and its associates' refers to the subsidiaries of the company, and not to its associates as defined in FRS 9, 'Associates and joint ventures'. Similarly, references to the 'Auditor and its associates' refer to members of the same network of firms as the company's auditor.

Where fees for services performed by other parts of the audit firm that assist in the audit are invoiced either as part of, or separately from, the audit fee, those fees are included within the audit fees disclosed.

The above disclosure requirements will still apply to parent company's individual financial statements where it chooses to take advantage of section 401 Companies Act 2006 exemption from consolidation for intermediate holding companies within a group headed by a non-EEA parent company (where the financial statements are drawn up in accordance with the Insurance Accounts Directive or in an equivalent manner).

Exceptional items

SI 2008/410 1 Sch 69(3)
FRS 3 p19

During the year, a few batches of one of the group's food products were found to have been contaminated with small pieces of glass. As a precaution, the group recalled all batches of this product made within six weeks of the contamination being discovered. The exceptional charge to cost of sales represents the cost of correcting the defective machinery, replacing the withdrawn product and meeting product liability claims.

FRS 3 p46
FRS 6 p31

The costs of £9.1m incurred in reorganising the businesses of Newsub plc arise from the integration and streamlining of the food products and health care divisions within the group's existing businesses. These costs relate to the project identified and controlled by management as part of the integration programme set up at the time of Newsub plc's acquisition.

5 Profit on sale of subsidiary

	Discontinued operations	2013 £m	2012 £m
FRS 10 p71(c)(ii)	Gain on disposal of subsidiary's net tangible fixed assets (note 32c) Goodwill previously eliminated against reserves (note 32c)	10.2 (3.9)	– –
FRS 3 p20	**Profit on sale of subsidiary (note 32c)**	**6.3**	**–**
SI 2008/410 1 Sch 67(1) FRS 3 p20	Taxation	0.7	–

FRS 3 p24
SI 2008/410
1 Sch 69(3)

On 1 December 2013, the group sold H Limited, a wholly-owned subsidiary, for £15.7m in cash. The consideration is due to be received in 2014. H Limited was the group's only poultry product manufacturing operation, and the disposal completed the exit from these activities. As a result of the material change in the nature and focus of the group's operations that this disposal represented, it has been treated as a discontinued operation in the profit and loss account.

6 Tax on profit on ordinary activities — analysis of charge in year

		2013 £m	2012 £m
	Current tax		
SI 2008/410 1 Sch 67(2)	**United Kingdom**		
FRS 16 p17(a)	Corporation tax at 23.25% (2012: 24.5%)	20.2	31.5
FRS 16 p17	Double tax relief	(0.9)	(13.1)
		19.3	18.4
	Foreign tax		
FRS 16 p17(b)	Corporation taxes	22.8	18.5
	Other current tax		
FRS 16 p17	Adjustment in respect of prior years	1.6	5.3
FRS 9 p21	Share of joint ventures	1.9	0.8
	Total current tax	45.6	43.0
	Deferred tax		
FRS 19 p60(a)(i)	Origination and reversal of timing differences:		
	– UK	18.1	2.5
	– Foreign tax	19.1	3.3
	Impact of change in tax rate	–	–
FRS 19 p60	Total deferred tax (note 20)	37.2	5.8
	Tax on profit on ordinary activities	82.8	48.8

		2013 £m	2012 £m
FRS 16 p17	**Tax on recognised gains and losses not included in the profit and loss account (note 25)** UK corporation tax at 23.25% (2012: 24.5%)		
	Current tax credit allocated to actuarial losses	3.6	–
	Current tax credit/(charge) on exchange movements offset in reserves	3.5	2.8
	Other deferred tax movement relating to pension scheme	2.8	(0.8)
	Impact of change in tax rate[2]	–	–
		9.9	2.7

FRS 19 p64(a) The tax for the period is higher (2012: higher) than the standard effective rate of corporation tax in the UK for the year ended 31 December 2013 of 24.5% (2012: 26.5%). The differences are explained below:

	2013 £m	2012 £m
Profit on ordinary activities before tax	108.7	112.2
Profit on ordinary activities multiplied by standard rate of corporation tax in the UK of 23.25% (2012: 24.5%)	25.3	27.5
Effects of:		
– Adjustments in respect of prior years	1.6	5.3
– Adjustment in respect of foreign tax rates	6.4	5.9
– Pension cost charge in excess of pension cost relief	–	1.3
– Capital allowances in excess of depreciation	(20.4)	(4.8)
– Other short-term timing differences	3.2	(2.3)
– Expenses not deductible for tax purposes	29.5	10.1
Total current tax	45.6	43.0

Factors affecting current and future tax charges

During the year, as a result of the changes in the UK corporation tax rate to 21% from 1 April 2014 and to 20% from 1 April 2015, which were substantially enacted on 2 July 2013, the relevant deferred tax balances have been re-measured.

PwC commentary

Where further changes to the tax rates and laws have been announced but not substantively enacted at the balance sheet date, disclosures explaining the changes and their effect should be made.

7 Earnings per share

FRS 22 p10
FRS 22 p20,
DV

Basic earnings per share is calculated by dividing the earnings attributable to ordinary shareholders by the weighted average number of ordinary shares outstanding during the year, excluding those held in the employee share trust (note 25), which are treated as cancelled.

FRS 22 p31

For diluted earnings per share, the weighted average number of ordinary shares in issue is adjusted to assume conversion of all dilutive potential ordinary shares. The group has two classes of dilutive potential ordinary shares: those share options granted to employees where the exercise price is less than the average market price of the company's ordinary shares during the year, and the contingently issuable shares under the group's long-term incentive plan. At 31 December 2013, the performance criteria for the vesting of the awards under the incentive scheme had not been met and consequently the shares in question are excluded from the diluted EPS calculation.

GAAP UK Group Limited – Year ended 31 December 2013

FRS 22 p70(a) Reconciliations of the earnings and weighted average number of shares used in the
FRS 22 p70(b) calculations are set out below.

		2013 Number of shares (millions)	2012 Number of shares (millions)
FRS 22 p70(b)	Weighted average ordinary shares in issue	1,137.8	881.6
FRS 22 p70(b)	Options	5.0	17.2
FRS 22 p70(b)	Diluted number of shares	1,142.8	898.8

		2013 Continuing	2013 Discontinued	2013 Total	2012 Continuing	2012 Discontinued	2012 Total
FRS 22 p70(a)	Earnings (£m)	17.6	7.8	25.4	58.2	5.0	63.2
	Earnings per share						
	– Basic (p)	1.55	0.68	2.23	6.6	0.57	7.17
	– Diluted (p)	1.54	0.68	2.22	6.48	0.55	7.03

8 Intangible fixed assets

		Goodwill £m
SI 2008/410 1 Sch Formats	**Group**	
SI 2008/410 1 Sch 51(1)	**Cost**	
FRS 10 p53(a)	At 1 January 2013	–
FRS 10 p53(c)	Additions (note 32)	1,151.5
	Exchange adjustments	(32.6)
FRS 10 p53(a)	**At 31 December 2013**	**1,118.9**
SI 2008/410 1 Sch 51(3)	**Accumulated amortisation**	
FRS 10 p53(b)	At 1 January 2013	–
FRS 10 p53(c)	Charge for the year	40.2
FRS 10 p53(b)	**At 31 December 2013**	**40.2**
FRS 10 p53(d)	**Net book amount at 31 December 2013**	**1,078.7**
FRS 10 p53(d)	Net book amount at 31 December 2012	–

GAAP UK Group Limited – Year ended 31 December 2013

9 Tangible assets

	Group	Land and buildings short leasehold £m	Land and buildings freehold and long leasehold £m	Fit-out, plant and equipment £m	Vehicles and office equipment £m	Total £m
SI 2008/410 1 Sch 51(3)	**Cost or valuation**					
FRS 15 p100(e)	At 1 January 2013	–	20.7	85.2	77.2	183.1
FRS 15 p100(g)	Exchange adjustments	–	(3.2)	(14.7)	(9.3)	(27.2)
	Additions at cost	1.2	10.9	54.3	30.4	96.8
	Acquisitions (note 32)	4.2	64.7	181.6	61.9	312.4
	Surplus on revaluation	–	3.1	–	–	3.1
FRS 15 p100(e)	**At 31 December 2013**	**5.4**	**96.0**	**278.9**	**135.4**	**515.7**
SI 2008/410 1 Sch 51 (1)	**Accumulated depreciation**					
FRS 15 p100(f)	At 1 January 2013	–	2.4	52.8	36.6	91.8
FRS 15 p100(g)	Exchange adjustments	–	(0.3)	(5.5)	(4.2)	(10.0)
FRS 15 p100(c)	Charge for the year	2.0	4.4	39.5	25.2	71.1
	Revaluation	–	(2.3)	–	–	(2.3)
	Disposals	–	(0.2)	(24.6)	(16.9)	(41.7)
FRS 15 p100(f)	**At 31 December 2013**	**2.0**	**4.0**	**62.2**	**40.7**	**108.9**
FRS 15 p100(g)	**Net book amount at 31 December 2013**	**3.4**	**92.0**	**216.7**	**94.7**	**406.8**
FRS 15 p100(g)	**Net book amount at 31 December 2012**	–	18.3	32.4	40.6	91.3

SSAP 21 p49,50 Assets held under finance leases, capitalised and included in tangible fixed assets:

	2013 £m	2012 £m
Cost	21.2	–
Accumulated depreciation	(2.6)	–
Net book amount	18.6	–

SI 2008/410 1 Sch 27 (3)(b) FRS 15 p31(b), (c), (e)

Note:
If the group capitalises finance costs directly attributable to tangible fixed assets, the amount added in the year and the cumulative total of such interest included at the balance sheet date should be disclosed. In addition, disclosure of the rate of capitalisation is required.

GAAP UK Group Limited – Year ended 31 December 2013

	Company	Land and buildings short leasehold £m	Land and buildings freehold and long leasehold £m	Total £m
SI 2008/410 1 Sch 51(1)	**Cost or valuation**			
FRS 15 p100(e)	At 1 January 2013	–	10.9	10.9
FRS 15 p100(g)	Additions at cost	0.1	0.6	0.7
	Surplus on revaluation	–	1.1	1.1
	Disposals	–	(0.3)	(0.3)
FRS 15 p100(e)	**At 31 December 2013**	**0.1**	**12.3**	**12.4**
SI 2008/410 1 Sch 51(3)	**Accumulated depreciation**			
FRS 15 p100(f)	At 1 January 2013	–	1.2	1.2
FRS 15 p100(g)	Charge for year	–	0.3	0.3
	Revaluation	–	(0.4)	(0.4)
	Disposals	–	(0.2)	(0.2)
FRS 15 p100(f)	**At 31 December 2013**	–	**0.9**	**0.9**
FRS 15 p100(g)	**Net book amount at 31 December 2013**	**0.1**	**11.4**	**11.5**
FRS 15 p100(g)	Net book amount at 31 December 2012	–	9.7	9.7

SI 2008/410 1 Sch 34 (2), SI 2008/410 1 Sch 52(a), FRS 15 p74(a)(ii)(iii), FRS 15 p74(a)(i), (v)
The group's freehold properties and long leasehold properties were revalued at 30 November 2013, on the basis of existing use value by independent qualified valuers. The valuations were undertaken in accordance with the Appraisal and Valuation Manual of the Royal Institution of Chartered Surveyors in the United Kingdom by Surveyor & Son, a firm of independent Chartered Surveyors and overseas by valuers having equivalent professional qualifications.

FRS 15 p74(a)(i) These valuations have been incorporated into the financial statements; the resulting revaluation adjustments have been taken to the revaluation reserve. The revaluations during the year ended 31 December 2013 resulted in a revaluation surplus of £5.4m (note 24).

FRS 19 p15 No deferred tax is provided on timing differences arising from the revaluation of fixed assets unless, by the balance sheet date, a binding commitment to sell the asset has been entered into and it is unlikely that any gain will be rolled over.

		Group		Company	
		2013 £m	2012 £m	2013 £m	2012 £m
SI 2008/410 1 Sch 53	**Analysis of net book value of land and buildings – freehold and long leasehold**				
	Freehold	87.1	18.3	10.8	9.7
SI 2008/410 10 Sch 7	Leasehold: (over 50 years unexpired)	4.9	–	0.6	–
		92.0	**18.3**	**11.4**	**9.7**

GAAP UK Group Limited – Year ended 31 December 2013

If the revalued assets were stated on the historical cost basis, the amounts would be as follows:

Freehold and long leasehold land and buildings

	Group 2013 £m	Group 2012 £m	Company 2013 £m	Company 2012 £m
At cost	88.8	17.1	10.5	9.1
Aggregate depreciation	(4.3)	(1.3)	(0.5)	(0.2)
Net book value based on historical cost	84.5	15.8	10.0	8.9

SI 2008/410 1 Sch 34 (3),(4), FRS 15 p74(a)(iv)

10 Investments in subsidiaries and joint ventures

SI 2008/410 1 Sch Formats, FRS 29 p29(b), SI 2008/410 1 Sch 51(1)

	Group 2013 £m	Group 2012 £m	Company 2013 £m	Company 2012 £m
Shares in group undertakings				
At 1 January	–	–	98.5	95.0
Additions in year	–	–	320.7	3.5
At 31 December	–	–	419.2	98.5
Interests in joint ventures				
At 1 January				
– Net assets	1.8	1.5	–	–
– Goodwill	–	–	–	–
	1.8	1.5	–	–
Exchange adjustments	(0.9)	(0.1)	–	–
Additions				
– Net assets	5.5	–	–	–
– Goodwill	8.5	–	–	–
Share of profits retained	2.5	0.4	–	–
At 31 December				
– Net assets	8.9	1.8	–	–
– Goodwill	8.5	–	–	–
	17.4	1.8	–	–
Accumulated amortisation of goodwill				
At 1 January	–	–	–	–
Charge for the year	(0.9)	–	–	–
At 31 December	(0.9)	–	–	–
Net book amount at 31 December				
– Net assets	8.9	1.8	–	–
– Goodwill	7.6	–	–	–
Total fixed asset investments	16.5	1.8	419.2	98.5

SI 2008/410 6 Sch 20(2)
FRS 9 p29
FRS 9 p29
FRS 9 p29

FRS 9 p57,58 Note:
Further disclosures are required for associates and joint ventures if the 15% and/or 25% thresholds are exceeded.

CA06 s410 (1),(2),(3) Investments in group undertakings are stated at cost. As permitted by section 615 of the Companies Act 2006, where the relief afforded under section 612 of the

Companies Act 2006 applies, cost is the aggregate of the nominal value of the relevant number of the company's shares and the fair value of any other consideration given to acquire the share capital of the subsidiary undertakings. The directors consider that to give full particulars of all subsidiary undertakings would lead to a statement of excessive length. A list of principal subsidiary undertakings and joint ventures is given in Note 40. A full list of subsidiary undertakings and joint ventures at 31 December 2013 will be annexed to the company's next annual return.

FRS 10 p55   The goodwill arising on the joint ventures acquired with Newsub plc is being amortised on a straight-line basis over five years. This is the period over which the directors estimate that values of the underlying businesses are expected to exceed the values of the underlying assets.

SI 2008/410
1 Sch Formats

11 Stocks

	Group 2013 £m	Group 2012 £m	Company 2013 £m	Company 2012 £m
Raw materials and consumables	6.1	4.3	–	–
Work in progress	3.0	0.8	–	–
Finished goods	24.7	11.9	–	–
	33.8	17.0	–	–

SSAP 9 p27
SI 2008/410
1 Sch Formats

SI 2008/410
1 Sch 28(3),(4)

Note:
If there is a material difference between the balance sheet amount of stock and its replacement cost, the latter amount should be disclosed.

FRS 29 p6

12 Financial instruments by category

The accounting policies for financial instruments on pages 21 to 23 have been applied to the line items below:

Group	Loans and receivables £m	Assets at fair value through profit and loss £m	Derivatives used for hedging £m	Available for sale £m	Total £m
Assets at 31 December 2013					
Available-for-sale investments	–	–	–	523.1	523.1
Derivative financial instruments	–	4.9	15.8	–	20.7
Current asset investments	25.3	–	–	–	25.3
Debtors	290.6	–	–	–	290.6
Cash at bank and in hand	74.8	–	–	–	74.8
	390.7	4.9	15.8	523.1	934.5
Assets at 31 December 2012					
Available-for-sale investments	–	–	–	410.0	410.0
Derivative financial instruments	–	3.1	4.0	–	7.1
Current asset investments	55.3	–	–	–	55.3
Debtors	109.6	–	–	–	109.6
Cash at bank and in hand	40.5	–	–	–	40.5
	205.4	3.1	4.0	410.0	622.5

Group	Liabilities at fair value through profit and loss £m	Derivatives used for hedging £m	Other financial liabilities £m	Total £m
Liabilities at 31 December 2013				
Borrowings	–	–	908.7	908.7
Derivative financial instruments	13.6	2.2	–	15.8
	13.6	2.2	908.7	924.5
Liabilities at 31 December 2012				
Borrowings	–	–	459.6	459.6
Derivative financial instruments	13.8	3.3	–	17.1
	13.8	3.3	459.6	476.7

Company

All financial assets of the company were categorised as loans and receivables at both 31 December 2013 and 31 December 2012. All financial liabilities of the company were categorised as other financial liabilities at both 31 December 2013 and 31 December 2012.

SI 2008/410 1 Sch Formats, FRS 29 p29(b)

13 Current asset investments

	Group 2013 £m	Group 2012 £m	Company 2013 £m	Company 2012 £m
Short-term deposits	25.3	55.3	–	48.7

FRS 29 p6 Short-term deposits are with major UK banks. The credit risk associated with these investments is considered to be low.

FRS 29p8(d), 25

14 Available-for-sale investments

	Group 2013 £m	Group 2012 £m	Company 2013 £m	Company 2012 £m
At 1 January	410.0	12.8	–	–
Exchange differences (note 27)	2.0	1.2	–	–
Additions	100.0	400.0	–	–
Disposals	(2.0)	–		
Revaluation surplus/(deficit) transfer to equity (note 27)	13.1	(4.0)	–	–
At 31 December	523.1	410.0	–	–

SI 2008/410 1Sch 40

FRS 29 p16 There were no impairment provisions on the available-for-sale investments in 2013 or 2012.

SI 2008/410 1 Sch 23-26, FRS 29p27(b), 31, 34(c)	Available-for-sale financial assets include the following:	

	2013 £m	2012 £m
Listed securities:		
– Equity securities – UK	459.3	377.0
– Debentures with fixed interest of 6.5% and maturity date of 12 August 2014[1]	39.2	21.1
Unlisted securities:		
– Debt securities traded on inactive markets	24.6	11.9
	523.1	410.0

FRS 29 p27(a) The fair values of unlisted securities are based on cash flows discounted using a rate based on the market interest rate and the risk premium specific to the unlisted securities 2013: 6% (2012: 5.8%).

	2013 £m	2012 £m
Listed securities:		
– Equity securities - UK	443.2	367.0
– Debentures with fixed interest of 6.5% and maturity date of 12 August 2014	35.2	21.1
Unlisted securities:		
–Debt securities	21.6	11.9
	500.0	400.0

15 Debtors

SI 2008/410 1 Sch Formats

	Group		Company	
	2013 £m	2012 £m	2013 £m	2012 £m
Amounts falling due within one year:				
Trade debtors (FRS 29p36)	230.2	100.6	–	–
Less: Provision for impairment of receivables	(8.0)	(7.0)	–	–
	222.2	93.6	–	–
Amounts owed by group undertakings	–	–	67.1	55.4
Amounts owed by joint ventures (*all trading balances*) (FRS 9 p55)	1.3	1.5	–	–
Amount due on sale of subsidiary (note 32(c))	15.7	–	–	–
Other debtors (see below)	39.4	5.8	–	–
Prepayments and accrued income	12.0	8.7	–	–
Dividends due from group undertakings	–	–	1.2	45.6
	290.6	109.6	68.3	101.0

FRS 29p25, 29(a) The carrying amount of debtors is a reasonable approximation to fair value.

---

[1] Effective interest rate was 7.3%.

Reference	Notes
SI 2008/410 1 Sch Formats	The amount falling due after more than one year must be shown separately for each item included within debtors.
UITF 4 p3	Debtors due after one year must be disclosed separately on the face of the balance sheet if material to net current assets.

Other debtors at 31 December 2013 include £7,000 in respect of loans to two officers of the company.

	2013 £m	2012 £m
3 to 6 months past due	8.5	7.3
Over 6 months past due	1.5	1.9
	10.0	9.2

FRS 29 p37(b) The debtors determined as individually impaired were mainly wholesalers, which are in unexpected difficult economic situations; it was assessed that not all of the debtor balance may be recovered.

FRS 29 p37(a)
FRS 29 p36 Trade debtors that are less than three months past their due date are not considered impaired. As of 31 December 2013, trade debtors of carrying value of £7.0m (2012: £5.8m) were past their due date but not impaired. These are balances from a number of independent customers and there is no history of defaults for these customers recently. The ageing of the trade debtors, which are past due but not impaired is the following:

	2013 £m	2012 £m
Up to 3 months past due	2.6	2.2
3 to 6 months past due	0.9	0.7
Over 6 months past due	3.5	2.9
	7.0	5.8

FRS 29 p31 Concentration of credit risk with respect to trade receivables is limited due to the group's customer base being large and unrelated. Management therefore believes there is no further credit risk provision required in excess of normal provision for doubtful receivables.

FRS 29 p36(c)) The credit quality of trade debtors that are neither past due nor impaired is assessed by reference to external credit ratings where available. Where no external credit rating is available, historical information about counterparty default rates is used.

Trade debtors that are neither past due nor impaired are shown by their credit risk below.

	2013 £m	2012 £m
Counterparties with external credit rating:		
A	56.7	20.3
BB	17.0	4.8
BBB	40.9	7.3
	114.6	32.4
Counterparties with no external credit rating:		
New customers (less than 6 months)	23.4	13.9
Existing customers with no defaults in the past	49.5	26.7
Existing customers with some defaults in the past	25.7	12.6
	98.6	53.2
Total neither past due nor impaired	213.2	85.6

FRS 29 p36(d) None of those trade debtors that are neither past due nor impaired have had their terms re-negotiated.

FRS 29 p31, 34(c) The carrying amounts of the group's debtors are denominated in the following currencies:

	2013 £m	2012 £m
Pounds	210.6	78.7
Euros	19.6	9.7
US dollars	50.4	15.2
Other currencies	10.0	6.0
	290.6	109.6

FRS 29 p16 Movements on the provision for impairment of trade debtors are as follows:

	2013 £m	2012 £m
At 1 January	7.0	6.0
FRS 29 p20(e) Provision for debtors impairment	22.3	18.6
Debtors written off during the year as uncollectible	(20.8)	(17.4)
Unused amounts reversed	(0.5)	(0.2)
At 31 December	**8.0**	**7.0**

FRS 29 p16 The other classes within debtors do not contain impaired assets nor items past due date. Of the amounts due in other classes, £34.6m (2012: £4.4m) have a credit rating of BB or better. The remaining £11.8m (2012: £2.9m) do not have external credit ratings but are long established customers of the company with no history of default.

16 Creditors – Amounts falling due within one year

SI 2008/410 1 Sch Formats, FRS 29 p8(f)

	Group 2013 £m	Group 2012 £m	Company 2013 £m	Company 2012 £m
Bank and other borrowings (note 18)	92.2	41.7	53.4	43.6
Trade creditors	55.7	15.3	–	–
Amounts owed to group undertakings	–	–	45.0	24.7
Amounts owed to joint ventures (all trading balances)	2.4	1.8	–	–
Corporation tax	60.2	29.4	1.4	–
Taxation and social security	38.7	20.5	–	–
Other creditors	45.7	7.4	–	–
Derivative financial instruments (note 19)	10.1	(10.7)	–	–
Accruals and deferred income	96.2	9.9	–	–
	401.2	136.7	99.8	68.3

FRS 9 p55

FRS 9 p55 Note:
Amounts owed to (or owing from) an associate or joint venture should be analysed between loans and trading balances, if applicable.

17 Creditors – Amounts falling due after more than one year

SI 2008/410 1 Sch Formats

	Group 2013 £m	Group 2012 £m	Company 2013 £m	Company 2012 £m
Bank and other borrowings (note 18)	816.5	417.9	240.5	17.0
Deferred consideration for acquisitions	0.8	0.6	–	–
Derivative financial instruments (note 19)	5.7	6.4	–	–
Other creditors	42.5	3.0	–	–
	865.6	427.9	240.5	17.0

FRS 29 p8(e)

FRS 9 p55 Note:
Amounts owed to (or owing from) an associate or joint venture should be analysed between loans and trading balances, if applicable.

18 Bank and other borrowings

		Group		Company	
		2013 £m	2012 £m	2013 £m	2012 £m
	Due within one year or on demand:				
	Bank loans and overdrafts				
SI 2008/410 1 Sch 61(4)	Secured (a)	21.2	–	–	–
	Unsecured (b)	66.4	41.6	53.4	43.6
		87.6	41.6	53.4	43.6
	Unsecured debenture loans due within one year (c)	1.3	0.1	–	–
SSAP 21 p51	Finance lease obligations	3.3	–	–	–
		92.2	41.7	53.4	43.6
	Due after more than one year				
	Bank loans:				
SI 2008/410 1 Sch 61 (4)	Secured (a)	0.1	–	–	–
	Unsecured (b)	738.6	414.0	237.5	14.0
		738.7	414.0	237.5	14.0
	Debenture loans (d)	65.0	–	–	–
	Other unsecured loans	–	0.9	–	–
SSAP 21 p51	Finance lease obligations	9.8	–	–	–
	Cumulative preference shares of £1 each 2,000,000 shares	3.0	3.0	3.0	3.0
		816.5	417.9	240.5	17.0
	Total borrowings	908.7	459.6	293.9	60.6

SI 2008/410 1 Sch 61(4)
(a) The secured bank loans and overdrafts are secured by a fixed charge over the group's freehold property in Exeter and by floating charges over the remaining assets of GAAP UK Group Limited.
(b) Group and company unsecured bank loans are stated net of unamortised issue costs of £4.2m (2012: £nil). The company incurred total issue costs of £5.3m in respect of the five-year committed multi-option facility entered into in June 2013 under which amounts have been drawn down to fund the acquisition of Newsub plc. These costs together with the interest expense are allocated to the profit and loss account over the five year term of the facility. Interest is calculated using the effective interest rate method.
(c) Debenture loans represents 6.5% unsecured loan stock, which is redeemable at par on 1 July 2016. Debenture loans issued during the year are stated at net proceeds.
(d) The debenture loans represent US$110m 7% bonds due 2015.

SI 2008/410 1 Sch 61(2)
Bank loans are denominated in a number of currencies and bear interest based on LIBOR or foreign equivalents, or government bond rates appropriate to the country in which the borrowing is incurred. In June 2013, as part of the interest rate management strategy, the company entered into one interest rate swap (2012: none) for a notional principal amount of £100m maturing in 2017. Under this swap, the company receives interest on a variable basis and pays interest fixed at a rate of 8.8%.

The group's borrowing limit at 31 December 2013 calculated in accordance with the Articles of Association was £973m (2012: £331m).

GAAP UK Group Limited – Year ended 31 December 2013

FRS 29 p31	The exposure of the group's borrowings to interest rate changes and the contractual repricing dates at the balance sheet are as follows.	

	2013 £m	2012 £m
6 months or less	85.1	40.0
6-12 months	3.8	1.7
1-5 years	457.1	62.3
Over 5 years	362.7	355.6
	908.7	459.6

FRS 29 p25   The carrying amounts and fair value of the borrowings due after more than one year are as follows:

	Group carrying amount		Group fair value	
	2013 £m	2012 £m	2013 £m	2012 £m
Bank borrowings	738.7	417.9	730.2	411.7
Preference shares	3.0	–	2.9	–
Debentures and other loans	74.8	–	73.9	–
	816.5	417.9	807.0	411.7

	Company 2013		Company 2012	
	Book value £m	Fair value £m	Book value £m	Fair value £m
Long-term borrowings	(237.5)	(205.6)	(14.0)	(12.6)
Preference shares	(3.0)	(2.9)	(3.0)	(2.9)
	(240.5)	(208.5)	(17.0)	(15.5)

FRS 29 p27(a)   The fair values are based on cash flows discounted using a rate based on the borrowing rate of 7.5% (2012: 7.2%).

FRS 29 p25   The carrying amounts of short-term borrowings approximate their fair value.

FRS 29 p31, 34(c)   The carrying amounts of the group's borrowings are denominated in the following currencies:

	2013 £m	2012 £m
Pounds	762.4	364.8
US dollars	71.3	8.1
Euros	53.4	54.0
Other currencies	21.6	32.7
	908.7	459.6

Borrowing facilities

DV FRS 29 p50(a) The group has the following undrawn committed borrowing facilities available at 31 December 2013 in respect of which all conditions precedent had been met at that date.

	2013 Floating rate £m	2013 Fixed rate £m	Total £m
Expiring within 1 year	110.5	–	110.5
Expiring between 1 and 2 years	199.1	323.5	522.6
Expiring in more than 2 years	100.0	–	100.0
	409.6	**323.5**	**733.1**

The facilities expiring within one year are annual facilities subject to review at various dates during 2014. The other facilities have been arranged to help finance the proposed expansion of the group's activities into Continental Europe. All these facilities incur commitment fees at market rates.

Note:
Where a company has issued convertible debt, that debt should be shown separately from other liabilities. Where such convertible debt is not shown separately on the face of the balance sheet but instead is shown separately in the notes, the relevant caption for liabilities in the balance sheet should state that convertible debt is included.

Preference share capital – authorised, issued and fully paid

	2013 Shares	£m
Group and company		
FRS 25 p 15 7% cumulative preference shares of £1 each at 1 January	2,000,000	3.0
FRS 25 p 18(a) At 31 December	2,000,000	3.0
SI 2008/410 1 Sch 47(2)		

The 7% cumulative preference shares, which do not carry any voting rights, were issued in 2007 at £1.50 per share and are redeemable at £1.50 at the option of the shareholders on 1 June 2017. Shareholders are entitled to receive dividends at 7% per annum on the par value of these shares on a cumulative basis; these dividends are payable on 22 December each year. On winding up, the preference shareholders rank above ordinary shareholders and are entitled to receive £1 per share and any dividends accrued but unpaid in respect of their shares. In the event that dividends on the preference share are in arrears for six months or more, holders of the preference shares become entitled to vote at general meetings of members.

SSAP 21 p 51, 52 The minimum lease payments under finance leases fall due as follows:

	2013 £m	2012 £m
Less than one year	3.3	4.4
Later than one year but no more than two	3.7	2.0
In more than two years but no more than five years	6.1	1.0
	13.1	7.4
SSAP 21 p53 Future finance charges on finance leases	–	–
Present value of finance lease liabilities	13.1	7.4

GAAP UK Group Limited – Year ended 31 December 2013

FRS 29p39(a),(b)

Maturity of financial liabilities

The maturity profile of the carrying amount of the group's liabilities, at 31 December was as follows:

	Debt £m	Finance leases £m	Other financial liabilities £m	2013 Total £m	2012 Total £m
Less than one year	88.9	3.3	–	92.2	41.7
In more than one year but no more than two years	94.0	3.7	–	97.7	10.0
In more than two years but no more than five years	347.0	6.1	–	353.1	52.3
In more than five years	362.7	–	3.0	365.7	355.6
	892.6	13.1	3.0	908.7	459.6

Company	2013 £m	2012 £m
Between two and five years	237.5	205.5
In more than five years	3.0	3.0
	240.5	208.5

	2013 £m	2012 £m
Amounts repayable otherwise than by instalment after more than five years	250.0	–

19 Derivative financial instruments

	2013 Assets £m	2013 Liabilities £m	2012 Assets £m	2012 Liabilities £m
At 31 December				
Interest rate swaps	4.9	(7.9)	3.1	(7.4)
Cross-currency swap – net investment hedge	7.2	–	1.8	–
Forward foreign currency contracts – cash flow hedge	8.6	(2.2)	2.2	(3.3)
Embedded derivative – operating lease renewal option	–	(5.7)	–	(6.4)
	20.7	(15.8)	7.1	(17.1)
Current portion	8.6	(10.1)	2.2	(10.7)
Non-current portion	12.1	(5.7)	4.9	(6.4)

In accordance with FRS 26, 'Financial instruments: Recognition and measurement', GAAP UK Group Limited has reviewed all contracts for embedded derivatives that are required to be separately accounted for if they do not meet certain requirements set out in the standard. In relation to the group head office, there is a renewal clause that determines the rent the group will pay from 2013 to 2022 based on a measure of the performance of construction companies as recorded in the London Stock Exchange. This is not cancellable or alterable without the payment of a significant penalty, which the directors believe would not be in the interests of the shareholders to pay. As at 1 January 2013, the fair value of this embedded derivative was a liability of £3.7m. This derivative is fair valued based on discounted future cash flows with gains and losses passing through the profit and loss account as hedge accounting is not available.

Amounts recorded in the profit and loss account are shown below.

	2013 £m	2012 £m
Gain/(loss) in profit and loss	0.7	(2.7)

FRS 29 p24(b,c) The ineffective portion recognised in the profit or loss that arose from cash flow hedges was not material in either 2013 or 2012. There was no ineffectiveness to be recorded from net investment in foreign operation hedges.

FRS 29p23(a) SI 2008/410 1 Sch 55(2)(b) The net fair value gains at 31 December 2013 on open forward foreign exchange contracts that hedge the foreign currency risk of anticipated future sales are £4.1m (2012: £2.3m). These will be transferred to the profit and loss account when the forecast sales occur over the next four months. There were no derivatives outstanding at the balance sheet date that were designated as fair value hedges.

Interest rate swaps

FRS 29p31 The notional principal amount of the outstanding interest rate swap contracts at 31 December 2013 was £100m (2012: £87m).

FRS 29p23(a),22 At 31 December 2013, the fixed interest rates vary from 3.3% to 8.8% and floating rates are 6.5% (LIBOR plus 275 basis points), 3.9% (US PRIME plus 215 basis points) and 4.5% (EUROBOR plus 200 basis points).

Hedge of net investment in foreign entity

FRS 29p22 SI 2008/410 1 Sch 35 The group has both dollar and euro denominated borrowings, which it has designated as a hedge of the net investment in its subsidiaries in the US and France. The fair value of the dollar borrowings at 31 December 2013 was £130.0m (2012: £120m), and the euro borrowings £32.1m (2012: £27.1m)

FRS 29p31 ### Fair values of non-derivative financial assets and financial liabilities

Where market values are not available, fair values of financial assets and financial liabilities have been calculated by discounting expected future cash flows at prevailing interest rates and by applying year end exchange rates. The carrying amounts of short-term borrowings approximate to book value.

20 Provisions for liabilities

Group	Vacant properties £m	Restructuring £m	Environment £m	Deferred tax £m	Total £m
At 1 January 2013 as previously reported	5.7	2.7	–	13.8	22.2
On acquisition (note 32)	68.1	3.8	18.3	22.5	112.7
Exchange adjustments (note 26)	(2.0)	(0.4)	–	–	(2.4)
Charged to the profit and loss account	–	13.1	–	–	13.1
Utilised in year					
– Existing	(0.5)	(15.2)	–	–	(15.7)
– Acquired	(3.8)	(0.7)	–	–	(4.5)
Amortisation of discount	0.3	–	0.1	–	0.4
Charged to the profit and loss account	–	–	–	37.2	37.2
At 31 December 2013	67.8	3.3	18.4	73.5	163.0

Company	Vacant properties £m	Restructuring £m	Environment £m	Deferred tax £m	Total £m
At 1 January 2013	–	–	–	0.5	0.5
Charged to the profit and loss account	–	–	–	(0.4)	(0.4)
At 31 December 2013	–	–	–	0.1	0.1

Vacant properties

Prior to the acquisition of Newsub plc, the group's vacant leasehold properties comprised the old Food Product's divisional head office in Swindon and a disused warehouse in Cleveland, Ohio. Full provision had been made for the residual lease commitments, together with other outgoings for the remaining period of the leases, which at 31 December 2013 is approximately 12 years. It is not expected that these premises will be sub-let.

With the acquisition of Newsub plc, the group has inherited a substantial number of vacant and partly sub-let leasehold properties arising from the significant downsizing and retrenchment undertaken by Newsub plc in the early part of the decade. The properties are primarily located in London and Bradford in the UK, and Los Angeles in the US. Provision has been made for the residual lease commitments, together with other outgoings, after taking into account existing sub-tenant arrangements. It is not assumed that the properties will be able to be sub-let beyond the periods in the present sub-lease agreements. This has resulted in increasing the provision already made by Newsub plc to bring its provisioning policy in line with the group's and has been reflected as a fair value adjustment. Investigations are still being made as to the extent that there might be other contractual arrangements separate from the sub-lease agreements that enable the sub-lessees to terminate their leases early. Should the investigations prove this to be the case, it may be necessary to increase the amount of the provision. In determining the provision for Newsub plc's properties, the cash flows have been discounted on a pre-tax basis using appropriate government bond rates.

Maturity profile of provisions	2013 £m	2012 £m
Within 1 year	8.4	0.5
Between 1 and 2 years	16.8	1.0
Between 2 and 5 years	13.8	1.0
Over 5 years	28.8	3.2
	67.8	5.7

FRS 12 p90 **Restructuring**

FRS 12 p90(b) The £3.8m provision in 2013 arises in respect of a re-organisation commenced by Newsub plc in November 2012 of its healthcare activities. The restructuring of the healthcare activities involves the loss of 125 jobs at two factories and the closure of the site at Newark, New Jersey. Agreement had been reached in October 2012 with the local union representatives that specified the number of staff involved and quantified the amounts payable to those made redundant and customers and suppliers of the Newark site were informed in early November 2012. The associated impairment charge for the write-down of the property and other fixed assets at the Newark site was recognised in Newsub plc's financial statements for its year ended 31 March 2013, prior to the acquisition. As indicated in note 32, the level of provision at the date of Newsub plc's acquisition was reviewed and considered insufficient to cover the costs envisaged in the plans drawn up by Newsub plc's management. Consequently, an adjustment was made as part of the fair value exercise. The provision is expected to be fully utilised during the first half of 2014.

FRS 12 p90 A group company, UK GAAP Limited, announced on 11 December 2013 a rationalisation of product processes at two of its factories. A provision of £0.1m has been raised in respect of the redundancies that will occur over the next few months.

FRS 12 p90 **Environmental**

As part of the group's normal acquisition review procedures, Environmental Appraisers, Inc of San Francisco have been commissioned to ascertain the extent of land contamination of Newsub plc's operational sites in the US. The interim report received from the appraisers indicates that four sites require remediation to deal with chemical spills that have occurred over the last decade. A provisional estimate of the cost of the remediation has been made as part of the fair value exercise on the acquisition of Newsub plc (note 32). It is expected that the decontamination work will take three years to complete. In determining the provision, the cash flows have been discounted on a pre-tax basis using appropriate US Treasury bill rates.

GAAP UK Group Limited – Year ended 31 December 2013

Deferred tax

		Group		Company	
		2013 £m	2012 £m	2013 £m	2012 £m
FRS 19 p61	Provision for deferred tax comprises:				
	Accelerated capital allowances	96.5	10.8	0.1	0.6
	Short-term timing differences	(23.0)	3.0	–	(0.1)
	Deferred tax provision	73.5	13.8	0.1	0.5
	Deferred tax liability on pension asset (note 34)	5.8	8.6	–	–
	Provision at end of year including deferred tax on pension asset	79.3	22.4	0.1	0.5
	Deferred tax liability relating to pension surplus				
	1 January			8.6	9.8
	Deferred tax charged/(credited) to profit and loss account			–	(1.3)
	Deferred tax charged/(credited) to the statement of total recognised gains and losses:				
	– on actuarial loss			(2.8)	0.1
	– change in tax rate[1]			–	–
	31 December			5.8	8.6

The deferred tax liability of £5.8m (2012: £8.6m) has been deducted in arriving at the net pension surplus on the balance sheet.

Factors that may affect future tax charges

In addition to the factors disclosed in note 6, the following factors may affect future tax charges.

FRS 19 p64(b)
- No provision has been made for deferred tax on gains recognised on revaluing property to its market value or on the sale of properties where potentially taxable gains have been rolled over into replacement assets. Such tax would become payable only if the property were sold without it being possible to claim rollover relief. The total amount unprovided for is £5.8m. At present it is not envisaged that any such tax will become payable in the foreseeable future.
- No deferred tax is recognised on the unremitted earnings of overseas subsidiaries, associates and joint ventures. As the earnings are continually reinvested by the group, no tax is expected to be payable on them in the foreseeable future. If tax were to be recognised, a provision of approximately £50m (2012: £40m) would have been required.

---

[1] The line item for change in tax rate is shown for illustrative purposes. Companies with 31 December 2013 year ends will need to consider the impact of the reductions in tax rates in the Finance Act 2013.

21 Called-up share capital

		Group and Company	
	Allotted, and fully paid	2013 £m	2012 £m
SI 2008/410 1 Sch 47(1)(a)	**Ordinary shares of 1p each**		
SI 2008/410 1 Sch Formats	At 1 January – 887,125,690	8.9	8.8
SI 2008/410 1 Sch 48(b)(c)	Allotted under share option schemes (10,008,001 shares)	0.1	0.1
SI 2008/410 1 Sch 48(b)(c)	Allotted on acquisition of Newsub plc (486,586,318 shares)	4.8	–
	At 31 December – 1,383,898,437 shares[1]	13.8	8.9

SI 2008/410 1 Sch 47(1)(a)

Potential issues of ordinary shares

SI 2008/410 1 Sch 49(1) FRS 20 p45(d)

Certain senior executives hold options to subscribe for shares in the company at prices ranging from 26.0p to 223.5p under the share option schemes approved by shareholders in October 2013 and September 2012. Options on 10,008,001 shares were exercised in 2013 and 70,300 options lapsed. The number of shares subject to options, the periods in which they were granted and the periods in which they may be exercised are given below.

Year of grant	Exercise price (pence)	Exercise period	**2013 Numbers**	2012 Numbers
2005	26.00	2006 – 2013	**197,777**	10,205,778
2007	50.00	2010 – 2014	**1,152,500**	1,152,500
2009	136.25	2012 – 2016	**3,182,866**	3,182,866
2012	185.75	2012 – 2017	**7,451,486**	7,451,486
2013	223.50	2013 – 2018	**8,630,316**	–
			20,614,945	21,992,630

SI 2008/410 1 Sch 49(1)

Under the group's long-term incentive plan for executive directors and former directors, such individuals hold rights over ordinary shares which may result in the issue of up to 466,439 1p ordinary shares by 2014.

22 Share-based payments

FRS 20 p45(a) FRS 20 p47(a)(i), FRS 20 p47(a)(iii

The Executive Share Option Plan (ESOP) was introduced in January 2013. Under the ESOP the remuneration committee can grant options over shares in the company to employees of the group. Options are granted with a fixed exercise price equal to the market price of the shares under option at the date of grant. The contractual life of an option is 10 years. Awards under the ESOP are generally reserved for employees at senior management level and above; and 107 employees are currently eligible to participate in this group. There are no reload features. The company has made annual grants on 1 January each year since January 2012. Options granted under the ESOP will become exercisable on the third anniversary of the date of grant, subject to the growth in earnings per share over that period exceeding an average of inflation plus 3% (for awards in January 2012 and January 2013, 4%). Exercise of an option is subject to continued employment. Options were valued using the Black-Scholes option-pricing model. No performance conditions were included in the fair

---

[1] Included in the total are 178,428 1p ordinary shares allotted to directors under the group's long-term incentive plan (2011: 148,447 1p ordinary shares) with a nominal value of £1,784 (2011: £1,484). [SI 2008/410 1 Sch 48(b)(c)].

value calculations. The fair value per option granted and the assumptions used in the calculation are as follows:

FRS 20 p46	Grant date	01 Jan 2013	01 Jan 2012
	Share price at grant date	£2.235	£1.8575
	Exercise price	£2.235	£1.8575
	Number of employees	107	85
	Shares under option	8,630,316	7,451,486
	Vesting period (years)	3	3
	Expected volatility	40%	40%
	Option life (years)	10	10
	Expected life (years)	5	5
	Risk-free interest rate	4.80%	4.80%
	Expected dividends expressed as a dividend yield	2.50%	2.50%
	Fair value per option	£0.73	£0.85

FRS 20 p47(a)(ii) The expected volatility is based on historical volatility over the last three years. The expected life is the average expected period to exercise. The risk-free rate of return is the yield on zero-coupon UK government bonds of a term consistent with the assumed option life. A reconciliation of option movements over the year to 31 December 2013 is shown below:

		2013		2012	
		Number (000)	Weighted average exercise price	Number (000)	Weighted average exercise price
FRS 20 p45(b)(i)	Outstanding at 1 January	21,993	£0.97	21,698	£0.49
FRS 20 p45(b)(ii)	Granted	8,630	£2.23	7,541	£1.86
FRS 20 p45(b)(iii)	Forfeited	–	–	(6,112)	£0.46
FRS 20 p45(b)(iv)	Exercised	(10,008)	£0.26	(1,134)	£0.50
FRS 20 p45(b)(vi)	Outstanding at 31 December	20,615	£1.85	21,993	£0.97
FRS 20 p45(b)(vii)	Exercisable at 31 December	1,350	£0.46	10,206	£0.26

FRS 20 p47(a) The weighted average fair value of options granted in the year was £6.3m (2012: £6.4m).

	2013				2012			
FRS 20 p45(d) Range of exercise prices	Weighted average exercise price	Number of shares ('000)	Weighted average remaining life: Expected	Contractual	Weighted average exercise price	Number of shares ('000)	Weighted average remaining life: Expected	Contractual
£0.00 – £1.50	£1.37	4,246	1.5	7.0	£0.35	10,254	2.2	7.7
£1.50 – £2.50	£1.97	16,369	2.8	8.8	£1.58	11,739	3.3	9.3

FRS 20 p45(c),50,51(a) The weighted average share price during the period for options exercised over the year was £0.46 (2012: £0.26). The total charge for the year relating to employee share-based payment plans was £3.2m (2012: £1.4m), all of which related to equity-settled share-based payment transactions. After deferred tax, the total charge was £1.8m (2012: £2.2m).

23 Share premium account

Group and Company	2013 £m	2012 £m
At 1 January	8.3	3.7
Premium on shares issued during the year under the share option schemes	2.5	4.6
At 31 December	10.8	8.3

SI 2008/410 1 Sch 59

24 Revaluation reserve

	Group £m	Company £m
At 1 January 2013	2.5	0.8
Exchange adjustments	(0.2)	–
Revaluation in year	5.4	1.5
Transfer to profit and loss account	(0.2)	–
At 31 December 2013	7.5	2.3

SI 2008/410 1 Sch 5

FRS 29 20(a)(ii)

25 Profit and loss account

	Group £m	Company £m
At 1 January 2013	141.5	154.6
Net exchange adjustments	(80.4)	(1.4)
Tax on exchange adjustments	3.5	–
Profit for the financial year	25.4	9.2
Dividend	(23.7)	(23.7)
Adjustment in respect of employee share schemes	3.2	–
Goodwill recycled on disposal of subsidiary	3.9	–
Transfer from revaluation reserve (note 24)	0.2	–
Actuarial loss on pension scheme (note 34)	(22.2)	–
Current tax deductions allocated to actuarial losses	3.6	–
Movement on deferred tax relating to pension asset	2.8	–
At 31 December 2013	57.8	138.7

UITF 19 p9

SI 2008/410 1 Sch 59(2)(b)

SI 2008/410 6 Sch 14
FRS 10 p71(a)(ii)
FRS 2 p53

Cumulative goodwill relating to acquisitions made prior to 1999, which has been eliminated against reserves, amounts to £172.2m (2012: £176.1m).

The reserves of subsidiary undertakings have generally been retained to finance their businesses. The ability to distribute £0.7m (2012: £1.2m) of consolidated retained profits of the group is restricted by exchange controls in certain countries.

Included in net exchange adjustments are exchange gains of £16.9m (2012: £2.4m) arising on borrowings denominated in, or swapped into, foreign currencies designated as hedges of net investments overseas.

26 Reconciliation of exchange differences recognised through the statement of total recognised gains and losses

FRS 23 p52(b)

	Note	2013 £m	2012 £m
Opening balance of cumulative exchange difference		8.9	(26.0)
Exchange adjustments on intangibles	8	32.6	26.3
Exchange adjustments on tangible fixed assets	9	27.2	24.1
Exchange adjustments on tangible fixed assets accumulated depreciation	9	(10.0)	(9.0)
Exchange adjustments on interests in joint ventures	10	0.9	1.5
Exchange adjustments on AFS investment	14	(2.0)	(1.2)
Exchange adjustments on provisions	19	(2.4)	(1.0)
Exchange adjustments on overseas subsidiaries		(69.4)	(5.8)
Closing balance of cumulative exchange differences		**(14.2)**	**8.9**

27 Other reserves

	Merger reserve £m	Other reserve £m	AFS revaluation reserve £m	Hedging reserve £m	Total £m
At 1 January 2013	–	(4.2)	10.0	–	5.8
Shares issued on acquisition of Newsub plc	933.6	–	–	–	933.6
Issue expenses	(1.4)	–	–	–	(1.4)
Exchange adjustments	–	(1.9)	2.0	–	0.1
Net revaluation to AFS investments	–	–	13.1	–	13.1
Net movement on foreign currency cash flow hedge	–	–	–	4.5	4.5
Net movement on cross currency net investment hedge	–	–	–	5.0	5.0
Movement on other reserve	–	7.6	–	–	7.6
Net movement on interest rate swap	–	–	–	(2.1)	(2.1)
At 31 December 2013	**932.2**	**1.5**	**23.1**	**7.4**	**964.2**

SI 2008/410 1 Sch 59, 40, 41
SI 2008/410 1 Sch 55(2)(b)
FRS 29 p20(a)(ii)

28 Cash flow from operating activities

Reconciliation of operating profit to net cash inflow from operating activities:

	Group 2013 £m	2012 £m
Continuing operations		
Operating profit	104.0	76.3
Depreciation charge (net of profit on disposals)	77.7	15.5
Goodwill amortisation	40.2	–
Difference between pension charge and cash contributions	(8.0)	9.3
(Increase) in stocks	(2.7)	(3.3)
Decrease/(increase) in debtors	15.0	(3.1)
(Decrease) in creditors	(47.5)	(13.5)
Other non-cash changes	3.2	1.7
Net cash inflow from continuing operations	**181.9**	**82.9**
Discontinued operations		
Operating profit	2.2	27.1
Depreciation charge	5.8	6.2
Decrease in stocks	1.0	2.0
(Increase) in debtors	(3.8)	(4.9)
Increase in creditors	2.3	3.3
Net cash inflow from discontinued operations	**7.5**	**33.7**
Total net cash inflow from operating activities	**189.4**	**116.6**

29 Analysis of net debt

	As at 1 January 2013 £m	Cash flow £m	Acquisition (excluding Cash and overdrafts) £m	Other non-cash changes £m	Exchange movements £m	At 31 December 2013 £m
Cash in hand and at bank	40.5	40.1	–	–	(5.8)	**74.8**
Overdrafts	–	(92.0)	–	–	5.0	**(87.0)**
Debt due after 1 year	(417.9)	(328.3)	(65.8)	(1.1)	9.4	**(803.7)**
Debt due within 1 year	(41.7)	57.1	(17.5)	–	0.2	**(1.9)**
Finance leases due after 1 year	–	–	(17.8)	8.0	–	**(9.8)**
Finance leases due within 1 year	–	10.8	(6.1)	(8.0)	–	**(3.3)**
Liquid resources	455.3	8.3	50.1	(1.0)	35.7	**548.4**
Preference shares	(3.0)	–	–	–	–	**(3.0)**
	33.2	**(304.0)**	**(57.1)**	**(2.1)**	**44.5**	**(285.5)**

Liquid resources comprise short-term deposits with banks which mature within 12 months of the date of inception and current asset investments that are traded in an active market.

Non-cash charges comprise amortisation of issue costs relating to debt issues and transfers between categories of finance leases.

Movement in borrowings	£m	£m
Debt due within 1 year:		
Repayment of part of bank loan	–	(57.1)
Debt due after 1 year:		
New secured bank loan	321.2	–
New unsecured bank loan	100.0	–
Repayment of part of bank loan	(87.6)	333.6
Increase in borrowings	–	276.5
Issue costs of new bank loan	–	(5.3)
	–	271.2
Capital element of finance lease payment	–	(10.8)
Cash inflow	–	**260.4**

30 Cash flow relating to exceptional items

FRS 1 p37

Operating cash flows include under continuing operations an outflow of £8.5m which relates to the reorganisation costs of £9.1m incurred in integrating Newsub plc. The balance of £0.6m was paid in January 2013. In addition, operating cash flows from continuing operations includes an outflow of £3.5m in respect of product remediation costs.

31 Major non-cash transactions

FRS 1 p46

Part of the consideration for the purchase of Newsub plc comprised shares. Further details of the acquisition are set out in note 32.

32 Acquisitions and disposals

(a) Acquisition of Newsub plc

SI 2008/410 6 Sch 13(2)
FRS 6 p21

The group purchased three companies during the year for a total consideration of £1,239.4m, of which £1,234.7m was in respect of the acquisition on 30 June 2013 of Newsub plc. The total adjustments required to the book values of the assets and liabilities of the companies acquired in order to present the net assets of those companies at fair values in accordance with group accounting principles were £106.2m, of which £105.5m related to Newsub plc, details of which are set out below together with the resultant amount of goodwill arising. All of these purchases have been accounted for as acquisitions.

FRS 6 p29
FRS 1 p45

Newsub plc contributed £77.0m to the group's net operating cash flows, paid £17.4m in respect of interest, £8.6m in respect of taxation and utilised £63.4m for capital expenditure.

FRS 6 p35

In its last financial year to 31 March 2013, Newsub plc made a profit after tax and minority interests of £56.6m. For the period since that date to the date of acquisition, Newsub plc management accounts show the following:

	£m
FRS 6 p36,83 Turnover	94.3
Operating profit	4.0
Profit before taxation	2.9
Taxation and minority interests	(1.2)
Profit attributable to shareholders	1.7
Exchange adjustments	(0.3)
Total recognised gains for the period	1.4

GAAP UK Group Limited – Year ended 31 December 2013

SI 2008/410 6 Sch 13 (4)	Newsub plc acquisition	Book value £m	Revaluations £m	Consistency of accounting policy £m	Other £m	Provisional fair value £m
FRS 6 p25	Intangible fixed assets	7.9	–	(7.9)	–	–
	Tangible fixed assets	330.5	(18.1)	–	–	312.4
	Investments in joint ventures	17.5	(1.9)	(1.6)	–	14.0
	Stocks	15.3	(1.7)	–	–	13.6
	Debtors	206.9	6.9	(0.3)	–	213.5
	Creditors	(244.2)	–	(3.4)	(30.9)	(278.5)
	Provisions:					
	– Vacant property	(13.9)	–	(54.2)	–	(68.1)
	– Environmental	–	–	–	(18.3)	(18.3)
	– Pre-acquisition restructuring	(1.0)	–	–	(2.8)	(3.8)
	Taxation					
	– Current	(6.2)	–	–	–	(6.2)
	– Deferred	(53.9)	–	–	31.4	(22.5)
	Cash	10.3	–	–	–	10.3
	Overdrafts	(25.7)	–	–	–	(25.7)
	Loans net of deposits	(54.0)	(3.1)	–	–	(57.1)
		189.5	(17.9)	(67.4)	(20.6)	83.6
	Minority interests	(0.8)	0.4	–	–	(0.4)
	Net assets acquired	**188.7**	**(17.5)**	**(67.4)**	**(20.6)**	**83.2**
	Goodwill					1,151.5
	Consideration					**1,234.7**
SI 2008/410 6 Sch 13(3) FRS 6 p24 FRS 1 p45	**Consideration satisfied by:**					
	Shares issued (net of issue costs of £1.4m)					932.2
	Cash					302.5
						1,234.7

FRS 6 p25
SI 2008/410 6 Sch 13(4)
FRS 6 p27

The book values of the assets and liabilities have been taken from the management accounts of Newsub plc at 30 June 2013 (the date of acquisition) at actual exchange rates on that date. The fair value adjustments contain some provisional amounts, as indicated below, which will be finalised in the 2013 financial statements when the detailed acquisition investigation has been completed.

Revaluation adjustments in respect of tangible fixed assets comprise the valuations of certain freehold properties.

Revaluations of investments and stocks reflect the write-down to estimated realisable value. The revaluation adjustment to debtors includes a revision to the bad debt provision to reflect an adjustment for an amount distributed in respect of a customer in receivership.

The revaluation of loans relates to an adjustment of £3.1m in order to reflect current market rate of interest on the Newsub plc US-dollar bond. Other adjustments to creditors of £30.9m relate to liabilities that were not fully reflected in the balance sheet of Newsub plc at the date of acquisition. These include adjustments to increase the creditor amounts for certain insurance and legal claims to reflect their final settlement shortly after 30 June 2013.

The fair value adjustment for alignment of accounting policies reflects the restatement of assets and liabilities in accordance with the group's policies including: the removal of capitalised in-store marketing costs (£7.9m); provision for the group's share of deferred consideration payable by an associated company for the acquisition of a business (£1.6m); establishing a creditor for outstanding holiday pay entitlement of employees and the alignment of general bad debt provisioning policy.

A provisional adjustment (£18.3m) has been made for the remediation of Newsub plc operational sites in the US. The final report from Environment Appraisers, Inc. will not be available until April 2014 and further provision may be required.

The book values of the net assets acquired included provisions for reorganisation and restructuring costs amounting to £1.0m. These provisions were established by Newsub plc in November 2013 and relate to an irrevocable reorganisation commenced by Newsub plc management before the acquisition. However, on review at the time of acquisition, the provisions were considered to be insufficient to cover the expected costs and have been increased by £2.8m. The adjustment in respect of vacant property is discussed in note 20.

No deferred tax has been recognised on fair value adjustments on non-monetary fixed assets as there is no intention to sell the assets concerned. However, the book value of deferred tax liability of £53.9m was reduced by a net deferred asset of £31.4m in respect of various fair value adjustments arising on the acquisition in accordance with FRS 19.

(b) Other acquisitions

	£m
Book value of net assets acquired (includes £0.3m cash)	0.2
Fair value adjustments	(0.7)
Goodwill	5.2
Consideration satisfied by cash	4.7

Co Limited and Sub SA were acquired by GAAPsub Ltd on 6 May 2013 and 12 July 2013 respectively. Fair value adjustments of £0.7m were made to align accounting policies in respect of fixed assets (£0.2m), stock (£0.2m) and creditors (£0.3m).

(c) Disposal of H Limited

	£m
Tangible fixed assets	1.4
Stocks	2.5
Debtors	6.5
Creditors	(4.9)
Goodwill previously written off to reserves	3.9
	9.4
Profit on disposal (note 5)	6.3
Deferred cash consideration	**15.7**

H Limited contributed £7.5m to the net operating cash flows, and paid £0.8m in respect of net returns on investments and servicing of finance and £0.9m in respect of taxation.

33 Employees and directors

	Staff costs for the group during the year	2013 £m	2012 £m
CA06 s411(5)	Wages and salaries	544.3	203.7
	Social security costs	62.0	22.3
	Other pension costs (note 34)	17.2	9.3
	Defined contribution pension cost (note 34)	0.2	–
FRS 20 p51(a)	Cost of employee share schemes (note 22)	3.2	1.7
		626.9	237.0

	Average monthly number of people (including executive directors) employed by the group	2013 number	2012 number
CA06 s411	**By business group**		
	Food products	18,630	7,602
	Personnel services	5,789	138
	Retail services	5,241	4,758
	Distribution services	13,735	915
	Property services	7,107	3,565
	Health care	9,368	3,499
		59,870	20,477

		2013 £	2012 £
SI 2008/410 5 Sch 2(1)	Aggregate emoluments, gains on share options exercised and benefits under long-term incentive schemes	200,000	180,000
SI 2008/410 5 Sch 2(2) (a)(b)	Defined benefit scheme:		
	– Accrued pension at end of year	30,000	25,000
	– Accrued lump sum at end of year	60,000	50,000

SI 2008/410 5 Sch 2(3) (a)(b)
The highest paid director exercised share options during the year and received shares under the executive long-term incentive scheme.

Notes:
Details should be given of all transactions or arrangements with the company or any subsidiary of it in which a person who was a director of the company or its holding company had a material interest.

SI 2008/410 5 Sch 3
Details should be given of any excess retirement benefits of directors and past directors.

SI 2008/410 5 Sch 4
Details should be given of the aggregate of compensation paid to directors or past directors for loss of office, including retirement.

SI 2008/410 5 Sch 5
Details should be given of the aggregate of any consideration paid to or receivable by third parties for making available the services of any person while a director. This includes benefits other than in cash.

GAAP UK Group Limited – Year ended 31 December 2013

34 Pension commitments

FRS 17 p77(a)
SI 2008/410
1 Sch 63(4)

The group has established a number of pension schemes around the world covering many of its employees. The principal funds are those in the UK: the GAAP UK Group Limited staff pension plan, the UK GAAP Limited pension scheme and the Newsub plc pension plan. The GAAP UK Group Limited staff pension plan and the UK GAAP Limited pension scheme are funded schemes of the defined benefit type, with assets held in separate trustee administered funds. The Newsub plc pension plan and schemes outside the UK are predominantly of the defined contribution type.

FRS 17 p77(a) The most recent actuarial valuations of the GAAP UK Group Limited staff pension plan and the UK GAAP Limited pension scheme were at 31 December 2013. The valuations of both schemes used the projected unit method and were carried out by Actuary & Actuary, professionally qualified actuaries. The principal assumptions for both plans made by the actuaries were as follows:

	2013 %	2012 %
FRS 17 p77(m) Rate of increase in pensionable salaries	3.6	3.0
FRS 17 p77(m) Rate of increase in pensions in payment and deferred pensions	3.0	4.0
FRS 17 p77(m) Discount rate	6.0	5.5
FRS 17 p77(m) Inflation assumption	3.6	3.3

FRS 17 p77(m) The mortality assumptions used in the group's actuarial valuations have been amended to assume that pensioners have a longer life expectancy. The mortality assumptions used in the valuation of the defined benefit pension liabilities of the group's UK plans are summarised in the table below and have been selected to reflect the characteristics and experience of the membership of those plans. This has been done by adjusting standard mortality tables which reflect recent research into mortality experience in the UK (PA 92 tables combined with the 2002 short cohort improvement factors) and the US (UP-94 tables using projection scale AA). In addition, the UK assumptions have been further adjusted to reflect the latest available trend information, which indicates that mortality relating in particular to blue-collar workers may not be improving as quickly as indicated by the standard tables. Based on an analysis of the mix of blue-and white-collar workers in the group's plan, the UK assumptions have been adjusted (using a scaling factor of 118.75%) to reflect a lower level of longevity amongst the blue-collar membership.

	UK 2013 Years	2012 Years
Longevity at age 65 for current pensioners		
– Men	20	18
– Women	22	21
Longevity at age 65 for future pensioners		
– Men	20	19
– Women	23	22

The assets of the schemes and the weighted average expected rate of return were as follows:

		Long-term rate of return expected 31 December 2013	Value at 31 December 2013	Long-term rate of return expected 31 December 2012	Value at 31 December 2012
		%	£m	%	£m
FRS 17 p77(i)	Equities	7.9	140.6	8.4	116.6
FRS 17 p77(i)	Bonds	5.4	94.2	5.6	81.0
	Total market value of assets		234.8		197.6
	Present value of scheme liabilities		(214.0)		(167.0)
FRS 17 p77(e)	Surplus in the scheme		20.8		30.6
	Related deferred tax liability		(5.8)		(8.6)
FRS 17 p77(e)	**Net pension asset**		**15.0**		**22.0**

FRS 17 p77(b) **Reconciliation of present value of scheme liabilities**

	2013 £m	2012 £m
1 January	167.0	136.9
Current service cost	17.2	8.3
Past service cost	–	1.0
Interest cost	10.0	7.8
Benefits paid	(49.5)	(32.7)
Actuarial loss	69.3	45.7
31 December	214.0	167.0

DV **Sensitivity analysis of scheme liabilities**

The sensitivity of the present value of scheme liabilities to changes in the principle assumptions used is set out below.

	Change in assumption	Impact on scheme liabilities
Discount rate	Increase/decrease by 1%	Increase/decrease by 9.5%
Rate of inflation	Increase/decrease by 1%	Increase/decrease by 4.5%
Rate of increase in salaries	Increase/decrease by 1%	Increase/decrease by 4.0%
Rate of increase in pensions in payment	Increase/decrease by 1%	Increase/decrease by 3.5%
Mortality	Increase by 1 year	Increase by 5.0%

GAAP UK Group Limited – Year ended 31 December 2013

FRS 17 p77(d) Reconciliation of fair value of scheme assets

	2013 £'000	2012 £'000
1 January	197.6	170.1
Expected return on scheme assets	14.4	11.8
Actuarial gains	47.1	48.4
Benefits paid	(49.5)	(32.7)
Contributions paid by employer	25.2	–
31 December	234.8	197.6

FRS 17 p77(j) Scheme assets do not include any of GAAP UK Group Limited own financial instruments or any property occupied by GAAP UK Group Limited.

FRS 17 p77(k) The expected return on scheme assets is determined by considering the expected returns available on the assets underlying the current investment policy. Expected yields on fixed interest investments are based on gross redemption yields as at the balance sheet date. Expected returns on equity investments reflect long-term real rates of return experienced in the respective markets.

FRS 17 p77(l) The actual return on scheme assets in the year was £61.5m (2012: £60.2m).

FRS 17 p77(f) The amounts recognised in the profit or loss account are as follows:

	2013 £m	2012 £m
Current service cost	17.2	8.3
Past service cost	–	1.0
Expected return on pension scheme assets	(14.4)	(11.8)
Interest on pension scheme liabilities	10.0	7.8
Total charge	**12.8**	**5.3**

£12.6m (2012: £6.3m) of the current service cost is included within cost of sales, and £4.6m (2012: £2.0m) is included within administrative expenses.

FRS 17 p77(o) Amounts for current period and previous four periods

	2013	2012	2011	2010	2009
Defined benefit obligation	(214.0)	(167.0)	(136.9)	(120.0)	(115.8)
Plan assets	234.8	197.6	170.1	165.0	156.7
Surplus/(Deficit)	20.8	30.6	33.2	45.0	40.9
Experience adjustments on plan assets					
Amount (£m)	47.1	48.4	40.6	40.4	20.6
Experience adjustments on plan liabilities					
Amount (£m)	(12.3)	(14.7)	(15.9)	2.9	5.2
FRS 17 p77(g) Total actuarial gains and losses recognised in statement of total recognised gains and losses					
Amount (£m)	(22.2)	2.7	7.8	6.3	(3.8)

FRS 17p75	The Newsub plc pension plan is a defined contribution plan. The contributions made to the plan from the date of acquisition were £242,000 (2012: £nil). At the end of the year, contributions of £21,000 (2012: £nil), representing the unpaid contributions for December 2013, were outstanding.
	GAAP UK Group Limited has no employees (the members of the group defined benefit scheme are or were employed by subsidiaries of GAAP UK Group Limited); consequently, no defined benefit scheme disclosures are given for the company.
FRS 17 p77(p)	The valuation at 31 December 2013 showed a decrease in the surplus from £30.6m to £20.8m. Improvements in benefits of £1m were made in 2012, and no additional improvements in benefits were made in 2013. From 1 January 2013, contributions were made to the pension scheme at a rate of 5% of pensionable salaries. It has been agreed with the trustees that contributions will remain at that level for the next three years.

35 Operating lease commitments

At 31 December 2013, the group has lease agreements in respect of properties, vehicles, plant and equipment, for which the payments extend over a number of years.

		2013		2012	
		Property £m	Vehicles, plant and equipment £m	Property £m	Vehicles, plant and equipment £m
SSAP 21 p56	**Annual commitments under non-cancellable operating leases expiring:**				
	Within one year	1.1	0.6	0.3	0.3
	Within two to five years	6.1	3.5	1.0	2.5
	After five years	6.9	0.5	0.6	1.2
		14.1	4.6	1.9	4.0

36 Contingent liabilities

FRS 12 p91 SI 2008/410 1 Sch 73 FRS 9 p53	The company has guaranteed bank and other borrowings of subsidiary undertakings and, jointly with its co-investors, of joint ventures amounting to £2.7m (2012: £0.4m) and £3.7m (2012: £0.7m) respectively.
SI 2008/410 1 Sch 63(2) FRS 12 p91	At 31 December 2013, the group was in dispute with one of its food suppliers over surcharges invoiced above the original contracted price for specialist ingredients. The directors are strongly resisting the payment of the surcharges and it is unlikely that the outcome of this dispute will have a material effect on the group's financial position.

37 Capital and other financial commitments

		Share of joint ventures		Group		Company	
FRS 9 p53		2013 £m	2012 £m	2013 £m	2012 £m	2013 £m	2012 £m
SI 2008/410 1 Sch 63(3)	Contracts placed for future capital expenditure not provided in the financial statements	2.1	0.7	12.9	2.4	0.1	0.1

GAAP UK Group Limited – Year ended 31 December 2013

38 Related-party transactions

FRS 8 p6,19
FRS 9 p55

During the year the group purchased food products from two joint ventures, ABC AG and DEF AG to the value of £19.5m (2012: £16.7m). At 31 December 2013 £2.4m (2012: £1.8m) was payable in respect of these purchases. During the year, the group sold healthcare products totalling £11.2m (2012: £13.4m) to HIJ SpA, a joint venture. At 31 December 2013 the outstanding balances receivable from HIJ SpA were £1.3m (2012: £1.5m).

CA06 s255(2)(5)
FRS 8 p6

Mrs S James, wife of Mr F James, a main board director and managing director of the healthcare division, owns the entire share capital of LMN Ltd. The nature of the business of the healthcare division necessitates the exporting of products to Saudi Arabia. LMN Ltd acts as an export agency on behalf of a group subsidiary company, OPQ Ltd. Throughout the year, CPS Inter Ltd has traded under the same terms as those available to other customers in the ordinary course of business. The value of export work performed during the year ended 31 December 2013 for OPQ Ltd amounted to £9.7m (2012: £8.4m). The amount owed to LMN Ltd at the year end amounted to £0.9m (2012: £0.8m).

39 Post balance sheet events

FRS 21 p21,
SI 2008/410
1 Sch 12(b)

On 15 February 2014, the company completed the purchase of RST, Inc for a total consideration of £75.1m. The company operates in North America providing healthcare services. At the date of acquisition it had estimated net assets of US$40m (£25m).

CA06 s409

40 Principal subsidiaries, joint ventures and associates

Subsidiary undertakings

Management should disclose the following:

SI 2008/410
4 Sch 1

Particulars of subsidiary undertaking:

(a) Name.

SI2008/410
4 Sch 17

(b) Country of incorporation, if incorporated outside Great Britain.

(c) If unincorporated, address of principal place of business.

SI2008/410 4 Sch 16(2)
SI2008/410 4 Sch 16(3)

(d) Description and proportion of the nominal value of the shares of each class distinguishing between shares held by the parent undertaking and those held by the group.

(e) Whether or not included in the consolidation and explain if not.

FRS 2 p34

(f) The specific definition of subsidiary undertaking that makes the undertaking a subsidiary – this need not be given if the reason is that the parent holds a majority of the voting rights and the proportion of shares and voting rights held are the same.

FRS 2 p33

(g) Where a subsidiary undertaking is consolidated on the basis of a participating interest with actual dominant influence, the basis of dominant influence.

(h) Proportion of voting rights held by group.

(i) Indication of nature of business.

Joint ventures and associates

For joint ventures and associates included in the group financial statements, give:

SI 2008/410
4 Sch 19
FRS 9 p52

(a) Name.

(b) Country of incorporation, if incorporated outside Great Britain.

(c) If unincorporated, address of principal place of business.

FRS 9 p52(a)	(d)	The identity and proportion of each class of shares held by the parent company and by the group, indicating any special rights or constraints attaching to them.
FRS 9 p52(c)	(e)	Indication of nature of business.
FRS 9 p52(b)	(f)	The accounting period or date of the financial statements used if they differ from the group's.

FRS 9 p56   *Notes:*

An explanation should be given to each case where either of the following presumptions is rebutted:

(a) An investor holding 20% or more of the voting rights has significant influence.

(b) An investor holding 20% or more of the shares of another entity has a participating interest.

FRS 9 p53   *Disclosure should be made of any notes or matters that should have been noted, had the investor's accounting policies been applied, that are material to understanding the effect on the investor of its investments, particularly in respect of contingent liabilities and capital commitments.*

41 Ultimate parent company

FRS 8, 5, Sch 4, 8, 9   The directors regard UVW-US Inc, a company incorporated in the US, as the immediate and ultimate parent company and ultimate controlling party[1]. Copies of the consolidated financial statements of UVW-US Inc can be obtained from The Company secretary, UVW-US Inc, 589 Fourth Avenue, New York 59361.

FRS 8p3   Advantage has been taken of the exemption in FRS 8 not to disclose transactions with entities that are part of the UVW-Inc group.

---

[1] Where the entity is itself a subsidiary, whether consolidated accounts are required to be prepared or not, will depend of on whether the exemptions in the Companies Act 2006, section 401, have been satisfied. For the purposes these financial statements, we have assumed that the exemption criteria have not be satisfied.

UK GAAP Limited – Year ended 31 December 2013

Example annual report under UK GAAP

Introduction

The example annual report that follows includes the financial statements of UK GAAP Limited, a wholly-owned private subsidiary company. Although UK GAAP Limited meets the size criteria for a medium-sized company, it is ineligible due to its ultimate parent company, GAAP UK plc, being a plc, and therefore it does not qualify as a medium-sized company.

> Significant changes to this illustrative annual report include:
> - The Strategic report requirements and related amendments to the Directors' report for private companies
> - Updated illustrative Auditor's report for private companies.

UK GAAP Limited is a fictitious company. The annual report has been prepared for illustrative purposes only and shows the disclosures and formats that might be expected for a company of its size that prepares its financial statements in accordance with the requirements of Part 15 of the Companies Act 2006 and 'The Large and Medium-sized Companies and Groups (Accounts and Reports) Regulations 2008' (SI 2008/410).

UK GAAP Limited does not apply the fair value accounting rules and therefore has not adopted FRS 23, FRS 26, FRS 29 or paragraphs 51 to 95 of FRS 25.

GAAP UK Group Limited is required to prepare a Strategic Report. It has prepared this on the basis of a private company. We have included an overview and the principles from the FRC Exposure Draft 'Guidance on the Strategic Report'. The Strategic report is intended to replace the operating and financial review. Guidance on an operating and financial review was given in the ASB's statement of best practice, 'Reporting statement: Operating and financial review (OFR)'. It is expected that, in due course, the FRC guidance will replace the ASB Reporting statement.

Guidance and information

References to source material are given in the left-hand margin. PwC guidance is presented in *italics*.

The intention is not to show all conceivable disclosures and this annual report should not, therefore, be used as a checklist. The suggested disclosures are not necessarily applicable for all private companies. These financial statements include many of the disclosure requirements contained in current Financial Reporting Standards, Statements of Standard Accounting Practice, Urgent Issues Task Force Abstracts and

UK GAAP Limited – Year ended 31 December 2013

Company Law, effective from 1 January 2013. Proposals included in exposure drafts at that date are not yet standard practice and have, therefore, not been reflected in these financial statements.

This illustrative annual report does not cover (amongst other items):

- Acquisition of a business.
- Cash flow statement.
- Discontinued activities.
- Exceptional items.
- Government grants.
- Impairment of fixed assets.
- Investment properties.
- Long term contracts
- Share-based payment, including ESOP and similar share-based payment schemes where the entity's employees are recipients.
- Sophisticated capital instruments.

The GAAP UK Group Limited example financial statements are consolidated financial statements for a group of companies that include many of the above items.

If you require further guidance on the UK law and accounting requirements affecting companies' financial statements, PwC's *Manual of accounting – UK GAAP 2012* may be of assistance.

UK GAAP Limited

Example annual report for the year ended 31 December 2013

UK GAAP Limited – Year ended 31 December 2013

Contents

Strategic report 1
Directors' report 3
Independent auditors' report 8
Profit and loss account 11
Statement of total recognised gains and losses 12
Balance sheet 12
Notes to the financial statements 14

UK GAAP Limited – Year ended 31 December 2013

Strategic report

Strategic report for the year ended 31 December 2013[1]

CA06 s414A The directors present their strategic report on the group for the year ended 31 December 2013.

Review of the business

The report should include a review of the business containing:

CA06 s414C(2)(a)
- a fair review of the business of the company; and

CA06 s414C(2)(b)
- a description of the principal risks and uncertainties facing the company.

Where non-GAAP numbers are disclosed, it should be clear that these differ from the GAAP numbers; the equivalent GAAP number should be disclosed; and there should be a reconciliation between the GAAP and non-GAAP numbers, together with relevant comment. This disclosure may be necessary to ensure that the annual report is fair, balanced and understandable

CA06 s414C(3) The review is a balanced and comprehensive analysis of:

- the development and performance of the business of the company during the financial year; and
- the position of the company at the end of the year,

consistent with the size and complexity of the business.

CA06 s414C(4) The review must, to the extent necessary for an understanding of the development, performance or position of the business of the company, include:

CA06 s414C(4)(a)
- analysis using financial key performance indicators; and

CA06 s414C(2)(b)
- where appropriate, analysis using other key performance indicators, including information relating to environmental matters and employee matters.

CA06 S414C(6) Note: For medium sized companies, where these indicators relate to non-financial information, disclosure is not required.

General

CA06 s414C(11); SI 2008/410 7 Sch 1A. Disclosure may include any matters that are directors' report disclosure requirements but considered by the directors to be of strategic importance to the company. (If this is the case, the directors' report includes a cross-reference to the relevant information in the strategic report.)

CA06 s414C(12) The report must, where appropriate, include references to, and additional explanations of, amounts included in the financial statements of the company.

CA06 s414C(14) The report need not disclose any information about impending developments or matters in the course of negotiation if, in the opinion of the directors, such disclosure would be seriously prejudicial to the interests of the company.

---

[1] A small company is entitled to exemption from preparing a strategic report if it is entitled to prepare accounts in accordance with the small companies regime or it would be so entitled but for being or having been a member of an ineligible group. [CA06s414B].

CA06 s414D(1) By order of the board

CA06 s414D(1) AB Smith

    Company Secretary[1]

    26 February 2014

---

[1] The strategic report has to be signed by the company secretary or a director after it has been approved by the board of directors. The copy of the strategic report that is delivered to the Registrar of Companies must be manually signed by the company secretary or a director.

Directors' report

Directors' report for the year ended 31 December 2013

The directors present their report and the audited financial statements of the company for the year ended 31 December 2013.

Future developments

An indication should be given of the likely future developments in the business of the company.

This disclosure is likely to be relevant to the strategic report. It could be included in the strategic report and incorporated into the directors' report by cross reference.

Dividends

Details of dividends paid and recommended should be included.

Political and charitable contributions

SI 2008/410 7 Sch(1)(b)
CA06s416(3)

If the company has made any political donation to any political party or other political organisation, any political donation to any independent election candidate or incurred any political expenditure and the amount of the donation/ expenditure exceeded £2,000, disclose:

- the name of each political party, organisation, or independent election candidate to whom any such donation has been made;
- the total amount given to that party, organisation or candidate by way of such donations in the financial year; and
- the total amount incurred in respect of political expenditure in the financial year.

SI 2008/410 7 Sch 3

Wholly-owned subsidiaries of companies incorporated in the UK are exempt.
[7Sch 3]

SI 2008/410 7 Sch 4

If the company or its subsidiaries have made any contributions to a non-EU political party disclose:

- the amount of the contribution; or
- if it has made two or more contributions in the year, a statement of the total amount of the contribution.

A non-EU political party means any political party that carries on, or proposes to carry on, activities wholly outside Member States.

Wholly-owned subsidiaries of companies incorporated in the UK are exempt.
[7Sch 4]

SI 2008/410 7 Sch 6

Financial risk management

The company's operations expose it to a variety of financial risks that include the effects of changes in debt market prices, credit risk, liquidity risk and interest rate risk. The company has in place a risk management programme that seeks to limit the adverse effects on the financial performance of the company by monitoring levels of debt finance and the related finance costs.

In order to ensure stability of cash out flows and hence manage interest rate risk, the company has a policy of maintaining 90 per cent of its debt (2012: 90 per cent) at fixed rate. The company seeks to minimise the risk of uncertain funding in its operations by borrowing within a spread of maturity periods. Given the size and nature of operations, the company's policy is to operate with 50 per cent of its debt being repayable within one year. At the year end, 52 per cent (2012: 43 per cent) of debt was repayable within one year. The company does not use derivative financial instruments to manage interest rate costs and as such, no hedge accounting is applied.

Given the size of the company, the directors have not delegated the responsibility of monitoring financial risk management to a sub-committee of the board. The policies set by the board of directors are implemented by the company's finance department. The department has a policy and procedures manual that sets out specific guidelines to manage interest rate risk, credit risk and circumstances where it would be appropriate to use financial instruments to manage these.

Price risk

The company is exposed to commodity price risk as a result of its operations. However, given the size of the company's operations, the costs of managing exposure to commodity price risk exceed any potential benefits. The directors will revisit the appropriateness of this policy should the company's operations change in size or nature.

Credit risk

Credit risk arises from cash and cash equivalents, and deposits with banks and financial institutions, as well as credit exposures to wholesale and retail customers, including outstanding receivables and committed transactions. For banks and financial institutions, only independently rated parties with a minimum rating of 'A' are accepted. If wholesale customers are independently rated, these ratings are used. If there is no independent rating, risk control assesses the credit quality of the customer, taking into account its financial position, past experience and other factors. Individual risk limits are set based on internal or external ratings in accordance with limits set by the board. The utilisation of credit limits is regularly monitored. The amount of exposure to any individual counterparty is subject to a limit, which is reassessed annually by the board.

Liquidity risk

The company actively maintains a mixture of long-term and short-term debt finance that is designed to ensure the company has sufficient available funds for operations and planned expansions.

Interest rate cash flow risk

The company has both interest-bearing assets and interest-bearing liabilities. Interest-bearing assets include only government securities and cash balances, all of which earn interest at fixed rate. The company has a policy of maintaining debt at fixed rate to ensure certainty of future interest cash flows. The directors will revisit the appropriateness of this policy should the company's operations change in size or nature.

Note: This disclosure is required by Schedule 7(6) to SI 2008/410. It is not required where such information is not material for the assessment of the entity's assets, liabilities, financial position and profit or loss. In addition, an exemption from making these disclosures is available to small companies.

Directors

The directors who held office during the year and up to the date of signing the financial statements are given below:

CA06 s416(1)(a)

C D Jones (Chairman)
E F Logan (resigned 6 July 2013)
J F King
I D Davies (appointed 31 July 2013)

CA06 s236 (1–5)

Qualifying third-party and pension scheme indemnity provisions

The directors' report should disclose whether:

(a) *at the time the report is approved any qualifying third-party indemnity provision and/or qualifying pension scheme indemnity provision (whether made by the company or otherwise) is in place for the benefit of one or more of the directors or one or more directors of an associated company; or*

(b) *at any time during the year any such provision was in force for the benefit of one or more persons who were then directors or directors of an associated company.*

SI 2008/410 7 Sch 7(1)(c).
(see also SSAP 13 p30, 31 for notes to financial statements)

Research and development

The directors' report should provide an indication of the company's research and development activities.

DV

Note: It is good practice to comment on the charge in the profit and loss account.

Post balance sheet events

SI 2008/410 7 Sch 7(1)(a)
(see also FRs 21 p19-22 regarding disclosure in the notes to financial statements)

Particulars of any important events affecting the reporting entity that have occurred since the end of the financial year must be disclosed.

Employees

SI 2008/410 7 Sch 11(1)

Note: This disclosure is required if the average number of employees during the year and working within the UK exceeds 250.

SI 2008/410 7 Sch 10(3)

Applications for employment by disabled persons are always fully considered, bearing in mind the respective aptitudes and abilities of the applicant concerned. In the event of members of staff becoming disabled, every effort is made to ensure that their employment with the company continues and the appropriate training is arranged. It is the policy of the company that the training, career development and promotion of a disabled person should, as far as possible, be identical to that of a person who does not suffer from a disability.

SI 2008/410 7 Sch 11(3)

Consultation with employees or their representatives has continued at all levels, with the aim of ensuring that their views are taken into account when decisions are made that are likely to affect their interests and that all employees are aware of the financial and economic performance of their business units and of the company as a whole. Communication with all employees continues through the in-house newspaper and newsletters, briefing groups and the distribution of the annual report.

Note: Where employee involvement in the company's performance is encouraged through an employee share scheme or some other means, details should be provided.

This disclosure is required if the average number of employees during the year and working within the UK exceeds 250.

Statement of directors' responsibilities

The directors are responsible for preparing the directors' report and the financial statements in accordance with applicable law and regulations.

Company law requires the directors to prepare financial statements for each financial year. Under that law, the directors have prepared the financial statements in accordance with United Kingdom Generally Accepted Accounting Practice (United Kingdom Accounting Standards and applicable law). Under company law, the directors must not approve the financial statements unless they are satisfied that they give a true and fair view of the state of affairs of the company and of the profit or loss of the company for that period. In preparing these financial statements, the directors are required to:

- select suitable accounting policies and then apply them consistently;
- make judgements and accounting estimates that are reasonable and prudent;
- state whether applicable UK Accounting Standards have been followed, subject to any material departures disclosed and explained in the financial statements; and
- prepare the financial statements on the going concern basis unless it is inappropriate to presume that the company will continue in business.

The directors are responsible for keeping adequate accounting records that are sufficient to show and explain the company's transactions and disclose with reasonable accuracy at any time the financial position of the company and enable them to ensure that the financial statements comply with the Companies Act 2006. They are also responsible for safeguarding the assets of the company and hence for taking reasonable steps for the prevention and detection of fraud and other irregularities.

Disclosure of information to auditors

CA06 s418(2) *Note: Section 418(1) to (4) of the Companies Act 2006 requires this disclosure within the directors' report. This section is applicable unless the directors have taken advantage of the exemption conferred by section 477(1) or 480(1). The report must contain a statement to the effect that, in the case of each of the persons who are directors at the time when the report is approved, the following applies:*

- so far as the director is aware, there is no relevant audit information of which the company's auditor is unaware; and
- he has taken all the steps that he ought to have taken as a director in order to make himself aware of any relevant audit information and to establish that the company's auditor is aware of that information.

Independent auditors

DV (see also CA06 s489(1),(2)) The auditors, PricewaterhouseCoopers LLP, have indicated their willingness to continue in office and a resolution concerning their re-appointment will be proposed at the Annual General Meeting.

CA06 s419(1) By order of the board

J F King
Company secretary 26 February 2014

CA06 s419(1) (a) The directors' report must be signed by the company secretary or a director after it has been approved by the board of directors.
(b) The copy of the strategic report and directors' report that is delivered to the Registrar of Companies must be manually signed by the company secretary or a director.

Note: Where the financial statements are published on a website, the statement of directors' responsibilities may also include a statement that:

- the directors are responsible for the maintenance and integrity of the web site; and
- legislation in the UK concerning the preparation and dissemination of financial statements may differ from legislation in other jurisdictions.

UK GAAP Limited – Year ended 31 December 2013

Independent auditors' report to the members of UK GAAP Limited

> Warning: This audit report format was current at the date of going to press. However it may not be the most up-to-date version. It should not be used without checking that it is the appropriate version.

Report on the financial statements

Our opinion

In our opinion the financial statements:

- give a true and fair view of the state of the company's affairs as at 31 December 2013 and of its profit and cash flows for the year then ended;
- have been properly prepared in accordance with United Kingdom Generally Accepted Accounting Practice; and
- have been prepared in accordance with the requirements of the Companies Act 2006.

This opinion is to be read in the context of what we say below.

What we have audited

The financial statements, which are prepared by UK GAAP Limited, comprise:

- the balance sheet as at 31 December 2013;
- the profit and loss account for the year then ended;
- the statement of cash flows and statement of total recognised gains and losses for the year then ended; and
- the notes to the financial statements, which include a summary of significant accounting policies and other explanatory information.

The financial reporting framework that has been applied in their preparation comprises applicable law and United Kingdom Accounting Standards (United Kingdom Generally Accepted Accounting Practice).

In applying the financial reporting framework, the directors have made a number of subjective judgements, for example in respect of significant accounting estimates. In making such estimates, they have made assumptions and considered future events.

What an audit of financial statements involves

We conducted our audit in accordance with International Standards on Auditing (UK and Ireland) (ISAs (UK & Ireland)). An audit involves obtaining evidence about the amounts and disclosures in the financial statements sufficient to give reasonable assurance that the financial statements are free from material misstatement, whether caused by fraud or error. This includes an assessment of:

- whether the accounting policies are appropriate to the company's circumstances and have been consistently applied and adequately disclosed;
- the reasonableness of significant accounting estimates made by the directors; and
- the overall presentation of the financial statements.

In addition, we read all the financial and non-financial information in the Annual Report to identify material inconsistencies with the audited financial statements and to identify any information that is apparently materially incorrect based on, or materially inconsistent with, the knowledge acquired by us in the course of performing the audit. If we become aware of any apparent material misstatements or inconsistencies we consider the implications for our report.

Opinion on matter prescribed by the Companies Act 2006

In our opinion the information given in the Strategic Report and the Directors' Report for the financial year for which the financial statements are prepared is consistent with the financial statements.

Other matters on which we are required to report by exception

Adequacy of accounting records and information and explanations received

Under the Companies Act 2006 we are required to report to you if, in our opinion:

- we have not received all the information and explanations we require for our audit; or
- adequate accounting records have not been kept, or returns adequate for our audit have not been received from branches not visited by us; or
- the financial statements are not in agreement with the accounting records and returns.

We have no exceptions to report arising from this responsibility.

Directors' remuneration

Under the Companies Act 2006 we are required to report if, in our opinion, certain disclosures of directors' remuneration specified by law have not been made.

We have no exceptions to report arising from this responsibility.

Other information in the Annual Report

Under ISAs (UK & Ireland), we are required to report to you if, in our opinion, information in the Annual Report is:

- materially inconsistent with the information in the audited financial statements; or
- apparently materially incorrect based on, or materially inconsistent with, our knowledge of the company acquired in the course of performing our audit; or
- is otherwise misleading.

We have no exceptions to report arising from this responsibility.

Responsibilities for the financial statements and the audit

Our responsibilities and those of the directors

As explained more fully in the Directors' Responsibilities Statement set out on page 6, the directors are responsible for the preparation of the financial statements and for being satisfied that they give a true and fair view.

Our responsibility is to audit and express an opinion on the financial statements in accordance with applicable law and ISAs (UK & Ireland). Those standards require us to comply with the Auditing Practices Board's Ethical Standards for Auditors.

This report, including the opinions, has been prepared for and only for the Company's members as a body in accordance with Chapter 3 of Part 16 of the Companies Act 2006 and for no other purpose. We do not, in giving these opinions, accept or assume responsibility for any other purpose or to any other person to whom this report is shown or into whose hands it may come save where expressly agreed by our prior consent in writing.

John Smith (Senior Statutory Auditor)
for and on behalf of PricewaterhouseCoopers LLP
Chartered Accountants and Statutory Auditors
London
26 February 2014.

UK GAAP Limited – Year ended 31 December 2013

Profit and loss account for the year ended 31 December 2013

			2013		2012	
CA06 s403(2) SI 2008/410 1 Sch Format 1 FRS3 p14	Continuing operations	Note	£'000	£'000	£'000	£'000
	Turnover	3		11,275		10,010
	Cost of sales			(8,734)		(7,305)
	Gross profit			2,541		2,705
	Distribution costs			(434)		(590)
	Administrative expenses			(1,536)		(1,220)
	Other operating income			13		11
FRS 3 p14	Operating profit	4		584		906
	Income from fixed asset investments			17		9
	Profit on ordinary activities before interest and taxation			601		915
	Interest receivable and similar income		21		13	
	Interest payable and similar charges	7	(166)		(97)	
	Other finance income	23	45		94	
				(100)		10
	Profit on ordinary activities before taxation			501		925
FRS 16 p17	Tax on profit on ordinary activities	8		(258)		(406)
	Profit for the financial year			243		519

Note: The above presentation of the profit and loss account follows format 1 as outlined in Schedule 1 to SI 2008/410. Alternatively, a company may present its profit and loss account such that expenses are classified by type using, for example, format 2. An example of presentation of expenses by type in line with format 2 using the above profit and loss account balances is shown below:

			2013		2012	
	Continuing operations	Note	£'000	£'000	£'000	£'000
SI 2008/410 1 Sch Format 2	Turnover	3		11,275		10,010
	Change in stocks of finished goods and work in progress			76		74
	Own work capitalised			11		9
	Other operating income			13		11
				11,375		10,104
	Raw materials and consumables		(6,519)		(5,537)	
	Other external charges		(293)		(278)	
	Staff costs	4	(3,277)		(2,921)	
	Depreciation		(202)		(200)	
	Other operating charges		(500)		(262)	
				(10,791)		(9,198)
	Operating profit			584		906

UK GAAP Limited – Year ended 31 December 2013

Statement of total recognised gains and losses for the year ended 31 December 2013

		Note	2013 £'000	2012 £'000
FRS 3 p27	Profit for the financial year		243	519
FRS 17 p57	Actuarial losses on pension scheme	23	(131)	(124)
FRS 16 p5,6	Current tax deductions allocated to actuarial losses		17	35
FRS 19 p34,35	Movement on deferred tax relating to pension deficit	18	22	2
	Total recognised gains and losses relating to the year		151	432

FRS 3 p26 — There are no material differences between the profit on ordinary activities before taxation and the profit for the financial year stated above and their historical cost equivalents.

Balance sheet as at 31 December 2013

SI 2008/410 1 Sch Formats		Note	2013 £'000	2013 £'000	2012 £'000	2012 £'000
	Fixed assets					
	Tangible assets	10	2,385		2,031	
	Investments	11	56		76	
				2,441		2,107
	Current assets					
	Stocks	12	1,908		1,779	
	Debtors (including £205,000 (2012: £56,000) due after one year)*	13	2,015		1,509	
	Investments	14	50		125	
	Cash at bank and in hand		91		159	
				4,064		3,572
	Creditors – amounts falling due within one year	15		(2,232)		(1,959)
	Net current assets			1,832		1,613
	Total assets less current liabilities			4,273		3,720
	Creditors – Amounts falling due after more than one year	16		(794)		(524)
	Provisions for liabilities	18		(234)		(48)
	Net assets excluding pension deficit			3,245		3,148
FRS 17 p47	Pension deficit	23		(150)		(93)
	Net assets including pension deficit			3,095		3,055
	Capital and reserves					
	Called-up share capital	19		508		505
	Share premium account	20		144		120
	Revaluation reserve	20		172		177
	Profit and loss account	20		2,271		2,253
	Total shareholders' funds	21		3,095		3,055

Notes:

*Debtors due after one year must be disclosed separately if material compared to net current assets.

FRS 21 p17
CA06 s414

The financial statements on pages 14 to 28 were approved by the board of directors on 26 February 2014 and were signed on its behalf by:

C D Jones

UK GAAP Limited Registered number xxyyzz

UK GAAP Limited – Year ended 31 December 2013

Notes to the financial statements for the year ended 31 December 2013

1 Accounting policies

SI 2008/410(1) These financial statements are prepared on a going concern basis, under the historical cost convention, as modified by the revaluation of certain tangible fixed assets and in accordance with the Companies Act 2006 and applicable accounting standards in the United Kingdom.

FRS18 p55 The principal accounting policies are set out below and have been applied consistently throughout the year.

FRS 18 p55(a),(b) *Note: A description of each of the accounting policies that is material in the context of the entity's financial statements should be disclosed. The policies must be the most appropriate. Where an accounting policy is prescribed by and fully described in an accounting standard, UITF Abstract or companies legislation, a succinct description of the policy should be given. Where an accounting policy is not prescribed by an accounting standard, a UITF Abstract or companies legislation, or an entity uses an option therein, a further description should be provided. In addition, there should be a description of those estimation techniques adopted that are significant (those where the range of reasonable amounts is so large that the use of a different amount from within the range could materially affect the view shown by the financial statements). The list of areas where companies might reasonably be expected to disclose accounting policies is not exhaustive.*

- Capital instruments.(FRS 4)
- Deferred taxation.(FRS 19)
- Depreciation and amortisation.(FRS15, FRS10, SSAP 13))
- Finance costs.(FRS 4, FRS15)
- Financial instruments.(FRS 4)
- Fixed assets.(FRS 15)
- Foreign currencies.(SSAP 20)
- Goodwill and intangible assets.(FRS 10, UITF 27, UITF 29)
- Government grants.(SSAP 4)
- Impairments. (FRS 11)
- Interest capitalisation.(FRS 15)
- Investment properties.(SSAP 19)
- Leases.(SSAP 21, UITF 28)
- Long-term contracts.(SSAP 9)
- Pensions.(FRS 17, UITF 48)
- Post-retirement benefits.(FRS 17, FRS 12)
- Provisions.(FRS 12, UITF 45)
- Research and development.(SSAP 13)
- Revaluation of fixed assets.(FRS 15)
- Stocks and work in progress.(SSAP 9)
- Revenue recognition.(FRS 5, UITF 40)
- Taxation.(FRS 16)

2 Cash flow statement and related party disclosures

FRS 1 p5(a)
FRS 8 p7B
SSAP 25 P34-45
The company is a wholly-owned subsidiary of GAAP UK plc and is included in the consolidated financial statements of GAAP UK plc, which are publicly available. Consequently, the company has taken advantage of the exemption from preparing a cash flow statement under the terms of FRS 1 (revised 1996).

The company is also exempt under the terms of FRS 8 from disclosing related-party transactions with entities that are part of the GAAP UK plc group. For details of other related-party transactions see note 26.

3 Segment reporting

The company's activities consist solely of the processing and sale of food in the United Kingdom.

4 Operating profit

		2013 £'000	2012 £'000
	Operating profit is stated after charging		
CA06 s411(5)	Wages and salaries	2,661	2,391
CA06 s411(5)	Social security costs	515	436
CA06 s411(5)	Other pension costs (note 23)	101	94
SI 2008/410 1 Sch Formats	**Staff costs**	3,277	2,921
FRS 15 P100	Depreciation of tangible fixed assets:		
	– Owned assets	159	158
SSAP 21 p50	– Leased assets	43	42
SSAP 21 p55	Operating lease charges:		
	– Plant and machinery	42	34
	– Other	55	48
SSAP 13 p31	Research and development – current year	15	18
SI 2008/489, as amended by SI 2011/2198, ICAEW Tech 04/11	**Services provided by the company's auditor**		
	– Fees payable for the audit	13	13
	– Fees payable for other services – tax compliance	5	5

5 Directors' emoluments

		2013 £'000	2012 £'000
SI 2008/410 5 Sch 1			
	Aggregate emoluments	210	206
	Aggregate amounts (excluding shares) receivable under long-term incentive schemes	5	7
	Sums paid to third parties for directors' services	2	–

Retirement benefits are accruing to three (2012: two) directors under a defined benefit scheme.

Notes:

SI 2008/410 5 Sch 2(2) (a)(b)   (a) If the company has a defined contribution scheme, a separate figure is to be disclosed showing the aggregate value of any company contributions paid or treated as paid to a pension scheme in respect of money purchase benefits. The number of directors to whom retirement benefits are accruing under each of money purchase and defined benefit schemes must also be disclosed.

SI 2008/410 5 Sch 2(2) (a)(b)   (b) For unlisted companies, the net value of assets received or receivable under a long-term incentive scheme excludes shares and, hence, such companies must disclose the number of directors entitled to shares under a long-term incentive scheme, if applicable.

SI 2008/410 5 Sch 3   (c) The aggregate amount of excess retirement benefits and the aggregate amount of compensation for loss of office must also be disclosed, where applicable.

SI 2008/410 5 Sch 2(1)   **Highest paid director**

	2013 £'000	2012 £'000
Total amount of emoluments and amounts (excluding shares) receivable under long-term incentive schemes	75	70
Defined benefit pension scheme:		
– Accrued pension at end of year	38	36
– Accrued lump sum at the end of the year	50	45

UK GAAP Limited – Year ended 31 December 2013

16

Note: Where the highest paid director exercised any share options, and where any shares under a long-term incentive scheme were receivable by him, these facts must be disclosed (Companies Act 2006 5 Sch 2(3)). Where he is a member of a defined contribution scheme, the amount of company contributions in respect of him must be disclosed.

6 Employee information

The average monthly number of persons (including executive directors) employed by the company during the year was:

	By activity	2013 £'000	2012 £'000
CA06 s411 (1)	Production	166	170
	Selling and distribution	32	30
	Administration	55	55
		253	255

7 Interest payable and similar charges

		2013 £'000	2012 £'000
SI 2008/410 1 Sch 66 (1)	Interest payable on overdrafts and bank loans	109	33
SI 2008/410 1 Sch 66(2) SSAP 21 P53	Interest payable on other loans	18	23
FRS 25 p35	Preference share dividend paid: 3.5p (2012: 3.5p) per £1 share	3	3
SSAP 21 p53	Finance lease interest	36	38
		166	97

8 Tax on profit on ordinary activities

		2013 £'000	2012 £'000
SI 2008/410 1 Sch 67(2)	Current tax:		
FRS 16 P17(a)	– UK corporation tax on profits of the year	211	339
FRS 16 P17(a)	– Adjustment in respect of previous years	25	36
	Total current tax	236	375
	Deferred tax:		
FRS 19 p60	– Origination and reversal of timing differences	22	31
FRS 19 p60	– Impact of change in tax rate[1]	–	–
	Total deferred tax (note 18)	22	31
	Tax on profit on ordinary activities	**258**	**406**

[1] The line item for 'Impact of change in tax rate' is shown for illustrative purposes. Companies with 31 December 2013 year ends will need to consider the impact of the reduction in tax rates in the Finance) Act 2013.

FRS 19 p64(a) The tax assessed for the period is higher (2012: higher) than the standard effective rate of corporation tax in the UK for the year ended 31 December 2013 of 23.25% (2012: 24.5%). The differences are explained below:

	2013 £'000	2012 £'000
Profit on ordinary activities before tax	501	925
Profit on ordinary activities multiplied by standard rate in the UK 23.25% (2012: 24.5%)	116	227
Effects of:		
– Expenses not deductible for tax purposes	117	141
– Accelerated capital allowances and other timing differences	(22)	(29)
– Adjustments to tax charge in respect of previous years	25	36
Current tax charge for the year	236	375

Tax on recognised gains and losses not included in the profit and loss account

	2013 £m	2012 £m
UK corporation tax at 23.25% (2012: 24.5%)		
Current tax deductions allocated to actuarial losses	(17)	(35)
Origination and reversal of timing differences relating to pension scheme	(22)	(2)
Impact of change in tax rate[1]	–	–
	(39)	(37)

Factors affecting current and future tax charges

FRS 19 p64(a) During the year, as a result of the changes in the UK corporation tax rate to 21% from 1 April 2014 and to 20% from 1 April 2015, which were substantially enacted on 2 July 2013, the relevant deferred tax balances have been re-measured.

PwC commentary

Where further changes to the tax rates and laws have been announced but not substantively enacted at the balance sheet date, disclosures explaining the changes and their effect should be made.

FRS 19 p64 (b)-(e) No provision has been made for deferred tax on gains recognised on revaluing property to its market value. Such tax would become payable only if the property was sold without it being possible to claim rollover relief. The total amount unprovided for is £53,100 (2012: £53,100).

Deferred tax liabilities have not been discounted.

---

[1] The line item for the change in UK tax rate is shown for illustrative purposes. Companies with 31 December 2013 year ends will need to consider the impact of the reduction in tax rates in the Finance Act 2013.

UK GAAP Limited – Year ended 31 December 2013

9 Dividends

	2013 £'000	2012 £'000
Equity – Ordinary		
Interim paid: 3.51p (2012: 2.57p) per £0.25 share	71	52
Final paid (2012): 3.32p per £0.25 share	67	–
	138	**52**

SI 2008/410 3 Sch 43 (b)

SI 2008/410 3 Sch 43 (a)
FRS 21 p13

The directors have proposed a final dividend for the year ended 31 December 2013 of 5.0p per share, which is a total of £102,000. This dividend has not been accounted for within the current year financial statements as it has yet to be approved.

10 Tangible assets

	Land and buildings £'000	Plant and machinery £'000	Total £'000
Cost or valuation			
At 1 January 2013	1,291	1,561	2,852
Additions	246	426	672
Disposals	(24)	(106)	(130)
At 31 December 2013	**1,513**	**1,881**	**3,394**
Accumulated depreciation			
At 1 January 2013	211	610	821
Charge for the year	45	157	202
Disposals	(6)	(8)	(14)
At 31 December 2013	**250**	**759**	**1,009**
Net book amount			
At 31 December 2013	**1,263**	**1,122**	**2,385**
At 31 December 2012	1,080	951	2,031

SI 2008/410 Sch Formats
SI 2008/410 1 Sch 51(1)
FRS 15 p100(e)
FRS 15 p100(g)
FRS 15 p100(g)
FRS 15 p100(e)
SI 2008/410 1 Sch 51 (3)
FRS 15 p100(f)
FRS 15 p100(g)
FRS 15 p100(g)

Analysis of land and buildings

	2013 £'000	2012 £'000
Analysis of land and buildings at cost or valuation		
At cost	1,224	1,002
At valuation	289	289
	1,513	**1,291**

The Company has taken advantage of the transitional arrangements in FRS 15 'Tangible fixed assets', and retained the book values of certain freehold properties that were revalued prior to implementation of that standard. Where an asset that was previously revalued is disposed of, its book value is eliminated and an appropriate transfer made from the revaluation reserve to the profit and loss reserve.

The transition rules set out in FRS 15 were adopted as at 31 December 1999; book values of property assets were frozen accordingly.

	2013 £'000	2012 £'000
SI 2008/410 1 Sch 53 **The net book amount of land and buildings comprises**		
Freehold	1,216	1,031
SI 2008/410 10 Sch 7 Long leaseholds	36	37
Short leaseholds	11	12
	1,263	1,080

SI 2008/410 1 Sch 34 (3),(4)
FRS 15 p74)(a)(iv)

If land and buildings had not been revalued, they would have been included at the following amounts:

	Land and buildings	
	2013 £'000	2012 £'000
Cost	1,326	1,104
Aggregate depreciation	(235)	(201)
Net book amount	**1,091**	**903**

	2013 £'000	2012 £'000
SSAP 21 p49-50 **Assets held under finance leases and capitalised in plant and machinery**		
Cost	349	396
Aggregate depreciation	(116)	(132)
Net book amount	**233**	**264**

11 Fixed asset investments

SI 2008/410 1 Sch Formats
SI 2008/410 1 Sch 51(1)

	£'000
At 1 January 2013	76
Disposals	(20)
At 31 December 2013	**56**

SI 2008/410 1 Sch 54 (2)

Fixed asset investments comprise equity shares in a trade investment with a cost of £56,000 (2012: £76,000). These are listed on the London Stock Exchange and had a market value of £145,000 (2012: £170,000) at 31 December 2013.

12 Stocks

SI 2008/410 1 Sch Formats
SSAP 9 p27

	2013 £'000	2012 £'000
Raw materials and consumables	873	820
Work in progress	209	182
Finished goods and goods for resale	826	777
	1,908	1,779

FRS 5 p30-31 £200,000 (2012: £100,000) of finished goods included above are consignment stocks that are held on a sale or return basis from the manufacturer. Title to these

UK GAAP Limited – Year ended 31 December 2013

stocks passes at the earlier of when they are sold and nine months from delivery date. On delivery a deposit of 30% is payable. The balance is included in trade creditors and bears interest at LIBOR plus 1.75% and becomes payable when title passes.

The replacement cost of stocks exceeds balance sheet values as follows:

	2013 £'000	2012 £'000
Raw materials and consumables	40	19

SI 2008/410 1 Sch 28 (4)

13 Debtors

SI 2008/410 1 Sch Formats

	2013 £'000	2012 £'000
Trade debtors	1,533	1,067
Amounts owed by group undertakings	389	367
Other debtors	32	21
Prepayments and accrued income	61	54
	2,015	1,509

SI 2008/410 1 Sch Formats

Trade debtors include £205,000 (2012: £56,000) falling due after more than one year. Amounts owed by group undertakings are unsecured, interest free, have no fixed date of repayment and are repayable on demand.

14 Current asset investments

SI 2008/410 1 Sch Formats

	2013 £'000	2012 £'000
Government securities	50	125

The market value of the government securities is not materially different from their carrying amount.

15 Creditors – amounts falling due within one year

SI 2008/410 1 Sch Formats

	2013 £'000	2012 £'000
Debenture loans (note 17)	349	12
Bank loans and overdrafts (note 17)	388	319
Trade creditors	876	1,005
Amounts owed to group undertakings	241	180
Finance leases (note 17)	27	31
Taxation and social security	243	291
Other creditors	15	12
Accruals and deferred income	93	109
	2,232	1,959

SSAP 21 p51 (Finance leases)
FRS 12 p11(b) (Accruals and deferred income)

Amounts due to group undertakings are unsecured, interest free and repayable on demand.

UK GAAP Limited – Year ended 31 December 2013

16 Creditors – amounts falling due after more than one year

	2013 £'000	2012 £'000
Debenture loans (note 17)	175	107
Bank loans (note 17)	166	52
Finance leases (note 17)	283	250
Cumulative preference shares of £1 each – 75,000 (note 17)	75	75
Other creditors	95	40
	794	524

17 Loans and other borrowings

	2013 £'000	2012 £'000
7% unsecured loan stock 2013/2014	349	12
10% unsecured loan stock 2018/2019	175	107
Bank loans and overdrafts	554	371
Finance leases	310	281
Cumulative preference shares of £1 each – 75,000	75	75
	1,463	846

Maturity of financial liabilities

	2013 £'000	2012 £'000
In one year or less, or on demand	764	362
In more than one year, but not more than two years	218	102
In more than two years, but not more than five years	211	168
In more than five years	270	214
	1,463	846

Note: The maturity time bandings are derived from paragraph 67 of FRS 25. This disclosure is suggested best practice for those companies that are not applying the disclosure requirements of FRS 25 as the equivalent disclosure requirements in FRS 4 have been deleted.

The 7% unsecured loan stock 2013/2014 is redeemable at par between 1 January 2013 and 31 December 2014. The 10% unsecured loan stock 2018/2019 is redeemable at par between 1 January 2018 and 31 December 2019.

Included in the bank loans is an amount of £300,000, which is payable in two annual instalments commencing 1 January 2014 and carries interest at 11% fixed. The balance of £254,000 carries interest at LIBOR plus 3% and is repayable in six quarterly instalments commencing 1 February 2014.

Finance leases

Future minimum payments under finance leases are as follows:

	2013 £'000	2012 £'000
Within one year	31	35
In more than one year, but not more than five years	302	243
After five years	25	37
Total gross payments	358	315
Less finance charges included above	(48)	(34)
	310	281

UK GAAP Limited – Year ended 31 December 2013

The total value of leases repayable by instalments any part of which falls due after more than five years is £24,184 (2012: £35,875).

SI 2008/410 1 Sch 61(4)

Debentures issued

The company issued the following debentures during the year.

Class	Amount issued £'000	Consideration received £'000
7% unsecured redeemable 2013/2014	337	337
10% unsecured redeemable 2018/2019	68	68

Preference share capital issued and fully paid	2013	2012
75,000: 3.5% cumulative preference shares of £1 each at 1 January 2013	75	75

The 3.5% cumulative preference shares carry a fixed cumulative preferential dividend at the rate of 3.5% per annum, payable half yearly in arrears on 31 December and 30 June. The shares have no redemption entitlement. On a winding-up, the holders have priority before all other classes of shares to receive repayment of capital plus any arrears of dividend. The holders have no voting rights unless the dividend is in arrears by six months or more.

Note: Although not applicable for UK GAAP Limited, companies that elect not to adopt fair value accounting for certain financial instruments must give additional disclosures relating to their derivative financial instruments. The following disclosure is required for each class of derivative financial instrument:

- *the fair value of the derivatives in that class, if such a value can be determined; and*
- *the extent and nature of the derivatives.*

[SI 2008/410 1 Sch 56 (a), (b)].

In addition, where:

- *a company has financial fixed assets that could be included at fair value;*
- *the amount at which those assets are included in the financial statements is in excess of their fair value; and*
- *the company has not made provision for diminution in value of those assets.*

The following disclosure must be made:

- *The amount at which either the individual assets or appropriate groupings of those individual assets is stated in the company's financial statements.*
- *The fair value of those assets or groupings.*
- *The reasons for not making a provision for diminution in value of those assets, including the nature of the evidence that provides the basis for the belief that the amount at which they are stated in the financial statements will be recovered.*

[SI 2008/410 1 Sch 57 (1), (2)].

18 Provisions for liabilities

		Pending litigation £'000	Reorganisation provision £'000	Environmental provision £'000	Deferred tax provision £'000	Total £'000
SI 2008/410 1 Sch Formats						
FRS 12 p89(a), SI 2008/410 1 Sch 59(2)(a)	1 January 2013	–	–	–	48	48
FRS 12 p89(b) FRS 19 p61 (b)	Charged to the profit and loss account	15	153	72	22	262
FRS 12 p89(b) FRS 19 p61 (c)	Utilised during the year	–	(42)	(34)	–	(76)
FRS 12 p89(a), SI 2008/410 1 Sch 59(2)(a)	31 December 2013	15	111	38	70	234

Pending litigation

FRS 12 p90   In December 2013, the company received a claim from Customer Limited that green colouring had been found in a batch of bread. A provision of £15,000 has been made for the costs of product recall and loss of profit claim from Customer Limited. The claim is expected to be fully resolved in early 2014.

Reorganisation

FRS 12 p90   A rationalisation of product processes at the company's two factories in London and Bradford was announced on 11 December 2013. This rationalisation involving the introduction of new technology will result in the loss of 15 jobs in total over the next few months. The provision is expected to be fully utilised by 31 December 2014.

Environmental

FRS 12 p90   In April 2013 a spillage of cleaning chemicals contaminated land surrounding the Bradford factory. The company is committed to a policy of environmental protection and immediate action is being taken to deal with the contamination. A provision of £72,000 has been recognised for those clean-up costs, which are expected to be incurred over an eighteen-month period.

		2013 £'000	2012 £'000
FRS 19 p61	**Provision for deferred tax**		
	Accelerated capital allowances	65	40
	Other timing differences	5	8
	Total provision for deferred tax	**70**	**48**
	1 January	48	21
	Deferred tax charged in profit and loss account (note 8)	22	27
	31 December	**70**	**48**

		2013 £'000	2012 £'000
FRS 19 p62	**Deferred tax asset relating to pension deficit**		
	1 January	36	38
	Deferred tax credit charged in profit and loss account	–	(4)
	Deferred tax credited/(charged) to the statement of total recognised gains and losses:		
	– On actuarial loss	22	3
	– Change in tax rate	–	–
	31 December	**58**	**36**

UK GAAP Limited – Year ended 31 December 2013

The deferred tax asset of £58,000 (2012: £36,000) has been deducted in arriving at the net pension deficit on the balance sheet.

19 Called-up share capital

	2013 £'000	2012 £'000
Allotted and fully paid		
2,032,000 (2012: 2,020,000) ordinary shares of £0.25 each	508	505

On 3 May 2013 12,000 ordinary shares were issued for cash. The nominal value of these shares was £3,000, and the consideration received was £27,000 after deducting expenses of £1,000.

20 Reserves

	Share premium account £'000	Revaluation reserve £'000	Profit and loss account £'000
1 January 2013	120	177	2,253
Premium on ordinary shares issued (net of £1,000 expenses)	24	–	–
Retained profit for the financial year (note 21)	–	–	105
Actuarial losses on pension scheme	–	–	(92)
Transfer to profit and loss reserve	–	(5)	5
31 December 2013	**144**	**172**	**2,271**
Pension deficit	–	–	(150)
Profit and loss reserve excluding pension deficit	–	–	2,421

21 Reconciliation of movements in shareholders' funds

	2013 £'000	2012 £'000
Profit for the financial year	243	519
Dividends	(138)	(52)
Retained profit for the financial year	105	467
Net proceeds of issue of ordinary share capital (note 19)	27	50
Actuarial losses on pension scheme net of tax	(92)	(87)
Net addition to shareholders' funds	**40**	**430**
Closing shareholders' funds	**3,095**	**3,055**

22 Contingent liabilities

The company has given a guarantee in respect of the bank borrowings of a fellow subsidiary, which amounted to £35,000 at 31 December 2013 (2012: £25,000).

An overseas customer has commenced an action against the company in respect of equipment claimed to be defective. It has been estimated that the liability should the action be successful is £2,000. A trial date has not yet been set; therefore it is not therefore practical to state the timing of any payment. The company has been advised by Counsel that it is possible, but not probable, the action will succeed; accordingly no provision for any liability has therefore been made in these accounts.

23 Pension commitments

The company operates a defined benefit pension scheme with assets held in a separately administered fund. The scheme provides retirement benefits on the basis of members' final salary. The company does not operate any unfunded schemes.

On 1 January 2012, the defined benefit pension scheme was closed to new entrants. At the same time, the company established a defined contribution scheme to provide benefits to new employees.

Defined benefit scheme

An actuarial valuation of the UK GAAP Limited pension scheme, using the projected unit basis, was carried out at 31 December 2013 by Actuary and Actuary, independent consulting actuaries. The major assumptions used by the actuary were:

	2013 %	2012 %
Rate of increase in salaries	4.3	4.0
Rate of increase in pensions in payment	3.0	4.0
Discount rate	5.2	5.0
Rate of inflation	2.8	2.5

The mortality assumptions used were as follows:

	2013 years	2012 years
Longevity at age 65 for current pensioners:		
– Men	19.7	18.4
– Women	22.4	21.3
Longevity at age 65 for future pensioners:		
– Men	20.4	19.3
– Women	23.1	22.3

The assets in the scheme and the expected rates of return were:

	Long-term rate of return expected at 31 December 2013 %	Value at 31 December 2013 £000	Long-term rate of return expected at 31 December 2012 %	Value at 31 December 2012 £000
Equities	8.2	5,852	8.4	5,341
Bonds	4.9	1,600	5.6	1,500
Total market value of assets		7,452		6,841
Present value of scheme liabilities		(7,660)		(6,970)
Deficit in scheme		**(208)**		**(129)**
Related deferred tax asset		58		36
Net pension deficit		**(150)**		**(93)**

UK GAAP Limited – Year ended 31 December 2013

Reconciliation of present value of scheme liabilities

FRS 17 p77(b)

	2013 £'000	2012 £'000
1 January	6,970	6,315
Current service cost	84	90
Past service cost	5	–
Interest cost	505	489
Benefits paid	(51)	(63)
Actuarial loss	147	139
31 December	7,660	6,970

DV, FRS 17 p77 (n)

Sensitivity analysis of scheme liabilities

The sensitivity of the present value of scheme liabilities to changes in the principle assumptions used is set out below.

	Change in assumption	Impact on scheme liabilities
Discount rate	Increase/decrease by 1%	Increase/decrease by 8.5%
Rate of inflation	Increase/decrease by 1%	Increase/decrease by 5.0%
Rate of increase in salaries	Increase/decrease by 1%	Increase/decrease by 3.5%
Rate of increase in pensions in payment	Increase/decrease by 1%	Increase/decrease by 3.0%
Mortality	Increase by 1 year	Increase by 4.5%

Reconciliation of fair value of scheme assets

FRS 17 p77(d)

	2013 £'000	2012 £'000
1 January	6,841	6,190
Expected return on scheme assets	550	583
Actuarial gains	16	15
Benefits paid	(51)	(63)
Contributions paid by employer	96	116
31 December	7,452	6,841

FRS 17 p77(j) Scheme assets do not include any of UK GAAP Limited's own financial instruments or any property occupied by UK GAAP Limited.

FRS 17 p77(k) The expected return on scheme assets is determined by considering the expected returns available on the assets underlying the current investment policy. Expected yields on fixed interest investments are based on gross redemption yields as at the balance sheet date. Expected returns on equity investments reflect long-term real rates of return experienced in the respective markets.

FRS 17 p77(l) The actual return on scheme assets in the year was £566,000 (2012: £598,000).

FRS 17 p77(f) Analysis of the amount charged to profit or loss is as follows:

	2013 £'000	2012 £'000
Current service cost	84	90
Past service cost	5	–
Expected return on pension scheme assets	(550)	(583)
Interest on pension scheme liabilities	505	489
Total	44	(4)

UK GAAP Limited – Year ended 31 December 2013

FRS 17 p77(f) Of the total current and past service cost, £63,000 (2012: £65,000) is included within cost of sales, and £26,000 (2012: £25,000) is included within administrative expenses.

Actuarial gains and losses

FRS 17 p77(h) The cumulative amount of actuarial losses recognised in the statement of recognised gains and losses is £536,000.

Actuarial valuation

FRS 17 p77(p)
FRS 17 p77(a) The full actuarial valuation at 31 December 2013 showed an increase in the deficit from £135,000 to £215,000. It has been agreed with the trustees that contributions for the next two years will be increased by £100,000 to make good the deficit. The total contributions expected to be made to the scheme by UK GAAP Limited in the year to 31 December 2014 is therefore £195,000. Further to this, as the scheme is closed to new entrants, the current service cost will increase as members approach retirement.

Amounts for current and previous four years

FRS 17 p77(o)

	2013 £'000	2012 £'000	2011 £'000	2010 £'000	2009 £'000
Defined benefit obligation	(7,660)	(6,970)	(6,315)	(6,115)	(5,987)
Plan assets	7,445	6,835	6,190	5,990	5,780
Deficit	(215)	(135)	(125)	(125)	(207)
Experience adjustments on plan assets:					
– Amount	16	15	50	41	(33)
Experience adjustments on plan liabilities:					
– Amount	(22)	21	98	45	66
FRS 17 p77(g) Total amount recognised in the statement of total recognised gains and losses:	131	124	150	245	160

Defined contribution scheme

FRS 17 p75 (b)
FRS 17 p75 (c) The cost of contributions to the defined contribution scheme amounts to £12,000 (2012: £4,000). There were no outstanding or prepaid contributions (2012: £Nil)

24 Capital and other commitments

	2013 £'000	2012 £'000
SI 2008/410 1 Sch 63(3) Contracts placed for future capital expenditure not provided in the financial statements	145	226

UK GAAP Limited – Year ended 31 December 2013

25 Financial commitments

SSAP 21 p56

At 31 December 2013, the company had annual commitments under non-cancellable operating leases for assets other than land and buildings expiring as follows:

	2013 £'000	2012 £'000
Within one year	12	20
Within two to five years	23	12
After five years	95	65
	130	97

26 Other related-party transactions

FRS 8 p6

Note: Information concerning transactions with related parties should be disclosed here, if they are not disclosed elsewhere within the financial statements. Information concerning transactions with directors and loans, etc, to officers should also normally be disclosed here. See note 2.

27 Ultimate parent undertaking

FRS 8 p5

The immediate parent undertaking is GAAP UK Intermediate Holdings Limited.

SI 2008/410 4 Sch 8, 9

The ultimate parent undertaking and controlling party is GAAP UK plc, which is the parent undertaking of the smallest and largest group to consolidate these financial statements. Copies of GAAP UK plc consolidated financial statements can be obtained from the Company Secretary at GAAP Towers, 2 The Square, London EC4Y 2DE.